Rationality and intelligence

Rationality and intelligence

JONATHAN BARON
University of Pennsylvania

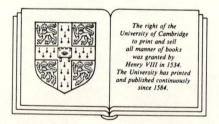

The right of the
University of Cambridge
to print and sell
all manner of books
was granted by
Henry VIII in 1534.
The University has printed
and published continuously
since 1584.

CAMBRIDGE UNIVERSITY PRESS

Cambridge
London   New York   New Rochelle
Melbourne   Sydney

Published by the Press Syndicate of the University of Cambridge
The Pitt Building, Trumpington Street, Cambridge CB2 1RP
32 East 57th Street, New York, NY 10022, USA
10 Stamford Road, Oakleigh, Melbourne 3166, Australia

First published in 1985

Printed in the United States of America

Library of Congress Cataloging in Publication Data
Baron, Jonathan, 1944–
   Rationality and intelligence.
   Bibliography: p.
   Includes index.
   1. Thought and thinking.   2. Intellect.   3. Reasoning
(Psychology)   I. Title.
BF455.B26   1985   153.4′2   84–27494
ISBN 0 521 26717 X

Contents

v

Preface

The roots of this book go back to the 1960s, when I began to worry about how to make experimental psychology relevant to the problems of the world, especially through the improvement of education (Baron, 1971). The two most salient figures of my undergraduate days, Skinner and Bruner, had made me think that this was possible, and that real advances in educational technology could grow out of psychological theory. Bruner (1957) also gave me — perhaps even more than he intended — a view of what aspects of human thinking need to be corrected, namely, a rigidity resulting from first impressions.

During the political turmoil of the late sixties, my wife gave me an article by Lawrence Kohlberg, and his ideas seemed to provide much enlightenment about the conflicts of those years. I spent a few years trying to work on moral reasoning, in the tradition of Kohlberg. Much of this work was done in collaboration with John Gibbs while we were both at McMaster University. I became dissatisfied with Kohlberg's scoring methods (for reasons I explain here), and I gradually diverged from Gibbs and developed a system much along the lines of Chapter 3 here.

My interest in intelligence was inspired by my wife and by the late Klaus Riegel (in graduate school) and later by Block and Dworkin's (1976) excellent collection. Earl Hunt and Robert Sternberg made the field a respectable one for experimental psychologists to enter, and for a while, I worked more or less in the tradition they established (Baron et al., 1980). Meanwhile, I had been an avid consumer of the work of Kahneman, Tversky, and others working on decisions and judgments. Although I never discussed the matter with my thesis advisor, David Krantz, I came to see the work much as he does (Krantz, 1981), as telling us where we need education — not where we (or the experimenters) are irremediably miswired. What I take to be the crucial insight behind this book came around 1980, when I saw the possible relevance of decision theory to the conduct of thinking itself. This step followed my reading of

Dewey (1933) — a book suggested to me by Jay Schulkin — and especially Nisbett and Ross (1980) with their repeated insistence on the need for normative models.

This book is written for serious students and workers in cognitive, developmental, clinical, personality, and social psychology, philosophy, education, and such related fields as decision sciences and artificial intelligence. Although there is a single thread of argument, the chapters do not draw heavily on one another, and readers should feel free to select their own path. However, chapters 1 and 3 are more central to what follows them, and one should read enough of these to get the idea before going on.

My main reason for publishing this book — despite its imperfections — is to enlist the help of others in the enterprise I describe. This enterprise is not just empirical; it is philosophical and technological as well: philosophical in its concern with normative and prescriptive theory as well as descriptive theory, and technological in its concern with educational methods.

I am grateful to many who provided comments and discussion about this book in its various stages. John Sabini read most of an early draft and steered me away from several dead ends. Robert Sternberg (as a reviewer) showed me where I was likely to be misunderstood, and provided many helpful suggestions. An anonymous reviewer gave good general advice about presentation. Barry Schwartz provided extensive criticism of a later draft from the point of view of one who both sympathizes and disagrees; I hope that the debate begun with him here will continue. More purely sympathetic, but equally helpful, criticism of that draft was provided by David Perkins and Jane Beattie. Peter Badgio, Dorritt Billman, Kathie Galotti, Lola Lopes, Harold Pashler, Marty Seligman, and Myrna Schwartz also provided detailed and helpful critiques of one or more chapters each. Of course, I have not solved all the problems my critics have raised.

I am also grateful to several people who have contributed to my education over the years: David Shapiro, Doug Davis, Dave Krantz, Lee Brooks, Henry Gleitman, John Sabini, and my wife, Judy Baron.

I dedicate this book to Judy, who exemplifies the traits this book extols, and to my son David, who I hope will live in times more rational than these.

1   Introduction

The main point of this book is that intelligent thinking is, among other things, rationally conducted. When we think intelligently, we do not hesitate to think about something when thinking can do some good. We consider possible conclusions — and possible goals for our thinking — other than the first one to enter our minds, and we are responsive to evidence, even when it goes against a possibility that we favor initially. When we seek evidence, we do not simply look for evidence that confirms our most favored possibility. We do not draw hasty and ill-considered conclusions, nor do we ruminate on irrelevancies.

When I speak of intelligence, I do not refer to just those qualities that make for high scores on IQ tests, or those that make for expertise in a particular field. Intelligent thinking can be effective in solving problems and making choices, even when pencil and paper must be substituted for a powerful memory or when the expertise of others must be relied upon instead of one's own. For example, we generally expect good administrators to think well in their work. Suppose you had to specify the intellectual traits of the president of the United States, or of whatever social unit you care most about, but without being able to specify his or her particular beliefs or knowledge. I think we would all want such a person to think rationally in the sense I have alluded to. Further, I shall argue that we would want the same traits in ourselves and in each other.

Consider some examples of errors in thinking:

> Case 1. A teacher gives a child a problem in mental arithmetic, and the child says, "I can't remember all the numbers."
>
> Case 2. The child takes a wild guess.
>
> Case 3. The child makes a mistake resulting from lack of knowledge, the teacher tries to explain the correct method, and the child insists that the first answer was correct.
>
> Case 4. A person makes a foolish life decision about a relationship, a job, or a place to live.
>
> Case 5. One person holds that capitalism is the only way to improve the

1

lot of people in poor countries, and another holds that Marxism is the only way; the two do not disagree about facts, but they remain unaffected by each other's arguments.

Case 1 is an ordinary failure of what I shall call narrow intelligence, a limitation of mental capacity. Cases 3, 4, and 5 are pure examples of irrationality in thinking. (In case 5, at least one of the two is irrational.) Case 2 is more like case 3 than like case 1; case 2 is a different but related kind of irrationality. Cases 2 through 5 seem to form a natural field of inquiry, which overlaps with the field treated in traditional work on intelligence (mostly cases 1 and 2); cases 2 through 5 are the ones dealt with in this book.

My aim is to define a conception of rational thinking, a conception that can serve as a basis for the teaching of good thinking, and to this extent the teaching of intelligence. By comparing people's actual thinking to this conception (or model), we may discover correctable deviations or biases, which we may then try to remedy through education. I shall argue that training in rational thinking could benefit all groups of people, regardless of their intellectual capacity or their cultural background. More generally, I believe that the nature and training of rational thinking are topics worthy of more attention than they now receive.

The main effort of this book is the development of a theory of the nature of good thinking (chapters 3 and 4). The theory serves to define what thinking is and to provide a framework for describing it wherever it is done. In this framework, thinking is analyzed into search for possibilities, search for evidence, search for goals, and use of evidence to evaluate possibilities. Each of these processes is characterized by various parameters, such as the thinker's willingness to carry out the various search processes. We can define the idea of well-conducted thinking in terms of the framework, by specifying that the parameters of thinking be set so as to maximize expected utility (chapter 2). (Utility is a measure of the extent to which an individual's goals are furthered.) There is an optimal range for each parameter of the thought process, so there can be a bias in either direction away from that range. However, I shall argue that biases are predominantly in one direction, and I shall provide evidence to support this claim. In particular, we tend to search too little, rather than too much, for possibilities other than the first ones to come to mind, for evidence, and for new goals. We tend to ignore evidence against possibilities that we find initially attractive. When we search our memories for evidence, we are biased toward finding evidence that supports such favored possibilities rather than evidence against them. One reason to think that these biases are more frequent than their opposites (too much think-

ing, etc.) is that most of them would be predicted from either of two principles, the overweighing of immediate costs and benefits as opposed to those more distant in time, and the difficulty of learning spontaneously to correct biases in these directions (chapter 3). There are no such general principles working in favor of biases in the other direction. Biases are also maintained by culturally transmitted standards, such as the belief that it ought to be embarrassing to change a judgment or decision or to discover an error in one's own thinking.

Such biases as these, if they exist, are especially detrimental to reasoning about moral questions. I include here not only questions that are obviously "moral," such as abortion, but also questions about general political philosophy, which often boil down to moral questions in a broad sense. Together, these biases may lead to hasty adoption of poorly considered beliefs about what is right, without adequate consideration of alternatives. Once such beliefs are adopted, they may resist change. Because moral beliefs are not merely matters of taste, but rather things that each of us would like to see everyone agree with us about, such a situation leads to endless conflict. Thus, education for rational thinking about moral issues is a particularly important function.

The point of view I develop may move forward several different traditions of research, and it may help to list these:

1. The study of the nature of intelligence. Here, my main claim (not a new one, I add) is that the part of intelligence having to do with the rational conduct of thinking is teachable, not without limit, but to a considerable extent. Put another way, although some of the qualities that constitute intelligence are surely biological limits on mental power, others may be seen as culturally transmitted inventions, like logic or arithmetic.

2. The study of human thinking and problem solving, as exemplified by the work of Woodworth and Sells (1935), Duncker (1935), Wertheimer (1945), Bruner, Goodnow, and Austin (1956), Bartlett (1958), Newell and Simon (1972), and Wason and Johnson-Laird (1972). A major tool of this tradition has been the use of protocols in which the subject thinks aloud while solving a problem. In chapter 3, I suggest how the present theory provides a new way of analyzing protocols. An additional consequence of the theory of chapter 3 is that there is much in common among such tasks as diagnosis, science, learning how to get about the world, decisions, and artistic creation (as argued also by Perkins, 1981). All these tasks involve the search for possibilities, evidence, and goals, and the use of evidence to evaluate possibilities. Because of these common phases, all the tasks are subject to the same kinds of systematic biases, or the same sources of irrationality.

    Beyond saying that there is much in common among these tasks, I urge that the study of thinking concern itself more with the comparison of what people do to what they should do. At present, the major approach to such prescriptive questions is the comparison of experts and

novices in a given task. Such comparisons, although useful, tend to reveal wide differences in specific knowledge of subject matter and to obscure possible effects of rationality of thinking. The novices in such comparisons (e.g., Larkin et al., 1980) often think quite well, and the experts, given the same problems, hardly have to think at all. I am thus urging a complementary approach, in which we focus on the quality of thinking while trying to hold constant the knowledge base.

3. The study of cognitive style as measured both by laboratory tasks (Kogan, 1983) and by verbal products (Schroder, Driver, & Streufert, 1967). The present theory, as presented in chapters 3 and 4, contains a conception of a more well-defined domain of styles than the open-ended list that has characterized previous literature. This domain consists of those styles that lead to the major biases I have mentioned (or their opposites). These styles could be measures, in principle, through laboratory tasks, thinking-aloud protocols (following Charness, 1981, and Voss, Tyler, & Yengo, 1983), or verbal products.

4. The study of biases in judgments (Kahneman, Slovic, & Tversky, 1982) and decisions (Kahneman & Tversky, 1984), and the related discussions in decision sciences (Simon, 1957; March, 1978) and in philosophy (Eells, 1982) about the nature of rationality (chapter 2). In order to show that people are somehow biased, it is necessary to compare their behavior to some sort of norm that must be established on other grounds. My position with respect to this tradition is that normative models are best applied to the conduct of thinking rather than to its conclusions. If thinking is conducted rationally, its conclusions may sometimes be wrong, even according to the same normative model used to evaluate the thinking; yet, the thinker can do no better. Thus, this book might make some contribution to the debate about what is needed to demonstrate human irrationality experimentally (Cohen, 1981). It might also, in some small way, contribute to the debate about the deeper question (Putnam, 1981) of whether there are context-free canons of rationality at all, and what form these might take. I shall argue that good thinking, as I define it, is more effective than poor thinking in serving the goals of the thinker; thus, people who want to further their goals by changing the way they think would be well advised to think well in this sense.

5. The study of moral reasoning, particularly the tradition of Kohlberg (reviewed by Rest, 1983). The essential claims of Kohlberg (e.g., 1970) are that moral reasoning can be studied separately from moral behavior, that reasoning nonetheless affects behavior, that the form of reasoning may be distinguished from its content, that the form nonetheless affects the content, and that the form of reasoning is both limited by development and improvable through education. I shall argue for all of these claims (although I shall have little to say about development). On the other hand, I shall suggest (along with other, e.g., Emler, Renwick, & Malone, 1983) that Kohlberg and his followers have done a bad job in distinguishing "form" and content, and the idea of form ought to be replaced with the idea of good thinking as defined here.

6. The teaching of thinking (chapter 7). My conception of rationally conducted thinking may serve as a goal of teaching. If this conception is correct, many efforts to teach thinking are off the mark, and cannot be

doing much good except by luck (e.g., de Bono, 1983); others (e.g., Blank, 1973) are very much on the mark, but still in need of a more complete justification, which I hope to provide.

Many of these efforts have been inspired by the belief that greater intelligence will make for a better world (Machado, 1980). It follows from the arguments I shall make here that this is unlikely, if we think of intelligence in the usual way. If we gave everyone a harmless drug that improved ability to learn, mental speed, mental energy, and so on (chapter 5), people would simply go about their usual business more quickly and accurately. On the other hand, getting people to think more rationally might really help (chapter 6). Right now, education seems to be the best way to do *this*.

In the rest of this chapter, I shall discuss the concepts of rationality and intelligence as I use them. I shall then briefly review some antecedents of the present theory. Finally, I shall review and criticize the traditional literature on intelligence.

Rationality

I take rationality to be a property of the thinking (or lack of thinking) that goes into belief formation or decision making. In particular, it is a property of the methods used, the rules followed (or not followed), not of the outcome of the process. Thus, we cannot determine whether an act or belief was rational without knowing how a person came to decide on it.

An *error* occurs when a false belief is held to be certain, or when a true belief is held to be certainly false. In the case of actions, an error occurs when the action chosen is in fact not the one that would have best served the thinker's goals. Errors are not necessarily irrational. A person may be deceived, may have bad luck, or may apply a rational thought process but make an unavoidable slip in carrying it through. If John steals a car to escape from the Mafia, which he thinks is after him, he is not necessarily irrational, even if we know he is wrong. Similarly, an irrationally made decision may turn out to be the correct one, as when a person avoids flying because it is Friday the 13th and the plane he would have taken turns out to crash. Rationality is not a matter of luck, although correctness and error may be.

When we say that a person has been irrational — for example, in ignoring our advice about investments — we mean that we think he could have used better methods in arriving at a conclusion. In particular, he could have weighed our advice more heavily. Usually we say this when we also disagree with the conclusion, but we quarrel with the conclusion in a

particular way, by criticizing the methods used to reach it rather than, say, the facts on which it was based (e.g., someone else's advice), or the *ability* of the thinker to use the evidence at hand. A charge of irrationality is thus a kind of admonition. Such a charge would be otiose if we had no hope of reforming the thinker's methods, at least enough to get him to reconsider the conclusion that prompted our charge. Thus, to say that thinking is irrational is to say that it should be changed, and this presupposes that it very likely *can* be changed. We do not admonish a person for being inept or unlucky (although we may admonish him for gambling). Similarly, one purpose of research on irrationality is to find ways in which human thinking may be improved (Krantz, 1981). The purposes of this research do not include the discovery of unalterable limits on human capacity, despite the fact that such limits surely exist.

Sometimes we say that a person is irremediably irrational, and the fact that we can say this seems to contradict the conclusion I have just drawn. I shall take such a usage to be an extension of the primary meaning of irrationality. When we say that a person is irremediably irrational, this is like saying that he has a habit (e.g., smoking) that cannot be broken. However, the difficulty of breaking the habit is a matter of choice. At any point, a person can decide to stop smoking, although by contrast he cannot decide to stop exhibiting a patellar reflex. Similarly, to say a person is irremediably irrational is to say that he does not listen to our advice when we criticize his thinking. However, we can never be sure that the person won't suddenly see the light, hence the term "irremediable" is never correctly applied. (When a person cannot take our advice because of true lack of capacity, e.g., inability to understand any language in which advice can be given, it would seem inappropriate to call him irrational in the first place.)

The purpose of rational thinking is to make decisions most consistent with the thinker's interests (Richards, 1971) or to arrive at beliefs whose strengths are in proportion to the evidence available. In *decision making*, the outcome of rational thinking depends on the thinker's goals and prior beliefs. Hence, the theory of rational thinking is "as applicable to the deliberation of the ignorant and inexperienced as it is to that of the knowledgeable expert; and it is as applicable to the deliberation of a monster as it is to that of a saint" (Eells, 1982, p. 5). Rational thinking is thus relevant to moral thinking only to the extent that thinkers take it as their goal to determine, by thinking, what is morally right. Since we sometimes do this, and might come to do it more, rational thinking is not irrelevant to moral thinking, and in fact the improvement of thinking in general might be one of the least difficult ways to improve the quality of

moral decisions. (Gewirth, e.g., 1983, has argued that there is a stronger link between rationality and morality; acceptance of his view would only strengthen my case, and therefore I have tried to see if I can do without it.)

The rationality of a decision depends on the way in which information about the possible consequences of different decisions is gathered and used. Rational decision making thus depends on the rational formation of beliefs about consequences.

In the case of *belief formation*, the outcome of rational thinking depends on prior beliefs, and we can ask whether these beliefs were themselves rationally formed. In general, consistent use of rational thinking will improve the effectiveness of rational thinking at any given point; rational thinking is useless if its premises are insane. However, it seems fruitless to attempt to define some sort of concept of perfect rationality, in which every step along the way, from first beliefs to present beliefs, is the result of rational thinking. In trying to do so, we would involve ourselves in an infinite regress, for the very first beliefs still have to come from somewhere. Because of this fruitlessness, rationality alone cannot determine what a person ought to believe, nor (consequently) what he or she ought to do. (Similarly, the correctness of any theory of rationality cannot be deduced from first principles. The construction of theories of rationality is at best a bootstrapping operation; see Daniels, 1979, 1980.)

Just as we can judge whether prior beliefs were rationally formed, we can also judge whether the goals served by rational decisions were rationally formed. One way to make such judgments is to examine a set of goals or policies that a person uses to guide decisions in general. We can ask whether some of the goals are inconsistent with other goals in a way that could be changed. For example, the goal of beating the record at Pac-Man could be inconsistent with the goal of getting into medical school, and, on reflection, it might turn out that a person would choose to give up the former goal for the sake of the latter (or vice versa). A second way to judge the rationality of goals is to ask whether the goals a person uses (in general or in a given case) are those that he or she would choose on reflection. Jane may choose a medical career because her parents wanted it for her, without asking whether she wants it for herself. Of course, in a deeper sense, "wanting it for herself" might amount to this goal being consistent with other goals she has, but, as I shall argue, it may not be helpful to look at things this way. Rather than trying to discover what a person's true goals actually are and then judge his other goals in terms of consistency with these, we might ask more simply whether the goals he uses are those that he would choose after an appropriate amount of

deliberation (chapter 2). If Jane thinks about her career for a reasonable amount of time and decides that she really wants to be a physician, despite the presumed external origins of this desire, then we cannot call her irrational in her choice of goal, even if some sort of deep examination of her unconscious mind should show that there is some sort of hidden conflict. The point is that it would, I assume, require an irrational amount of time and effort — so much as to conflict with her goals as she sees them — for her to try to discover this conflict when she is not even sure it exists. (Without involving ourselves in another regress, we must say here that the appropriate amount of time is what Jane herself would regard as appropriate, and the critical test is asking herself whether she has deliberated enough.) In sum, deliberation about goals may be considered as a type of decision making, and goals may be judged as rationally formed or not, just as decisions may be so judged. All this assumes, of course, that goals are in fact under control; to the extent they are not, there is no question of irrationality.

Rational thinking is generally taken to have certain properties. Rational thinkers are self-critical, open to alternatives, tolerant of doubt, and purposeful in their thinking. When we say a person is irrational, we generally mean that one of these properties is missing. We imply that there is some norm from which the person deviates. The theory of rationality is concerned with specifying that norm.

Models of rational thinking: descriptive, normative, prescriptive

I distinguish among three kinds of models in the theory of rational thinking: descriptive, normative, and prescriptive. Descriptive models describe the process or product of thinking. Normative models are usually taken to concern the conditions that the products of rational thinking should meet, although I shall take a slightly different view here. Prescriptive models specify how the process of thinking should go on. The distinction between normative and prescriptive models is my own (so far as I know), although I shall try to show how it is implicit in the ideas of Simon (1957).

Examples of descriptive models abound in the psychological literature. Such models can either be step by step accounts of the internal processes of thinking, the chain of causes and effects that leads to overt behavior (e.g., Newall & Simon, 1972) or more formal systems of rules that characterize the behavior without specifying the temporal sequence of internal states in detail (e.g., Kahneman & Tversky, 1979).

Normative models are usually taken to be standards to be met by sets of decisions or beliefs. For example, the theory of expected utility

(chapter 2) holds that the relative attractiveness of behavioral choices should be determined by the expected utility for each choice, which is (roughly) the sum over possible outcomes of the (subjective) probability of each outcome times its (subjective) utility, given the decision maker's goals. Failure to conform to the rules of utility theory makes us subversive of our own ends. For example, if we prefer A to B, but we choose a .5 chance to win B over a .5 chance to win A, we are acting inconsistently with our basic preference.

Much research has been devoted to the question of whether such normative models as these are also descriptive models of the products of human thinking. As I shall discuss, it frequently turns out that the normative models are not good descriptive models. People deviate from them not just because behavior is variable, but also because we seem to be systematically biased to act against them. Education in prescriptively correct processes of thinking may reduce some of these systematic biases.

Normative models are constructed by trying to reach "reflective equilibrium" about them (Rawls, 1971, ch. 9; Richards, 1971; see also Daniels, 1979, 1980; Stich & Nisbett, 1980). In essence, we try to find principles that account for our strong intuitions about what is rational. We try to systematize these principles by deriving some of them from others; for example, one strong intuition is that rationally held beliefs tend to be consistent with one another, and this principle of consistency does a lot of work in justifying other principles of rationality. We repeatedly test our principles against other intuitions. When the principles and the intuitions conflict, we try to change the principles or we try to convince ourselves to give up the intuitions. We may wish, at this point, to bring in other considerations, such as psychological explanations of why the conflicts might occur.

Each normative model I shall discuss here can be stated as procedures designed to ensure that the relevant conditions will be satisfied. For example, the procedure corresponding to utility theory would involve assignment of probabilities and utilities to all possible consequences of each possible decision, multiplying each possible utility times the corresponding probability, and adding. Such procedures are usually impractical. For example, in any complex decision, such as a chess move, any attempt to imagine all possible consequences of all possible courses of action would take so much time that the cost of the time would not be compensated by the benefit gained from the deliberation (as pointed out by Simon, 1957). Although the derived procedure is not a good prescriptive model for ordinary people, it can be seen as a good prescriptive model for some sort of idealized creature who lacks some constraint that people really have,

such as limited time. We may thus think of normative models as prescriptive models for idealized creatures (of a specified sort), rather than as conditions on products. This way of looking at normative models may help us in the task of evaluating normative models themselves, for it will be clear just what the model is supposed to do. In particular, this view will help us get over the temptation to think that there is only one normative model, which is that one should be correct all the time.

We need normative models to evaluate prescriptive models. The best prescriptive model is the one that is expected to yield the best decisions, as evaluated according to the normative model. For example, Simon (1957) proposes that it is often sufficient to classify outcomes as acceptable or not, and then choose the first alternative course of action that will invariably lead to an acceptable outcome. In chess, an acceptable move might be one that strengthens one's position (and does not lose pieces needlessly). The nature of the best prescriptive model might depend on circumstances; for example, Simon's proposal might maximize utility (on the average) in some situations but not in others. In general, it is a safe bet that the best prescriptive model will be based on some sort of simplification of the normative model by which it is evaluated. It is often impossible to specify uniquely a single best prescriptive model, so that even when the normative model specifies a unique best decision, there might be several rational prescriptive models, all leading to different decisions. Prescriptive models are, by definition, possible to follow, which is to say that there is in principle some way to educate people to follow them more closely than we do. A prescriptive model may therefore be challenged by showing that people do not learn to follow it under conditions that are, on other grounds, thought to be suitable for learning.

The basic role I see for psychology is the demonstration of biases and the evaluation of methods for correcting biases. Biases may be defined in terms of normative models or prescriptive models; in either case, the bias is a systematic deviation from what the model specifies. Biases in meeting the conditions of normative models may give us clues about the biases that exist in following prescriptive models. However, I can think of no guarantee that following the best prescriptive models, without any biases at all, will eliminate all biases in conforming to the normative models. For example, following Simon's prescriptive model for chess (last paragraph) does not guarantee utility maximization. All we can say is that there is no way of guaranteeing that we can come any closer to this goal than we can come by following a rational prescriptive model. Thus, the focus of psychological investigation should be on the prescriptive models, with the

normative models acting as behind-the-scenes justifications of the prescriptive models. We cannot claim that a person is irrational on the basis of evidence that his behavior does not conform to a normative model, for he might be following a perfectly rational prescriptive model. On the other hand, we can show that people are irrational if there is no conceivable prescriptive model that fits what they do.

Cohen (1981) has argued that it is impossible to demonstrate human irrationality in the psychology laboratory (and presumably elsewhere). His basic argument is that any such demonstration involves showing that human intuitions conflict with the dictates of a normative model, yet, it is such intuitions that are the basis of any such model. By his account, all adults are entitled to have their intuitions about rationality respected (just as linguists claim to respect their intuitions about grammaticality, etc.), and, presumably, all of an individual's intuitions are equally worthy of respect (even if they conflict with one another, and even if one of them is that beliefs about rationality should not conflict).

It seems to me that this view has been successfully refuted by many of the commentaries that appear along with this article, even when the argument is limited to normative models rather than prescriptive ones. Most importantly, both Krantz and Nisbett point out that Cohen's view gratuitously rules out the possibility of improvement in conformity to normative models, either within the individual or within society. If a person ignores chance factors when explaining a statistical fact, and if labeling his behavior irrational is part of an educational process that leads the person to attend to those factors (with no loss in time or effort, say), thus bringing the person's behavior into conformity with statistics as a normative model, the label can hardly be misapplied.

One possible objection to some purported demonstrations of irrationality is that the subject is incapable of being rational without expending an unreasonable amount of time or effort. For example, it might take too much time to make the calculations required to meet the conditions of utility theory or probability theory as normative models. This objection cannot be made when we use a good prescriptive model as our standard, for violation of such a model cannot be excused on the grounds that the model is impractical as a guide to behavior, by definition. A good prescriptive model takes into account the very constraints on time, etc., that a normative model is free to ignore. In sum, although the use of prescriptive models as standards makes it harder for the researcher to show irrationality, they make it easier to defend the claim that people are irrational.

Intelligence and its relation to rationality

Intelligence has received far more empirical study than has rationality, yet its status as a concept is confused. Jensen (1982) typifies the approach of most researchers when he says (p. 257):

It is a mistake to waste time arguing about the definition of intelligence, except to make sure everyone understands that the term does not refer to a "thing." Nearly everyone understands its lexical meaning . . . Scientifically, intelligence is perhaps best characterized at present as an unclear hypothetical construct (or class of constructs) that has sprung from observations of individual differences in a class of behaviors called "abilities" . . .

a term Jensen then defined more carefully. In the case of intelligence, reliance on our intuitive concept seems insufficient, for it has led to endless conflict about such things as whether IQ tests do measure intelligence, whether there are different kinds of intelligence, and so on.

In order to develop a clearer definition, we need to distinguish between criterial and explanatory statements about the nature of intelligence. A criterion tells us what is to be explained, that is, what behavior we should classify as intelligent. Criterial statements correspond to the use of the term "intelligent" as a term of commendation. We speak of an intelligent chess move or an intelligent decision as a way of expressing approval and admiration. As a description, such a statement says that the behavior meets certain evaluative criteria. An explanatory statement tells us what accounts for success or failure (or individual differences) in meeting such criteria. An explanation must not restrict itself to a description of ways in which intelligent behavior is successful. It must tell us how that success is achieved (or not) in terms that refer to mental states and processes, not to the success itself. We cannot explain success in investing by saying that good investors buy low and sell high; such a statement is, rather, a criterion for what we take a good investor to be.

Two kinds of descriptive criteria seem to underlie most current thinking about intelligence. In one, intelligence is viewed as adaptation. For example, Sternberg & Salter (1982, p. 17) argue that "a social context (be it a classroom, a tribe, a family, a profession, or whatever) sets up a variety of problems, and intelligence consists in large part of the ability to solve these problems." By this criterion, a bee is intelligent because it has evolved to meet the demands of its social context. There are some problems with this crtierion. First, the criterion is incompletely stated, for the idea of adaptation presupposes goals. To say that an organism is adapted to an environment is to say that it is achieving certain goals in that environment. It is these as yet unstated goals that actually define this

criterion. (Usually, the goals are assumed to be things like survival and reproduction, but then we make it impossible to say that a monk or a daring fighter for a good cause could be well adapted. If we try to state the goals more completely, we can dispense with the idea of adaptation itself; it buys nothing.) Second, adaptation to a social context seems to imply that the goals intelligent people pursue are those set for them by other people. However, rebels and loners need not (as implied) be unintelligent, and it also seems likely that even well-adjusted people have some goals that are distinctly their own. Intelligence is surely involved in the successful pursuit of those goals, as well as the social ones.

The second kind of criterion is performance on intelligence tests themselves, leading to the well-known remark that "intelligence is what the tests test" (E. G. Boring, in *The New Republic*, 1923). The problem here is that a criterion ought to clarify our reason for being interested in intelligence. Without an explicit reason, we cannot evaluate a test itself as being good or bad (except in terms of its ability to meet certain minimal criteria of reliability). Let us now consider the criteria and types of explanations we ought to adopt.

We often think that intelligent people ought to do better, other things equal, not just at schoolwork but also at doing their jobs, managing their finances, getting along with their spouses, and raising their children. We make fun of otherwise intelligent people who fail in some of these areas, as if we expect them to know better. Thus, when we try to define intelligence as a criterion in a way that does justice to our natural concept, it would seem reasonable to say that intelligence is whatever helps any person, in any natural human environment, to achieve their rationally chosen goals. These goals would include the goal of choosing goals rationally (since anyone would have that as his goal, whatever else his goals might be). (If we can explain the achievement of rationally chosen goals, we can probably also explain the achievement of all goals—e.g., self-destruction, etc.—whether rational or not. However, an explanation of rational goals alone will serve our purposes here. If some component of mental processes were found to help people achieve only their irrational goals, we would surely not want to help people develop this component.) This criterion allows us to ask what properties of mental states and processes might make for such success, regardless of circumstances. An explanatory theory of intelligence is a partial answer to this question.

It is usually assumed that an explanatory theory of intelligence will contain statements about cognitive processes, but no statements about motives and emotions. It is more to the point to say that explanatory statements generally concern *abilities*, which are statements about

whether a person can meet certain criteria of speed, accuracy, or appropriateness in certain component processes. For example, intelligent people might be successful in achieving their rational goals because they are more accurate in learning tasks, faster in processing information, or more appropriate in allocating the right amount of effort to a task. These abilities are not just other criteria (although they are that too), for they are embedded in a general theory of psychological functioning. We think of intelligence as cognitive because we do not usually speak of abilities in the domains of motivation and emotion. Other than this, however, there is nothing to exclude these domains from a theory of intelligence. It may at times make sense to speak of abilities to control emotions and motives, and it may also make sense to think of motives and emotions as important influences on cognitive processes. Thus, I see no reason to exclude these areas from theories of intelligence by definition. However, it does make sense to exclude factors such as physical condition, muscular tone, etc., which do not concern mental processes of any sort. Although such factors surely help us to achieve our goals, they do so in a way that need not complicate the theory concerned with mental processes alone.

To be more precise, in this book I shall use the term "effectiveness" to refer to the criterion of interest. The terms "intelligence" and "rationality" are reserved for (still to be provided) explanations of whether this criterion is met or not—in a given case or, more generally, by a given person. Intelligence, in turn, is seen as a set of characteristics, which can be subdivided into capacities and dispositions, and rationality comprises an important subset of these dispositions. More specifically:

Capacities are ability parameters within a psychological theory (however rudimentary) that affect success at tasks and that cannot be increased by instruction. Examples are things like speed of discrimination, working-memory capacity, learning capacity as measured by some parameter in a model of learning, or ability to adopt a cheerful mood. It would do no good to tell people to increase their working memory capacity (even if they knew what that was). Capacities become relevant only when a person is voluntarily trying to meet some standard of performance, such as responding quickly and accurately in an experiment. However, capacities are unlikely to be measurable in any direct way. For example, reaction time in a discrimination task may be affected by effort and by carefulness, both of which are under control, as well as by the (theoretical) capacity of discrimination speed, which is not. The important property of capacities is that they are not under control at the time a task is done. Capacities may be affected by prior practice, which may, of course, have been under control.

Dispositions are parameters in a psychological theory that affect success in tasks and that *are* subject to control by instruction (including verbal commands, modeling, or reward) or self-instruction. Examples might be the disposition to weigh new evidence against a favored belief heavily (or lightly), the disposition to spend a great deal of time (or very little) on a problem before giving up, or the disposition to weigh heavily the opinions of others in forming one's own. Although you cannot improve working memory by instruction, you can tell someone to spend more time on problems before she gives up, and if she is so inclined, she can do what you say. Because dispositions may be affected by admonition, it is these, and not capacities, that are at issue when we say that someone is thinking irrationally. (Of course, a disposition, such as the disposition to persist at a problem, may be only partly controllable; in this case, we may analyze it into a capacity and a disposition, or we may say that it is both — the choice having no bearing on anything else here.)

Effectiveness is the achievement of rationally chosen goals that are difficult to achieve, the difficulty resulting from such factors as complexity or the number of goals pursued at once. Effectiveness may involve success in earning a large income, forming stable personal relationships, improving the state of the world (or preventing it from getting worse), or simply ensuring the survival of self and family (which, for some, is not a trivial problem), depending on one's goals. Effectiveness may be affected by capacities as well as dispositions, and of course, by other factors having nothing to do with a person's mental processes.

Rationality is following the rules of a good prescriptive model of decision making or belief formation (as defined above). A good prescriptive model is one that maximizes our conformity to a good normative model. Because a good normative model is one we would want to conform to, rational thinking helps us to achieve our goals, insofar as following any rules of thinking would do so. That is, if I make my decisions rationally, I cannot blame the way I carried out my thinking for any failure of my plans. In this way, the idea of rational thinking relates to the idea of rational and irrational reasons for action (Richards, 1971): The fact that the thinking behind a decision is good provides good reason (to a person who respects rationality itself) to take that action.

Rationality makes for rationality of goals. I assume here that people can and do think about their goals, and that such thinking may itself be rational or irrational to varying degrees.

Intelligence is the set of properties within a psychological theory that make for effectiveness, regardless of the environment a person is in. A "component of intelligence" is any property in this set. Intelligence dif-

fers from rationality in that it includes other factors, besides rationality, that affect success. Where rationality alone permits one to do the best one can given one's goals and personal endowments (capacities, knowledge, environment, etc.), intelligence includes the endowments themselves, and thus enlarges the set of environments and life plans in which one can expect success. Because it allows a person to pursue successfully a wide range of rational plans in any environment, intelligence is something that anyone would want, if he did not know what his environment and his goals would be.

The advantage of defining intelligence this way is that it makes explicit both the criteria and the kinds of explanations that count. It also implies that intelligence can be defined cross-culturally, and that it can, in principle, be affected by experience. It does not imply, however, that intelligence is a single dimension; rather, it is a set of qualities, which may differ in importance in different contexts.

It may be argued that I have settled a number of controversial issues by fiat, through the definitions I have given. I would reply that these definitions are at least reasonable ones, because they provide structure to psychological inquiry and because they explicate at least one meaning of the common-sense view of intelligence.

It may be deduced from what I have said that rationality is entirely a function of the dispositional components of intelligence. This is a consequence of the relation between rationality and control through instruction: As noted, to say that a person is irrational is to imply that he could be rational if he tried. If a person fails some task because of limited capacity, however, there is nothing he can do about it.

It also follows that rationality is part of intelligence; that is, all the properties of rational thinking are properties of intelligent thinking. Rationality in thinking makes for both rationality in choosing goals, which I have defined as a condition for effectiveness, and success in achieving those goals, which is effectiveness itself.

Components of intelligence, in order to play the role assigned to them, must be relatively *general*. That is, they must affect performance in a sufficient variety of situations so that we can expect them to affect success in some situations in any realistic culture or environment, so as to increase effectiveness in that environment. This condition is met for things like discrimination speed or the disposition to weigh evidence appropriately, but not for perfect pitch, or size of English vocabulary. (It is, of course, possible to imagine environments in which any given component is unnecessary or even harmful. The term "realistic" is meant to exclude such cases. The term "intelligence" is thus tied to some sort of notion of

"possible human culture." Without this limitation, a culture-free theory of intelligence would very likely be impossible, and a concept of intelligence that could include Martians or computers, as well as humans, would very likely be quite different from the one I am trying to develop, if could be framed at all.) The point of this restriction is to make the theory manageable. Without it, the explanatory theory of intelligence would have to refer to anything people could possibly know and anything we could possibly do. Intelligence is not just the sum total of a person's knowledge and abilities, for some of these are thought to be the result of intelligence, not its essence.

When I say that a component is general, I mean that it is meaningful to ask about its level in a great many situations. This does not imply that a high level of this component in one situation will predict a high level in another for the same person. If speed of counting is uncorrelated (across individuals) with speed of searching memory, speed (in general) might still be a component of intelligence, for it may still allow us to explain (and possibly influence) successful performance in each situation where it can be measured. It is this that I take to be the primary function of the theory of intelligence, rather than the explanation of correlations among performances. The question of whether components account for correlations can be asked later. (For dispositions, I shall argue, the answer to this question is to some extent not empirical, but it is a matter of how we as a culture choose to teach or inculcate dispositions in the first place. If we teach general dispositions to some people but not to others, we shall thereby create correlations, however if we teach everyone the same general dispositions, the correlations might disappear. Thus, if the theory's truth depended on correlations, its application might bring about its demise.)

General components of intelligence may be subdivided into capacities and dispositions, and capacities may be further subdivided into components that are affected by practice and those that are not. Dispositions and practiceable capacities together may be called *experiential* components. In this book, I shall be concerned mainly with dispositions, and I shall have little to say about practiceable capacities. Dispositions might be teachable with some generality, so that they might be good targets for educational efforts to improve intelligence, even when we do not know exactly what our students' future goals and environments will be. Practiceable capacities, on the other hand, seem to be situation specific (Thorndike & Woodworth, 1901; Baron, 1985). For example, practice does improve the memory span, but practice with digits does not affect the span for letters (Eriksson, Chase, & Faloon, 1980). Thus, although

practice helps because it improves the speed and accuracy of the task practiced, there is no reason to provide practice in hopes of improving performance in other, unrelated tasks. Practice should thus be provided in tasks a person is expected to do, such as reading and calculation, but practice in "thinking in general" will not help, except as a way of inculcating dispositions.

Narrow intelligence is the part of intelligence consisting only of unpracticeable capacities. Some people use the word "intelligence" for this. However, intelligence as defined here is not the same as narrow intelligence. For example, there are dispositions that affect how thoroughly a person searches for possibilities, evidence, and goals, and how he or she uses the evidence found.

The approach I have taken here helps us to clarify and justify the teaching of rational thinking as part of the teaching of intelligence, insofar as that is possible. There ought to be a few dispositional components that could be identified and taught, possibly taught in general so that they would affect behavior in most situations a student would encounter in the future. I shall argue that the dispositions of rational thinking are among the most important of these. In everyday language, by teaching people to think well, we might improve their lives, individually and collectively.

Antecedents of the present approach

The view I shall present here is closely related to a number of previous traditions of thought, and I shall briefly review the major ones: Dewey's theory of reflective thinking, Simon's concept of bounded rationality, the developmental tradition of Piaget as exemplified in the work of Kohlberg and Perry, and the more recent concern with the role of strategies in intelligent behavior.

Dewey

Dewey (1933) tried to characterize a type of thinking, which he called "reflective thinking." This term refers to thinking that tries to reach a goal, resolve a state of doubt, or decide on a course of action, in contrast to thinking as the content of the stream of consciousness, or to "think" as a synonym of "believe." Reflective thinking is the kind of thinking one ought to do whenever easily applied or habitual rules of behavior do not suffice. Reflective thought involves an initial state of doubt or perplexity (a problem), and an active search of previous experiences and knowledge for material that will resolve the doubt.

There may, however, be a state of perplexity and also previous experiences out of which suggestions emerge, and yet thinking may not be reflective. For the person may not be sufficiently *critical* about the ideas that occur to him. . . . To many persons both suspense of judgment and intellectual search are disagreeable; they want to get them ended as soon as possible. They cultivate an over-positive and dogmatic habit of mind, or feel perhaps that a condition of doubt will be regarded as evidence of mental inferiority. . . . To be genuinely thoughtful, we must be willing to sustain and protract the state of doubt which is the stimulus to thorough inquiry, so as not to accept an idea or make positive assertion of a belief until justifying reasons have been found. (p. 16)

One advantage of reflective thought over "merely impulsive and merely routine activity" is that it "enables us to act in a deliberate and intentional fashion to attain future objects or to come into command of what is now distant and lacking." Reflective thinking allows us to choose courses of action that enable us to succeed in attaining otherwise unattainable goals, and it makes us more confident in beliefs that are true and less confident in beliefs that are false. When it is done successfully, it allows us to improve on our initial hunches, which we would otherwise follow. A theory of good thinking must not confine itself to the form of the thinking itself:

Ability to train thought is not achieved merely by knowledge of the best forms of thought. . . . Moreover, there are no set exercises in correct thinking whose repeated performance will cause one to be a good thinker. The information and the exercises are both of value. But no individual realizes their value except as he is personally animated by certain dominant attitudes in his own character. (p. 29)

Dewey includes such "attitudes" as open-mindedness, whole-heartedness, and "responsibility" as necessary. ("To be intellectually responsible is to consider the consequences of a projected step; it means to be willing to adopt these consequences when they follow reasonably from any position already taken. Intellectual responsibility secures integrity; that is to say, consistency and harmony in belief." p. 32)

As for the form of reflective thought itself, Dewey suggests five phases:

1. Suggestion of an initial solution or action, which is not carried out because of a feeling of doubt.
2. Intellectualization of the difficulty into a problem to be solved (what we would now call formation of a problem representation).
3. The use of one suggestion after another as hypotheses, which guide further reasoning.
4. Reasoning in the narrow sense, that is, "the mental elaboration of the idea or supposition as an idea or supposition."
5. The testing of the hypotheses in action and in thought.

These phases are intended as descriptions of actual steps taken, not as formal constraints.

Dewey's theory is a descriptive theory of an idealized kind of thinking. Dewey speaks as if "reflective thinking" can actually be found, but he wishes it were found more often. Thus, although reflective thinking is idealized, it is achievable. In this sense, Dewey's theory is closest to what I have called a prescriptive model, rather than a normative or descriptive one.

The theory described in chapter 3 is derived directly from Dewey's. I find it necessary, however, to be more explicit about the terms of the theory, and I modify the list of phases considerably. I collapse phases 1 and 3 into a single phase of search for possibilities. I replace phase 2 with a more general conception of search for goals, which may occur at any time during the process of thinking — although it need not occur at all if the goal is taken over from the activity out of which thinking emerges. I replace Dewey's fourth and fifth phases with two others, one concerned with searching for evidence and the other concerned with use of the evidence thus found. I believe that Dewey's term "elaboration" is imprecise, and it has the unfortunate connotation of random embellishment. The precise statement of the phases of thinking is, as we shall see, not something that can be etched in stone, for it is partly a matter of analytic convenience. In addition to these modifications, I propose some parameters for each phase, the optimal setting of which can be specified by a normative model.

Dewey had a great influence on the "progressive" movement in education. In his later years, he came to feel that this movement had gone awry; indeed, such feelings were apparently behind his decision to reissue *How we think* in revised form in 1933. In retrospect, it certainly seems that much of progressive education was more concerned with the elimination of constraints than with instilling the values and discipline needed for reflective thinking. Perhaps we are now ready for a new attempt to put his ideas into practice (Baron, 1981a). (See also Brim et al., 1962, and D'Zurilla & Goldfried, 1971, for some other modern attempts to use Dewey's ideas about thinking.)

Simon

Simon (1957, part IV) began his work on "bounded rationality" during the height of the influence of the theory of expected utility as put forward by von Neuman and Morganstern (1947). This theory was being advocated not only as a normative model of decision making, but as a descriptive and prescriptive model as well, especially in the disciplines concerned with administrative decisions. Simon argued that the model is essentially

useless in these contexts, just as it is in chess, because of the complexity of the problems that we face. Thus, "the intended rationality of an actor requires him to construct a simplified model of the real situation in order for him to deal with it." We must "replace the goal of *maximizing* with the goal of *satisficing*, of finding a course of action that is 'good enough.' " (p. 204) For example, for many purposes, the utility of outcomes may be represented as satisfactory or unsatisfactory, and a precise utility need not be assigned. Likewise, probabilities may be represented as certain, possible, or impossible. When we are trying to decide among several possible actions, for example, moves in chess, we need not consider all the possibilities at once. We might, for example, consider actions one at a time until we find one that is certain to lead to a satisfactory outcome, that is, an action that leads to a satisfactory outcome given any possible event. "Aspiration level" will determine the level of value that we consider to be satisfactory (or, put another way, the size of the set of satisfactory outcomes). In general, the higher the aspiration level, the more actions we consider before we find one that leads to a satisfactory outcome. For example, in buying a house, we may have a long list of criteria, and if we try to satisfy every one, we may end up looking at many more houses than if we allow some leeway. In repeated decisions of the same type, such as moves in chess or hiring of job applicants, we can adjust our level of aspiration so as to be consistent with the time we are willing to spend on each decision. Even in a single decision, we can decide to lower our criterion as more alternatives are considered. However, such simplified methods as these are not guaranteed to yield a decision in any given problem. Most importantly, they are not guaranteed to produce the best decision as defined by expected-utility theory. Thus, we must settle for something less than the optimality defined by normative models such as expected-utility theory.

I believe that Simon makes essentially the distinction between normative and prescriptive models, as I stated it earlier:

If the pay-off were measurable in money or utility terms, and *if* the cost of discovering alternatives were similarly measurable, we could . . . speak of the optimal degree of persistence in behavior. . . . But the . . . organism does *not* in general know these costs. . . . It is precisely because of these limitations on its knowledge and capabilities that the less global models of rationality described here are significant and useful. [However,] in many situations we may be interested in the precise question of whether one decision-making procedure is more rational than another, and to answer this question we will usually have to construct a broader criterion of rationality that encompasses both procedures as approximations. Our whole point is that it is important to make explicit what level we are considering in such a hierarchy of models . . . (Simon, 1957, p. 254)

Such a hierarchy is just what I had in mind in my earlier discussion of normative and prescriptive models.

I do take issue slightly with Simon's conclusion about the possibility of determining an optimal degree of persistence, an issue I shall discuss at some length in chapters 3 and 4. The determination of optimal persistence or optimal level of aspiration is best seen as a matter of policy or rule, not a matter to be decided each time a problem is solved. When we tell a person that he is irrational, we do not mean that he has failed to calculate the optimum thought process for the situation he is in. Rather, we suggest that he is not following some policy, such as adopting a certain degree of persistence, that is suitable for a certain class of cases that includes the case in question. The policy can be of varying levels of generality; that is, the size of the class of problems governed by a given policy can vary. For any given class of cases, it is possible at least to define a range of persistence levels (or whatever) that are appropriate for that class, given our knowledge of the thinker's behavior in that class of situations. Although we do not know the optimum exactly, we can say with some confidence that it falls within that range. If the thinker is outside that range, we may call him irrational. Of course, rationality in this sense does not guarantee optimality of persistence from the viewpoint of an omniscient observer, for the case may be an exception to the general rule. But it is not the omniscient observer that we need to worry about, but only a somewhat idealized replica of the thinker himself, in particular, a replica who has no time constraints for setting policies. In sum, although neither the thinker nor his critic could possibly divide up the world finely enough to know exactly how long he ought to persist in any given case, it may still be possible — despite Simon — for a critic to be right.

It is important to note that my view here agrees with Simon's in holding that there is not necessarily a single optimum level of persistence. In addition to the problems already mentioned, it is impossible to consider all possible classification systems to use as the basis of policy, so one must always settle for what one has, and there may be several acceptable alternatives. It may also be difficult to decide which category a given situation belongs to. Thus, rationality is defined with respect to a classification system, and there may be several acceptable systems, hence several specifications of optimal persistence. However, there may also be levels of persistence that are irrational by any classification of situations. By this view, then, the criterion of rationality does not divide thinking into a single optimum on the one hand and everything else on the other, but rather into two sets, the rational and the irrational, each with several

members. These arguments apply to a great many parameters of thinking, aside from level of aspiration or persistence (chapter 3).

There is an ambiguity in Simon's presentation of his views, which has affected the way psychology has responded to them. It shows up in passages of the following sort:

It may be said in defense of the theory of games and statistical decisions that they are to be regarded not as descriptions of human choice but as normative theories. . . . Even this position seems to me untenable, but I shall not pursue the matter here. We are interested in the prediction and description of human behavior, rather than the normative rules of conduct.

The problem, as I see it, is that the the rest of Simon's account, as just cited, for example, seems incompatible with an exclusive interest in descriptive models.

Despite the neglect of prescriptive models in modern cognitive psychology, Simon has not forgotten his earlier interest in them. Writing for economists (1978a, p. 10), he points out that it is possible "not only to *take account* of human bounded rationality, but to *bring it within the compass* of the rational calculus." Some recent work in psychology is exactly in this spirit, in particular, that of Beach and Mitchell (1978), Christiansen-Szalanski (1978), and Russo and Dosher (1983). These authors have analyzed the costs and benefits of various simplifying strategies for solving problems of various sorts, including problems involving the maximizing of expected utility (for example, in investment and gambling decisions). Some of the strategies involve exactly the kinds of simplifications suggested by Simon, for example, coding outcomes as acceptable or not rather than using their actual dollar values. The optimal strategy to be used is affected by the cost of thinking itself, which can be included the same framework of the overall normative model. Prescriptively, the thinker does best by choosing a *method* with the highest expected utility — taking the cost of thinking into account — even though this does not generally lead to the *outcome* with the highest expected utility. This is the approach I take here.

At this point, a summary of my views of rationality, which are close to Simon's, is in order. I shall give it in the form of some questions and answers:

Is there only one rational choice for any situation? Not necessarily, there may be more than one, but there is always at least one.

Is there only one best complete normative theory? There may be, but it depends somewhat on the kinds of idealized creatures we imagine in framing normative models. Certainly, if two conflicting normative models arise from the same idealization, we have not done our job of stating the

models well, and further reflection will surely lead us to modify one or both.

Can the following of a prescriptive model lead to a violation of the normative model that justified it? Yes, even to systematic violations when the classification of a repeated situation is inappropriate.

Stage theories

The work of Piaget (Flavell, 1963, 1977; Gelman & Baillargeon, 1983) has been central in developmental psychology, and has also been associated to varying degrees with the study of the nature of intelligence (Siegler & Richards, 1982). Piaget's interest in development was, apparently, inspired in part by his early work with Simon, Binet's collaborator in developing the first useful intelligence test. Many of the tasks Piaget designed are like the items in Binet's tests. For example, Piaget's test of conservation of length, in which a child is asked which of two lines is longer after the shorter one is moved forward, is very similar to one of Binet's items. Piaget's tests of object constancy in infants, in which the question is whether the subject thinks that an object will reappear where it was (as opposed to its usual location) after being obscured, would be a reasonable item in a test of infant intelligence by any of Binet's criteria. However, many other tasks were of the sort that might be more revealing of the nature of intelligence as I speak of it here, except that these items have not been included in most intelligence tests, probably because their scoring would be too subjective and because they might take too long to administer. In this category, I would place Piaget's studies of moral judgments, conceptions of the physical world, and hypothetico-deductive reasoning (with Inhelder). Even Piaget's tests of conservation of number and other quantities across transformations of length and shape were presented as interviews rather than yes-no questions.

Piaget was not interested in the development of test items but rather in the underlying "schemes" and "operations" that accounted for children's inferences, and in the developmental processes that accounted for the progression of these underlying structures with age. It is worthy of note that he does not ask his subjects to think aloud—a practice now in common use. Rather, he asks for reasons, justifications, and extrapolations to hypothetical and changed situations, designed to reveal the premises that govern the subject's inferences. (There are some exceptions; for example, Inhelder & Piaget, 1958, examine what might be called the process of testing hypotheses about physical principles. But even here, the results are explained in terms of differences in underlying premises or

"structures.") Piaget's concern was with the processes of development leading to the formation and change of these premises, not with the process of thinking (using one's knowledge to solve new problems). Indeed, Piaget and his followers do not usually distinguish between problems in which the subject has no doubt about which premises are relevant (or how to apply them) and those in which doubt is present from the start. Only the latter would involve thinking as discussed here.

Piaget's writings on the nature of intelligence have ranged from unclear to incoherent (see Osherson, 1974; Carey, 1985, for critique and analysis). However, we might gain some insight by trying to piece together a Piagetian theory from the empirical work done by Piaget and those who work in the same tradition (as recently reviewed by Gelman and Baillargeon, 1983). Many of these studies are concerned with the rules of inference by which children extend what they have learned to novel cases, in essence, the assumption the child makes. Do children assume that objects will stay where they are put, or move back to where they ought to be? Do they assume that numerical equality of two rows is unaffected by a change in the length of one of the rows? Do they assume that objects that move on their own are alive, so that they therefore have other properties of living things such as desires or hearts? If such experimental studies were seen as directed at a theory of intelligence, it seems reasonable that such a theory would take inferential rules as central. The development of intelligence might be seen as the replacement of an early set of rules that led to inconsistencies and discrepancies with a more internally consistent and useful set. An example of a mature rule of inference, useful for conservation tasks of all sorts, might be as follows: Whether or not a transformation (such as movement of objects) affects a dimension (such as numerosity) depends only on the transformation and the dimension, not on the values of the dimension in question or of other dimensions. Young children do not follow this rule, for they take changes in length of a row to affect relative numerosity when numerosity is high but not when it is low (Lawson, Baron, & Siegel, 1974). (If they took length to affect relative numerosity in all cases, we would simply say that they were treating questions about number as if they were about length, but the problem seems deeper than this.) Further, the kinds of rules studied by Piagetians are (usually) applicable in any culture or environment, so that they would qualify as general components by my definition. Thus, we might say that the Piagetian theory holds intelligence to depend on rules of inference, which are probably dispositional although they are surely (like other dispositions) affected by capacities and by the maturation of those capacities. (It is also necessarily true, as pointed out by Keil, 1981,

that there are innate constraints and biases that affect the development of rules of inference. The extent to which these constraints are "high level" as opposed to perceptual and motor, their complexity, and the proper terminology for describing them, however, are matters of heated — but not necessarily lighted — discussion. Fortunately, these questions are beyond the scope of this inquiry, since my concern here is with the movement, through thinking, from where one is to where one goes next, not with the total course of development from the beginning.)

I do not disagree with this kind of theorizing, and it is by no means irrelevant to my present goals, for it may be appropriate to try to teach such rules of inference explicitly as a way of increasing intelligence. In chapter 3, I shall make some suggestions about how such rules of inference are used in thinking. However, I feel that the Piagetian approach is less fruitful than the one I have adopted, largely because the acquisition of rules of inference may be affected by the quality of thinking and its application to learning. Thus, teaching children to think will help them to acquire more adequate rules of inference. Moreover, the most basic rules of inference (the rules of natural logic), those that I presume to be necessary for thinking to occur at all, are probably well known even to toddlers, and I suspect that no special effort is needed to teach them other than the opportunities for practice afforded by thinking itself (chapter 8). Finally, the rules of inference studied by Piagetians are much more numerous than the processes I discuss here, and I am led to question whether a distinction can be made in Piagetian theory between intelligence and the totality of belief. In sum, I have no principled objection to the Piagetian tradition as an approach to the problems I am trying to solve; I have simply chosen another tack, which I think is more likely to work.

Despite these quibbles with the Piagetian tradition, I must also say that part of it was a more direct inspiration for the present effort, namely, one part concerned with the stages of intellectual development. Piaget himself proposed that the basic rules of inference he examined could be organized into stages, which are roughly associated with ages. The final stage, formal operations, was characterized by an ability to think abstractly, and it was supposed to begin in early adolescence. Findings that Piaget's own measures of formal operations were not passed by many adults led to some modification (Piaget, 1972), in which it was suggested, in essence, that formal operations might be domain specific, and their presence in any domain at all could be counted as evidence for their existence.

Others went further, suggesting that there were other kinds of stages.

In particular, Kohlberg (1969, 1970) proposed a sequence of six stages for development of reasoning about morality and related issues. In a similar vein, Perry (1971) proposed a sequence of nine stages (subdivided into three main ones) of intellectual and ethical devlopment in the college years. In both of these theories, development moves from stages in which morality (and truth, for Perry) are believed to be defined by authority and convention to stages in which they are believed to be objects of individual reflection. These workers argue that the higher stages are normatively more correct than the lower ones, and that appropriate education can promote movement through the stages.

Although these approaches are (as noted earlier) related to my approach, they differ in a couple of respects. First and most importantly, they do not concern themselves much with the process of thinking itself. Rather, in the Piagetian tradition that inspired them, they are concerned with the kinds of principles appealed to at different stages. I shall argue that development of principles is to some extent the result of the use of good thinking. Thus, the teaching of the processes of good thinking, rather than some of its consequences, might be more fruitful in the long run.

The second difference is that these traditions concern themselves with development. I have nothing against this approach. Indeed, my own first steps on my present path (Baron, 1973, 1975) were entirely within this framework. However, I now feel that the assumption that thinking develops, although likely, is gratuitous. Conceivably, thinking does not develop "naturally" at all after a very early age. It is undeniable that thinking in most domains becomes more successful with development, but this might have more to do with the accumulation of specific knowledge or with increased capacities than with dispositional components of intelligence. Thus, educational efforts to increase intelligence might do better if they were not limited to attempts to mimic or accelerate natural developmental processes (or, for that matter, attempts to reduce individual differences). If it turns out that efforts to improve thinking succeed by mimicking a natural deveopmental process, so be it, but it should not be assumed that this will happen.

Strategies

It has long been known that young children learn less quickly than older children (with the possible exception of language, but even this is not certain; see Snow & Hoefnagel-Höhle, 1978) and that retardates learn less quickly than normals. It seemed reasonable to suppose that some sort of capacity was at issue. However, in the late 1960s and 1970s, several

findings began to suggest that these developmental and group differences were caused by differences in the use of strategies (methods) for learning, such as rehearsing the material to be learned, looking for relationships within the material that would make it more memorable, self-testing combined with concentration on what has not yet been learned, and so on. Young children and retardates were found not to use such strategies. When these groups were taught to use the strategies, memory performance improved immediately, often to the level of older or normal children. Further, there were some memory tasks in which even normal subjects failed to use any obvious strategies for learning, and in these tasks, effects of age or retardation were generally not found. (These findings are reviewed by Flavell, 1970; Brown, 1975; Baron, 1978; and Campione, Brown, & Ferrara, 1982.) What was impressive about these results was that they showed the possibility that a fundamental sign of intelligence, the ability to learn, could be affected by voluntary, teachable strategies, which must be dispositions rather than capacities. Thus, unless we were to give up the idea that ability to learn is a direct manifestation of intelligence, we had to accept the possibility that intelligence itself involves learned strategies.

What is meant by a strategy? A strategy is essentially a method, a way of trying to reach some goal. Strategies can be as simple as picking up a spoon or as complex as a strategy in chess. A natural way of describing a strategy is as a rule for actions, a rule consisting of statements of the form, "when condition C holds, do action A," where the condition may include information about goals in effect, and where the action might consist of adding new conditions, including goals to be achieved. Knowledge of strategies is measured by looking at the probability that a strategy is successfully completed by a certain person in a certain situation. (If a person knows a strategy, say, for tying a shoe, but cannot execute it quickly enough, I would say that he knows the strategy but lacks sufficient *skill*.) It sometimes makes sense to speak of the strength of a strategy as a hypothetical variable that determines either its probability of use in a given situation or in which situations it will ever be used at all.

One way of classifying or analyzing strategies is as plans (Miller, Galanter, & Pribram, 1960). A plan is described in terms of its goals and the subgoals needed to reach each goal or subgoal. Knowing a plan consists of knowing what subgoals must be achieved in order to achieve another goal or subgoal, and, ultimately, what elementary acts must be carried out to achieve a given subgoal.

Strategies might also be related to the rules of inference studied by Piagetians, but they are not the same thing. I take the idea of a strategy

as one possible explanation of how inference rules are used. Another explanation is that each inference rule corresponds to something more like a belief, or to a representation in terms of propositions rather than actions. There might be more general strategies or action rules for making use of such propositional representations, but new inference rules might be acquired without any changes in these action rules themselves.

Strategies can be specific or general. Specific strategies such as shoe tying or addition of decimal numbers are not good candidate components of explanatory intelligence, because they are useful only in certain environments and because they do not explain other manifestations of intelligence.

Baron (1978) suggested that it might be possible to identify a set of *fundamental* strategies. By definition, these strategies would be the basic tools of the intelligent person. They would either suffice in their own right for ensuring optimal performance, or they would suffice for the construction of other tools (strategies or bits of knowledge) that would suffice to perform the task at hand, or perhaps to construct still other tools. Baron (1978) made some suggestions about what these fundamental strategies might be. Two of these were called "checking" and "relatedness search" (and the third major one was "stimulus analysis," which now appears unlikely to be a strategy at all— see Baron, Badgio, & Gaskins, 1983). In retrospect, I find these strategies to be defined vaguely, and I believe that the prescriptive model of chapter 3 incorporates them both explicitly. Relatedness search is replaced by search for possibilities, and particularly by search for evidence (especially evidence that will suggest a possibility). Checking is replaced by search for evidence and its use to modify the strengths of possibilities (or to eliminate them which is to reduce their strengths to zero). In sum, my present view is that the rational conduct of thought plays the role I had previously assigned to fundamental strategies. It is correct, although not necessarily helpful, to view the scheme of chapter 3 as a single basic strategy for thinking, which may be modified for different kinds of tasks.

The comments just made apply to the idea of fundamental strategies only, and there still might be some general strategies that are well worth teaching. In particular, as I shall discuss, strategies might serve as heuristics for search processes (for possibilities, evidence, and goals) within particular domains.

Biases in judgment

A final influence on my approach is the recent literature on the extent to which our judgments conform to normative models of rational judgment

(see Nisbett & Ross, 1980; Kahneman & Tversky, 1984; Kahneman et al., 1982, for reviews). Most of this literature concerns the extent to which our judgments are consistent with the dictates of probability theory and statistics. It turns out that they are not, for two sorts of reasons. One is that although our judgments are affected in a qualitatively correct way by variables such as sample size and goodness of evidence — so that we trust large samples more than small ones and good data more than bad data — the effect of these variables is not quantitatively correct. In essence, we show biases that can be accounted for by the addition of fudge factors to normative models without changing the nature of the models. The other source of error seems to be that we sometimes completely ignore variables that ought to affect our judgments. For example, there are many cases in which we are completely insensitive to sample size, goodness of evidence, or characteristics of the population from which an individual we are judging is drawn. In these cases, it seems that we go about solving these problems in a way that is qualitatively wrong, that is, we use an incorrect strategy.

The contribution this tradition makes to the present approach is in the emphasis on the comparison of our behavior to the dictates of normative models. The approach I take, as I have said, is to apply these models to the process of thought rather than its products, so as to derive prescriptive models. I shall argue that there are systematic biases that prevent us from following these prescriptive models. Note that these biases in thinking are of the quantitative sort just described; I assume that everybody thinks in the same way except for parameter settings. (This is not to deny that quantitative effects can have qualitative causes.)

Biases in thinking may explain directly some of the biases observed in studies of judgments and decisions (as I shall explain; this idea has also been proposed by Kruglanski & Ajzen, 1983). Biases in judgment may in some cases be reduced, for example, by more careful thinking about the problem (Koriat, Lichtenstein, & Fischhoff, 1980). But other biases in judgment may be present even when thinking is optimal at all points. In particular, the subject might not have learned a strategy for avoiding the bias, it might be unavoidable, or the use of a correct strategy might require inordinate (irrational) expenditure of time or effort. In the last two cases, we cannot really say that a person is irrational for failing to conform to a normative model of the products of thinking.

I thus agree with the argument of Cohen (1981) and others that the existence of deviations from normative models in judgment need not always reflect irrationality. On the other hand, I disagree with Cohen's more sweeping claim that irrationality cannot be demonstrated in the

laboratory. I would argue that there are two kinds of irrationality that can be experimentally demonstrated. First, we may show irrational parameter settings in the thinking that generates a judgment. Second, we may show that a person has simply not had the opportunity to learn a correct strategy. In this case, he would presumably use the strategy and find it beneficial once he was successfully taught how to use it. In saying that a person is irrational, we are not accusing him of any irremediable flaw, but, rather, just urging him and people who think like him to reform.

The study of intelligence: history of IQ tests

In the rest of this chapter, I want to examine the major traditions in the study of intelligence. The first tradition I shall discuss is that of the psychometricians, the developers and validators of tests. The early history of this tradition has affected current views of intelligence measurement, so a brief sketch of this history is needed. The tradition began with the work of Galton (e.g., 1883) and Cattell (1890). These workers sought to measure individual differences in basic processes of association and memory, using tasks such as speed of color naming and memory span (the number of digits or letters a person could repeat after a single presentation). Wissler (1901) found that scores on such tests failed to correlate with class standing among Columbia University undergraduates. Although Spearman (1904) found that simple tests did correlate with teacher ratings of children's intelligence, Wissler had already convinced most workers that tests based on simple processes were impractical. (Spearman also pointed out serious flaws in Wissler's work.)

When Binet and Simon (1905) set out to develop a practical intelligence test, they tried a different approach. Binet was a member of a commission charged with making recommendations about what to do with apparently retarded children in the (French) public schools. Binet and Simon put together a test — partly out of other tests previously used by Binet to study intellectual development — for the purpose of distinguishing what we now call mild retardation from other possible causes of school failure. The practical problem was immediate, and these workers had little time to develop new theory. Because they were convinced by Wissler's work that measurement of simple processes alone was insufficient, they tried to make up items to measure higher-level abilities, such as memory, judgment, the ability to maintain a set for a task, the ability to follow instructions, and the ability to check one's answers. Their criterion for a good item was that it be able to distinguish older children from younger children; they thus assumed that intelligence, or at least its measurable pro-

ducts, increased with age. In order to meet this criterion, it may have been necessary to choose items that were largely dependent on the acquisition of specific facts, despite the avowed aim of Binet to avoid too much dependence on schooling and cultural background. Their final test included such items as identifying body parts, the memory span (again), finding rhymes, interpreting pictures, comparing the meanings of words, filling in missing words in a story, and answering questions about relative length. The items were grouped so that the average child of a given age would pass most items in one group and fail most in the next group. Intelligence was thus expressed in terms of level of development, corresponding roughly to the typical age at which a test would be passed (much as we now classify children by grade in reading and arithmetic). Binet recommended that a child who was two years behind be considered as subnormal. Interestingly, Binet also developed and partially implemented a program of "mental orthopedics" for those diagnosed as behind by his test. It included exercises in attention span — such as maintaining a "frozen" position for successively longer periods — and in speed. It must have been one of the first attempts to increase intelligence, to "teach children how to learn" before asking them to do the real thing.

Later workers (Stern, 1912; Terman, 1916) developed a precise measure of mental age, and defined the intelligence quotient (IQ) as [mental age/chronological age] x 100. Terman's (1916) "Stanford Binet" improved on Binet's test only in making the scoring more exact. Some new types of items were added, but the spirit was not changed. Terman's test, after several more revisions, is still widely used.

When the IQ test took hold in the United States, the view became widespread that it measured innate intelligence. For example (Pintner, 1931, pp. 520-521; quoted by Carroll, 1982): "Intelligence tests have done much to show that all children are not created free and equal with respect to their mental abilities. A child's abilities are determined by his ancestors, and all that environment can do is to give opportunities for the development of his potentialities." So far as I can determine, there was no empirical basis for this belief except for the finding that intelligence was correlated among family members, and the fact that environments are similar within families seems not to have given much consideration (however, see the exchange between Lippman and Terman in *The New Republic*, ca. 1922, reprinted in Block & Dworkin, 1976).

Several other kinds of tests have been devised, including tests that do not depend on language and tests that can be given to groups of people using pencil and paper alone. New kinds of items were developed for these tests, such as geometric analogies, mazes, and puzzles. "Aptitude"

tests are also similar to IQ tests, except that they make no effort to avoid material explicitly taught in school. However, in other respects these tests take over the properties of IQ tests, particularly the need to be easily scored. Like most IQ tests, these tests measure the products of previous learning rather than learning itself.

Despite these modifications, most of our current tests are rather direct descendants of Binet's test and the conceptions behind it. This has led to certain limitations that are common to practically all of these descendants. For one thing, Binet's test was designed to provide as much information as possible in as short a time as possble. Thus, it consisted of items that could all be answered in a few seconds. It excluded, for example, difficult problems that might take an hour (or a week) or so to solve, or tests of actual learning and recall of material of the sort to be learned in school. Another constraint is required by the need for easy objective scoring. The test contains no items that require the subject to form a belief or make a decision in any sort of realistic context, even though such items might be useful in measuring what Binet called "judgment," which, at times, he regarded as the heart of intelligence. For example, the test contains no requests for moral reasoning or personal decision-making. The selection of items was thus dictated by practical needs first, and only secondarily by any clear explanatory or criterial concept of intelligence. (Dörner and Kreutzig, 1980, provide a similar critique.) Our present view of intelligence may be so influenced by Binet-type tests that it is hard for us to see how constrained it is, how arbitrary the selection of test items is from a theoretical point of view. Finally, IQ tests are not based on any clearly defined criterion of success, except for correlation with each other and with measures of intellectual success (such as school grades). For example, they are not designed to predict school learning as well as possible; if they were, they might include actual teaching within the test session (Campione et al., 1982). Nor are they based on a cohesive or coherent theory of the nature of intelligence. Most importantly, we cannot look to them to find out what intelligence is, descriptively or theoretically.

Factor analysis

In the absence of a theory of intelligence, attempts were made to derive a theory from empirical study of IQ tests themselves. This effort has been largely associated with a single method of investigation: factor analysis, a statistical technique for inferring underlying causes from a pattern of correlations. Indeed, factor analysis, a method that is useful in other

sciences (see Gould, 1981, ch. 6), developed largely in connection with the study of intelligence.

The roots of factor analysis go back to Spearman's (1904) paper, the same one in which he showed that perceptual measures correlated with teachers' ratings of children's intelligence. The main point of that paper was to present and explain Spearman's finding that every measure correlated with every other measure. Ability to discriminate pitches of tones correlated with ability to discriminate weights about .31; sensory discrimination, in general, correlated about .38 with teacher-rated intelligence; and so on. [Correlation is measured on a scale from 1 (perfect) to 0 (no correlation) to -1 (perfect negative correlation). These particular correlations would be much higher if they were corrected, as Spearman recommended, for errors of measurement.] Spearman proposed that these correlations are the result of a general factor, *g*, or general intelligence. The tests are correlated with each other because they are all correlated with *g*. If the effect of *g* is removed from the correlations, most of the correlations fall to around zero. The methods of factor analysis, applied to this situation, allow us to postulate an underlying source of individual differences, such as *g*, and ask about the correlation between that source or factor and each item or subtest score within a test. This correlation is called a loading of that test on that factor. If the loading of two tests on a given factor is known, the effect of that factor on the correlation between the two tests can be removed by the technique of partial correlation.

Spearman and others applied the new technique to Binet-type tests, once these tests had been developed. The *g* factor was still found; that is, every test, indeed, every item, correlated with every other test or item. When the effect of the *g* factor was removed, groups of tests correlated with each other. For example, on the Wechsler test, tests of general information, similarities, and vocabulary correlate with one another after *g* is removed, as do tests of block puzzles, object assembly, and digit coding. It was proposed that these correlations could be explained by "group" factors, factors that characterized groups of tests. For example, the former correlations may be accounted for by a factor that we might call verbal comprehension; the latter, by a "perceptual speed" factor. Names such as these did not come from any theory, but from examination of the list of loadings on each factor found in the analysis.

Once it became apparent that a pattern of correlations among tests could be analyzed into several factors, a disturbing fact emerged. It turned out that the factors, and hence the loadings of each test on each factor, were not unique. A factor analyst need not begin by extracting the *g* factor and then looking for remaining group factors. Instead, as proposed by Thur-

stone (1938), he might seek a set of factors in such a way as to maximize the number of zero or near-zero loadings in the entire table of loadings. This criterion, called "simple structure," would result in an analysis in which each factor had high loadings for a few tests and essentially zero loadings for others. It could then be said that those tests were the ones that measured that factor. When Thurstone applied this criterion to his own tests, he found seven major factors, which he called verbal, number, spatial, word-fluency, memory, perceptual speed, and reasoning.

Given this sort of analysis, one could ask about the correlations among the factors themselves. Most studies indicate that the factors still intercorrelate, suggesting that there is a *g* factor in addition to the primary factors arising from a simple-structure analysis. However, even the factors themselves seem to fall into higher groups, such as "verbal" versus "performance." Each of these higher factors accounts for a group of correlations among lower factors. When factor analysts speak of the "structure" of intelligence, they often mean a kind of hierarchy of factors, factors of factors, and so on. For example, Vernon (1950) proposed a general factor at the top of the hierarchy. Below this, there were two factors, "verbal-educational" and "practical"; that is, the general factor accounted for the fact that these two factors correlated with each other. The verbal-educational factor was subdivided into a purely verbal factor, a number factor, and so on; the practical factor subdivided into mechanical information, spatial ability, manual ability, and so on. Each of these factors could contain others; for example, the verbal factor contained a vocabulary factor, which could contain separate factors for different domains of vocabulary.

There is no one best way to produce such a model of intelligence by looking at data. A model of this sort can be produced only after certain assumptions are made, each of which imposes a constraint on the factor analysis. For example, one might decide in advance that the factors should be uncorrelated with each other (thus preventing the discovery of a *g* factor). Or one could decide that the factors ought to be uncorrelated after the *g* factor is removed. Or one could decide that there ought to be two major factors, each subdivided into others, in the sense that each major factor accounts for correlations among some of the other factors. Each set of assumptions or constraints that one adopts will produce a different pattern of loadings, but ordinarily there will be no way to decide, by factor analysis alone, which set of loadings is best. Thus, the use of factor analysis to study the structure of intelligence requires the use of considerations outside of factor analysis itself.

A related problem is that the results one gets depend on the tests one chooses to analyze. For example (Carroll, 1982, p. 102), many factor

analyses are based on test batteries in which all of the tests are time limited. In these cases, there will probably be a general factor that can be explained in terms of individual differences in speed of working. If there are some tests in the battery that are untimed, their scores might not correlate at all with the others, so there will be two factors, one for the time-limited tests and one for the untimed tests. As a result of this fact, the enterprise carried on by factor analysts is a kind of bootstrapping operation. One tries to find simultaneously a set of tests, a set of constraints on the analysis, and a resulting set of factors that together will make sense.

The most ambitious effort of this sort is that of Guilford (1967, 1982), who devised a kind of periodic table of tasks, which allowed him to propose kinds of tasks not yet included in batteries examined by others. Guilford tried to devise tasks such that each measured a single ability. He classified tasks, and hence abilities, according to a three-dimensional scheme. One dimension concerned content: figural (designs, etc.), symbolic (letters, etc.), semantic, and behavioral (interpretations of behavior). Another concerned types of mental operations: memory, recognition, convergent production (getting the right answer when there is only one), divergent production (many right answers required, scored for quality and number), and evaluation (judgments of goodness or appropriateness). The third dimension concerned the type of product: units of information, classes of units, relations between units, systems of information, transformations, and implications. The 120 different combinations of these attributes are supposed to yield 120 different factors. If pains are taken to pick tests that are relatively pure for each factor, the tests for each factor do indeed correlate highly with one another, and not as highly with tests for other factors. However, it is impossible to say how much these results are due to selection of tests for each factor on the basis of some good intuition that the tests of the same factor should correlate highly. It is apparently impossible to provide rules for assigning tests to factors, and it is often hard to predict, from looking at one of Guilford's tests, which factor he will assign it to.

The most interesting use of the factor analytic approach, I think, is that of Raymond Cattell (e.g., 1963) and Horn (e.g., 1978). This approach proposed a distinction between "fluid" and "crystallized" intelligence, which, under appropriate conditions, show up as superordinate factors. Fluid intelligence is measured by tests of speed, energy, and quick adaptation to new situations: e.g., memory span, copying symbols, and solving abstract problems (as on the Raven's matrices). Crystallized intelligence is measured by vocabulary, tests of social reasoning, and problem-solving

that depends on knowledge. Scores on fluid tests decline with age after adolescence, whereas scores on crystallized tests continue to increase throughout the life-span. (Total score may remain approximately the same over the life-span, on the average, but this must be seen as a coincidence. If more crystallized items were used, IQ would increase with age, if fewer, it would decrease, and there is no principle for deciding on the appropriate mixture.) Performance on fluid items, but not crystallized items, is improved by administration of stimulant drugs (Gupta, 1977). Cattell suggests that crystallized intelligence is the result or product of prior fluid intelligence, since the former represents abilities useful in learning and the latter measures what has been learned. Although this seems to be an attractive conception of test design, I should point out that there is not a sufficiently developed theory to allow us to make up items that we know in advance will measure one type of intelligence or the other. Further, the attractive simplicity of the original formulation I have described has been complicated by subsequent findings and reconceptualizations (Horn, 1978).

Summary and critique of the IQ testing tradition

Our current concept of IQ, and indeed our concept of intelligence, has been largely shaped by the followers of Binet and by the factor analysts. From Binet and his followers, we inherit the idea that intelligence can be reasonably measured by a test taking only an hour or two, the idea that such a test should include a variety of tasks, and the idea that intelligence is related to rate of development. From Spearman and the followers of Binet, but not Binet himself, we inherit the idea that intelligence is a single trait, or, more conservatively, that there is a "general factor" underlying it all. From later factor analysts, we inherit the somewhat contradictory idea that intelligence actually consists of a mixture of traits, which can be classified as verbal versus performance, or crystalline versus fluid, etc.

I have two main criticisms of the theory we have inherited. First, the selection of items for IQ tests has been based on tradition rather than on a well-justified criterion of what intelligence is good for (a criterion) or what causes it (an explanation). As a result, it is likely that the factors discovered reflect the biases inherent in this tradition, and there is little reason to think that a more adequate theory would yield the same results. Second, although the traditional conception of intelligence may serve certain purposes—such as the diagnosis of retardation—there are others that it is unlikely to serve, because it has not been developed with these in mind. In particular, it makes no distinction between general capacities

and general dispositions, a distinction we need if we are going to try to improve intelligence through education.

One answer to my first criticism is that various intelligence tests all correlate highly with one another. Thus, it is argued, some sort of true intelligence comes through, despite the variety of measures. But is the variety really that great? I have pointed out that the various IQ tests, because of their ancestry, share many assumptions, which, together, could lead to considerable overlap in the kinds of items used in different tests. To see how this might be, consider the kinds of tasks that are not usually included in IQ tests: learning new material of the sort taught in school, inventing or creating a novel product such as a poem or a machine, making moral arguments, memorizing large amounts of arbitrary material, or solving a real interpersonal problem. Such evidence as there is suggests that correlations are not all that strong when very different kinds of tasks are intercorrelated. For example, Wallach (1976) points out that measures of real-world creativity do not correlate that highly with measures of academic performance or IQ. Similarly, Kohlberg's (1970) score for maturity of moral judgments does not correlate much with IQ when IQ is above average, although it does correlate when IQ is below average, as if an IQ of 100 were a kind of prerequisite for a high score; and Dörner and Kreutzig (1980) report essentially zero correlations between intelligence measures and success in very complex problem-solving (such as governing an imaginary town successfully in a computer model).

Thus, the *g* factor may arise from lack of variety in the selection of tasks, most of which are short tasks that require some general knowledge (but not specific school subjects) and that can be timed and easily scored for quality. There is no reason I can think of, other than convenience, for selection of just this kind of item as a measure of "intelligence." We simply do not know how much of this "common *g* factor" phenomenon is due to the basic similarity of the items used. Indeed, it does not even make much sense to ask the question of whether there is a *g* factor without some clear criterion for selecting items, and there is basically no such criterion except for convenience and tradition.

Even if this problem could be solved, there are other problems with the idea of a *g* factor. One basic argument goes back to Thomson (Brown & Thomson, 1921). Suppose that there is really no *g* factor at all, but rather a set of 10 or 100 or 1000 specific abilities that have no correlation with each other. For example, some of these might be the capacities of mental speed, available effort, learning, and accuracy of retrieval from memory. Suppose further that because of our ignorance of what these specific abilities are, we have not yet hit upon pure measures of more than a small

proportion of them. (A pure measure is a measure affected by no other abilities.) The tasks we actually use are each affected by several different abilities. For example, the digit span will be affected by speed and available effort, vocabulary will be affected by speed and retrieval, the Raven's matrices will be affected by learning and retrieval, and so on. Any two tasks are likely to be affected by one or more common abilities. Thus, their scores will correlate because the scores on both tasks will be affected by the common abilities. At base, it is just such correlations among pairs of tasks that provide the evidence for the *g* factor. Yet, we see that such correlations can be explained without any reference to such a factor. These underlying abilities do not emerge as factors in a factor analysis because there are so many of them, and because they are swamped by other factors that happen to be measured with greater purity by the tasks we have. Nor can it be said that these specific abilities constitute the *g* factor itself. A test made up on the basis of a theory of these underlying abilities, with direct measures of each one, would show no *g* factor; hence, when the *g* factor appears in other tests, it would be an artifact of the tests themselves, not a necessary property of intelligence tests in general.

This point is accepted by workers such as Humphreys (1979) and Jensen (1980), who still feel that the *g* factor is a useful concept. They apparently assume that IQ test items are a fair sample of the tasks that life provides, and the interesting fact is then that people who are good at one task are good at another. However, these workers tend to downplay or ignore the problem of unbiased test selection. In fact, given the history I have sketched, there is little reason to think that IQ tasks are a representative selection of important tasks.

To put factor analysis in perspective, it may help to think about those cases in which the statistical technique is clearly appropriate. Suppose we know that several chemical factories along a river are dumping chemicals into the river illegally, and we want to find out how many there are by sampling river water repeatedly from different places at different times. Each chemical factory is known to have its own "signature" expressed as a certain mixture of chemicals, and each is known to vary somewhat independently of the others in rate of dumping. For each sample, we measure the various illegal chemicals in the river, of which there are a great many. We correlate the amount of each chemical with the amount of every other chemical in each sample. In this case, assuming no other influences, the number of separate factors will correspond exactly to the number of factories dumping illegally. Here, the underlying factors have a real causal meaning: Each one represents a factory.

By comparison, the use of factor analysis in the study of intelligence seems inappropriate. Correlations among items may be affected by spurious influences, such as correlations among learning opportunities (Carroll, 1982, p. 101) or environments. For example, arithmetic tests may load on the same factor only because arithmetic is taught all together. The common factor exists because of differences in teaching (as well as learning). If some people were taught addition and others subtraction, there would be two factors instead of one.

It is often said that these problems are unimportant, because factor analysis is only a discovery procedure, and its results admittedly need to be checked by other methods. But what methods? The problem is that the psychometric tradition has given us neither criteria nor possible explanations, and without these, it is not clear what kind of inquiry will be able to use the results that the tradition has given us. Moreover, when we arrive at some criteria, of the sort I have proposed here, or explanations (of the sort I propose later), it is not clear that the results of factor analysis provide any help at all.

Is there anything that the IQ test is good for? One answer is that it is a research tool, to be used for such purposes as making sure that two groups of subjects are equal in "general ability." Clearly, from what I have said, it cannot legitimately be used in this way. Two groups — e.g., dyslexics and normals — may have identical IQ scores only because they excel or fail on different parts of the test. A different mixture of items in the test, one that included more of the strengths of one group and the weaknesses of the other, would show the groups to be unequal. And there is no principled basis for choosing any particular mixture of items.

On the other hand, the IQ test is good for some things. One is that it helps us predict which children will benefit most from which kind of instruction. In many cases, low-IQ students benefit most from more "structured," step-by-step instruction in a subject, whereas high-IQ subjects benefit most from less structured instruction (Cronbach & Snow, 1977; Snow & Yalow, 1982). However, even here, there is reason to think that better predictions are possible using tests in which the student was actually asked to learn something during the course of testing (Campione et al., 1982). Thus, IQ tests might not be as good for prediction as tests designed exactly for that purpose.

In some cases, IQ tests may be considered as stand-ins for cognitive tasks in general. Thus, we can use IQ tests legitimately to ask such questions as whether (and why) birth order affects cognitive skills (Zajonc & Markus, 1975); here, any measure of cognitive skills would do, and IQ happens to be available. Beyond this, IQ seems to play much the

same role in our thinking as do many indexes in economics, such as the Gross National Product, or M1. These measures are proxies for things that are of real interest, such as the material quality of life of the people now and in the future, or the relative attractiveness of investment versus purchases, or the total demand for goods and services. Better measures are impractical or theoretically beyond our reach, so we use what we have for the time being. The danger, in psychology as in economics, is that we may come to think of the measures themselves as representing our real concerns.

A comment on the controversy about the inheritance of IQ

Before leaving the IQ test, I should address briefly the issue that has been the source of much controversy about the test, namely, the inheritance of IQ, and hence, in the minds of many, of intelligence. Most of the early workers who made up intelligence tests — except Binet — thought that intelligence was largely inherited. Furthermore, inherited abilities were assumed to be unaffected by education or child rearing. Thus, a good IQ test would try to measure abilities that we could not easily imagine teaching. Of course, some abilities were thought to be measured most easily by testing knowledge of material everyone supposedly has a chance to learn, such as vocabulary. In this case, one could try to subvert the test by teaching the vocabulary that would be on it. But this sort of thing has always been considered subversion, because one did not teach the underlying ability that leads to large vocabulary, one only coached students on the test. (The attitude of teachers is less clear when they try to convince their students to learn vocabulary on the grounds that "vocabulary is the best measure of IQ," to quote my 10th grade English teacher. Did he really think he was raising our intelligence by increasing our vocabulary? Or did he want to help us fool anyone who gave us an IQ test?) For the same reason, extensive practice at items of the type used on a test is thought to make the test invalid.

Given this conception of what the test is supposed to measure, it is not surprising that much effort has been expended on finding out whether test scores are genetically determined. Scarr and Carter-Saltzman (1982) provide a current review. It is very hard to do good genetic research on human beings. Any such research requires comparison of IQs of pairs of people who are either closely related or distantly related, holding constant the difference between the environments of the members of the pairs. We cannot hold environment constant, as would be possible in agriculture or animal breeding, and there are all kinds of reasons why

genetically related people will live in similar environments, no matter what pains we take to avoid this. Nor can we try to measure the relevant environmental differences and take account of their effect, because we do not know what they are. The evidence that there is, for example, from identical twins separated at birth, suggests that IQ is somewhat heritable. Perhaps half the variation in IQ is genetic; some say more, some say less. (One can even argue that IQ is not heritable at all; see Kamin, 1974.)

Arguments about the inheritance of IQ have always been bitter (Block & Dworkin, 1976), because people have thought them to be related to various issues in public policy. This is particularly true recently, because it has become known that American blacks score 10-15 points lower than whites, on the average, even during recent times, when most blacks attend schools. Jensen (1969) suggested that the black-white difference accounted for the supposed failure of compensatory education programs for blacks in the United States. To make this argument, Jensen had to argue that the black-white difference in IQ is itself genetic, and thus not something that compensatory education could itself correct. Now if IQ is not heritable at all, it follows that the black-white difference is not genetic. However, if IQ is somewhat heritable, then the black-white difference may or may not be genetic. The best guess (Scarr & Carter-Saltzman, 1982) is that IQ *is* somewhat heritable but race differences in IQ are not genetic. Race differences are probably due to such factors as expectations of blacks for themselves, expectations of others for them, prejudice, effects of economic factors on intellectual development, and perpetuation of cultural and linguistic patterns that lead to low performance on academic tasks.

One undercurrent in this debate concerns the relation between the validity of IQ tests and their heritability. One view, which I think is secretly held by those who emphasize the inherited component of IQ, runs roughly as follows. We admit that IQ is partly determined by experience. However, look for a moment at the IQ test. It is clearly the sort of test that would be influenced by things that one has learned, such as vocabulary and test-taking skills. This is purely a matter of the testers' convenience, and it has nothing to do with intelligence itself. It seems a safe assumption, then, that *real* intelligence is much more heritable than that measured by the tests. Thus, if the IQ score is only 50% heritable, real intelligence is probably a lot more heritable than that. Further, if real intelligence is nearly 100% heritable, it is hard to imagine (goes the argument) that it might be influenced by changes in education or child rearing.

There are two problems with this argument. First, high heritability does

not imply lack of malleability. It has been claimed, for example, that the heritability of height in human populations is nearly perfect, within a given generation, yet the mean height has increased steadily over several generations in the United States and Japan (Crow, 1969, p. 158). Presumably, some environmental factors have changed that vary little within each generation, for example, general awareness of children's need for fluoride. There may be analogous factors that would increase everyone's intelligence, even if intelligence differences are mostly genetic. Second, even if high heritability did rule out malleability, there is no reason to assume that the "true" intelligence hidden behind the test is highly heritable (or that it is not malleable). The assumption that IQ would be perfectly heritable, or not malleable, if only the tests were better is completely gratuitous.

Cross-cultural research

Another relevant tradition is that concerning cultural effects on performance of abstract tasks, such as memory tasks using arbitrary material, free classification tasks, and problem solving. It is generally found that people who grow up in cultures without Western-style schooling perform poorly on such tasks, even when efforts are made to exclude tasks that might have been done in school. Recently, with increased but as yet not universal schooling in many cultures, it has become possible to ask whether these cultural differences are due to schooling itself or to other aspects of the cultures in question. In every case I know of in which this question has been asked, the answer is that the effects are due primarily to schooling. For example, Wagner (1974, 1978) found that rural Mexican and rural and urban Moroccan children showed no improvement with age in a serial memory task, unless the subjects had been to school. The schooled subjects showed the same age trends that had been found in other studies in the United States, trends of the sort usually explained in terms of increasing use of strategies such as rehearsal. Sharp, Cole, and Lave (1979) asked Mexican subjects to sort a set of cards into classes. The cards varied in three dimensions, e.g., color, shape, and number of figures per card. Schooling affected the probability of sorting the cards according to a consistent rule that could be described in terms of the attributes that were manipulated. This result occurred as well when the stimuli were made up of corn kernals, with the attributes reflecting the local classification scheme. Years of schooling, in contrast to age and sex, was also the main determinant of performance on most of the subtests of Thurstone's (1938) test of Primary Mental Abilities (a kind of IQ test)

and on a set of problems from Raven's Matrices. This study was also noteworthy for its careful measurement of the determinants of who went to school and who did not. The main determinants of years of schooling were the number of years of school available in the subject's town, and other economic factors such as number of siblings. Parental schooling had little effect. The evidence indicated that there was little if any selection for schooling on the basis of mental abilities. (See also Stevenson et al., 1978.)

I take these studies to be the best evidence there is for the possibility of raising intelligence through education, and, therefore, the best evidence there is for experiential causes of intelligence. It is noteworthy that most of these effects of schooling are on tasks that are not directly taught in school, and that do not in any obvious way depend on the learning of reading, arithmetic, etc. Hence, whatever is responsible for these effects is somewhat general. In some cases, as in the corn kernals task, and Wagner's memory experiments, pains were taken to make sure that the materials were familiar to the unschooled subjects. Testing was often done by members of the subjects' cultural group. Although the tasks were not measures of basic components of intelligence, the most likely explanation of these results is that true intelligence (in the explanatory sense) is affected by schooling. Most likely, schooling affects various dispositions — some specific and some general — in addition to imparting specific knowledge. It would be worthwhile, for example, to examine the time taken by the schooled and unschooled subjects in these tasks and others; conceivably, schooling affects the disposition to search thoroughly and plan fully.

In view of the straightforwardness of my interpretation of the data, it may seem strange that many workers in cross-cultural psychology have resisted this interpretation (e.g., Greenfield, 1978), and that the strongest resistance has come from those with the strongest results (Sharp et al., 1979). In a historical context, this resistance is understandable. Many early workers in cross-cultural psychology seemed to operate under blatantly racist assumptions, and took poor test performance as a sign of genetic inferiority. Under the influence of anthropology, a field that had dealt with this sort of approach much earlier, cross-cultural psychology reacted against these early workers by making sure to respect its subjects and their culture; hence the resistance to the idea that Western schooling, an invention of the psychologists' culture, can make people generally intelligent. Although the resistance is understandable, it may still be out of place, even given the liberal values the psychologists profess to hold.

The resisters make two main arguments. The first is that task perfor-

mance of unschooled people is highly sensitive to the conditions of testing. For example, in one experiment, Cole, Gay, Glick, and Sharp (1971) showed their subjects a set of objects for subsequent recall. The subjects failed to take advantage of the fact that the items could be grouped into a few categories. When the experimenter insisted that the subjects recall the items by category, however, performance improved and was comparable to that of American schoolchildren left to their own devices. Thus, the unschooled subjects in this study could be taught to use what I have been calling a strategy, and when they used it, their deficit disappeared. This sort of result is usually interpreted as evidence that there is no "real" deficiency. It is indeed evidence of this, but only if we take "real" to refer to a capacity deficit. From my perspective, the most straightforward explanation for this sort of result is that the deficit *is* real and that it is the result of an effect of culture on dispositions (e.g., to use strategies).

There is another sort of finding that has suggested to people that results are not real. This is that performance is affected by some variable that does not affect performance in control subjects in, for example, the United States. Greenfield, for example (in Bruner et al., 1966), found that her African subjects often failed to give correct answers in the conservation of liquid task, when the experimenter poured the liquids, as is usually done. But when the subjects were allowed to pour the liquids, performance improved considerably. This manipulation had no effect on North American subjects. Apparently, the African children went into the experiment with the assumption that it was more like what we would call a magic show than what we would call a test. When they poured the liquids themselves, they realized that there was no trick. This sort of result shows up repeatedly in anecdotes. Glick (1975, cited by Goodnow, 1976), for example, described one subject who did a sorting task in a way that we would consider less mature, putting a knife with an orange instead of with other silverware. When the subject said he was doing the task the way a wise man would do it, the experimenter asked him to do it the way a fool would, and the subject proceeded to do it "correctly."

These sorts of results and anecdotes seem to raise more serious problems for my interpretation. However, I think that the problem is not as great as it appears. Most of the results of this sort that I know of have to do with certain kinds of tasks, specifically, tasks in which the experimenter is not explicit about the criterion for success. In sorting tasks, for example, both kinds of responses are correct, in the sense that the experimenter has presented the task as a test of the subject's judgment, not his or her ability to solve a problem. We consider the categorical grouping to be more mature because it is the one that Western adults give. But there

is no other good argument that this is the more intelligent response. (There are post hoc arguments, but I suspect that equally good ones could be given if the results were reversed.) The important point is that the general effects of schooling that I have described are not confined to this sort of task. They occur as well in memory tasks and concept learning tasks, where the criterion for success is usually clear. More generally, the more recent studies I have mentioned have taken considerable pains to avoid such effects as these.

The second argument made by those who resist my interpretation is more serious. This is that the tasks used for the reseach are not representative of anything important, such as "intelligence," and that they reflect no more than arbitrary cultural biases. The results thus mean no more than a demonstration that Texans would fail a test devised by Eskimos, in which most of the items consisted of fine discriminations of different kinds of snow. Sharp et al. (1979), for example, admit that their results are consistent with the claim that education fosters "the development of flexible problem-solving routines and rules for their application," but they feel that this impression is "an illusion produced by the narrow range of tasks, all of them derived from school contexts." (p. 82) Cole, in his reply to comments, indicates that more valid tasks would sample domains of work that are relevant to the culture. "Do rural Yucatecans who have been to school more rapidly adopt advantageous strains of corn?" (p. 112)

What is going on here? The same tasks that I have found so convincing just because they are not typical of what is taught in school are maligned because they *are* "derived from school contexts." What could Sharp et al. mean by this? It seems to me that when they say "derived . . . ," they mean that the tasks are abstract and novel, and they are ready to grant that schooling might help people perform such tasks. But, they would argue, the ability to solve abstract, novel problems might itself be seen as a task valued by our own culture (Laboratory of Comparative Human Cognition, 1982, p. 688 and fn. 11), but of no particular value in others. What is thus denied is the possibility of a cross-culturally valid conception of intelligence, such as the one I have suggested here. In particular, these workers would deny the possibility that certain ways of thinking (such as considering alternative possibilities, or gathering adequate evidence before making a decision) could both be culturally acquired and be helpful to people in achieving their rational goals, whatever these might be. Such a denial seems gratuitous, and perhaps it is not even intended.

At issue is what we take intelligence to be. Many cross-cultural psychologists, and others, seem to take descriptive intelligence to be a matter

of adaptation to one's environment. Hence the emphasis on tasks that the culture does. Any other emphasis, it seems to these workers, would put us in the position of using our own cultural standards to make judgments about the value of other people.

In reply, I note that making a judgment about the level of intellectual abilities in a certain group is not the same as making a judgment of the value of the people in that group in any other sense — although we must of course be wary of slipping into this error. In fact, such judgments may be a necessary part of any program to help people make the most of their capacities to achieve their own rational goals, and thus in the end might be a sign of respect for humanity rather than arrogance.

Further, descriptive intelligence ought to be a broader concept than adaptation to one's environment. One of our reasons for being interested in general intellectual abilities is exactly that we cannot prepare people fully for their environments with specific knowledge alone, that we cannot fully anticipate their environments. This is now certainly as true for members of rural societies around the world as it is for our own; perhaps it was always more true than the idea of long-term cultural stability would lead us to believe. The use of abstract and novel tasks as criteria is thus partly justified by the role of these tasks as proxies for unanticipated tasks people will be called on to do, such as (I hope) to make decisions among political candidates on the basis of abstract statements the candidates make or to decide whether to adopt new agricultural methods.

At another level, the whole idea of adaptation (to tasks that are antici- pated or not) is, I think, a stand-in for some other concept, such as goodness of life. The idea of adaptation seems sufficiently neutral and noncommittal that it allows us to talk about other cultures without much worry that we are imposing our own values on them. But this is an illusion. It is simply not clear that the average Yucatecan, on reflection, would want nothing more than to be "adapted" within the standards of his or her culture, that is, to have a good corn crop, or whatever. (By "on reflection," I mean with a kind of awareness of other possibilities that it may be difficult for the Yucatecan to acquire.) To assume that only the current values of the culture are relevant to questions about the value of intellectual abilities and traits is, in a way, as presumptuous as it is to assume that only our own current values are relevant. We must, in the end, face squarely the question of what is rational to want in oneself and in others as thinking beings.

In sum, it would seem that the controversies surrounding cross-cultural findings are explicable in the framework I have outlined. The claim that cultural effects are not "real" is related to the belief that only narrow

intelligence is real intelligence, a belief I take to be gratuitous. The claim that the tasks used by cross-cultural psychology are arbitrary is related to the assumption that descriptive intelligence is fully captured by the idea of adaptation, a belief I take to be unfounded. The cross-cultural evidence, in fact, provides encouragement for the view that some components of intelligence are acquired from experience in a general form. The theory outlined in the rest of this book should permit more conclusive tests of this claim to be made.

Conclusion

Let me conclude by trying to sketch a view of how the theory of intelligence might develop. We must begin with a criterial definition of intelligence, stated in general terms. I have argued that this definition should be as broad as possible, so that intelligence includes whatever makes for effectiveness regardless of environment.

Next, we propose general explanatory components that can reasonably be thought to lead to intelligence in the criterial sense we have chosen. These explanatory components must also be described in general terms. They may be dispositions, practiceable capacities, or unpracticeable capacities. Experimental tests may be made of the existence of the proposed components as sources of individual differences. Studies of malleability can be done to determine whether a proposed component is experiential, and, if so, whether it is malleable through instruction or practice, and whether general training is effective. Such studies are also of obvious practical interest.

Once components are isolated, it then must be shown that they can account for criterial intelligence, that is, that they are consequential. The simplest way of doing this is to find correlations between a measure of a causal component and a measure of a criterial aspect, for example, a correlation between, on the one hand, a measure of mental resources or impulsiveness, and, on the other, a measure of school success or happiness with one's work. (Any measure of effectiveness must obviously make assumptions about what is effective in a given cultural context.) For example, one possibly inconsequential component is the ability to learn and recognize items, when strategies used at the time of learning and recognition are held constant (Baron, Freyd, & Stewart, 1980). This ability is uncorrelated with academic success, which is at least roughly related to any descriptive definition of intelligence in our culture. In general, it is difficult to establish with certainty a relationship between an explanatory component of intelligence and an aspect of a criterial definition. In the

case of capacities, one must rely on correlational evidence. Even in the case of experiential components, it is difficult to manipulate only a single component with enough power so that it might have an observable effect on a person's effectiveness, adaptation, or academic success. Demonstrations of relationships between explanatory components and criterial aspects of intelligence will have to rely largely on arguments of plausibility.

My task here is only to propose a part of this theory, the part dealing with dispositions. This part is of particular interest because of its relation to the question of educational goals.

2   Rational choices and plans

Consider a student caught in a conflict between working some more on a homework problem in statistics, which he has so far failed to solve, and playing his favorite video game on his personal computer. On the first side is his desire to learn statistics, to get a good grade in the statistics course, to get into graduate school, to have a successful career, and to convince himself that he really is smarter than his sister. On the other side is his desire to play Pac-Man. The student might admit that the rational course of action would be to continue working on the problem, but he might give in to temptation anyway. In this chapter, I shall try to say why the first course might be the rational one (when it is). I want to try to say what it means to be rational in balancing expected costs and benefits when choosing alternative actions—especially when one choice involves thinking and the other does not—given one's goals. Beyond this, I shall ask what it means to have rational goals. In the next chapter, I shall use the ideas developed here to justify some prescriptive rules for the conduct of thinking. As in the present example, these rules will involve tradeoffs of different kinds of consequences of thinking or not thinking. I shall argue that the rational conduct of thinking involves a kind of expected-utility maximization. Thus, this chapter will contain a limited defense of expected-utility theory as a normative theory of action, at least for this case.

I have argued that rational thinking is thinking that follows a prescriptive model, and that prescriptive models are justified in terms of normative models applied to the process of thinking (not its products). In this chapter, I deal with the normative models that provide the justification, particularly the principles of *deliberative rationality* and *utility maximization*. In the next two chapters, I use some of these models to develop prescriptive rules. The normative models are idealized, and it is not necessarily rational for a real person to try to follow them; the prescriptive models, on the other hand, are exactly what we should strive to follow.

50

Discussion of normative models is dangerous, for we can quickly become detached from reality. In such discussion, there is no requirement that a normative model be feasible; unlike the case of prescriptive models, "ought" does not imply "can" (for mortals). The evaluation of normative models is done from the perspective of idealized creatures who are not constrained by various factors that constrain us mortals, such as lack of time for deliberation, or fear of risk taking. We may construct different creatures by imagining the removal of different constraints. A good normative model for mortals is a good prescriptive model for one of these creatures. (Occasionally, as when we are willing to spend a great deal of time on a decision or other thought process, or when we design a computer program to help us, we may ourselves approach the situation of an idealized being, and the normative model may be useful prescriptively for real people.) I shall try to be explicit here about what kind of creatures I am discussing.

Given the perspective of an idealized creature, we may evaluate normative models by reflecting about the principles we would want ourselves and others to follow, if we were all idealized. The test of a normative model is whether it fits our strong intuitions, whether we find it clarifying, especially in developing prescriptions, and whether it allows us to give advice to ourselves and others that we could not have given otherwise. For a normative theory to be helpful in this way, the creatures we imagine must be as close as possible to real humans. We ought to be able to set real goals for our own thinking by asking what we would do if we were idealized in the ways assumed. This method of reflecting about hypothetical situations is the only method we have for developing normative models. There is no authority we can appeal to, no set of axioms from which such principles can be derived (for how would we know that the axioms are true?), and no empirical data that will settle the question. (To try to derive a normative model from data, without additional normative assumptions, would be to commit a form of the naturalistic fallacy, the attempt to derive "ought" statements from "is" statements alone.) Moreover, such a reflective theory — although necessarily imperfect — can be taken as the best basis we have for construction of prescriptive models for making decisions about our lives, and, in our role as educators, about the lives of others.

I shall refer to two idealized beings as the educator and the student, respectively. The educator may be thought of as a parent, teacher, or friendly critic, and the student may be a child or adult. The prescriptive model of the next chapter is primarily a theory of what advice a real educator should give to a real student. This *educator's perspective* is the one from which we might say, "You may think you really want to play

Pac-Man now, but in the long run, it is learning your statistics that is in your true interest, so you should spend more time thinking about it." Thus, the crucial question is not what the student should take as being rational, but rather what the educator should take as rational for the student on the student's behalf. I deal with this question by asking what an idealized educator would assume.

Rational plans

Utility maximization is roughly the idea that the relative desirability of an action may be computed by multiplying the probability of each of the possible consequences of the action by the utility of that consequence and adding up these products. The being who uses this theory is assumed to be mortal except for having unlimited time to list possible consequences, estimate their probabilities, and estimate their utilities. No special knowledge is assumed for any of these tasks, although the estimations need not be done directly (as I shall explain). (The theory allows flexibility in what is considered a "consequence." Each consequence can potentially be analyzed in to subconsequences, each with its own utility and probability. However, if our idealized creature applies the theory successfully, it should not matter how fine an analysis he performs; he should come up with the same answer concerning the expected utility of an action. The point of the analysis into consequences is to compare actions whose consequences can be analyzed similarly.) The theory seems to be a good one for investment decisions, if all one cares about is maximizing income in the long run, but its extension to decisions about careers, marriage, public policy, or even whether to play Pac-Man may seem arrogant, unwarranted, or impossible. The critic may well ask why he should follow this simple rule, and whether it is possible to do so in any meaningful way. I believe that some of these questions may be answered in terms of a general theory of rational plans of the sort proposed by Rawls (1971, ch. VII) or Richards (1971). Thus, a broad theory of the rational course of living life can help us to understand the sense in which it is rational to maximize expected utility. I shall begin by sketching such a theory, drawing heavily on Rawls and Richards. My aim is not to develop this theory with all its ramifications, but rather to show how such a theory might be developed and how it is relevant to the questions I discuss in this book.

A theory of rational choices and goals should be concerned with plans or rules as well as individual decisions, for plans may set up the goals that individual actions are intended to satisfy. Further, it is reasonable to

speak of *life plans* as well as short-term plans, for a rational short-term plan is intended to satisfy some higher goal, and the basic goals and policies of a person may be taken to constitute his or her life plan. A theory of rational life plans goes beyond utility theory in saying what is rational. Utility theory assumes that utilities of consequences already exist for an individual. A theory of rational life plans says something about whether the utilities themselves are rational; that is, it allows an educator to criticize a student's utilities, and for the student to criticize his own. Of course, to criticize utilities as irrational is to presuppose that they are to some extent under an individual's control. This is true to the extent to which people choose their goals, which then motivate their day-to-day actions. It does not seem unreasonable to assume that people can follow advice about goals—a necessary condition of their goals being evaluated as rational or not—even if most people neither seek nor follow such advice. We may advise someone else, or advise ourselves, to listen to more classical music in order to develop a liking for it, to participate in politics in order to acquire an interest in social reform, or to get over a taste for chocolate by eating less of it. We might even be advised to create (or weaken) lasting motives by single acts, which we might call plan-forming decisions. For example, it may help a person to stop smoking to decide that she doesn't like cigarettes anymore. (Irwin, 1971, would describe these as initiations of extended acts.) Because we believe that goals are somewhat corrigible, we frequently criticize people's goals (e.g., those of our children). Of course, sometimes we are wrong to think that a goal is corrigible—but, importantly, we are not always wrong.

It can be argued that that the process of coming to value, say, classical music really involves a *discovery* that classical music satisfies some value already present within us, so that no new value is created (Williams, 1981, ch. 8). However, the main implication of this argument for rational living is that we ought to discover and try to satisfy all the values within us. If the argument does not have this implication, the difference between discovery and creation is a matter of terminology. If the argument does have this implication, it seems too strong. If I am satisfied with my life as it is, why should I try to "discover" my latent interest in punk rock? Undoubtedly, there are many values that each of us could discover or invent; decisions about life plans involve a choice among these. The theory of rational plans is supposed to help us make the right choice or to help an educator decide what sorts of choices will be right for a student.

A life plan need not be explicitly formulated, nor need it be fixed at some point in time. It makes sense to think of many elements of our life plan as innate and beyond our control; thus, it also makes sense to say

that the rationality of *all* our actions is dictated by our life plan. We also set precedents for ourselves by making a certain decision for a certain reason (Hare, 1952, ch. 4). If we do nothing more than act according to the same reason in a subsequent situation, we can be said to be following a principle or part of a plan. If we later act according to a different principle, it is fair to say that our plan has changed. Thus, a plan is an abstraction from the rules we follow, not necessarily something that we consciously hold in mind — although it may be that too. Usually, the term "plan" connotes a complex structure of contingency plans, goals, and subgoals (Miller, Galanter, & Pribram, 1960). However, in the sense used here, it need not have this connotation. The principle, "take things as they come," can be the main principle of someone's life plan (if he or she is sufficiently "laid back").

Rawls's most important concept for a normative theory of life plans is the principle of deliberative rationality (ch. 64). An idealized form of this principle "characterizes a person's future good on the whole as what he would now desire and seek if the consequences of all the various courses of conduct open to him were, at the present point in time, accurately foreseen by him and adequately realized in imagination." The best plan for a person, then, is the one he would choose under this hypothetical condition. It is important to note that the condition *is* hypothetical, which is why this principle is normative without necessarily being prescriptive. As stated so far, the theory involves an idealized being with infinite time for imagining possible consequences and weighing sets of them against one another. For our purposes (going beyond Rawls), this ideal being is free to declare himself unable to decide among alternative plans, in which case they would all be considered rational. He may make judgments about whole plans or about features of plans (such as the rules of utility theory I shall discuss). Importantly, he makes judgments holistically, without analyzing consequences into different dimensions of utility; one purpose of the plan might be to specify the nature and importance of such dimensions, so they cannot be presumed to exist.

The final form of the principle of deliberative rationality takes into account the cost of deliberation. As Rawls points out (p. 418), "deliberation is itself an activity like any other, and the extent to which one should engage in it is subject to rational decision. The formal rule is that we should deliberate up to the point where the likely benefits from improving our plans are just worth the time and effort of reflection." In this form, the only idealization required is that the person in question actually deliberate the right amount of time about his life plan, and choose one of the best ones given this amount of deliberation.

Actual deliberation about life plans is most easily understood as a matter of constructing one's values so as to take the facts of one's nature, one's past history, and one's likely future circumstances into account. For example, when I decide to have a child, I do not do so just because I expect the child to further my current values. In addition, I adopt new values, such as concern for the child's welfare, and these new values stand alongside my old ones. In making such a decision, I would like to know whether I would prefer a life with the new values, given what chance of satisfying them exists, to a life without them. Since I do not have these values yet, I cannot make a decision simply by consulting my values (except in the sense in which all decisions about values are viewed as discoveries and all apparent new values are merely consequences of old ones). However, choices about values or goals are not totally arbitrary; if I want to take the time to deliberate, I can rely on such aids as imagination of what the new life would be like, aided by the reports of others, and my knowledge of the effects of my circumstances on the satisfaction of various values. Actual deliberation is not required for me to have a rational plan (or, more realistically, some parts of one). What is required is that I would find my plan to be acceptable if I did deliberate to a sufficient extent.

A consequence of trying to follow a rational plan is that one need not blame oneself for making bad plans in the past, no matter how things turn out (Rawls, 1971, p. 422). This is because a plan chosen rationally is the best that can be done. If things turn out badly, this is because some turn of events could not have been foreseen, or it could have been foreseen only as a result of an excessive amount of deliberation. Faced with the same decision, we would make it the same way; there is nothing to be learned.

Rational plans are not ordinarily formed in a social vacuum, and the fact that we are social beings places additional, moral, constraints on our plans. Rawls defines "self-respect" as the personal good that is furthered by carrying out a plan that fits into some social order. Self-respect, which is something that anyone can be assumed to want, is more likely to be achieved if a person's plan leaves room for the development and exercise of abilities. This is because people appreciate the exercise of each other's abilities, and because (it is reasonable to assume) people have a natural motive to develop their abilities (Rawls's "Aristotelian principle"). In a utopian remark that seems worthy of pasting on one's wall, Rawls goes on to say,

Putting all these remarks together, the conditions for persons respecting themselves and one another would seem to require that their common plans be both

rational and complementary: they call upon their educated endowments and arouse in each a sense of mastery, and they fit together into a scheme of activity that all can appreciate and enjoy. (pp. 440-441)

For Rawls, integration of one's plans into a potential scheme of cooperation is what any rational person would do as a matter of fact, but not as a logical necessity (although others, such as Gewirth, 1983, have argued that morality is to some extent a matter of logical necessity as well).

In general, the principle of deliberative rationality is useful not only in deciding among conflicting plans, but also in justifying other principles. The question we might usefully ask, when reflecting on other principles of rational planning, is whether everyone would adopt them under the ideal conditions specified by this principle. This is the approach I shall take to the justification of utility theory. (I believe that it also works for some other principles of rationality proposed by Rawls, which he calls "counting principles," such as: Other things equal, choose the plan more likely to succeed.)

The practical value of a theory like this one is apparent when we consider some of its competitors, such as hedonism. The idea that the good life involves the pursuit of pleasure is either useless or wrong. The view is useless if we define pleasure (or some surrogate term) as "whatever one seeks." Such a view prevents us from giving advice (the product of the kind of normative theory we want) other than "seek what you seek." The other form of hedonism, the idea that we should pursue pleasure as distinct, say, from achievement, enlightenment, service to others, or eternal salvation, seems to conflict with our intuitions so strongly that most of us will quickly grasp at any alternative theory. Such a view would hold that most of the people we admire are highly irrational, and that most of us, in the ambitions we consider most important, are irrational as well. The principle of deliberative rationality, of course, permits these other goals, and hedonism (type 2) does not. Perhaps the attraction of type 2 hedonism is that it may be confused with the first: We do pursue pleasure (type 1), hence we should pursue pleasure (type 2). I hope I have made it clear why this is, in fact, confusion.

On the other side are what might be called culture-bound theories of the good life, such as those put forth to us by religious missionaries who come to our door or confront us on the street. Unlike the first form of hedonism, which tells us nothing, these theories tell us too much. They cannot be justified by arguing that the potential convert, on reflection, would want to live by them. (Usually they depend, instead, on some supposed external fact such as the revealed word of God or some earthly prophet.) The theories of the good life that most of us learned from our

parents (or from popular psychology) are probably mild forms of the same thing. A theory such as that of Rawls tries to steer a middle course between these two extremes. Unlike the overly restrictive theories, it admits that what is rational is up to each person (taking into account the person's circumstances), and the only criterion is deliberative rationality. This criterion says in essence that a person should choose according to the values he would like to use under ideal conditions of deliberation. What these values will turn out to be may well differ from person to person. This point, of course, owes much to the writings of the existentialists.

Utility theory

I now turn to a discussion of the theory of expected utility, which forms the basis of the decision-theoretic approach to plans and decisions. This discussion will at first seem to have little to do with the kinds of questions I have just discussed. However, utility theory aspires to be a general theory of rational decisions. As such, it provides a framework for further discussion and clarification of the theory of rational plans, and, at the same time, that theory clarifies utility theory, both by justifying it and by showing us its limitations.

Utility theory originated in the analysis of gambling. The basic idea is that the expectation of a bet is the sum of a set of products, one for each outcome of the bet. Each outcome is the probability of the outcome multiplied by the payoff if that outcome occurs, which may be positive, for gains, or negative, for losses. Formally,

$$(1) \qquad E(v) = \sum_i P_i \cdot V_i$$

where $E(v)$ is the expected value of the gamble, P_i is the probability of outcome i, and V_i is the value of outcome i. In the long run, if many gambles of the same type are played, the average payoff approaches $E(v)$, and this fact has been taken to justify the use of $E(v)$ in deciding which of several gambles is best.

The values in Equation 1 refer to something like money values. An interesting problem, called the St. Petersburg paradox (because of the journal containing the paper about it), was discussed by Bernoulli (1738/1954). Suppose I toss a coin as many times as necessary to get one head. I will give you \$1 if I get a head on the first toss, \$2 if it takes two tosses, \$4 if three, \$8 if four, and so on, by powers of 2. How much will you pay me to play this game? Most people say a few dollars at most. In fact, the $E(v)$ is infinite according to Equation 1, since each outcome has an expected value of \$0.50, and there is an infinite number of outcomes.

(For example, for the outcome "3 tosses," the payoff is $4 and the probability is 1/8.) Bernoulli suggested that people do not in fact maximize $E(v)$, but rather what we would now call "expected utility." Thus, the expected utility of a gamble is

$$(2) \qquad E(u) = \sum_i P_i \cdot U_i$$

where $E(u)$ is the expected utility and U_i is the utility of outcome i. What is crucial here is that U_i is subjective, and it need not be the same as money value. Bernoulli accounted for people's behavior by assuming that U_i is a negatively accelerated function of money value (V_i), so that the added (marginal) utility of a dollar decreases as the total number of dollars increases. Savage (1954) argues — using examples like Bernoulli's — that the utility of money must be bounded.

  $E(u)$ maximization not only describes behavior in the St. Petersburg situation and elsewhere, but it also seems to be normatively superior to $E(v)$ maximization. Thus, it seems rational not to stake one's fortune on the St. Petersburg game, and it seems rational to buy insurance even though the insurance company makes money. (In the case of insurance, the expected disutility of the loss insured against is presumably great enough to outweigh the certain loss of the premium.)

  Although expected utility seems normatively superior to expected value, we may ask why we should follow even the former principle. The main argument for accepting utility theory as a principle of rational choice is somewhat indirect. This is that this principle has certain mathematical implications, which we shall call (because they are implied by Equation 2) "necessary axioms." Although the utility formula itself (Equation 2) is not self-evidently rational, the necessary axioms are, when properly interpreted. That is (going somewhat beyond what others have said), these axioms would be accepted by anyone under conditions of deliberative rationality as formal constraints that must not be violated by the substance of a plan. Further, these axioms, together with other axioms that have no substantive implications for behavior (for example, axioms that assert the existence of outcomes with certain utilities or events with certain probabilities), imply that a person who conforms to them also conforms to expected-utility theory as expressed in Equation 2. Thus, if one accepts the necessary axioms as normative rules, one logically accepts utility theory. Finally, given the entire set of axioms, it is possible to calculate, from a person's choice behavior observed in a sufficient number of cases, what utilities he (behaves as if he) assigns to outcomes and what probabilities he (behaves as if he) assigns to events.

(The utilities thus calculated have arbitrary units and an arbitrary zero point.) When we say that the ideal creature for whom utility theory is designed can assess his utilities and probabilities, we mean only that he can make this calculation, and that his choices conform to the axioms, so that the calculation can be made. (See Keeney, 1977, for an example of a real human going through the time-consuming process of assessing utilities in this way.) We do not require that the creature have direct access to his utilities.

There are different axiom systems, some of which are mathematically equivalent in essential respects (but which differ in the transparency of their axioms), and some of which make different substantive assumptions. For example, the system of von Neuman and Morganstern (1947) assumes that probabilities are known, whereas the axioms of Ramsey (1931), Savage (1954), and Krantz et al. (1971) do not. The last of these systems considers preferences among acts rather than outcomes, but it is essentially equivalent to other systems. I shall ignore these distinctions, for my purpose is simply to illustrate the kinds of axioms proposed:

1. For any two outcomes A and B, either $A > B$, $B > A$, or $A = B$, where $>$ and $=$ indicate preference and indifference, respectively. In other words, you cannot prefer A to B and B to A at the same time, and if you do not prefer one to the other, you must be indifferent. According to the theory, to say "I have no preference, but I'm certainly not indifferent" amounts to not having discovered one's preference yet. This seems reasonable to assume for our idealized creature, even though true indecision might be allowable for mortals with limited time.

2. If $A > B$ and $B > C$, then $A > C$. In other words, preference is transitive (for preferences determined at the same time). (Axioms 1 and 2 together mean that preference is a "weak ordering.") Suppose I violate this axiom, so that I prefer C to A. Then I would pay you a little to give me a B in return for my C (since I prefer B), I would pay you again to give me an A for my B, and again for a C (since I prefer C to A). By repeating this cycle, you could turn me into a money pump, unless my preferences changed. More generally, if I violate this axiom, I subvert my own ends. By trading B for C and A for B, I commit a complex act that works directly against my preference for C over A. This in itself may not be a sufficient argument, for we (or an idealized creature) may prefer to subvert this particular preference rather than make our preferences consistent. However, it is hard to imagine situations in which we would really want to do this. Most apparent counterexamples involve true indifference among the three alternatives, changes in preferences over time, choices

that we would not make if we deliberated enough, or easily recognized incorrect descriptions of what the alternatives are. An example of the last is that I might prefer a left shoe over a left sock if I have a right shoe, a left sock over a left glove, but a left glove over a left shoe if I have a right glove. Of course, the correct description here is in terms of pairs of shoes and gloves, not single shoes and gloves. Another example is that someone might choose intransitive preferences for the sake of showing that Jon Baron is wrong about transitivity. But here, the real preference is not C over A, but C-plus-the-satisfaction-of-showing-me-wrong over A. Hence, the satisfaction would be a false one!

3. If A = B, then B may be substituted for A in any gamble or choice situation without changing the choice made there. Once again, if you can change my preferences by substituting equivalent outcomes, you can make money from me. This axiom may be rephrased so as to mean that the relative preference value of an outcome is unchanged by the gamble or set of choices it is embedded in. It seems fair to take this axiom as part of our definition of outcome, so that if we appear to violate it, we have not analyzed the situation correctly. For example, if I prefer $10 to my friend's fancy ball-point pen, but I prefer to win the pen rather than the $10 in a bet on a tennis match, then we would say that the possible outcomes of the bet are not the objects themselves, but rather the satisfactions of winning the objects in a bet.

4. If we prefer outcome F to outcome G, then we would prefer a gamble with outcome F at probability p and H at probability $1-p$ to a gamble with G at probability p and H at probability $1-p$. For example, if I prefer a trip to Europe to a trip to the Caribbean, then I will prefer a lottery with Europe as the first prize to a lottery with the Caribbean as the first prize, provided that the two lotteries are otherwise identical. This is a form of what has been called the "sure-thing principle": Outcomes that are determined only by events other than the choice I make should not affect my choice. This one, to me, seems so compelling as to need no justification. It can be taken as a statement of what we mean by event, outcome, and preference. (In fact, however, it is clearly violated, as I shall explain.)

5. Suppose that S is my current state, and that I prefer R (e.g., a pin, plus my current state) to S, and I prefer S to T (e.g., being shot at dawn). Then there is some probability—greater than zero but possibly very, very small—such that I will prefer to risk T at that probability for the sake of R. (This is a consequence of what is called the Archimedian assumption of most versions of utility theory.) This at first seems difficult to accept,

for it seems that some outcomes are so bad that we would never risk them. But in fact, we risk such outcomes all the time, as when we bend down (thus taking a .0000000001 probability risk, let's say, of having a stroke) to pick up a pin. As I shall explain later, however, we can dispense with this axiom and still have a useful version of utility theory.

6. Suppose I regard the utility difference between C and D as equal to that between C and D, so that, concretely, I would be exactly indifferent between a 50-50 gamble between B and C and a 50-50 gamble between A and D. (In essence, the mean utility of B and C, the expectation of the gamble, equals the mean utility of A and D. We can imagine A, B, C, and D, lined up in a row as follows:

A B . C D

Here, the "." represents the expected utility of both gambles.) And suppose I regard the utility difference between C and D as equal to that between E and F, in the same behavioral sense. Then, I must regard the utility difference between A and B as equal to that between E and F. In other words, utility differences, defined in this way, are transitive. It is this axiom (Ramsey, 1931), or some similar axiom, that permits construction of the utility scale. It serves to give a behavioral definition for a difference between utilities, and any such difference can provide a unit for a utility scale. To deny this axiom would be to say that it was meaningless to compare differences in utilities of outcomes. To see that it is not meaningless to do so, compare this kind of judgment to one that the theory holds *is* meaningless: *Ratios* or utilities cannot be compared, because the assignment of "zero" to an outcome is arbitrary. In fact, if weak ordering holds for gambles of the sort given above (involving A, B, C, and D), then comparison of utility differences is always possible.

In sum, the kinds of axioms from which utility theory can be derived do seem to be acceptable to a creature of the sort postulated by the principle of deliberative rationality. When we are inclined to violate them, it seems that we have either not defined our decision problem correctly, our preferences have changed, or we are taking decisions that are merely difficult to be impossible. Of course, to follow the axioms requires that we describe our choices in terms of acts and outcomes, which have utility, and events that cause the outcomes, which by themselves do not. Despite claims to the contrary (Jeffrey, 1965), this does not seem hard to do either, especially given the ideal creature to whom the theory is supposed to apply. All that is crucial here, however, is that we should be able to describe situations involving thinking in this way.

Was Bernoulli right?

Let us return briefly to the origin of the idea of subjective utility, namely, the need for a diminishing marginal utility of money. None of the axioms compel us to accept this idea, for we may simply say that the utility of money is proportional to its value, and be completely consistent.

In fact, we may argue in favor of the principle of expected *value* along the following lines: In the long run, probabilities convert to frequencies. If a gamble is repeated over and over, the average payoff will approach the expected payoff. Because we have no reason to treat any occurrence of that gamble as different from any other, our choice on any one occurrence sets a policy for the rest. To set a policy based on decreasing marginal utility is to fail to maximize long-run gains. For example, suppose I refuse to pay \$5 for an even chance to win \$12 — a bet with an expected value of \$1. By doing so, I set a precedent; I would have no reason to change my mind if offered a similar bet in the future. I would thus decline all such bets, and thus fail to win \$1 per bet in the long run. On the other hand, suppose I decide to accept any bet with positive expected value. By doing so, I would maximize my income in the long run. In this case, if I followed the axioms of utility theory, I would be committing myself to expected value theory as well (for bets in the appropriate range). Extending this argument, I can view every decision I make as part of a sequence of similar decisions, in which case the right course of action would be to convert all outcomes to their monetary value (for me) and then maximize expected value.

One qualification must be acknowledged: Life is in fact finite, so there are some decisions involving gains and losses so large that only a few such momentous decisions are likely to be made in a lifetime. Thus, the more momentous the decision, the less applicable is the long-run argument for expected value as a normative model.

Two arguments may still be made against expected value. First, we may refuse to accept gambles with positive expected value because we are truly averse to risk; in other words, we have a negative utility for risk itself, which must be included in any expected-value calculation. One way this could happen is that we could try to avoid situations in which we might regret making the "wrong" choice (considering the actual outcome rather than anything even an ideal creature could know); see Thaler (1980) and Bell (1982). Is this rational? The answer seems to hinge on which ideal creature we are talking about. If the creature has complete control of its emotions — including fear of regret — then risk aversion is indeed irrational, for the creature can realize more value in the long run

without it than with it. Such a creature will be able to convince itself, when it gambles and loses, that it made the best decision for the long run, and there is no reason to feel bad. On the other hand, if the creature cannot control its emotions, it must deal with them as a fact, and risk aversion is completely rational. If, like most people, I would guess, the creature is not sure whether it can control its emotions or not, it must include this uncertainty along with others in its calculations. (This argument illustrates a way in which emotions may be taken into account more generally in normative and prescriptive models of rationality. Because emotions are sometimes controllable, with some amount of effort and some degree of success, the possibility of controlling them must be considered as part of the decision to be made, and, to the extent to which they will not be controlled, they must be considered as outcomes with utilities of their own.) Accepting this view leads to the conclusion that risk aversion may be rational, depending on the individual — but it must be taken as a true disutility for risk rather than a true declining marginal utility for small gains and losses. Although risk aversion may lead to behavior that is indistinguishable from that predicted by declining marginal utility for money, it is not a true violation of expected-value theory, for the negative value of risk can be converted to money value and added into the equation.

The second argument against expected value as normative is that we do not in fact regard all decisions as setting precedents for one another, even when they involve gains and losses of comparable magnitude. Our life plan might specify a set of domains, perhaps organized around different goals or activities such as work, personal relationships, social service, etc., each with subdomains and sub-subdomains. Although we must ultimately make tradeoffs among such goals, just as we must make tradeoffs among the goals of different individuals, there is no more reason for a decision in one domain to set a precedent for a decision in another domain as there is for my decision to set a precedent for yours. We may thus be unwilling to be bound by precedents except within decisions of the same type, and the number of such decisions may in fact be small enough so that the finiteness of life comes into play. The long run is not so long. In the extreme case, no decision would set a precedent for any other, and the argument for expected-value theory in terms of long-run gains would completely evaporate.

It does not seem irrational (for any idealized creature) to take such limited decisions as setting precedents only for decisions within the same domain or subdomain. In sum, then, it seems that there are really only two reasons not to follow expected value as a normative model: First,

some decisions are so momentous that they will not be repeated; second, we cannot argue against a person who chooses to divide his life into domains, which are treated like separate lives in the sense that precedents do not apply from one to the other. Of course, neither of these reasons makes following expected value a mistake; they only give our idealized creature more freedom than expected value would give.

Multi-attribute utility theory (MAUT)

The second reason just given calls attention to the need for a normative theory of tradeoffs among different goals or dimensions in decision making. Many, if not most, of the decisions we make involve such conflicts. The conflict may be among such goals as health, wealth, and wisdom, or between the pleasure of Pac-Man and the satisfaction of statistics. Multi-attribute utility theory, or MAUT, is concerned with the tradeoff between such attributes. Its basic claim is that such attributes can and should be traded off in a consistent way. Although such consistency implies that all the dimensions can be — if we like — converted to a common scale, this is not the crucial part of the theory. Rather, the import of the theory is to allow the dimensions to be distinct, while at the same time allowing consistent tradeoffs among them. In a sense, the common scale is a by-product rather than a goal of the system.

MAUT is best known as a prescriptive theory for making serious public-policy decisions involving tradeoffs among multiple objectives (Keeney & Raiffa, 1976; Keeney, 1977; Gardiner & Edwards, 1975), such as where to locate an airport or what kind of power plant to build. (However, some adaptations have been made for everyday decision making: see Beach & Beach, 1982; Janis, 1982.) To use the theory, for example, for choosing among alternative plans for generating electric power, a decision maker such as a public official (or an idealized creature) evaluates each plan on several dimensions, such as amount of land required, cost, expected loss of life (e.g., from mining accidents), and pollution. The decision maker makes judgments of the form, "The difference between 0 and 200,000 acres of land use is equivalent to the difference between 0 tons of pollution and how many million?" In other words, "What is X, such that you are indifferent between the combination of X tons and 0 acres and the combination of 0 tons and 200,000 acres?" To make such judgments, the decision maker starts with values that are clearly too high and then lowers them, and starts with values too low and raises them. When a range of indifference is encountered, the middle of the range is chosen as the best guess. Suppose X is 10 per day. Then we

can say that the difference between 0 and X is equal in utility to the difference between 0 and 200,000 acres. We then ask about Y, such that the difference between X and Y tons is equal to the difference between 0 and 200,000 acres. Proceeding in this way, we may mark off equal utility intervals on the pollution scale, using land use as a standard of measurement. (There are more accurate ways to mark off the scale, but this one is the easiest to understand.) So far, we have asked the decision maker to imagine that all other values (lives, cost, etc.) were held constant at some imagined value. The next step is to ask him to change these drastically and repeat the whole procedure for trading off land use and pollution. If the tradeoff is the same, regardless of the values of the other dimensions, we say that the tradeoff is *preferentially independent* of the other values. If all the pairs of dimensions are preferentially independent of other dimensions, it is possible to assign utility values to every dimension on a common scale. Each value of each dimension has a utility on that scale, and the total value of any alternative is simply the sum of the values of its attributes.

The normative status of MAUT may again be evaluated by considering its necessary axioms from the point of view of the same sort of idealized creature as the one who uses utility theory, namely, one who has unlimited time for weighing choices and for calculating utilities. Would such a creature want to adopt these axioms as general constraints on his plan? The main axioms are these:

> Weak ordering (i.e., either A > B, A = B or B > A; plus transitivity).
> Preferential independence — tradeoffs among dimensions are unaffected by the values of other dimensions.
> The Archimedian axiom: If two consequences have different utilities, no matter how small the difference, we can string together differences of the same size so that the sum will equal any other difference we find. For example, if there is some utility to having a pin, as opposed to not having it, there is some number of pin-sized utilities equivalent to the utility of not being hanged at dawn. (Note that I said pin-sized utilities, not pins, for the marginal utility of pins is surely decreasing.)

If we can accept these conditions (and a few others of less importance), we ought to be willing to accept MAUT as a normative standard for all decision making. To begin, weak ordering presents special problems for MAUT. Our most difficult decisions seem to violate this condition, for example, those in which we must trade off the welfare of a child against success in our work, love against money, or morality against self-interest (in choosing a career of public service versus a more lucrative one, for example). In such decisions, we often have no clear preferences, but it does not seem correct to say that we are indifferent either. However, this

may be an illusion. The true state of affairs may be better described by saying that our preferences are *difficult* to determine (or to construct), not impossible. Surely, there is no difficulty in comparing across dimensions as such. We find it difficult to decide whether to give up our chosen career in order to marry our true love, but it is not difficult at all to choose the career over a brief infatuation (at least in a state of reflective equilibrium!). The difficulty arises when the alternatives are relatively close, and this is not a peculiarity of comparing across dimensions. (There may be special problems in comparing across dimensions, as pointed out by Shepard, 1964, but these problems still do not render such comparisons impossible, only especially difficult.) Thus, for an idealized creature willing to take the time to make a difficult judgment (e.g., by making repeated judgments and then taking an average), weak ordering would be acceptable, but for a less idealized creature — or a real one — we may want to drop this assumption (in which case we could be sure that at least some of our decisions would be underdetermined by whatever version of MAUT emerged).

Preferential independence at first appears to present some problems. For example, the tradeoff between right shoes and right gloves will depend on whether we have left shoes or left gloves already. But this is a silly example. What it shows is not that the theory is wrong, but that we have to choose appropriate dimensions, e.g., pairs of socks and pairs of gloves. However, it is clear that MAUT cannot be applied to just any arbitrarily chosen set of dimensions, but rather those a decision maker takes to be preferentially independent. If a person says there are no such dimensions (truly, rather than out of orneriness), we cannot call him irrational, and we must advise him to make all his decisions holistically, rather than by decomposing into dimensions. In the case of thinking, however, it would seem that such benefits as furthering one's long-term goals and such costs as mental effort would be preferentially independent of each other and of other factors affecting the decision to think, such as the pleasures of Pac-Man, at least for an idealized creature.

The arguments for the Archimedian axiom are the same as before. However, it turns out that dropping the axioms is not a disaster for MAUT. Hausner (1954) showed that without this axiom, we can still have a system in which dimensions are "lexically ordered." Only when we were sure that two options were identical on a more important dimension, such as probability of losing life, would we consider a less important dimension lower in the ordering. This situation may be seen as a kind of limit that is approached as one dimension is weighed more and more heavily relative to others, that is, as larger and larger differences on the

latter are required to compensate for smaller and smaller differences on the former. The sort of theory that Hauser proposed is suitable for our purposes here, although it seems unlikely to be relevant in tradeoffs involving the consequences of thinking.

If MAUT is normative, then we can assume that a rational person (i.e., one who follows MAUT) would have optimal sets of tradeoffs among dimensions of utility. It would be possible, for example, to say that there is some point at which it is no longer worthwhile to abstain from Pac-Man in order to work on a statistics problem. We might not be able to say what that point is for any individual, but it is important to know that it exists, for we can then advise a person to try to behave appropriately, given his own values.

In sum, MAUT permits us to have a conception of preferentially independent goals (or subgoals) as part of a life plan. The theory tells us when we can expect meaningful tradeoffs among these goals. Although the theory does not require even an idealized creature to conform to all the axioms, it is reasonable to expect that preferential independence, at least, would hold for some of the major goals of anyone's life plan, including the goals involved in thinking. (These goals could occur in different domains, but they need not.) Because MAUT allows goals to be traded off, we can make an analogy between a life plan and a policy for consumption in economics (as made by Becker, 1981). As a consumer, there are various commodities we might consume, just as there are various goals we might pursue in our lives. Each commodity has a decreasing marginal utility, let us assume. Economists have shown us that given this assumption, there is an optimal pattern of consumption, in which the marginal utilities of all commodities are equal. (If the marginal utility of one commodity were higher than that of another, we could realize a net gain by trading some of the latter for the former.) By analogy, a life plan can specify our utility functions for the various goals we might pursue (including moral goals), and, specifically, the tradeoffs among them. In essence, a life plan can specify a consumption policy for the things that life has to offer.

Utility theory as a descriptive model

There have been many attempts to evaluate utility theory as a descriptive theory of choice behavior. These are of interest here for a few reasons. First, consideration of the problem of testing utility theory in practice may shed light on its normative significance. Second, some apparent deviations from utility theory raise questions about its normative status.

Third, other results, particularly those of prospect theory (Kahneman & Tversky, 1979) suggest some relationships between utility theory and the theory of life plans as described above.

Both expected utility theory and MAUT are reasonably good descriptive models in stripped-down laboratory situations. For example, in Tversky's (1967) study, subjects were asked to choose between a gamble and a sure outcome, or between two sure outcomes, involving cigarettes and candy, which may be regarded as attributes in MAUT. For example, the subject might be asked to choose between a .4 probability of 4 packs of cigarettes or 2 packs of cigarettes for sure. Subjects generally followed the axioms, so that their choices were consistent. Utility scales for candy and cigarettes could be derived either from the gambling data or the data in which these goods were traded off (as in MAUT). However, the utility functions for the two methods were not the same. The same outcome seemed to have a higher utility when it was part of a gamble than when it was a sure thing. For example, the analysis based on certain outcomes might show that two packs of cigarettes had less than twice the utility of one pack of cigarettes, but the subject might prefer a .5 chance of two packs to one pack for sure. One explanation of this result is that the subject might have a utility for gambling, which made the gamble more attractive than the sure thing. This would allow us to continue to believe that utility theory is a good description of the subject's behavior. However, the assumption of a utility for gambling makes it difficult to test utility theory as a descriptive model. It seems that we can make up some assumption of this sort to explain any kind of observed violation of the theory.

The problem for us is this: It appears that utility theory is empty as a descriptive theory. As Popper has argued, a theory that cannot be shown to be false by any conceivable data is not a scientific theory. If utility theory is indeed empty descriptively, how could it be adequate as a normative theory?

One answer to this is that utility theory is untestable — if it is — only from a narrow behavioristic point of view. For example, we might test the utility-of-gambling account by asking the subject why he appeared to be inconsistent (and showing him the relevant examples of inconsistency). He might tell us that he liked to gamble. For a hard headed psychologist, this is not great evidence, but it is evidence. Further, since we all know what he means, perhaps one of us, one day, will figure out a way to measure the utility of gambling independently of the experiment just described.

A second answer is that falsifiability is not logically required for a normative model. It would be required if the normative model were a

standard to be applied to results, for then, if the model were not falsifiable, it would be impossible to tell whether the standard applied. However, I have taken the view that a normative model is a prescription for an idealized creature, and a prescription might be followable without anyone being able to tell from its result whether it was followed or not.

Some results concerning deviations from utility theory raise questions about the theory's normative status, and others shed light on its relation to the theory of rational plans. Both of these kinds of results are best presented in the context of prospect theory (Kahneman & Tversky, 1979), which is a *descriptive* theory that attempts to explain many apparent violations of utility theory in subjects' choice behavior. (Usually, subjects are given hypothetical choices rather than real ones. However, there is no reason to think they would behave differently in real cases, and there is some evidence that they do not; see Thaler, 1980.) For convenience, I shall sketch the theory first, and then the evidence.

Prospect theory shares with expected utility-theory the idea that the value of a gamble is determined by one factor having to do with probability and another having to do with the outcome. The theory speaks of "subjective value," $v(.)$, rather than utility, $U(.)$. The difference between the two concepts is that, in the case of money, utility is usually based on a person's total wealth, but in prospect theory, the utility of the outcome of a gamble is a function largely of the change from a starting point. (Most experimenters who study gambling behavior seem already to assume this, as they assign utilities to winnings and losses in the experiment rather than to their subjects' total wealths.) The shape of the function relating $v(x)$ to the amount of money won or lost is shown in the left part of Figure 1. One aspect of this function is that losses are taken more seriously than gains; thus, people generally prefer their current state to a situation in which they may gain or lose $100 with equal probability. A second aspect is that marginal subjective value is decreasing for *both* gains and losses. Bernoulli noticed that this was true for gains, but if we view gains and losses as movements along a continuum of wealth, then the opposite should hold for losses calculated from a given point on the continuum. That is, a small increase in wealth would have a *larger* effect, the greater the loss. The fact that marginal value decreases for both gains and losses explains the "reflection effect," for example ($300, .9) > ($600, .45) although ($-$600, .45) > ($-$300, .9), where > indicates preference by most subjects, and ($300, .9) means a .9 probability of winning $300, versus nothing. The latter choice (in which the outcomes are $-$600 or $-$300) can be converted into the former, and hence reversed, if the subject imagines that he has already lost $600, so that $-$600 translates into $0.

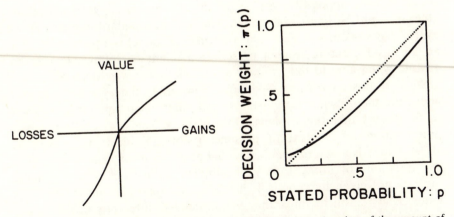

Figure 1. The left panel shows the value, $v(x)$, as a function of the amount of money (or some other good), x, gained or lost, according to prospect theory (Kahneman & Tversky, 1979). The right panel shows how probabilities given to subjects, p, are distorted by the function $pi(p)$ before being used as decision weights. (Reprinted by permission.)

According to the theory, subjects use a "decision weight," $pi(p)$ in place of the probability p. The theory applies to situations in which probabilities are given to the subjects, and this part of the theory holds that subjects distort those probabilities before using them. The right part of Figure 1 shows $pi(p)$ as a function of p. Some relevant aspects of this function are:

1. By convention, $pi(0) = 0$ and $pi(1) = 1$.
2. Very low probabilities are overweighed, so that $pi(p) > p$ when p is near 0. This can explain the fact that some people are willing to buy lottery tickets, thus assuming risk, and to buy insurance, thus passing risk on to others. Concretely, both ($500, .001$) > (50 cents), as in a lottery, and (-50 cents) > ($-\$500$, $.001$), as in insurance, despite the fact that the opposite is predicted from the declining marginal value of gains and losses.
3. Over most of the range of the function, the reverse is true, so that $pi(p) < p$. This implies that $pi(p)$ shows "subcertainty," which means that $pi(p) + pi(1-p) < 1$. It also implies that subjects will overweigh certainty itself, relative to uncertainty. For example, ($\$30$) > ($\$45$, $.8$), although ($\$45$, $.2$) > ($\$30$, $.25$), a result inconsistent with utility theory, which would hold that only the ratio of the two probabilities ($1/.8$ for the first case, $.25/.2$ for the second) is relevant.

Finally, according to the theory, before the subject applies these functions to maximize expected subjective value, he uses a number of simplifying heuristics. Most of these heuristics would not affect the decision if

the subject were following expected-utility theory (and, for some, if the utility of money were a linear function of its value), but they do affect the decision in combination with the other mechanisms of prospect theory.

The first of these heuristics concerns the choice of the zero point. Essentially, subjects adopt whatever point is most consistent with the situation as described (although see Fischhoff, 1983, on the difficulty of determining what this will be). For example (Tversky & Kahneman, 1981), "Imagine that the United States is preparing for the outbreak of an unusual Asian disease, which is expected to kill 600 people. Two alternative programs to combat the disease have been proposed . . . :"

> Problem 1.
> If Program A is adopted, 200 people will be saved.
> If Program B is adopted, there is a 1/3 probability that 600 people will be saved and 2/3 probability that no people will be saved.
>
> Problem 2.
> If Program C is adopted, 400 people will die.
> If Program D is adopted, there is a 1/3 probability that nobody will die, and 2/3 probability that 600 will die.

Subjects given problem 1 tended to choose A as the better program, and those given problem 2 chose D. Of course, these choices are inconsistent, and the only difference is whether subjects see the situation as starting with 0 lives lost or with 600 lives already as good as lost. The decreasing marginal value of both gains and losses induces the different judgments.

A second heuristic is that components seen as being shared by two gambles (or prospects) are ignored in deciding between the two. For example, recall that ($45, .2) > ($30, .25), but ($30) > ($45, .8). However, the first gamble may be redescribed as a two-stage game in which the subject has a .25 chance of playing at all, but if he gets to play, he is offered the second gamble. When the first gamble is described this way, subjects will choose the $30 rather than the $45. Expected-utility theory, of course, would specify that subjects ought to make the same choice ($30 or $45) in the two gambles.

The effects described by prospect theory can work together, as in this classic example from Allais (1953):

($500,000) > ($2,500,000, .10; $500,000, .89; $0, .01), but
($2,500,000, .10) > ($500,000, .11).

(In this notation, semicolons separate possible outcomes, each given as a value with its probability.) In the first gamble, subjects are unwilling to take the risk of getting nothing at all, even if it means a .10 chance to get

$2,500,000. In the second gamble, the larger amount seems worth the slightly increased risk of getting nothing at all. However, the increase in the risk of nothing at all is the same in the two gambles, .01, so utility theory would dictate that subjects should either choose to gamble for the larger amount of money, or not, consistently in the two gambles. To see this, note that the first gamble may be redescribed (Savage, 1954) as

($500,000, .01; $500,000, .10; $500,000, .89)
versus ($0, .01; $2,500,000, .10; $500,000, .89).

Looked at in this way, we see that the third term, $500,000 at .89, is common to the two gambles, and therefore may be ignored (by the sure-thing principle, Axiom 4 above). If this term is replaced with $0 at .89, the first choice of gambles is identical to the second, so the same choice should be made. One might think of a lottery with 100 tickets. For each choice, one outcome is assigned to 1 ticket, a second outcome is assigned to 10 tickets, and a third outcome to 89 tickets. Your decision should not depend on what is assigned to the 89 tickets, for the outcome is the same for those 89, no matter what you decide. Prospect theory explains the conflict between the two choices: The choice of the sure outcome in the first gamble is accounted for by the certainty effect. In addition, the overweighing of low probabilities may make the subject take the .01 probability of no gain more seriously than it ought to be taken.

The interesting thing about this example, called Allais's paradox, is that it is quite compelling to many people (Slovic & Tversky, 1974). Because people resist the idea that they ought to make the two choices consistent, the paradox has been taken as a counterexample to the normative status of expected-utility theory, specifically, to the sure-thing principle. It has inspired various attempts to modify utility theory so as to account for choices in the paradox, with the idea that the resulting theory might be normative (e.g., Bell, 1982). Before we leap at such an opportunity to tailor the normative to the descriptive, we should note that a good descriptive theory such as prospect theory can actually help to justify utility theory as normative. By displaying the separate factors that lead to our choices in independent situations, where they may be more easily overcome by reflection, prospect theory helps us to see why the usual choices in Allais's paradox might be wrong. A psychological explanation of our choices in terms of various cognitive illusions — i.e., certainty and overweighing — is surely not sufficient reason for us to give up our strong intuitions in favor of a normative theory consistent with other intuitions, namely, utility theory. However, the psychological explanation does provide some reason for this capitulation. The use of this sort of reason is consistent with the view

(roughly that of Daniels, 1979, and Stich and Nisbett, 1980) that normative models must be based on a "wide" reflective equilibrium, which can take into account social and psychological factors, as well as our raw intuitions and the principles we find to explain them. In sum, prospect theory can help us to see why some possible counterarguments to utility theory are weaker than they appear at first to be.

At this point, one might ask whether the certainty effect itself is irrational. Could we not argue that certainty can have a utility, just as we invoked a utility for gambling? (Note that if we did this, we would not be giving up utility theory; we would just make it harder to test, once again.) One argument (based on Borch, 1968) against accepting the certain $500,000 in the first gamble is this: Certainty itself is an illusion. For example, money is not a primary end for most of us, but a means to other ends, which are attained with some probability less than 1 even if the money is in hand. Even if we had the $500,000 in hand, most of us would spend a part and invest the rest. The investment itself is a gamble; even if the banks never fail, we still might die before we can use the money. Putting this another way, a consequence with probability 1 can be further analyzed as a set of consequences, each of which has probability less than 1. In sum, the claim that any outcome is a certainty is the result of a particular way of framing the situation, and therefore we would not want to let this enter our decision.

On the other hand, as suggested earlier, we may want to take into account our anticipated regret if we lose the chance to win big (as Bell, 1982, suggests). This could be described as taking into account the anticipations of uncontrollable emotions (the utilities of which could be included in our calculations). This would not argue against utility theory as normative, but it would make the data in question (e.g., responses to Allais's paradox) irrelevant as a test of its descriptive adequacy.

Is using the reference point rational?

The effect of subjective changes in the reference point is one of the more interesting fallacies derived from prospect theory. This effect is clearly irrational when the position of the reference point is affected by the experimenter's instructions. No one wants his decisions to be affected by the way in which situations are described to him . However, it may not be irrational at all to take one's reference point as one's current position, so long as one determines correctly what one's current position is. Consideration of this possibility will lead us to qualify or constrain utility theory as a normative model.

Let us consider two versions of utility theory as normative models. In one, the traditional theory, utility is analogous to total wealth. In the second version, utility is determined by the frequency of events consistent or inconsistent with one's goals (as determined by one's plan). By this view, money has utility because of the expectation that it will lead to events consistent with one's goals, for example, it will allow one to take trips, buy records, and so on. For some people, wealth accumulation is itself a goal, of course, but for these people, we may simply say that their goals consist of increases in wealth. The point is that this need not be true of everyone. We need not assume any utility for wealth as such.

Now according to the theory of rational life plans, fulfillment is found in the successful realization of such a plan, and in the expectation of continued success. We can see, then, why winnings and losings — in the sense dealt with by prospect theory — contribute to or detract from fulfillment.

First, if a plan is achieving a moderate degree of success — as is probably true for most plans — then a boost in income might allow it to achieve more complete success, for a short time at least. If my plan includes occasional visits to exotic places, a lucky investment can permit me to pursue that part of my plan for one or two vacations at least. Conversely, a financial loss can set back this part of my plan for a while.

Second, gains and losses of the same type affect my expectation of future gains and losses of the same type (except, perhaps, in gambling, but see Gilovich, 1983). Each success increases my expectation for further success, and each failure increases my expectation for future failure.

A third possible effect of gains and losses is that they may force me to reconsider my plan. An unexpected achievement may lead me to consider trying to repeat it, and a lucky investment may make me reconsider my consumption patterns. An unexpected achievement failure, or a serious financial loss, may, on the other hand, cause me to give up some part of my plan for the indefinite future.

For all three of these effects, the appropriate reference point is one's current position, defined as one's current expectations for success in one's plans. If there is reason for there to be decreasing marginal utility for gains, then there is reason for there to be decreasing marginal disutility for losses as well. In either case, the primary concern of the plan is with the smaller, everyday gains and losses, and larger gains and losses might play roughly the same role in a plan, despite their greater size. Thus, this aspect of prospect theory is not irrational.

Further, the third reason — the possibility of changing plans — may help us understand the fact that losses are treated more seriously than gains (in prospect theory, and probably in life). Many of our plans are

"open ended at the top." Most scientists, for example, are reasonably happy if they can make some contribution and earn the respect of a few of their colleagues, but none would say that winning the Nobel prize was definitely outside their plans. In this sense, great success and great luck is part of everyone's plan, requiring no major revision, but large losses or failures may lead a person to give up even a fundamental part of his plan.

In sum, the subjective-value function of prospect theory, by itself, need not be seen as irrational (except, perhaps, for the decreasing marginal disutility of losses). Moreover, the fact that we can understand it in terms of the event-frequency version of utility theory provides an argument for the analytic usefulness of this version, and for its consistency with the theory of rational life plans. In any case, the second version is easier to apply to real plans and life events. It is not always easy to interpret experiences — such as hearing a piece of great music — as a change in wealth, but it is easy to think of changes in wealth as experiences. Thus, consideration of the rationality of prospect theory has led us to a clearer conceptualization of utility theory as a normative model of the sort that might be relevant to life as well as gambling. This is not to say that all of prospect theory is normative, however. For example, the effect of framing on the reference point is clearly not (Kahneman & Tversky, 1984).

Is conformity to utility theory required?

How far must a person with a rational plan go in conforming to the necessary axioms of utility theory? The arguments made earlier imply only that an idealized creature should not make plans that will necessarily lead to violations of the axioms (in situations that might come up). Thus, we leave two ways in which utility theory may still be violated: having an incomplete or incompletely formed plan, and not conforming to the plan one has.

We consider this question from two points of view, that of the person whose plan is at issue — let us call him the student — and that of the educator. The student's task is to develop a life plan that satisfies the principle of deliberative rationality. The questions for him are whether his plan must be one he can fully conform to, and whether — given the cost of planning itself — it must specify utilities completely.

The educator's task is to ensure that all students have life plans that include properties that anyone would want in his own plans or the plans of others. These properties include moral goals that might not be weighed sufficiently in each student's plan, if the students were left on their own, so there can be conflict between the two points of view. The educator

need not consider the cost of planning, for he sets his policies for large numbers of students. Although the student is concerned with every aspect of his plan, the educator is concerned with more limited policies, such as, "Think about a problem until the expected long-term benefits of doing so are equal to the costs." Note that for this policy, the idea of expected benefits implies balancing uncertainty against the utility of possible benefits, and the idea of weighing costs against benefits implies some sort of tradeoff of utility dimensions. The educator's question is whether this implication is warranted, that is, whether an educator is justified in giving advice that involves tradeoffs like these.

Must a student's plan be one he can follow? The fact that a person habitually violates the policies he has set for himself (perhaps with consequent feelings of guilt or shame) might seem to be sufficient reason to change the plan. However, it may be better (from the viewpoint of deliberative rationality) to live with a little guilt and shame than to live by policies that are so easy to follow that violations never occur. Thus, a student's plan need not be one he can fully conform to.

A student's plan could fail to specify the relative importance of different dimensions of utility. A student might waver back and forth between two kinds of behavior—playing Pac-Man one night, getting down to work the next— without ever thinking that he was being inconsistent (and without attempting to reconcile the conflicting behavior in terms of a higher-level plan, e.g., one in which variety or level of fatigue played a role). From the point of view of the student's ideal life plan—formed under conditions of ideal deliberative rationality—this behavior would be irrational. This is because it is inconsistent with utility theory, and I have already argued that a plan formed under these conditions should be consistent with utility theory. On the other hand, a plan formed under conditions of ordinary deliberative rationality—where planning time is an issue—might well be incomplete enough so as to allow some behavior of this sort. The time and effort involved in bringing order into one's life might not be compensated by the benefit (specifically, living in closer approximation to one's ideal plan).

Although the cost of deliberation is irrelevant to the educator, his involvement with a student's plan is limited for other reasons, because most of a student's policies are of no concern to the educator. The educator may legitimately want the student to appreciate many different kinds of music, for example, but if the student continues to listen only to punk rock, no great harm is done. The educator need concern himself only with those aspects of a student's plan that serve the educator's purpose, such as those aspects having to do with the student's conduct of his

thinking. If, as I argue, rational thinking is something that anyone would want in himself and others, it is a proper concern of the educator. For the utility dimensions relevant to rational thinking, the educator should be concerned with complete consistency. The plan of the well-educated student should be expected to specify tradeoffs among the various properties of thinking tasks, such as time spent thinking versus different kinds of benefits from thinking. This is because we describe the principles of rationality in terms of such tradeoffs, and it is reasonable to do so, given the rationality of utility theory from the point of view of ideal deliberative rationality. (Note that the rational student still need not conform fully to this plan, and the educator still need not require him to do so.)

What counts as "rational" here might differ somewhat for the student and the educator. The student's rational life plan might give less weight to moral concerns than does the educator's rational plan for that student. Thus, an educator might want that student to do more thinking, for the benefit of others, than the student would want to do, given his own preferred life plan. A student might not care to think about public policy issues, for example, although it would be better for everyone if everyone thought more about such issues. (Nothing in the definition of rational life plans requires students to weigh the interests of others as much as we all might like.)

In sum, the educator's point of view does not require complete conformity to utility theory, for most parts of a student's plan are outside of an educator's concern. However, it does require sufficient consistency for certain dimensions so that the student would never be at a loss for how to resolve conflicts among these dimensions (if he could follow his plan). If the student were left on his own to resolve the conflicts in the future, he might not resolve them ideally. Thus, the educator should try to get the student to conform to utility theory for the relevant parts of the plan.

The important point here is that—with considerable qualifications—utility theory is required by the theory of rational life-plans. Insofar as a plan specifies choice policies at all, and insofar as cost of planning is not a factor, it is rational to specify choices in terms of utilities. The educator has a right to assume that students will conform to utility theory with respect to certain dimensions. For example, if the educator thinks it is rational for a student to think about a problem up to the point where the expected benefits are equal to the cost of further thinking, this policy is meaningless unless the student follows the axioms of utility theory with respect to this tradeoff. Yet, this does seem to be a legitimate goal for an educator to have.

Plans, investments, and self-control

The relation between plans and utilities might be clarified by considering another question: Why shouldn't we behave according to our immediate preferences (e.g., playing Pac-Man) when doing so conflicts with our plan? In these cases, the plan itself dictates that the immediate preferences should be ignored, for our own long-term good, as decided on with more deliberation than we are willing to spend on the choice at hand. (Assume that our "long-term good" includes the following of policies adopted for moral reasons. Moral goals are no less real than other goals we have that might conflict with our immediate preferences.) In the economic sense, a plan permits investment, the forsaking of immediate consumption for longer-term gain (including "moral" gain). To withdraw investment prematurely is to be unfair to ourselves in the future as we ourselves see it. Thus, the various methods we use to "control ourselves" (Elster, 1979) are legitimate parts of a plan: avoiding distractions, making schedules, making "side bets" (e.g., that we will not smoke) with others or even ourselves (Ainslie, 1975), etc.

If we find that an actual temptation is more tempting than we anticipated, we are of course free to change our plan and give in. (Or we may give in without changing our plan, in which case our plan loses some of its force.) For example, a dieter may decide, on reflection, that it is really better to eat ice cream every day than to be thin. In such a case, we might say that the original plan did not adequately foresee the consequences — unless, of course, this "reflection" occurred in an ice-cream store. More generally, my deliberation about my plans is not performed in one sitting; it is a recurrent part of my life. It would be irrational *not* to change my plan if I believed that my new plan was, on reflection, superior. It may even be rational to make decisions that render past investments worthless; for example, a person may work hard to prepare for a certain career, and then decide it is not what she really wants.

On the other hand, there are reasons for sticking to plans even when we would not choose these plans if we were to start over. For example, if we give up one plan, we may reduce our own expectation that we will, in the future, be able to stick to other plans, so we may thus be hesitant to make other investments of time and effort (Ainslie, 1975). Also, reneging on an announced plan may make others less prone to trust us (just as we are less prone to trust ourselves).

The reason we should stick to rational plans is that we want to be fair to ourselves in the future, and rational plans represent our best guess

about how to do that. Except for this need for fairness, there is no need for plans at all (Elster, 1979). In addition, one person's plan is part of an interrelated set of plans of self and others, from which all benefit, so that fairness to others is involved as well as fairness to oneself in the future. Thus, moral goals—if we have them—often provide reasons for sticking to plans.

Interpersonal and intrapersonal comparison of utilities

It is often argued that there are special problems in weighing one person's utilities against another's. This claim is frequently used as an argument against utilitarian moral philosophy, the use of some principle of maximizing average welfare to decide moral questions such as the appropriate distribution of income. For example, if Jane claims that her need for champagne and caviar is just as important as some other person's need for beans and tortillas, how can we prove her wrong? If interpersonal comparison of utility is impossible (or merely difficult), then so is comparison of utility across time for a single individual (March, 1978; Williams, 1981). If Dick claims that his need for a BMW this year is much greater than his need for a retirement pension, we have the same problem with him as with Jane. Utilities change over time, so that Dick will be—in terms of his utilities—a somewhat different person at the time of his retirement. The same problem comes up in the Pac-Man versus statistics example that began this chapter. The problem of intrapersonal comparison (across time) is made even more complex by the fact that a person's future utilities are affected by his current plans (as already noted).

The answer to Dick and Jane is this. First, we cannot prove to them that they are wrong, but that is not the issue. The issue is a matter of advice, not proof. The real question is whether we can give them reason for changing their beliefs, or whether they can find such reason for themselves. In fact, the weighing of utilities across people is not a totally indeterminate process; we do have evidence. We can imagine what it would be like to be constantly hungry, or to be stuck in a small apartment in one's old age, unable to travel or to afford the entertainment that one finally has time to enjoy. We can listen to the reports and complaints of others who find themselves in the situations we are imagining, and we can even discount reports on grounds that some people are complainers and others are stoics. A creature who has unlimited time for calculation and comparison—the creature who uses utility theory prescriptively—can imagine, as best she can, herself existing at one time with concurrent

goals of two or more people at once, and she can ask how she would resolve the conflict among different goals if she had them all concurrently as her own. This is the sort of decision we make when we weigh different dimensions of utility against one another (Hare, 1981). (However, there are some problems that arise in the intrapersonal case that do not arise in the simplest form of the interpersonal case. In particular, when I imagine myself at time 2, the future, I may want to consider the preferences I will have at that time for myself at time 1, the present, just as I consider my time 1 preferences for myself at time 2. Hare (1981) suggests that we limit our deliberation to now-for-now, now-for-then, and then-for-then preferences as best imagined now, but the issue is not settled. I assume, as he does, that it can be settled without disturbing the general outlines of the argument just made.) In sum, if a person desires to be fair to others, or to himself in the future, there are sources of evidence he can draw on so as to make a best guess about the relative weights of utilities across people or times. A best guess is all that can be achieved, but it is all that is needed for planning. The problem of weighing utilities across people and times is no more a problem than the problem of weighing different attributes of utility at the same time. As noted earlier, this is often difficult, but there is no reason to think that it is impossible — especially in view of the fact that such judgments are sometimes made rather easily — and difficulty alone is no reason to eliminate a type of judgment from a normative theory.

Probabilities and beliefs

Rational plans are made and carried out on the basis of knowledge and belief, including belief expressible in degrees. What can we say about what a rational planner would want for himself, or what an educator would want for him, in these areas? There are really three separate questions here: (1) Why have true beliefs as opposed to false ones? (2) Why have probabilities that accurately reflect the information available? (3) Why have probabilities that are mutually consistent?

First, true beliefs, and accurate probabilities, may be helpful in accurately foreseeing the consequences of actions and plans, hence, in choosing plans that will succeed, so as to maximize utility as determined by those plans. The value of such foresight may seem limited when viewed from the perspective of narrow self-interest, for which little knowledge may be required (relative to the knowledge that schools and colleges routinely try to impart). But when plans concern themselves with the long-term welfare of society or humanity, for moral reasons, the practical

value of knowledge—of the sort obtained from science and history, for example—is considerable.

Second, the attainment of true beliefs and accurate probabilities could be a goal in its own right in each of our plans. If there is such a goal—and there is every reason to think that people are innately curious—it would be worthwhile for the educator to encourage its development, because of the other benefits of having accurate beliefs. Traits that lead to accurate beliefs are traits that we would want to encourage in ourselves and others, regardless of our other ends or theirs.

Note that these arguments apply to probabilities as well as other beliefs. When we are trying to decide whether to carry an umbrella, we will maximize utility if we act as if we know the true probability of rain. If the utility difference between getting wet and staying dry is exactly three times the utility difference between walking without an umbrella and carrying one needlessly, then we should carry one when the probability of rain is more than 25%, but not otherwise.

Of course, like any other criterion of rationality, this must be balanced against the cost of achieving it. Inaccuracy in belief is rational if the cost of removing that inaccuracy is greater than the expected benefit.

If we are *coherent*, our judgments (or the behaviors based on them) follow the axioms of probability theory. The most important one of these is additivity: if A and B are mutually exclusive events, then $p(A \text{ or } B) = p(A) + p(B)$. (In addition, by convention, the probability of an impossible event is 0 and the probability of a certainty is 1.) Coherence is assured by the axioms of utility theory that were cited earlier. This does not mean that a person who follows utility theory can state probabilities coherently, but it does mean that he behaves as if he follows probabilities that are coherent. The fact that coherence is implied by utility theory is related to the fact that a "Dutch book" can be made against a person with incoherent probabilities (Freedman & Purves, 1969). A Dutch book is a set of bets such that the person will lose overall no matter what happens.

Aside from these reasons for coherence, I believe that there are no others. If I am right, the reasons for coherent probabilities stem entirely from the role of probabilities in utility theory. To the extent that we seek accurate probabilities out of a goal of acquiring knowledge for its own sake, coherence by itself is unimportant. If the most effective methods for acquiring knowledge (for this purpose) lead to incoherent probabilities—or to representations of degrees of belief for which coherence cannot be defined in the usual way—this is no problem. The question of what type of coherence is required for these purposes, if any, must rest on a more complete analysis than is possible here.

Summary

We may view the theory of rational choices and plans as a hierarchy. At the top level is the choice of a rational life plan, taking into account long-term personal and moral interests. There are two versions of this plan, the student's and the educator's; the latter is complete about those parts of a plan that anyone would want in themselves and others, and is otherwise silent about the parts that are matters of "personal choice." The choice of a life plan is made without appeal to utilities, for one of its results is just the specification of dimensions of utility and their weights. A student's life plan may be incomplete, because it may take too much time and effort to complete it. (What counts as "too much" is again a holistic judgment made hypothetically at the highest level.) Examples of actual choices made at this level might be the choice of a career or the choice of sexual orientation. (Alternatively, a career might be chosen because it is instrumental to the achievement of deeper goals.) The point here is that a student's decision to be a psychologist, for example, cannot be criticized by appeal to her utilities. It *can* be criticized by appeal to the principle of deliberative rationality, that is, by the argument that she would not have chosen it if she had deliberated sufficiently about her choice. It can also be criticized, from the educator's perspective, by the argument that it is not sufficiently moral, that it does not do enough to further the interests of humanity. Note that such criticisms can be made without anyone fully being able to determine whether they apply. They are not descriptive statements to be verified or falsified, but exhortations to rethink the plan in certain ways (or to regret that the rethinking was not done earlier).

The output of this highest level includes a person's specific policies, including dimensions of utility and the relative weights of those dimensions. These policies, in turn, guide the making of rational decisions in individual cases. But the way in which this occurs is not always by direct appeal to utilities. Rather, these policies might define an intermediate level of *activities*, which may include rules for classifying situations so as to decide which activity is appropriate. For example, a psychology student sets policies concerning the time and effort put into different work and play activities, such as coursework, research, and video games. These policies also specify, to some extent, how various actions will be classified, for example, whether seeing the movie *Freud* is education, entertainment, or both. People make (and revise) these policies on the basis of a set of basic utilities or goals, such as curiosity, helping others, and the attainment of education and advancement that permits the achievement

of other goals. (The utilities may also be revised on the higher level, of course.) This level of a plan can be criticized only by arguing that the specification of activities does not conform to the utilities or to (other aspects of) a life plan.

Policies may define activities in such a way that only some utilities are relevant within each activity. For example, in the activity of doing statistics homework, utilities of other parts of a plan, such as those concerning love relationships, may be irrelevant. Thus, a plan might define *local* utilities that apply within certain activities, as distinct from the *global* utilities specified by a whole plan. One of the things that happens because of this local-global distinction is that a person can discover additional goals within an activity. For example, a student might think of asking his girlfriend for help with his statistics homework, perhaps with some expected sacrifice of efficiency in getting the homework done.

The lowest level is the level of individual decisions. Does our student persist on his statistics problem, go on to the next problem (a matter of local utilities), or play Pac-Man (a matter of utilities governing the choice of activities)? At this level, a person can be criticized for violating the local utilities that apply within each activity, or for failing to search sufficiently for other utilities that would be relevant. For example, a student might underestimate the utility of continuing to work on a problem. The student, from his own perspective, cannot be expected to make such decisions errorlessly, for to do so would require too much deliberation. Thus, our student would have no reason to regret an error here if the situation in question (an unsolved problem) came up so rarely that it would require too much effort to decide on a policy for it. However, from the educator's perspective, certain policies, such as those governing the conduct of thinking, should be complete, so there is always room for criticism of decisions governed by such policies.

3   A theory of thinking

Consider an executive caught in a dilemma: How should she respond to her colleagues' unanimous decision to increase their expense accounts without informing the central office (which is unlikely to notice)? First, she wants to go along, imagining the nice restaurants she could take her clients to, but then she wonders whether it is right to do so, from the corporation's point of view. She is still tempted to go along, for it has been argued that other departments in the corporation are allowed higher accounts, and that increased entertainment and travel opportunities will benefit the corporation in various ways. However, she thinks of reasons against this view, such as the argument that any other department could do the same, on the basis of other flimsy excuses, and if all did so, the corporation would suffer considerably. (She makes use here of a heuristic or schema for moral arguments that she recognizes as one she has used before.) She considers reporting the decision to the central office, but rejects this both because of the personal danger it would involve and her feelings of loyalty to her colleagues. She decides not to go along, and to keep careful records of her own actual use of her expense account, because she has imagined what would happen if the scheme were in fact discovered.

This episode of thinking has much in common with other thinking. *Possibilities*, in this case possible actions, are considered in turn; in some cases these arise only as a result of search, but in other cases (as in the case of going along) they present themselves. *Evidence* is sought—or (like the arguments of the colleagues) makes itself available. The evidence may consist of arguments, imagined scenarios, examples, etc. The function of the evidence is to increase or decrease the *strengths* of the possibilities, as when the moral argument weakens the possibility of going along. For this purpose, each piece of evidence has a *weight* with respect to a given possibility and goal. *Goals* are present, or are sought, as when the moral goal of serving the corporate interest is considered as a possible

84

goal to be served in the decision. The search for possibilities, evidence, and goals is governed by the thinker's subjects *costs* and *expectations* for success of each search process, and the costs of thinking and the value of success are a function of her utilities. If our executive does not care much about moral goals, or if she finds thinking about them aversive, she will not think much (and in this case will be more prone to go along).

In this chapter, I show how such terms as these can provide a scheme for analysis of all goal-directed thinking. I also show how formal and informal prescriptions can be derived from this scheme. Formally, pre-scriptive rules for classes of thinking may be derived from normative models, particularly utility theory (a suggestion developed in chapter 4). Informally, the scheme can lead to suggestion for changes in thinking. If our executive did not consider the possible action she chose, it would have been fair to suggest that she consider other possibilities; or if she ignored the moral argument after thinking of it, it would be fair to suggest that her initial temptation to go along was distorting her evaluation of the evidence (the argument). I argue that we should expect deviations in particular directions from the prescriptive rules that thinkers ought to follow. Namely, if we assume that people overweigh the immediate costs of thinking relative to the long-term benefits, people can be expected to think less than they should, to gather and interpret evidence in a way that does not challenge possibilities about to be adopted, and to change goals less often then they should. I conclude with a loose taxonomy of thinking tasks, designed mainly to illustrate the range of tasks to which the present theory may apply.

The basic idea of the present theory, then, is to analyze thinking into phases or functions. This analysis provides a way of categorizing the moves a thinker makes in the course of thinking. A given move may be a member of two categories, as it may have two functions. The phases should be thought of as usually *conscious*, in the sense that a thinker would be able to follow instructions stated in terms of the phases, and to recognize whether he has succeeded in doing so. Thus, the descriptive language of these phases can be used both to instruct a person in thinking and to analyze his reports of his thinking. Some phases may be missing from some episodes of thinking, in the sense that their work is done subconsciously, that is, without such a potential for instruction and recognition. When all phases occur subconsciously, no thinking has occurred (in the sense in which I use these terms), but the work of thinking has been done by subconscious processes. For example, when we swerve to avoid a pothole while driving, we are not aware of any evaluation of alternative possible actions, and it is immaterial here whether we say that such evaluation occurred subconsciously or not at

all. I concentrate on conscious thinking, in the sense I defined, because this is what can be influenced by advice about rationality, in such a way that the thinker can cooperate in such an educational enterprise by observing his own thinking.

The theory I present here has been arrived at by reflection, e.g., by modification of other possibilities (see the section on Dewey in chapter 1, for example). It has not been deduced logically from first principles, and although it is consistent with much empirical evidence (both formal experiments and less formal observations of protocols), its empirical consequences have not been fully tested. It is, first, a method of analysis, which is neither true nor false but rather useful (or less useful) in specifying what we mean by good thinking, and, second, in combination with other assumptions, a way of deriving empirical predictions.

The phases

A given episode of thinking may be analyzed into phases, and some of these phases may contain or require still other episodes of thinking. For example, the phase of gathering evidence might require thinking about what evidence to gather or how best to gather it. Thus, a given episode may be part of a still larger episode. The theory is thus hierarchical (in the same way as is the theory of Miller, Galanter & Pribram, 1960): Some episodes are included as parts of other episodes, which are included in others, and so on.

The analysis takes knowledge, capacities, and unmodifiable emotions (see chapter 2) as givens. Thus, the exact behavior that is counted as rational will differ from person to person, depending on these things. Most discussion of the effect of knowledge and capacities on thinking, and of the effect of thinking on the acquisition of knowledge, is put off until chapter 5.

There are three kinds of terms in the theory: objects of search processes, quantities, and rules.

Objects of search processes

The objects are as follows:

Goals. A goal is a criterion for ending the thinking process. It is reached when we find an acceptable answer to a question, such as, "What should I do?" We may think of a goal as a set of local criteria to be satisfied, e.g.,

attributes in MAUT (chapter 2). Formally, we may wish to represent the goal as an evaluation function of the sort used by MAUT, with attributes corresponding to the different factors. For our executive, her initial goals are to serve her own interests in food and travel; later, she adds the goals of concern with her immediate colleagues and concern about the corporation. Often, a goal is present before thinking begins, and an impasse in progress toward achieving it is the stimulus for thinking. The goal determines what evidence is sought and how it is used. For example, it is not until moral goals are adopted that the "what-if-everybody-did-that" schema is used to search for evidence. (A computer model of thinking would draw on different knowledge bases, or organizations, for different goals, as discussed in chapter 5. It is noteworthy that a great deal of work in artificial intelligence avoids this problem by concerning itself with single-goal models.)

Possibilities. These are possible answers to the question implicit in the goal, e.g., possible actions our executive might take. Possibilities (like goals and evidence) may be in mind before thinking begins, or they may be added in the course of thinking.

Evidence. Evidence is defined by its function in changing the strengths assigned to possibilities, i.e., the thinker's tendency to adopt them. Evidence may come from the thinker's own memory or imagination, it may come from a question asked of the outside world (e.g., asking about expense accounts in another department), or it may come passively, needing only to be noticed, e.g., the arguments of a colleague. One possibility can serve as evidence against another, as when we challenge a scientific hypothesis by giving an alternative and incompatible explanation of the data.

In sum, the classification of a given move in thinking depends on its function: Goals determine when thinking is successful, possibilities are potential satisfiers of goals, and evidence is used to evaluate possibilities.

Quantities

The *quantities* are properties of the basic propositions for a given thinker. Quantities vary in degree, and for purposes of modeling it may be useful to assign numbers to them. Quantities are also a function of the thinker's knowledge and abilities. They are assumed to be conscious in the sense that a person can be instructed to use them as guides for action. The quantities are:

Strengths. These represent the extent to which each possibility is seen as satisfying the criteria that constitute the goal. Strength is a function of the possibility, the goal, and the evidence available, the function itself depending on the thinker, given his knowledge and abilities. When the goal of thinking is to determine the truth (as in diagnosis, or in detective work), strengths may be interpreted as probabilities. However, there is no reason to expect a person, even a person who follows prescriptive rules exactly, to be able to translate strengths (which are subjective) into numerical probabilities without training. In decision making, strengths correspond to expected utilities of the possible courses of action (possibilities), given the goal of maximizing expected utility. In general, if the goal is conceived as a multidimensional evaluation that can be applied to each possibility, then the strength of each possibility can be decomposed into strengths on the separate dimensions. For example, our executive might feel that the possibility of informing the central office is high on the dimension concerning the corporate interest but low on the dimensions concerning herself and her colleagues, hence low overall. Her chosen solution to her problem was moderate on all relevant dimensions but high on none. These dimensional strengths can be used to guide the search for new possibilities: for example, our executive might consider trying to persuade her colleagues to inform the central office, thus ameliorating the deficiencies of her chosen possibility. We may define *confidence* as a measure of the closeness of thinking to its goal; often, confidence is simply the maximum of the strengths of the possibilities under consideration.

Weights of evidence. These represent the degree to which a given piece of evidence supports (or weakens) a given possibility with respect to a given goal. The weight is thus a function of the possibility, the evidence, and the goal. (Later, I shall discuss various normative models for the interpretation of such strengths.) Weights may be available immediately with the evidence, or they may be the results of a subepisode of thinking, for example, when our executive evaluates the form of her colleagues' arguments by appealing to the "what-if-everybody-did-that" schema (which is, in this case, also a direct piece of evidence as well as part of a subepisode for assigning weight to another piece). A weight by itself does not determine how much the strength of a possibility is revised; rather, the thinking controls this revision. Thus, a thinker may go wrong either in a subepisode whose goal is the assignment of a weight or in the use of weights to revise strengths (or both ways). The latter error occurs in a bias to underweigh evidence against an initial possibility.

Expected gains and costs. These govern the time and effort put into the search for evidence, possibilities, and goals; we stop searching when we feel that it will not "pay off." They are functions of many properties of the current state of thinking, e.g., the number of possibilities under consideration, the amount of time spent thinking so far, etc. There is an expected gain and cost associated with each phase of thinking. For example, our executive might stop thinking of still other possible actions because of a feeling that she is unlikely to find one, so that the expected gain from further search is low. Gains and costs depend on a thinker's utilities, and here is where the normative models described in chapter 2 enter the theory. Both the goals of thinking and its costs are assumed to have utilities dictated by a thinker's life plan (including those parts of it that are biologically determined). The plan defines what dimensions of costs and benefits are relevant and how these dimensions are weighed; for example, our executive might perceive her situation in terms of such dimensions as getting along with her colleagues, serving the corporation, and so on. The goals of her thinking are, in general, a subset of the goals of her life plan, the dimensions on which she evaluates outcomes.

Formally, gains may be represented as expected increases on a scale of confidence (closeness to the goal). Expected gains may be a function of both the probabilities of different levels of confidence (after further thinking) and the utility of each level of confidence as determined by immediate goals (which, in turn, may depend on the life plan).

Costs are a function of the utilities assigned to time and effort and such other factors as the anticipated effect of success or failure on self-esteem, given a certain level of effort. The utility of time may in turn depend on what other activities are competing for attention at the moment: Our executive is more likely to mull over her problem while waiting for a train than while watching a movie. We may define costs for different purposes in terms of the thinker's actual life plan or the plan he ought to have (from the educator's perspective); for example, in the latter case, the value of thinking for others might be weighed more heavily. Costs may also depend on biological factors associated with thinking. For example, underaroused people (extraverts, perhaps) may find it difficult (costly) to attend to a given goal for a long period of time (Eysenck, 1967). Such people may give up quickly on an episode of thinking, and thus appear to be impulsive, because thinking, in fact, becomes subjectively costly. However, it must be noted that such costs should still be weighed (with other costs) against benefits in determining whether thinking is worth continuing.

Thinkers do not usually *calculate* expected gains and costs of thinking; rather, the role that these quantities play in thinking is that they are reasons for continuing to think or not. It is quite reasonable to say, as an expression of one's true reasons, "I gave up because I felt I was not going to think of anything better" or "I kept at it because I felt I would." As in the case of weights, a person may go wrong in responding to a given quantity (by continuing to think or not).

Why just the phases I have listed: search for possibilities, evidence, and goals, and use of evidence? The idea is that thinking is, in its most general sense, a method of choosing among potential possibilities, that is, possible beliefs or actions. Hence, there must be possibilities to choose among, and if thinking is conscious, the possibilities must enter the mind; hence, search for possibilities is essential. For any choice, there must be a purpose or goal, and the goal is subject to change. We can search for (or be open to) new goals; hence, search for goals is always possible. There must also be objects that can be brought to bear on the choice among possibilities; hence, there must be evidence, and it can always be sought. Finally, there must be rules for using the evidence. The phases I have outlined are necessary in this sense.

This is not to say that all the details of my analysis are necessary. Indeed, there are a host of variants of this basic description, and the choice among the variants is a matter of convenience. (For example, in an earlier version of this scheme, I suggested that there should be an overall expectation and cost for thinking, and then separate parameters governing which of the phases was to occur; this now seems less elegant to me, although it is technically equivalent to the present approach.) Nor do I mean to imply that there is no other correct way to analyze thinking. Rather, given the starting point of taking thinking as a means of resolving doubt, an analysis into possibilities, evidence, and goals is always possible (even if these categories overlap). By analogy, utility theory analyzes decisions into actions, states of the world, and outcomes (which depend on actions and states); this is not the only way to analyze decisions, but it can always be done, and when it is, no other terms are required.

There are several advantages of this scheme. First, it is useful as a descriptive model. In particular, I shall suggest that it can provide a framework for the development of more detailed systems for analyzing verbal protocols of thinking, of the sort collected by Newell and Simon (1972), Perkins (1981), and others. The extra details in each scheme come from the enumeration of different kinds of possibilities, evidence, and goals, and of

standard moves involving subepisodes, etc. Second, it lends itself to a description of biases in thinking., The rule for each phase is specified by a normative model, i.e., utility theory as described in chapter 2, and there are likely to be deviations (biases) from the normative rule. Such biases might be specific to a certain topic or they might tend to be general across all topics for a given thinker. In the latter case (at least), we might want to speak of a cognitive style characteristic of that thinker. Third, it is general; it is a kind of description that can be reasonably applied to all thinking, even though its details may change with each application. Fourth, it provides an easily understood language for prescriptions, and for those people who neglect to think at all in certain situations it may serve as a prescription by itself; that is, it may tell them what they need to do (consider alternative possibilities, gather evidence, etc.).

Purely normative or descriptive models do not have these advantages. The prescriptive value of normative models is limited to cases in which we approximate the idealized creature for whom the model is intended. Descriptive models, on the other hand, contain no standard of performance or evaluation, except perhaps the implicit standard of correctness versus error. The prescription to "be correct" is not helpful. By contrast, the prescriptive model to be developed here is stated in terms a thinker can use to guide, and thus improve, his own thinking.

Here is a more complete description of the phases.

Search for possibilities

Possibilities may be sought directly from memory under the guidance of the goal and the evidence available. When our executive tries to think of solutions to her dilemma, she may ask herself, "What will serve the goal of being loyal to my colleagues, given the evidence I have of their commitment to the expense-account scheme?" Possibilities may also be suggested to us from outside, for example, by a friend, and the fact that we are searching is then indicated only by our readiness to add them to the set under consideration. We may think of each possibility as coming with a strength already attached. This strength is based on the contents of memory, and hence on prior evidence, although the evidence on which it is based may itself be forgotten, and the strength need not be a normatively correct reflection of that evidence. For example, our executive may feel that her idea of informing the central office is a good one when she first thinks of it, perhaps because of her admiration for "whistle blowers" she heard about—the memory of which need not be recalled. Subsequent evidence can, of course, change the strength.

Search for evidence

The search for evidence is affected by the goal, the possibilities under consideration (and their strengths), and the evidence already available. Our executive may ask herself, "Can I think of any reason why my plan (possibility) will not serve my goal given the evidence I already have about my colleagues, etc.?" There are different types of evidence:

1. Signs, or correlated events, are the most typical kind of diagnostic evidence. For example, "patients with such and such a disease typically have such and such an appearance." If the appearance is observed, it is a sign of the disease, even if the link between the two is not understood.
2. Reasons, that is, rules or generalizations brought to bear on a given case, are relevant to almost any type of possibility.
3. Examples constitute evidence for or against a possibility that is a general statement, a statement meant to apply to a class of examples (e.g., "Absence makes the heart grow fonder").

Other possibilities may themselves constitute evidence against a given possibility. If we can think of another possible disease, the strength assigned to the first possibility might be legitimately reduced as a result. When other possibilities are used as evidence, phase 2 and phase 1 are combined, since the move of thinking of a new possibility serves two different functions. Likewise, the discovery of a goal may serve as evidence, as when our executive rejects her original impulse to join the scheme by finding her goal of serving the interests of the corporation.

Use of evidence

In this phase, new strengths are assigned to the possibilities as a function of their original strengths and the weights of the evidence obtained. The possibility of joining the scheme becomes less attractive to our executive, for example, when she thinks of the moral argument against it, but it is still not out of consideration, so its strength is reduced, but not to zero.

It is worthy of note that true thinking cannot occur in a domain, in the course of development, unless the thinker has some rules of inference, however simple, that can be applied to that domain. It seems likely that there is a small set of "natural deduction" rules that are used from an early age, as suggested by Braine and Rumain (1983). These rules might be able to handle most thinking in which a separate subepisode is not required for use of evidence and in which hypotheses may be confirmed or falsified conclusively (given the thinker's beliefs). It may be useful to express these rules in terms of the objects of the present theory, for example (with examples from clinical diagnosis):

R1. If we find some evidence that is implied by only one possibility, that possibility is confirmed. For example, if auditory hallucinations occur only in schizophrenia, then their presence is sufficient to diagnose that disease.

R2. If a possibility implies that D is true, and D is false, the possibility may be eliminated. If all schizophrenics have inappropriate affect, then absence of that symptom rules out schizophrenia.

R3. If two possibilities are mutually exclusive, then confirming one rejects the others. If no depressives are schizophrenic, then we can rule out schizophrenia by confirming the diagnosis of depression.

R4. If some observed evidence implies that some possibility is true, then the possibility is true (another version of R1, suitable for a person who has learned that auditory hallucinations imply schizophrenia).

There are surely also some basic rules of inductive reasoning, as suggested by Tversky and Kahneman (1983) or Collins and Michalski (1984), for example: If one possibility is similar to a second possibility, and the second serves the goal, then the first is likely to serve the goal as well.

Search for goals

There are several ways in which the goal of thinking is modified during the course of thinking.

1. Duncker (1945) noted that problems are often solved by "formulating the problem more productively" in a series of phases, each of which "in retrospect, poses the character of a solution, and, in prospect, that of a problem." For example, in Duncker's classic tumor problem, a subject is asked how to destroy a tumor with some tissue-destroying rays, without destroying the surrounding tissue. Subjects generally proceed by thinking of general types of solutions, such as weakening the rays as they pass through the surrounding tissue, protecting that tissue, or focusing the rays. Each solution type then becomes a new goal, for example, "How can I focus the rays?" Newell and Simon (1972) have described this process as creation of a subgoal.

2. A different kind of subgoal may be formed when the thinker identifies a particular discrepancy (a kind of evidence) between the current goal and the current best possibility. Then, the thinker forms a subgoal of reducing that discrepancy by changing the possibility. (In Newell and Simon's terms, this kind of goal change operates in means-ends analysis, but not in hill climbing, where the goal remains the same.)

3. Polya (1945) points out that an important "heuristic" for mathematical problem-solving is the creation of "auxiliary problems," e.g., the current problem minus one of the requirements of its goal. A solution to the auxiliary problem will either suggest a solution to the main one or allow the main one to be reformulated again in terms of a simpler goal.

4. In the three types of goal search described so far, the local goal remains in force, and new goals are introduced only for the purpose of achieving the goal as initially assumed. There are other cases in which goals are found that are drawn from outside the local context. For example, Reitman (1965) and Perkins (1981) have pointed out that artists, engineers, and others who solve "ill defined problems" frequently "discover" the goal in the course of working. This discovery may amount to recognition that the problem at hand is relevant to parts of a higher-level plan, or life plan, parts which had not been involved as motivation for the action out of which the thinking arose. This recognition, and hence the goal change, is triggered by evidence; therefore one purpose of seeking evidence may be to discover one's goal.

5. In the course of searching for evidence or goals we may find that one of the goals in our plan conflicts with a possibility. For example, our executive found that her goal of serving the corporation conflicted with the possibility of going along with the scheme. We may thus add an element or attribute to our original goal, such as the requirement that the solution serve the corporation. In this case, as well as case 4, it may be useful to think of our life plan as one gigantic thinking episode, with several goals. To achieve these goals, we pursue a few subgoals at a time; hence the distinction between local and global goals that was suggested in chapter 2. But in the midst of our pursuit of local goals, it may be useful to search for the global goals of which our life plan consists (perhaps even just a part of our life plan, such as our aesthetic values). Such a search for higher-level goals — in contrast to the effortful search for subgoals (1 through 3 above) — is usually a kind of openness or receptivity. We cannot go through life exploring actively the ethical implications of every action we take. What we can do is to be willing to revise our decisions (about actions or policies) when we perceive that they may affect the achievement of some goal.

The theory as a framework for description

If, as I claim, the present scheme corresponds to the actual processes of thinking, it may be used as a framework for scoring verbal protocols of thinking, that is, records of someone "thinking aloud." This is possible to the extent that the objects and quantities are conscious, hence available for report.

Verbal protocols must not be seen as ways to make thinking overt, for two reasons. First, the task of reporting one's thinking itself may change the thinking process. For example, a thinker may search more thoroughly

when he knows his thinking is being observed. Second, conscious thoughts may go unreported. This may be particularly true for quantities. We are probably capable of making much finer discriminations among degrees of strength, weight, and expectation than we do spontaneously in reports of our thinking.

The answer to these objections is that their seriousness depends on the purpose to which protocol analysis is put. In the study of individual differences (e.g., Charness, 1981), we may often assume that these differences are uncorrelated with differences in the effect of verbalization instructions on thinking or on the tendency to report fully. In the diagnosis of individual difficulties in thinking (Lytle, 1982), verbal protocols may be the most revealing diagnostic tool available. For example, when a reader repeatedly does nothing to figure out the meaning of unfamiliar words, it would seem worthwhile to suggest that the thinker search for some possible meanings and some relevant evidence (from the text or a dictionary). We cannot tell from protocols whether such a suggestion will help, but protocols might give us good reason to try it out.

I shall present some protocols here for yet another purpose, to show that the phases I have listed provide a useful and flexible framework for description of various kinds of thinking. For this purpose, it is important only that you, the reader, recognize the protocol as similar in relevant respects to your own thinking (or to thinking you think you have observed in others) and thus appreciate the relevance of the analysis. In particular, it will be seen that some of the quantities are represented in protocols, a fact not previously recognized in other analyses such as those of Newell and Simon (1972). Second, they show how objects such as possibilities and evidence may be subdivided into types peculiar to the type of thinking at issue. Third, they show — for anyone who doubts it — that there are cases in which thinking does indeed help to reach correct conclusions, or at least conclusions more acceptable to the thinker.

The reader who is willing to accept these points (and who does not enjoy reading protocols) may skip the protocols themselves without missing any of my argument. And the reader who is totally uninterested in the use of protocols may skip the rest of this section completely.

The first example comes from Lytle (1982), who, with my advice, developed a system for scoring protocols of students reading difficult texts. A subject is asked to read a passage one sentence at a time and to talk aloud about what he does to understand each sentence in context. The scoring system was based on the idea of a "move," a basic function of thinking, such as a search for possibilities, finding a possibility. The term corresponds to what Newell and Simon would call a change of state,

except that it may include the initiation of a search for possibilities or evidence as well as the success of the search in finding its object. Since a move was a function, a given part of the protocol could be scored as two different moves at the same time. There could be several moves per text sentence, but, by definition, one move could not extend over several text sentences. The unit of analysis was specified by the definition of the various categories of moves themselves, not by such units as sentences or phrases of the protocol.

The major scoring categories were monitoring, reasoning, signaling, judging, elaborating, and analyzing. Each of these was divided into subcategories.

Monitoring statements indicate that the subject doubts his understanding, and has initiated a search for possibilities or evidence. Examples are: "I'm not sure what a ganglion is." "This is in a way a contradiction of what they said earlier."

Reasoning statements indicate more explicitly what is being done to try to resolve some doubt. One type involves the finding of a possibility or hypothesis (with explcit doubt still remaining), e.g., "I guess it means something physical but I'm not sure." Another type involves a prediction, a combination of a hypothesis and the initiation of search for evidence of its confirmation, e.g., ". . . so they're going to talk about the problems people have who like to act and who like to write." Another type involves a question, the intiation of a search for evidence, e.g., "I'm wondering how they're sensed and all through the past sentences I guess I've been wondering how the animals, how the insects do this." Another type involves the use of evidence to draw a conclusion, e.g., ". . . clearly they're doing it for even more a reason than the ants did what they did because they [the author] said that the termites are even more extraordinary." A special scoring category was used when the conclusion involved the rejection of an earlier hypothesis, e.g., "So that — okay you can die — excuse me — that's not the idea at all — the idea is that some people can go through an illness and then finally die with dignity and it's you know it's spiritually meaningful but that assumption is taken to mean that everyone is capable of doing that which I guess the author is going to say is not the case. What was my other idea about this? Oh well." The last two types of reasoning moves illustrate how thinking can help in comprehension, to the extent the conclusions reached are correct (which they usually are).

Analyzing and elaborating moves consisted of search for, and discovery of, evidence, but without the guidance of specific possibilities on which the evidence might bear. Elaborating moves were scored when the reader

reported being reminded of something, having an emotional reaction, etc. Analyzing was scored when the reader reported noticing features of the text such as unusual working. Much of our initial groping about, in many different thinking tasks, is of this sort; it is an attempt to gather more evidence in order to help the search for possibilities, or to distinguish among possibilities not yet found.

Judging involved the drawing of (tentative or final) conclusions about the correctness or appropriateness of the text. It indicates the presence of other goals than merely "comprehending" the text, and it therefore may indicate that a search for goals has occurred.

Here is an example of part of a protocol, generated by me (as the subject) before either Lytle's system or the present theory was developed. I choose it because of the high density of reasoning moves, and because it illustrates how reading may sometimes involve the consideration and rejection of several possibilities before a satisfactory one is found. It therefore suggests indirectly that a reader who fails to think will fail in cases in which someone equally ignorant but more willing to think might succeed. I present the protocol in entirety because it may be surprising how much thinking can occur in a domain, reading comprehension, in which the role of thinking has not received a great deal of attention. The text sentences are in parentheses, and my comments in brackets:

(While naturally respecting the sincerity of Rex Raab's comments against euthanaisa (April 16), I feel his own gentle sermonizing is not without incoherence.)
Well Rex Raab must have written an article against euthanasia. "gentle sermonizing" - must have given a gentle sermon against euthanasia. The letter says it's "not without incoherence." That means "with incoherence." So that means it was incoherent, .. although it was a gentle sermon, okay.
[Mostly summarizing and drawing conclusions from evidence, indicated by "must have" and "so that means."]
(The "right to live," however vague a concept, certainly refers not only to being born, but also to developing into, and existing as, a mature and rational person.)
I guess this is an argument that the letter is making against Rex Raab. Let's see, Rex Raab was *against* euthanasia. That means Rex Raab is *for* the right to live, but this seems *consistent* with an argument for the right to live. Maybe this is a quotation of Rex Raab. Maybe this person's paraphrasing the argument now. But that doesn't make sense because it's a new paragraph. (Experimenter intervenes.) Oh, okay, it's not a new paragraph. But, on the other hand, if the person says that what Rex Raab says is incoherent, then this person wouldn't be able to paraphrase it. So it's probably a *counter*argument. This says, this is an argument for euthanasia. The right to live .. (rereads) .. ah, so the crucial words might be "mature" and "rational." That is, this person is gonna argue that euthanasia is okay when people are not rational, or mature, or something like that. Let's see.
[Here the reader proposes a hypothesis that the letter opposes Raab, rejects this hypothesis by finding a conflict with evidence, then proposes the hypothesis

that the writer is paraphrasing, rejects that on the basis of poor evidence, returns to the first hypothesis, looks for consistent evidence, and finds the words "mature" and "rational, which lead to a hypothesis about the subsequent argment.]

(Presumably, it is this rationality that underpins the claim to choose euthanasia, a rationality a baby clearly does not have.)

Now I'm lost again. The person who's writing this is against . . . Let's see, Rex Raab is *against* euthanasia, so this person is *for* euthanasia, and (rereads) . . . *Who* chooses? So a baby doesn't have rationality, but the baby never decides to kill anyone, so that's not what this means. (rereads) Maybe . . . ah! the choice of euthanasia is made by the person who wants to *die*, so now we're taking about not killing people in a coma but killing people they are dying of cancer, and they can't stand the pain or something like that. Now a baby doesn't have this rationality to choose. I – see. So this phrase "mature and rational person" must mean that the right to live depends on developing into a mature and rational . . . The right to live exists because it allows people to become mature and rational, but once they become mature and rational then their life is in their own hands. Now a baby doesn't have this right, so it's not okay to kill babies because you want to protect its potential. But once it gets that right, once it gets the rationality, then it can decide for itself. Let's see if that . . .

[The reader begins with monitoring, caused by failure of his last hypothesis. He searches for evidence ("Who chooses") so as to form a new hypothesis, rejects the idea that it is the baby, finds the possibility that it is a sick person, and then looks for evidence in favor of that possibility. This leads to a complex hypothesis about the argument to follow.]

(That we cannot choose when and where to be born is true but trivial: the fact is that we *are* capable of choosing the circumstances of death— whether we should do so being a separate issue.)

Rex Reed must have said that. I do not know why he'd say that. (rereads) When we're rational . . . This is reinforcing the argument about rationality. When we're rational, we can choose. But I do not know . . . I do not understand this first part, "we cannot choose when and where to be born . . ." Reed must have given that as an argument against euthanasia. How can you make that into an argument against euthanasia? I guess I do not see that.

[The last hypothesis is held in abeyance while a new source of difficulty is uncovered and a search for possibilities initiated.]

(The relevant parallelism between birth and death that Rex Raab rhetorically implies does not exist.)

Ah! Rex Raab must have drawn a parallel between birth and death, saying that since we cannot choose "when and where to be born" therefore we cannot choose when and where to die, but that's silly! I can't believe it's that silly.

[Possibility discovered. Judgment made.]

(There is a similar confusion in Mr. Raab's own "arbitrary human decision" that the pain caused to the mother at birth "justifies" the pain of terminal illness (an anesthetized birth thus deserving eventual euthanasia, presumably?).)

Wow! It sounds like another stupid argument here. (rereads) So Raab must have said that people should have to suffer no matter how much the pain because their mothers suffered to bring them into the world. And this is a good argument here: if you anesthetize the mother during birth then it's okay for the patient to choose death. But that was another silly argument and this person who's writing the letter is absolutely right. This Rex Reed guy must be pretty stupid.

[Conclusions from evidence, and more judgments.]

(To apply justification in such an area is simply inappropriate.)

Well, I do not know about that. Now the person who's writing the letter seems to be saying that you can't argue about whether euthanasia is justified or not, but you *can* argue about it.

[More conclusions and judgments.]

(Behind the account of patients suffering and finally dying with dignity can only rest the assumptions that voluntary euthanasia would prevent anyone choosing to undergo such a spiritually meaningful process, and/or that everybody is capable of "dying well" without euthanasia.)

Oh boy, this is a complicated sentence, I've got to read it again. (rereads) I see. Reed must have said that patients should suffer and die with dignity and should not chicken out and they should be prevented from chickening out. (rereads) Oh boy, I still can't unravel the syntax. Ah! Reed then is assuming "that voluntary euthanasia would prevent anyone choosing to undergo such a spiritually meaningful process." The reason that the syntax is hard is that this is badly written. (rereads) The "choosing" could either be modifying "anyone" or it could be "prevent anyone *from* choosing." I can't figure out which of those is meant. (rereads) Ah! That must be it. That makes sense. And also there's no other "from." So that must be it. So Reed is assuming that voluntary euthanasia . . . Reed is *mistakenly* assuming that voluntary euthanasia would prevent the people from choosing against euthanasia, and Reed also seems to be assuming that everyone is capable of dying well without euthanasia, which might be wrong. Okay, this makes sense.

[Of interest here is the finding of two possibilities about the meaning of "choosing" before evidence search is begun.]

(Of course, neither assumption is true.)

That's true.

Lytle gave this passage and two others of comparable difficulty to a group of seniors at a private school. Good readers (as determined from their summary retellings of the passages they read) tended to use more analysis moves than poor readers, thus suggesting that poor readers fail to search for evidence that might help them. Good readers did not use more reasoning moves than poor readers, but they had less occasion to do so, as they expressed doubt less often. Good readers are surely good in part because they have relevant knowledge (of grammar, vocabulary, and the topic) and skills, which decrease the need for thinking. If the need for thinking—as indicated, for example, by monitoring moves, were held constant, we would expect to find that good readers do more reasoning; indeed, Fullerton (1983) has found this in a elementary-school sample even without equating groups on need for thinking.

Here is a protocol of moral reasoning done in response to a class assignment to think through a moral issue and analyze one's thinking. Unlike previous examples, the thinker here was somewhat familiar with the analytic scheme outlined in this chapter [half a lecture plus a reading of Rawls's (1971) chapter on reflective equilibrium], but the example

seems realistic nonetheless. It illustrates a kind of reflective thinking in which a principle is tested against examples one retrieves or constructs for the purpose. In particular, the examples come with intuitions about rightness or wrongness (or, for the linguist, of grammaticality or ungrammaticality), and the thinker may sometimes change the intuition about the example rather than give up an otherwise useful principle. Such changes in intuition may be considered as the consequence of a subepisode of thinking concerned with the phase of using evidence: The evidence first seems to weigh against a possibility, but the evidence itself is changed by this subepisode. Because the analysis is especially transparent, I shall keep my comments to a minimum. The question here was one of several options provided with the assignment:

When does the state have a right to intervene in childbirth or child rearing? First of all, I think any time the child's life is in danger, like with a child abuser, or when there's a good chance that a mother is going to have a difficult delivery and she wants to have it at home, or something like that . . . I'm thinking of examples . . . I do not think they have a right to in a case like having to send your kid to school. [Use of an intuition about an example as evidence to support the initial possibility.] I think that should be a parent's decision . . . If a parent . . . It's hard . . . I think in general the only time the state really has a right to intervene is when a child's life is in danger, or not even life, really, but physical well-being; or, in a sense, psychological well-being, but I do not mean schizophrenia, or if your parents are a little nutty people can live with that. [Continued search for possibilities even though no counterevidence is apparent.] I guess they have a right to intervene there, but they shouldn't because it isn't practical. But if a child is continually left alone or locked up in a closet or something like that they should. So when a child's physical or psychological well-being is significantly threatened, that's when. [After an aborted subepisode about practicality, the thinker finds a positive example to support the new possibility, a revision of her original one.] Now for more specific. Like an example of a questionable case would be a kid who grows up somewhere in farm country and his parents do not want to send him to school, they just want him to work on the farm. That's hard because I would want the kid to go to school to try to have a "better life," but I do not think that anyone can judge for another what a "better life" is. [Here, she rejects her intuition on the grounds of another principle, which may be seen as evidence bearing on the interpretation of the original intuition, hence a subepisode.] So in a sense a parent has every right to keep his kids at home if they do not think that school will do him well. I do not know 'though. I think I'm gonna have to revise my principle because I think that every kid has a right to learn to read and do basic arithmetic just so they can make it in society, regardless of what their parents want them to do. [The subepisode continues, and changes its conclusion about the weight of this example.] I think there are skills that you have to have to have any choice of what you are going to do with your life. So maybe that's part of it: a parent has to provide some means of a kid doing that. I do not know how you could test it or anything. So, the state has the right to intervene when a kid is in serious danger of physical or psychological danger or when . . .

but also has a right to set minimal standards on a child's abilities, but I do not think they have a right to say how they must be obtained. Parents could teach their own kids how to read. [The possibility is again modified to take into account the evidence against the old one.] (The student continues beyond this point to think of a couple of examples that do not lead to major changes and then to try to state the principle clearly once and for all.)

Now here is a brief excerpt from Galotti, Baron, and Sabini (1984), which shows that thinking, as I have defined it here, is used in solving syllogisms. Such analysis as this may help us to clarify the relation between logic and thinking in general. I shall suggest that there is a basic logic used in thinking, but most logical problems are best understood in terms of the thinking process itself, as I describe it here.

Some orange books are not philosophy books. Some philosophy books are not long. Oh, well, um, some orange books aren't the long philosophy books. .. Um, but I do not know if anything has to follow from that. Let's see. OK. [S tries to make inferences that will serve as evidence suggesting a possibility.] (What are you thinking?) Oh, well, let's see. I'm thinking whether .. there's anything in the first sentence that has to equal anything in the second sentence. If I could substitute in anything. [Indicates a search for a certain kind of evidence.] Um, and let's see, well, there's .. okay. Only some of the orange books are not philosophy books. And some of them could be.. Um, and the ones that *are* philosophy books could be the philosophy books that aren't long. But they could also be the philosophy books that *are* long. So I do not think anything follows from this one either." [The subject makes two inferences about possible relations, which, together, imply that nothing follows. The weight of the evidence for this possibility is sufficiently great that the subject feels no need to continue thinking. The subjects seems to know the general rule: If A could be C and if A could be not-C, then nothing follows about A and C.]

As a final example, let me indicate how I might analyze a protocol that Newell and Simon (1972, pp. 274 ff) found somewhat troublesome (although not impossible). In this protocol, the subject is given the cryptarithmetic problem LETS + WAVE = LATER, in which he must discover the digit that each letter stands for. Of interest in this protocol is that the subject tries out several different problem spaces before settling on one that can lead to the answer. First, he tries to solve it on the basis of trial and error; he had just solved a simpler problem (AA + BB = CBC) in this way. He then rejects this method and tries to find general constraints on the size of the numbers. Next, he tries to look for hints from the meanings of the words. At other points he tries to set up algebraic equations, or discover a code in which letters correspond to digits in a regular way. He returns to methods given up several times. Finally, he settles on the correct method of making inferences about individual letters, but does not finish before the time limit.

Newell and Simon describe this protocol in terms of changing problem spaces. Although this description is reasonable, nothing in their theory says anything about how a subject does this, since the problem space itself is considered fundamental. (In principle, it might be possible to talk about a problem space for finding a problem space, but I suspect this would begin to look like the scheme I suggest here.)

All of the attempted problem spaces in this example may be described in my scheme as searches for subgoals. (Indeed, Newell and Simon might be happy with such a description, except that the idea of problem spaces does not contribute to arriving at it.) For example, the subject explicitly mentions trying to find algebraic equations or letter-number codes before attempting to achieve this subgoal. Following Duncker (1945), I conceive of a subgoal as both a possibility, a general statement of the answer to the problem, and a goal to be satisfied by completion. The question of how this search is directed is a question, in part, of how memory is organized, and this question will be addressed in chapter 5.

In general, it is possible to develop a scoring system for a given type of thinking by classifying different types of evidence, possibilities, and goals. Separate scoring categories may be needed for initiations of search processes and for the success of those processes in finding their object. Successes may be subdivided into those that occur as a result of effort and those that do not (e.g., where an idea is suggested, or occurs to a thinker while he is pursuing another object). Finally, separate categories may be used for moves that are inconsistent with the various biases I shall describe; e.g., searching for an alternative possibility or a counterexample is inconsistent with biases not to do these things.

I hope that these examples have shown how the phases of thinking might plausibly correspond to the actual thinking that lies behind these protocols, even if much of that thinking is unreported and hence hard to fathom. I also hope it is apparent that feelings of strength, weight, etc., are sometimes represented even in the protocols themselves, as well as in the thinker's mind. Finally, it should be clear that general parameters of the phases — which I shall describe in more detail shortly — can affect the outcome of thinking. For example, giving up the search for possibilities, or evidence, too early might have led to failure in place of the successes we have seen in these examples. This is not to say, by any means, that these parameters are the only, or even the main, determinant of success in thinking, or that specific knowledge — of rules of inference, of examples, etc. — is unimportant. It is to say that the way we carry out our thinking, given our knowledge and abilities, can make a difference too.

The prescriptive theory

The scheme, as outlined so far, specifies what thinking is and how it is to be analyzed. The prescriptive *rules* of thinking specify what *good* thinking is. In brief, thinking is good when it follows policies that can reasonably be expected to maximize utility, as defined by the thinker's long-term plan or by the plan he ought to have.

Specifically, each search process — for possibilities, evidence, and goals — may be considered as a type of action to be carried out. The thinker should carry out each of these actions so long as it is worthwhile in terms of utility, that is, as long as the expected gain is greater than the cost. The expected gain, in turn, should depend on confidence in the thinking done so far, expectation of improvement from the thinking yet to be done, and the utility of the goal as specified by the thinker's plan. For our executive, confidence is not high until the last possibility is found, expectation of improvement is probably moderate throughout, and utility is very high, since the goals involved are important. The cost should depend on the (negative) utility of search and by the utility of whatever action would be done (according to the thinker's immediate appraisal) as an alternative.

In addition, evidence should be sought and used in a way that is fair to all possibilities.

Optimal search

What determines the optimal amount of search? Several comments are relevant to this question:

1. Each episode of thinking need not take the full life-plan into account, for the plan itself may reasonably specify that local goals may operate in certain classes of situations: our executive need not think about her hobbies in trying to work through her dilemma.

2. We want our prescription to be useful to a thinker, so it can be based only on what is available to him. We cannot take the point of view of an omniscient observer who knows just how much more thinking it would take for a student to solve a statistics problem. We must accept the student's own categorization of the problem, his own subjective costs and expectations, and his own appraisal of alternative actions he might take. (We may still question those judgments, which may themselves be formed by irrational thinking; in particular, we can question the thinking that went into a student's plan or into his learning how to think in a given type

of situation. But this is not the same as saying that the student failed to optimize thinking in the statistics problem itself.)

3. There is no general method a person can use to ensure optimal search in all situations, including new ones. Whether a person continues searching or not will depend on different policies, habits, or heuristics for different classes of situations. In each class, there will usually be feelings of cost, expectation, and confidence in the thinking done so far and in that still to be done. Feelings may be similar in two different classes, yet it may still be optimal to continue thinking in one class but not in another. A person may learn that perseverance in statistics usually pays off, even when the situation seems hopeless, yet the same feeling of hopelessness elsewhere may be a good signal to give up. Expectations and confidence do not come with labels on them indicating the true probability of being right or or succeeding with further efort. What is judged as rational or not is the way the thinker responds to his expectations and costs, not these quantities themselves. Further, the success of a rational policy will be affected by the validity of feelings of confidence (which affects feelings of expectation). For example, it might be that when my spelling confidence is at its ceiling, I am still correct only 90% of the time. If I needed to do better, I would have to look up every word, at considerable cost. There is a limit to what good thinking can accomplish.

4. The allocation of effort to each search process is best seen as a matter of degree rather than an all-or-none dichotomy. To oversimplify slightly, it may be useful to think of two types of search. One type consists of active search that excludes other activities, the type that occurs when a person is playing chess. For this type of search, the optimum is defined by asking whether the thinker should give up the search at any given time. The other type consists of a postponement of a judgment or decision while other activities are pursued. In the meantime, the thinker remains open to whatever possibilities, evidence, and goals occur to him in the course of other activities (or are suggested by others). That is, the thinker will incorporate these objects into his thinking as they come up, making the appropriate revisions in strengths of possibilities. This is the sort of thinking our executive might do. This passive type of search is essentially without cost — except when there is external time pressure. In the absence of such pressure, there is no good reason to discontinue this sort of passive search, hence no good reason to make final judgments and decisions that are not subject to revision. In this sense, a good thinker is never intolerant of ambiguity or doubt for its own sake, and while he is able to make judgments and decisions, he is also always open to "new ideas." (Within active search, there may be an optimal *amount* of effort

as well as an optimal time to give up, and within passive search, there may be degrees of openness; but to a first approximation such issues may be ignored.)

5. The rules of good thinking specify when allocation of effort should begin as well as when it should end. For example, in spelling, I can set a criterion (on my feelings of confidence) for when I search for evidence by using a dictionary. If the critical level of confidence is too high, I will waste time. If the critical level is too low, consequential errors will result from failing to think enough. For example, my paper will be rejected because the editor thinks I am illiterate.

6. In saying that the thinker should maximize expected utility by using expected cost and benefit, I do not mean that he should calculate how to do this. His position is like that of a driver who must decide his speed by balancing the need to reach his destination quickly against the probability of accident (or arrest for speeding). It would be possible to analyze this situation mathematically, by plotting the driver's (personal) probability of accident as a function of speed, and assigning utilities to time and accidents. Although the driver does not do this calculation, he would be willing to regard it as a criterion of his success in optimizing his speed (assuming the calculation were done correctly, by an idealized creature of the sort discussed in chapter 2). When the driver's wife (for example) criticizes him for driving too fast, she is asserting that he is failing to optimize his speed, according to the calculation, if it were to be performed, given the utilities he ought to have. The question of the driver's (or thinker's) rationality is thus the question of whether such a criticism is true. To say that a driver or thinker is irrational is thus to say that he would benefit from advice to change, where benefit is defined by the hypothetical analysis that he would himself accept (on reflection) as a criterion for optimality. (In some cases, it may be possible to show that groups of people are irrational even when we cannot show this for any individual; e.g., Svenson, 1981.)

7. It is unlikely that there is a uniquely optimal amount of effort or time allocated to a search process; there may be a range of acceptable values. There are of course clear cases of irrationality, as when a driver repeatedly gets into accidents by speeding, or when an executive repeatedly makes disastrous decisions by failing to think at all about them. But there are other cases in which different idealized creatures (of the same type) may reach different conclusions. For example, there may be several ways of calculating the probability of an accident, each leading to a different conclusion about the optimum speed. The driver's (idealized) estimate of probability may depend on how he classifies situations—snowy, rainy,

sunny; high visibility versus low; etc. The classification of a thinking task may also be ambiguous in this way.

Interrelations among phases

In general, the considerations just mentioned apply to each of the three search phases separately. As we shall see later, different types of tasks are characterized by different relative importance of the three phases; for example, search for goals may be particularly important in creative tasks. There are also some relationships among the phases within a single task, which should be considered in a prescriptive model.

The utility of evidence search may depend on the number of possibilities under consideration. In some cases, as suggested by Simon (1957), it might be optimal to consider one possibility at a time, gathering evidence before considering another. In other cases, it is best to find at least two possibilities before searching for evidence. This is the essential wisdom in the "method of multiple hypotheses" in science (Chamberlain, 1890/1965; Platt, 1964), and it seems to be the common practice among experienced physicians (Elstein et al., 1978), although they do not usually share their hypotheses with the patient early on. When a scientist or diagnostician has only a single hypothesis in mind, she is likely to seek evidence that would not distinguish this hypothesis from any of the alternatives she would have thought of if she had tried. On the other hand, it is sometimes best to search for evidence before possibilities, because the evidence may suggest possibilities. This is especially true when the expected gain of evidence-search is high and that of possibility-search is low, in particular, when it is difficult to think of any possibilities at all.

An important property of the goal is its complexity, roughly, the number of attributes specified. Goals tend to become more complex as search proceeds, as a local goal is expanded by the discovery of other relevant goals from a higher-order plan, as in the case of our executive. People are described as "single-minded" when they generally pursue simple goals. (Social institutions sometimes serve to protect people against having to pursue complex or multidimensional goals; e.g., the good soldier completes his mission, the good academic need consider only intellectual quality.) In general, the more goals, the more difficult the rest of the process will be, hence the higher the cost. It is easier to think about the operation of one's department than about the operation of the whole corporation — easier to think about national interest than about world interest. The effect of number of goals is exerted because of the way our knowledge is organized: Different bodies of knowledge are ordinarily

brought to bear on different dimensions of evaluation. As the number of goals increases, the cost of thinking increases steadily, but the marginal benefit may decrease. There is thus some optimum point, often involving some simplification. In general, the optimum is a function of the expected value of further thinking and its cost (e.g., the amount of time required to reach an acceptable level of strength). These principles provide most of the rationale for the adoption of local goals as part of a plan.

Fairness to possibilities

Aside from optimal search, good thinking involves being fair to all possibilities — including those not currently strong — when searching for evidence and using evidence. In making a decision, for example, we should look for evidence against our current favorite as well as evidence in favor of it. If we look only for evidence that favors our current favorite possibility, we are likely to find it and thereby strengthen that possibility; in this case, we might as well not have bothered to search at all. When our favored possibility is a general assertion, such as "Dictatorships never turn into democracies," only negative evidence, that is, counterexamples, are relevant. Likewise, in using evidence to revise the strengths of possibilities, we should not ignore evidence that goes against possibilities that are already strong, nor evidence that favors possibilities that are weak.

I have assumed that the costs of using evidence are negligible in the simplest cases. (However, when the weight of evidence must be determined by a subepisode, the costs of that subepisode are relevant. For example, when a thinker must use logic or probability theory to figure out what a piece of evidence means, the cost of these methods becomes relevant, and a thinker who gives up without carrying the method through to completion is not necessarily irrational.) For the simple case in which the weight of the evidence is immediately apparent, however, the prescriptive model for use of evidence is equivalent to whatever normative model is appropriate (since no costs are involved).

It seems that there is no single normative model for use of evidence that includes all cases treated by the present theory. (Shafer, 1976, comes close, but the application of his theory — the rules an idealized creature would follow to use it — have not been spelled out, nor has its normative status been fully clarified.) In cases in which beliefs are the object of thinking, and in which subjective probabilities may be meaningfully assigned, probability theory itself may provide a normative model. In the absence of a complete normative model, we must content ourselves with a few constraints, to which any normative model of use of evidence ought

to conform. The most important of these constraints is a general one that the effect of evidence on the strength of a possibility should not create a bias toward (or, less likely, away from) possibilities that are already strong. Concretely, the order in which two or more pieces of evidence are presented should not affect the final strength of any possibilities. If bias were present, a piece of positive evidence could render the strength of a possibility insensitive to a second piece of negative evidence; if the order were reversed, the negative evidence might render the possibility less sensitive to the same positive evidence. (In some cases, the order of evidence is evidence in its own right, as when we are told the most important things first. In this case, the order should be analyzed as another piece of evidence, and then the order in which this piece and all the others are presented should still not matter.)

Many previous discussions of the nature of good thinking have concentrated exclusively on the use of evidence and especially the calculation of weights. Implicitly, these views define thinking as the making of inferences from evidence. Although the view I have presented implies that such views are severely limited, the use of evidence is surely of great importance in thinking.

Rules, parameters, and biases

A systematic deviation from the optimum may be called a bias, and if a person is consistently biased in one direction in some class of situations (or consistently unbiased), I shall say that that person has a *cognitive style* for that class. Styles defined in this (novel) way are actually abilities, because there is a definition of success and failure. This is what allows me to say that styles may be part of intelligence, which I have defined as a set of abilities (chapter 1). Styles differ from other abilities in that success occurs at an intermediate point on a continuum, so that failure may consist of a deviation in either direction. For example, some people may overweigh favorable evidence, and some may underweigh it. Of course, this does not imply that biases in both directions will be equally common.

Although there may be many possible biases, there are some that can be expected to go generally in one direction rather than another, and these are the ones of particular interest here, for it is just these biases that are likely to be in need of remediation. This is the claim of Dewey and other critics of human nature (see chapter 1). I shall argue that general biases are the result of two common causes (among others that are not necessarily common): (1) "intellectual laziness," that is, trying to minimize the cost of thinking, even when the cost is worthwhile in terms of

long-term benefits; (2) the detrimental effect of the biases themselves on the learning of optimal parameter settings. In general, these causes lead to too little thinking (search) and too little self-criticism in the search for evidence and use of evidence. Education may work against these biases, so that the biases may decrease with age in some societies. However, so long as education works against these biases haphazardly, without a clear sense of purpose (and without effective methods, if these are lacking), success in reducing them is likely to be uneven and incomplete.

The benefits of thinking are mostly in the future, and the costs are immediate. People in general tend to overweigh immediate costs relative to long-term benefits (Ainslie, 1975; Elster, 1979), and there is no reason to think that thinking will be an exception. This problem goes to the heart of every serious discussion of rationality (e.g., Richards, 1971; Ainslie, 1975; Elster, 1979; Hare, 1981, as well as Socrates and Aristotle). If there were no question of binding ourselves to follow rules for the sake of our long-term interest, despite possible conflict between these rules and our immediate interest, the question of rationality would never arise. Much of our education and rearing is designed to help us to overcome the temptations of the moment, both for moral and prudential reasons, and it is generally thought that a great deal of human folly (and immorality) results from lack of sufficiently effective education. (This is not to deny that a few people are oversocialized, so that they postpone gratification more than they should.)

The second cause can be described as a difficulty in learning, given the opportunity that one has; it has been discussed in a context much like the present one by Einhorn and Hogarth (1978). In general, certain biases in thinking make it hard to discover the adverse effects of the same biases or other biases, so that simple repeated exposure to a situation is insufficient to bring about rational parameter settings. This effect tends to operate on biases that lead to too little thinking rather than those that lead to too much. If people think too little, they cannot easily compare their conclusions to those that would have been reached with more thinking, but if people think too much, their earlier, tentative conclusions are available for comparison. Thus, it is possible to discover that one is thinking too much, by finding that extra thinking does not change one's early conclusions, but it is more difficult to discover that one is thinking too little. This is the same direction of bias that is caused by intellectual laziness.

These mechanisms cause three major biases: insufficient search or low allocation of effort to search processes, oversensitivity to positive evidence, and biased search for positive evidence.

Insufficient search (low allocation). The basic problem here is that people think too little: We do not search hard enough for possibilities, evidence, and goals; we make irrevocable decisions too hastily; and we are not receptive to the objects of search even when a final decision has not been (or need not be) made. One explanation of this bias, when it occurs, is that we learn to allocate effort to search processes on the basis of the immediate cost of thinking compared to the immediate gain. But the long-term gain of thinking is often much higher than its immediate gain. Thus, we are irrational, viewed from the perspective of our own rational plans, but not from the perspective of immediate pleasures and pains, particularly the pain of thinking itself. (An exception consists of thinking games such as chess, in which thinking is fun rather than costly. If all thinking could be made gamelike, the biases at issue might disappear.)

A second source of insufficient search is the difficulty of obtaining immediate and unambiguous feedback about erroneous conclusions. This problem can operate so as to produce insufficient search in two ways: (1) by creating *overconfidence* in conclusions reached with little search, and (2) by creating low expectations for success of further search, i.e., *low efficacy*. If Dr. Rosen makes misdiagnoses because she fails to think of a sufficient number of possibilities, and if she does not always follow up her cases, she will believe she has been correct more often than she has, and she will have no reason to change her diagnostic methods, e.g., by making a greater effort to think of more possibilities. Moreover, she will have no reason to question her accuracy, because the failure to think of alternative possibilities will make her highly confident in her favored diagnoses (once she has ruled out the alternatives she *does* consider). She will thus be overconfident, and therefore have a low expectation for the gain from further thinking. In particular, she will not seek evidence about the outcome of her cases. On the other hand, if she does extensive testing, she will easily discover that extra tests do not change the diagnosis that could have been arrived at earlier.

If Jon repeatedly fails in his attempts to write decent poetry because he never searches for new goals or modified goals, he may come to believe that he is simply unable to write poetry (because of lack of knowledge or capacity) and that it is not worth his while to try. Once again, his initial bias makes it hard for him to learn to change that bias, because he does not experiment with different settings of the parameter in question. In this case, however, efficacy is decreased, rather than confidence being increased. If, on the other hand, he searches too much, he will have the opportunity to observe that his search after a certain point does not help his poetry, and he will learn to search less.

Note that nonoptimal search can have other causes. A person might simply misweigh expected costs and gains against one another, because it is hard to compare them (perhaps because the costs may be certain and the gains uncertain). A related fact is that thinking generally involves risk, since success is rarely assured. Some people may like taking such risks, and others may dislike them. Finally, people may differ in confidence and in efficacy for a variety of reasons. A person may for no good reason think that he is totally inept at some task, or that he is a great genius at it, and thus think less, or more, than the facts warrant. (In such cases, the original misperception may come to be, in time, less of a misperception; for example, a person who spends a great deal of time working on something, despite the objective fact that he is initially not much better at it than anyone else, may become better at it as a result of spending the time.) However, there is no reason to think that any of these factors will operate in a particular direction; thus, there is no reason to think that the biases these factors produce will be consistent across people or situations.

The two remaining major biases are a matter of lack of self-criticism rather than insufficient thinking, but they may have the same causes as insufficient search.

Confirmatory search. The two mechanisms I have described will lead to a tendency to search for evidence that will support one's favored possibility, as opposed to evidence that will impugn it. This bias can occur only when the thinker can ask (e.g., his memory) for evidence by specifying its significance. For example, if I believe that Southern politicians tend to be conservative, I can test this by trying to think of conservative Southerners, and then increase the strength of my belief every time I think of one. If I try to think of Southerners in general (e.g., by mentally scanning a map of the United States), I will avoid this bias.

We may think of a parameter governing the direction of search: evidence for a favored hypothesis, neutral evidence, or evidence against it. (It may be somewhat easier to try to think of supporting evidence, because our memories may be organized in such a way that such evidence is most directly elicited by the possibility itself. Thus, the cost of setting the parameter toward this side may be lower. As long as the setting is not too extreme, it may not make much difference if the parameter is set a bit on the positive side.) A thinker may compensate for confirmatory bias, if he has it, by being suspicious of evidence he thinks of himself — but it might be easier not to have it. The worst case, which may often occur, is when a person thinks mostly of confirming evidence and then revises strengths as if he had searched in an unbiased way.

Confirmatory search for evidence saves immediate cost. When John makes a tentative decision to buy a Buick, he can save himself a great deal of thinking by trying to think of a few more reasons why he should buy that car, so that he is sufficiently confident to take action. (For this mechanism to work, the increase in confidence has to fail to take into account the biased nature of the search for evidence.) If, instead, he thinks of reasons not to buy it, he is in danger of finding them and then having to consider other cars, other reasons, and so on.

There is also a learning problem. Once he buys the Buick, it may be hard for him to learn that a Dodge would have been better. Thus, this bias produces overconfidence in incorrect decisions, so that there is no opportunity to learn that the decisions were wrong, hence no opportunity to use this feedback to improve one's parameter settings. The opposite bias, on the other hand, would produce obsessive alternation among decision alternatives, and would, because of this symptom, become apparent to the thinker. (I assume that knowledge of a bias is helpful in correcting it, but not sufficient, so that there is in fact a small minority of obsessive people.)

Belief perseverance, or oversensitivity to supporting evidence. Here, the thinker *uses* evidence in such a way as to favor a possibility he already favors: He overweighs evidence in its favor and underweighs evidence against it. He can thus be led to violate the normative rule given above: early evidence would render him less sensitive to later evidence in the opposite direction.

Once again, laziness may be the culprit. If the strength of a favored possibility is lowered, more thinking must be done in order to decide which possibility is best. (That is, more thinking is required to bring the strength of the most favored possibility up to a point sufficiently high so that the expected gain from further thinking is sufficiently low so that thinking can stop.) As long as the favored possibility is in considerable doubt, the expected gain from further thinking is high.

This bias can also prevent learning of more optimal parameter settings in the same way that insufficient search did in the case of Dr. Rosen described above. Overconfidence in incorrect decisions can prevent us from gathering further evidence about their correctness and thus learning to correct our biases.

The setting of parameters and the demonstration of irrationality

When we attempt to ask whether a person thinks irrationally, we must take into account the possibility (discussed above) that, in general, the

rule for optimal setting of each parameter will depend on the situation. Thus, in general, a thinker must learn the optimal setting for each type of thinking situation: playing chess, writing a paper, buying a piece of furniture, etc. When faced with a novel situation, the thinker must set the parameters on the basis of some more general rule; for example, parameters may be set to the values learned for situations similar to the novel one. Thus, each rule for parameter setting applies to a set of situations, and there are rules for sets that are subsets of other sets (e.g., buying furniture is a subset of buying things in general). When there are rules for both a subset and the set containing it, there is conflict between the rules. With sufficient experience with the subset, it becomes optimal to resolve this conflict in favor of the subset rule. In the early stages of experience with a certain type of task, the more general rule might be reasonable to use. In between, either rule is reasonable.

People are likely to differ in the complexity of rules they can learn. For some, a fine categorization of tasks may be used, but for others, any more than a coarse categorization would make learning of the policy impossible. Once again, there are cases in which several different levels of analysis are reasonable, and these may lead to somewhat different parameter settings.

If we are evaluating the rationality of a thinker in a given situation, there are two standards we might use: the optimum for a broad class of situations that includes the current one, or the optimum for a narrow class. If we find the thinker to show a bias by the narrow criterion, this is not necessarily a cause for calling him irrational and trying to correct his behavior, for the narrow class may be so small and infrequently occurring that it would be useless for the thinker to develop a rule specific to it. The rule for the broad class, which includes that class, may be the appropriate one to follow. (This is the argument of those who criticize purported laboratory demonstrations of irrationality by arguing that the subject's methods serve the subject well in general, but not in the task in question.) On the other hand, if the narrow class is one a thinker will encounter frequently (possibly because we make sure to present it repeatedly), we are justified in trying to help him to optimize his behavior in it. One way to do this might be simply to provide him with experience in it; he might learn on his own to set his parameters more rationally. In sum, the term "irrational" or "nonoptimal" should be employed when we want someone to change in his own interest, and this, in turn, should depend on our expectation about his future. If we expect a person to encounter certain situations involving probabilistic reasoning, it is reasonable to try to teach that person to do that kind of reasoning correctly.

On the other hand, if I am correct about the general causes of biases (laziness and lack of corrective feedback), the biases I have listed ought to be found no matter which standard is used, the broad or the narrow. If we can find evidence for the operation of these causal mechanisms, or for the generality of these biases across different domains (regardless of breadth), we shall be able to demonstrate irrationality in a stronger sense, a sense that is not dependent on the way we analyze situations.

The practical problem of measuring bias (except in confirmatory search and weighing evidence) is that we need to know, or control, the relevant utilities. Another approach, more useful in educational settings, is to look for signs of suspected irrationality and teach a person how to become more rational according to our suspicion. If we have not simply brainwashed the person, and if he continues to use what we have taught him and to extend it to new situations, it is a fair bet that he has found his new parameter settings helpful in realizing his own goals (as he has come to perceive them), and was thus appropriately called "irrational" before the change. Because laboratory experiments (chapter 4) and educational experiments (chapter 7) suffer from different kinds of indeterminacy, they are best carried out in conjunction.

Heuristics

Many of the rules and policies I have mentioned may take the form of heuristics (or strategies), which may be defined as rules for directing search processes or for using evidence in a certain class of situations (which need not be well defined). Heuristics may play several roles in the present theory. First, they may affect the chance of success of a search process. For example, in searching for possibilities, there are classes of situations in which it is more effective to search "forward" by using available evidence as a cue, asking oneself, "What possibilities are suggested by the evidence?"; there are other cases in which it is more effective to search "backward" by using the goal as a cue, asking oneself, "What possibility can achieve this goal?" In general, the latter method is more effective when the goal can be achieved in only a few ways, but the evidence does not constrain the generation of possibilities, as in much practical problem solving. The former method is effective when the reverse holds, as when a scientist tries to think of an explanation for some results (the goal here being to find the truth about some phenomenon). Another heuristic is, "When trying to think of a possible solution to a problem, think of a similar problem you have already solved." This one

may be more useful in some situations (e.g., a field in which the thinker is experienced) than in others. The expectation of success of a search process should depend on the heuristics used, and the choice of heuristic is under the thinker's control. Thus the real choice facing a thinker at any given point is not just whether to continue a search, but to continue using heuristic A, continue using heuristic B, etc., or give up.

There are a great many heuristics, and they vary in their generality (see Polya, 1945; Lenat, 1983; and Newell, 1983; for enlightening discussion). Detailed discussion of the great variety of heuristics is beyond the scope of the present enquiry. However, it is worth noting that it is possible to classify heuristics according to the type of process for which each is used; some heuristics are used for each of the three search processes, and others are used in using evidence. Thus, the present theory might slightly reduce the disorder in our current knowledge of heuristics.

A major role of the present theory is the evaluation of heuristics. For a given type of situation, heuristics may differ in the extent to which the thinking they govern conforms to the normative model (taking into account the cost of thinking itself). In this sense, a heuristic may cause a bias (as argued frequently in the articles in Kahneman et al., 1982). To say that a heuristic causes a bias, however, we must argue that there is some other heuristic that would lead to a smaller departure from the normative model in the class of situations under consideration. For example, in chapter 4, I shall argue that biases in the search for evidence and use of evidence may result from heuristics that consider only a single possibility at a time. Such an argument requires the assumption that other heuristics, which involve considering two or more possibilities, are worth the extra effort they require (if any).

Note that the factors I have suggested as causes of biased thinking may influence the learning of heuristics. People may acquire heuristics that involve less search, and less self-criticism, than other heuristics that would be more rational to use from the thinker's long-run point of view.

The use of the theory in education

In chapter 4, I shall indicate how the theory can be made more precise, so that it can be used to measure biases in laboratory experiments. However, the measurement of biases need not be done in such a precise way. In schools and clinics, it is often sufficient to measure biases in informal ways and then to try to correct these biases through instruction. The measure of bias, used repeatedly during teaching, serves as a standard

and a check for our efforts. For the major biases I have listed, measurement might not be necessary at all, for it may be assumed that biases would be present in most students without appropriate education.

Measurement of biases may be "informal" in that we assume that (1) our subjects have certain common knowledge and goals in the tasks we use; (2) the biases of interest (or our efforts to correct them) are general across content areas; and (3) variations in measures are unaffected by the subject's perception of the task and the situation. Given these assumptions, it ought to be possible to design an informal test for the major biases described here. Such a test would not suffice to demonstrate the existence of biases for scientific purposes, but it could be used by a teacher to examine the strengths and weaknesses of an individual student (as informal reading inventories are used by reading teachers) or to measure the effects of an instructional program on a large number of students. In the latter case, many potential contaminating factors could be assumed to be constant between a pretest and a posttest with comparable forms.

Here are some examples of types of items that might be used (some of which have been suggested by Eric Kraut):

1. The subject is presented with a list of words (or other items) one at a time. His task is to discover a simple category that includes all the items in the list. He announces the hypotheses (usually one) he has in mind after each item. The lists begin with clear members of a given category (e.g., trout, flounder, sardine), but marginal items are introduced (shark, dolphin), and occasionally an outright exception (whale, seal). If the subject maintains his original hypothesis (e.g., fish) despite the counterevidence, we have some first-blush evidence for persistence of belief.

2. The subject is given only two words from a category, and he is asked to discover the category by giving examples one (or more) at a time, announcing his reasons for each example. The experimenter provides feedback designed to confirm the subject's favored hypothesis. If the subject makes no effort to think of alternative hypotheses, we have evidence that he terminates his search for possibilities too soon.

3. The subject is asked to ascertain the truth of general statements, such as "All words ending in -itis are names of diseases" or "All five-letter words that end in -ght have i as their second letter (so that they end in -ight)." The subject thinks aloud while doing this. If the subject makes no effort to think of counterexamples, or even if he spends substantial effort thinking of confirming examples, we have evidence that his search for evidence is biased toward confirmation. In cases in which the subject cannot find counterexamples, we can measure the time he spends look-

ing, and thus get some indication of whether he allocates sufficient time to the search for evidence.

Clearly, many more item types of this sort can be constructed, and even informal tests can be refined by trying them out, calculating reliabilities and validities, etc.

Within specific content areas, biases may sometimes be inferred from verbal protocols, given the same assumptions we made for the informal test just sketched. For example, here is a protocol (collected by Jane Beattie) of a subject doing Wason's (1968a) four-card problem. The subject is shown four cards, with A, B, 2, and 7, showing. He is told that each card has a letter on one side and a number on the other, and he is asked which cards he might have to turn over to test the rule, "If there is an A on one side, there is a 2 on the other side," for all four cards:

Look at card A, see if there's a 2. If not, this rule's false, I mean it's true. If there's not a 2, then it's false. I would turn over the A. [The subject rates his confidence at 100%. He is then asked, "If you found A 2, is the rule true?"] Oh! We could also turn over the 2 and there'd be something on the back of that that could negate that. I'm just thinking out loud. Huh. I would've been sure before, but right now I'm questioning my reasoning because I didn't consider the 2, turning over that. Seeing if there was an A on the 2. [Pause.] If there was a C on the 2 then the rule wouldn't be true. I didn't consider that on the other boards, nor did I consider it on this one until just now, so my confidence is dwindling, but stubborn as I am I'll stick to my guns and say it's true." [The correct answer is A and 7.]

The subject terminates his search for possible cards prematurely (assuming he wants to solve the problem) twice. The second time, he admits that he is "stubborn" in his insensitivity to the evidence against his initial conclusion, and it can be inferred that he terminates his search for possibilities and evidence because he does not want to see his initial conclusion challenged.

Informal tests of this sort, in the hands of a good teacher or clinician, might be helpful in the formulation of prescriptions for individuals. But there are other prescriptive uses of the present theory. I shall discuss these more extensively in chapter 7, but some suggestions at this point may help to clarify the relevance of the present chapter. First, the theory can tell us what we ought to pay attention to when we are learning how to do a new task, if we want to set our parameters optimally for that task. In essence, *learning* to think in a certain kind of situation can be an instance of thinking itself. The thinker may try to discover the optimal settings of the various parameters for the task at hand.

For example, consider an English major who has his first confrontation with serious mathematics, in the course of filling a college requirement.

One problem is to learn the math, and to learn certain relevant concepts peculiar to the field, such as the concept of a function, an axiom, a theorem, a proof, etc. But another problem is to figure out how to think about the new area. In part, this is a matter of learning some specific strategies, such as indirect proof. But in part it is also a matter of learning to adjust one's thinking parameters, particularly allocations. In the humanities, it may indeed be true that understanding comes fairly quickly or not at all, so that one's expectation of the benefit of further thinking may be legitimately low after one has worked on a problem unsuccessfully for a few minutes. However, in math, one may be surprised to find that success often comes only after a protracted period of effort. One might learn this by essentially asking oneself what the appropriate amount of effort is, by doing experiments with oneself which are designed to ascertain this.

Another way in which the theory can be prescriptively useful is that we might derive from it some general qualitative rules of thinking. These rules are designed to help us avoid the common biases postulated by the theory. (Each such rule might be more useful in some domains than in others.) Here are some examples:

> Ask if you are performing this task too habitually, without thinking enough. Have you gotten stale?
>
> Ask if your goal is too simple.
>
> Ask if it would help you to select evidence if you evaluated more than one possibility at a time.
>
> When thinking about the truth of a general statement, look for counterexamples.
>
> When thinking about a set of alternatives, look for negative evidence (reasons against each alternative) as much as for positive evidence about each one.
>
> When weighing evidence, do not weigh early evidence any more heavily than later evidence, unless there is good reason to trust it more. In particular, do not regard possibilities suggested by early evidence as having any special status because you thought of them first.
>
> Keep track of evidence. This is a way of avoiding the situaton just referred to, in which the possibility is given special status because the evidence for it is forgotten. It is simply easier to compare weights (of evidence) to other weights than to adjust strengths (of beliefs) exactly to the right extent in response to certain weights. I believe that this is a routine practice of scholars. Because scholars are sometimes called upon to defend their beliefs (about their field) against challenge, they must keep track of the evidence for their beliefs, and also the evidence against them, and their answers to that evidence. A side benefit of this is that a good scholar may incorporate new evidence in an unbiased way, so as to change his favored beliefs, should the evidence turn against them.
>
> Before you stop, ask yourself if there are other possibilities you have not

thought of, or other evidence that might be relevant. This question might bring to mind some other possibilities or evidence fairly quickly and easily, with very little cost.

Ask if you should be pursuing a different goal. Are you being rigid about your view of what you are trying to do?

The most general heuristic of all is to ask whether you are avoiding thinking because of laziness, that is, whether you are ignoring possible long-term benefits for the sake of avoiding short-term costs.

Finally, it might be possible to develop heuristics for particular domains that serve the purpose of optimizing the rules followed in the domain. One attempt to do this is Polya's (1945) description of the heuristics used in mathematical discovery. Some of these heuristics are descriptions of goals or generally useful subgoals, such as: Understand the problem, ask what are the givens and what is the unknown, and devise a plan. One heuristic, try to generalize the solution, seems to be a general prescription for changing the goal. Most of the others are subgoals for subepisodes concerned with the phase of search for possibilities: Think of a related problem, solve a simpler problem, break the problem into parts, etc. Again, these are generally useful subgoals to set up when possibilities do not come immediately to mind. They serve the purpose of keeping the search for possibilities going, so that it does not end prematurely. In general, when we design a set of heuristics, we should make sure to try to design some to help people avoid the general biases I have listed, within the particular domain at hand.

It might also be possible to give more explicit rules for thinking in the various domains I have discussed, such as reading comprehension or moral thinking. Here is an example from Carol Brown's (personal communication) work on teaching reading comprehension, based on the scoring system of Lytle (1982) described above:

When you do not understand something:

1. Determine what it is you do not understand.
2. Decide if it is important to know.
3. Form a hypothesis.
4. If you can't form one, look for evidence to form one.
5. Ask yourself, "Does it make sense?"
6. Check it from your own memory and the previous text.
7. If it does make sense, read on, keeping the hypothesis in mind.
8. If it doesn't make sense, go back to step 3.
9. When you have drawn a conclusion, try to look back at unanswered questions you had and answer them in the light of your conclusion.

This heuristic is not taught to the student directly. Rather, it is used by the teacher to evaluate a student's verbal protocol and suggest things a student might try, by looking for steps that the student leaves out. Brown

has also devised a tutorial method designed to help the student follow this kind of prescription.

Examples and suggestions for a taxonomy of thinking tasks

Although the present framework can be applied to all thinking tasks, these tasks differ from one another in various ways, some of which may also be described in terms of the framework. (Here, I follow, to some extent, Perkins, 1983; however, his analysis covers a broader set of tasks, not limited to those that involve thinking in my sense.) Each search process may be considered as a request for objects (possibilities, evidence, or goals), and thinking tasks may differ in the degree of *control* the thinker has over this search. In some cases, the success or failure of the search may be largely independent of the effort allocated to it; in other cases, the phase may operate so quickly that it is even insensitive to the amount of time allowed for it to occur by itself. For example, in problems involving "insight," the evaluation of a possibility is often immediate, once the possibility is found. Each request for objects specifies certain of their properties, and in some cases, some of these properties in the request may have no effect on the result. For example, a scientist may ask for a piece of evidence (in an experiment) that supports his theory (as one property), but he can do nothing to compel nature to obey such a request.

Thinking tasks may also be distinguished in terms of the *representation* or nonrepresentation of objects or quantities in consciousness, that is, the extent to which they can be used to guide further thinking. An element that is clearly represented can be easily measured without distorting the reasoning process (Ericsson & Simon, 1980). If none of the elements is represented consciously, the whole process is subconscious, and the present analysis is useless. Representations may also differ from one another in clarity; for example, in some cases, a subject may be able to classify possibilities only as strong or weak, but in others, he may be able to assign numbers indicating relative strength.

In what follows, I discuss a number of tasks from the point of view of control and representation. I shall be discussing my stereotype of each class of tasks, and I note in advance that there may be substantial variation within each. The categories of thinking I present are intended neither as exhaustive nor mutually exclusive. My purpose is to show how the present theory can be applied to a broad variety of tasks, while still allowing for the differences among them.

Diagnosis

In diagnosis—including medical diagnosis and troubleshooting of all sorts—search for possibilities (diseases, sources of malfunction) is under considerable control. Search for evidence is only partially under control, both because some of the evidence is provided by the patient (or situation) without being requested, and because there is some limitation on the kinds of requests that can be obeyed. In particular, the import of the evidence cannot usually be specified as part of the request (e.g., "give me any evidence supporting a diagnosis of ulcers"—unless the patient knows what this would be!). In the purest form of diagnosis, the goal is essentially never changed, although there may be subepisodes of thinking directed toward subgoals such as obtaining a certain kind of evidence. Thus, search for main goals is out of control, although search for subgoals is controlled. (I have spoken as if the goal of diagnosis were simply to determine the most likely disease, but this is surely oversimplified. More often, the goal is to determine treatment, and the probabilities of different diseases may be seen as evidence bearing on this choice.)

All elements are represented. Indeed, strengths, weights, expectations, and costs usually figure explicitly in the diagnostician's thinking.

Elstein et al. (1978) describe a scoring system for the analysis of verbal protocols of medical diagnosticians that maps neatly into the present scheme. Subjects were asked to diagnose simulated patients, and they were scored in terms of which of a set of reasonable hypotheses they thought of and which findings (symptoms and test results, evidence) they discovered at what point in the process. They were also scored with respect to inferences about the hypotheses on the basis of the evidence, i.e., use of evidence to revise strengths. An expert had previously assigned a weight ranging from +3 to −3 to the effect of each finding on each hypothesis, and the subjects' inferences were compared to this weight. Common errors were the use of irrelevant evidence (assigned weight of 0) as support for a hypothesis ("overinterpretation," p. 107), failure to generate the correct hypothesis (p. 110), misinterpretation of evidence (use of weights opposite in sign to the correct one, indicating lack of knowledge, p. 207), and performance of useless tests, often at considerable expense and risk (p. 207). (Happily, the last error was found mostly in medical students, not in experienced physicians, it seems.) Note that these errors may be the result either of lack of sufficient knowledge or of poor thinking, or both. For example, overinterpretation could result from biased use of evidence, generation failure could be due to insuffi-

cient search for possibilities, and performance of useless tests could be due to failure to choose tests that discriminate likely possibilities; and all these errors could also result from lack of knowledge of relevant possibilities or of the relations between possibilities and evidence.

Hypothetico-deductive science

A great deal of science involves testing hypotheses about the nature of some phenomenon, such as the spread of a disease, typically by seeking evidence from experiments or observations. Science differs from diagnosis in that the search for goals is largely under control and goals are frequently changed. Scientists (at least those I know) frequently "discover" the "real question" they were trying to answer in the course of trying to answer some other question. There is — in experimental science — the same limitation on control over the evidence-search phase; the scientist cannot pose an evidence-search of the form, "Give me a result that supports my hypothesis." (Of course, the unscrupulous scientist may instruct a research assistant, "If it comes out the wrong way, do not tell me." But this is not my stereotype.) This limitation does not apply when evidence is sought from the literature or from one's memory. Representation is usually explicit for all elements. In a great deal of science, strengths are represented not on a continuous scale but rather on a three-level scale: impossible, possible, and certain. Thus, the various possibilities are initially represented as possible, and are then ruled out or confirmed by experiments. Likewise, the bearing of a piece of evidence on a possibility is that the evidence either rules out the possibility, does nothing to it, or rules out everything else. In chapter 4, I shall suggest that this way of representing strengths and weights in science is inspired by a criterion according to which it is only certainty that makes for success. With such a criterion, only subjective probabilities of 0 and 1 are meaningful, and the other values might as well be treated as alike. However, this way of thinking may be inappropriate to some kinds of science.

Reflection

Reflection includes the essential work of linguists, philosophers, and others who try to arrive at general principles or rules on the basis of evidence gathered largely from their own memories rather than from the outside world. In reflection, the search for evidence is more controllable than in diagnosis and experimental science; in particular, a thinker may direct his memory to provide evidence either for or against a given possi-

bility (in this case, a generalization). Because of this, the bias of confirmatory search can always occur in reflection, although it usually cannot occur in diagnosis or experimental science. I shall discuss this distinction at greater length in chapter 4, and I shall discuss the limits on the control of search in chapter 5.

A common characteristic of reflection (which may occur in diagnosis and science as well) is that new possibilities are often modifications of old ones, designed to take certain troublesome evidence into account. This is one way in which evidence affects the generation of possibilities.

Insight problems

These are problems whose solution usually comes suddenly and with some certainty. Many are used on intelligence tests, e.g., Raven's Matrices. Much of the older literature on problem solving is concerned with them almost exclusively (e.g., Köhler, 1925); although, curiously, they are almost totally ignored by recent literature (e.g., Newell & Simon, 1972; but see Sternberg & Davidson, 1982, and Weisberg & Alba, 1981). Insight problems are also, apparently, fun to solve, as attested to by the popularity of crossword puzzles and games such as Scrabble. Often, when thinking occurs in the form of a subepisode of other thinking, e.g., trying to think of a possibility or question in science, or a principle or counterexample in reflection, the subepisode is of this type.

In insight problems, essentially the only phase under control at all is the search for possibilities. Often, it is difficult to come up with any possibilities at all. In other cases, possibilities present themselves readily and are rejected even more readily. In either case, search for evidence and use of evidence (acceptance or rejection) are essentially immediate and subconscious (or at least quite easy), and the goal is fixed by the problem statement. It is this immediate occurrence of the other phases, which are essentially effortless, that gives insight problems their unique quality of sudden realization of the solution. In many insight problems, the only elements represented are the possibilities themselves, their strengths (which are coded simply as adequate or inadequate), and the expected value and cost of continued search for possibilities. In other insight problems, such as Scrabble, the strength varies more continuously (and it can even be a numerical point value).

Search problems

Newell and Simon's concept of a problem space works best for certain kinds of problems, which include mazes, the Towers of Hanoi, and chess.

In this problem, there are states (positions in the maze) and allowable moves between the states. What is sought is a path through the maze. This description works best for "forward search," but it is easily modified for problems (such as the Towers of Hanoi) in which we can proceed by searching backward from the goal; in this case, we simply redefine the given problem so that the starting point and goal (of the maze) reverse.

I see no harm in assuming that the thinking occurs at each state, so that the possibilities consist of possible moves away from that state. The evidence consists of the imagined or anticipated effects of the action under consideration. Many of these imagined consequences are simply other descriptions of states from which one might move, i.e., other problems identical to the original problem. To determine more accurately the weight of this evidence, I can go through a subepisode of thinking in which I consider the possible moves I might make out of *that* state, and I evaluate the best of these. Ultimately, I must be able to use some other criterion, such as winning the game or getting into a good position as evaluated by other criteria (as in chess). In sum, the assignment of a new strength to each possibility involves solving a subproblem of the same form as the original problem, up to a point.

One issue in search problems is the choice of a "depth first" versus a "breadth first" strategy. In chess, for example, at one extreme, one might consider only one move at a time, and only one move following that one, and one move following that one. At the other extreme, one might consider several different moves at once, but not many moves beyond each of these. These two strategies correspond to the choice between possibility-search and evidence-search. (Charness, 1981, finds that the better the player, the deeper the search, but there is no relation between ability and the number of base moves considered. Thus, ability differences may reside in part in the thoroughness of the search for evidence, although it is also clear that memory and knowledge are extremely important in this task; see de Groot, 1965; Chase & Simon, 1973.)

Creation

I refer here specifically to artistic creation, although, of course, many other thinking tasks are similar to artistic creation in many respects. (Perkins, 1981, argues convincingly that the similarities are much greater than usually supposed.) In cases of "spontaneous creation," such as jazz improvisation, most of the creative thinking occurs during the hours of practice in which the basic patterns of the skill are devised; the creative product is in part the skill itself.

Possibilities are possible parts of the work, e.g., possible words or phrases in a poem. Evidence consists largely of these parts themselves. The weight of the evidence is determined by the artist's critical reaction to the evidence itself (see Perkins, 1981, ch. 4). A negative reaction indicates a kind of discrepancy between the possibility and the goal, and in creation, it can be responded to by searching for new possibilities and goals (including modifications of old possibilities and goals). Creative tasks are almost unique in the extent to which the search for goals is under control; indeed, part of out concept of creativity may include the idea of pursuing novel goals (or novel variations of traditional goals). The artist examines a particular possibility with the (partial) purpose of generating an additional part of the goal, which can guide the search for the next possibility. The possibilities (like those in reflection) are often modifications of other possibilities, and the goals are modifications of other goals.

The possibilities are also often hierarchically arranged. For example, we can think of an entire work of art (or even a career plan) as a possibility, or a part of that work, or a part of that part, e.g., a line or word in a poem. Each kind of part may be the object of thinking, and the choice of that part usually affects the evaluation of (assignment of strengths to) higher- and lower-level parts. This hierarchy of parts leads to a hierarchy of goals and subgoals, and a corresponding hierarchy of episodes and subepisodes of thinking.

It has been suggested (e.g., Osborne, 1953) that people are biased toward generating too few possibilities before evaluating them (searching for evidence and using it) in creative tasks. However, Johnson, Parrott, and Stratton (1968) found that in creative tasks such as thinking of original plot titles, subjects instructed to produce more possibilities before choosing the best did not improve the judged quality of their final choice. It would thus appear that there is no general bias of this sort. However, it should be noted that the subjects were limited to 7 minutes per problem (after some complained that 5 minutes was not enough); thus the tasks may have been unrealistic. Also, as Perkins (1981) points out in different terms, there are two ways to increase allocation of effort to the search for possibilities: We may either try to think of more possibilities, or we may use more specific instructions for search. Subjects instructed to search for more possibilities might have (necessarily) used more general instructions, which would reduce the chances of finding high-quality answers overall.

The tasks discussed so far, in their stereotypic forms, require thinking almost by definition. In the remaining tasks I discuss, the stereotypic

forms do not require thinking, although thinking may be done. Thus, in these tasks, no effort may be allocated to search processes, and possibilities may be adopted without even any period of openness to other possibilities, evidence, or new goals. Biases may thus manifest themselves as total absence of search, rather than low allocation of effort or premature cessation.

Prediction

Prediction of likely future events is like reflection in form, although the search for goals may not be as controllable. The evidence often consists of memories of other situations the thinker knows about, which are used as the basis of analogies.

Decision making and planning

Here, once again, all phases are under control and all elements and feelings are represented. The possibilities are courses of action, and the evidence, usually from memory, may consist of imagined consequences, based on analogies. Subepisodes of prediction may be required in the evidence-search phase. That is, in imagining consequences, one may have to try to predict them.

An interesting subclass of planning and decision making is the selection of strategies (rules for performance) for other mental tasks, including other thinking tasks. In some cases, such strategies might be selected as a result of thinking about what to do. Once a decision is made about a strategy for use in a thinking task (e.g., a strategy for making a decision), the carrying out of that strategy becomes largely mechanical, and there is no need for further thinking. In other cases, the strategy is not used for a thinking task itself, but for some other task in which the resolution of doubt is not at issue, such as a task of memorizing. The use of thinking to decide on a strategy for another task may be related to the discussion of "executive control" over strategies in the literature on memory and learning (e.g., Campione, Brown, & Ferrara, 1982).

Behavioral learning

I use this to mean "learning about the effects of one's own behavior." This is one of the most important kinds of learning. In every realm of our lives, in social relationships, work, etc., we learn how to control events through our behavior. Much of what constitutes our personality may be

seen as a set of learned patterns, often ones that have become habitual. The success and failure of our plans depends in large part on the effectiveness of this kind of learning. When thinking occurs as part of such learning, each action is a search for evidence (the outcome of the action), and each possibility is a policy concerning what action to take in some class of situations.

As pointed out by Schwartz (1982), this kind of learning can have much in common with science. Each action in a particular environment can be an experiment designed to find out what happens as a result of taking that action in that environment. Of course, the learning in such cases differs from that occurring in science in that the latter seeks general principles. But the biggest difference is that where science is a pure activity, with a single goal, behavioral learning has two goals: learning about the situation and obtaining immediate success or reward in the task at hand. These goals often compete. We are often faced with a choice of repeating some action that has served us reasonably well in the past, or taking some new action either in hopes that it might yield an even better outcome or in hopes of obtaining evidence that will help us decide what to do in the future. In the long run, many people probably choose the former course too often, and, as a result, achieve adaptations less satisfactory to them than what they might achieve if they experimented more. In terms of life plans, such suboptimal adaptation can affect either the expectations on which plans are based, or the success of plans already formulated.

One example of behavioral learning is the learning of heuristics and strategies for thinking tasks themselves. The effectiveness of thinking may depend largely on the number and quality of these heuristics and strategies. This, in turn, may (or may not) depend on the quality of the thinking that went into the learning of those heuristics. At issue here is the importance of thinking in such learning; it is possible that heuristics are learned "implicitly," without conscious gathering of evidence and revision of strengths. If thinking can be brought to bear on the learning of heuristics, however, it can be an extremely powerful determinant of intellectual growth (Lenat, 1983). (Note that the crucial question, for education, is "can be" rather than "is.")

Learning from observation

This includes all cases in which we learn about our environment from observation alone, without voluntary experimentation. As such, it can include behavioral learning without experimentation, namely, learning in which we simply observe that certain actions (done for reasons other than

to get evidence) are followed by certain events. It may also include a large part of the learning of language, including word meanings, and other culturally transmitted bodies of knowledge. To take a classic example, Bruner, Goodnow, and Austin (1956) studied two kinds of "concept attainment" tasks, in both of which the learner had to discover a rule concerning the attributes of a class of stimuli, e.g., cards with large triangles. In the selection task, which was analogous to science or behavioral learning, the subject chose cards one at a time and asked the experimenter whether each chosen card was in the class. In the reception task, which is a pure case of learning by observation, the experimenter chose cards at random and told the subject whether each card was in the class. The subject had to discover the rule without being able to seek his own evidence, without being able to choose his own cards. Clearly, the distinctive property of learning by observation is that the evidence is not under control at all.

Summary

Goal-directed thinking may be analyzed into search for possibilities, evidence, and goals, and the use of evidence to change the strengths of possibilities. Thinking tasks differ in the extent to which the search phases are under control, the extent to which their success or failure depends on the thinker's behavior. The analytic scheme is complete in the sense that no other phases are required for any tasks that are reasonably called *thinking*, and in the sense that differences among tasks may be usefully described in terms of these phases. This scheme is thus an improvement over earlier schemes that apply well to certain tasks (such as search problems, or scientific reasoning) but not to others.

The operation of each phase is specified by a prescriptive model (except when the model is moot because of limited control). The allocation of effort to the search phases should be set so as to maximize expected utility, taking into account the real costs involved (as viewed from the educator's perspective). The prescriptive model for use of evidence is equivalent to whatever normative model applies, since we analyze thinking so as to make this cost-free. Likewise, the setting of the parameter governing search for evidence — whether evidence should be neutral or negative with respect to a favored possibility — is determined by the normative model for the task.

Two factors, intellectual laziness and an asymmetry in the availability of corrective feedback, lead to departures from the prescriptive model in the direction of overconfidence in initial possibilities and low allocation to

search processes. People will in general think too little, search for evidence to confirm what they already favor, and use evidence the same way — unless corrective education has been provided. We may thus expect people (without corrective education) to exhibit biases predominantly in one direction, and therefore to be generally irrational. This is the main empirical prediction of the present theory. Individual differences in the extent (and direction) of these biases may be described as cognitive styles.

The prescriptive model, coupled with the theory of consistent biases, can form a basis for training in thinking. It is not just a set of criteria (in the sense of chapter 1) but a basis for change. The terms of the prescriptive theory are all available to the thinker; they do not refer to the success he is supposed to achieve without telling him how to achieve it. (For confirmatory search and persistence of belief, instruction may be given directly, and followed straightforwardly. For optimizing search, the educator may tell the student to search more, without saying exactly how much, or he may measure the degree of bias, or he may simply try to get the student to learn from feedback. Although the student must discover something for himself, such as how much time to spend on a statistics problem before giving up, he knows exactly what he is supposed to discover and how to discover it.) Of course, following the prescriptive model so as to eliminate biases is not sufficient for effective thinking, but it ought to help.

4   The scheme fleshed out: a decision–theoretic analysis of thinking

In the present chapter, I explore the possibility of interpreting the prescriptive scheme of chapter 3 in terms of some mathematical models. If we can fix (or assume, or measure) the utilities of a subject in a laboratory experiment, and if we can fix (or measure) various subjective probabilities or degrees of belief, we can prescribe his behavior in the experiment. By comparing his behavior to what we prescribe, we can find out whether he is performing optimally, and, if not, we can perform experiments to find out why not. In addition, these models may enlighten us about the interpretation of experiments that have already been reported.

I shall begin by considering some experiments that purport to show biases in the search for evidence, other than the kind of confirmation bias I discussed in chapter 3. I shall suggest that there are other interpretations of these experiments, in terms of other biases I have mentioned, some biases I have not mentioned yet, or no biases at all. This section of the chapter also lays out a general framework that will be useful in the rest (although it need not be understood in detail). In the rest of the chapter, I discuss the experimental study of the biases discussed in chapter 3: impulsiveness, confirmation bias, and belief perseverance.

Choice of evidence

In many situations, such as those involving diagnostic or scientific reasoning, we have an opportunity to gather evidence from the outside world before we adopt a belief or make a decision. We can describe these situations in terms of a set of possibilities (e.g., possible diseases) and a set of questions we might ask (e.g., medical tests); the asking of the questions constitutes the search for evidence. Each possibility may be assigned a degree of belief. Each question can yield one of a set of answers (e.g., test results, often just "positive" or "negative"), and some answers can affect our belief in the different possibilities. In some cases,

the answer will rule out a possibility from further consideration. When we choose a question, we know at least roughly how the answer would affect our belief in different possibilities, but we do not know in advance what the answer will be; if we did, there would be no point in asking. A normative model of choice of evidence would dictate that we choose as if we considered what the answers might be and how they might affect our ultimate decision. We can evaluate heuristics for choosing evidence by comparing their results to those of such a normative model.

This general form of reasoning applies to any situation in which we gather evidence in the course of making a decision that hinges on which of several possibilities is true. As noted in the last chapter, such situations occur often, and many of them are important. For the scientist, the possibilities are hypotheses, and the questions are often experiments. For the diagnostician, the possibilities are diagnoses, and the questions are tests to be given. For the ordinary person in social situations, or for the interviewer, the questions are things we do to size up another person. Even more generally, the acquisition of all of our behavior in any domain — including skills, habits, and rules we make for ourselves — may involve experimentation designed to find out what behavior produces the most desired outcome. Each such experiment is thus a choice of evidence bearing on this question.

In this section, I shall describe a normative model for choice of evidence and show how this model may be applied to psychological experiments that ask whether people are rational in their choice of evidence.

The 2 4 6 experiment

In one such experiment, Wason (1960, 1968b) asked subjects to discover a rule concerning the relation among three numbers. On each trial, the subject gave the experimenter a sequence, and the experimenter told the subject whether the sequence followed the rule or not. Before the first trial, the experimenter told the subject that the sequence 2 4 6 followed the rule. Typically, subjects began with a hypothesis such as "numbers ascending by two." They tested their hypothesis by giving more sequences that conformed to their hypothesis, such as 7 9 11, −5 −3 −1, 2.5 4.5 6.5, and so on. After several such sequences, all of which indeed followed the rule, subjects announced that they had discovered the rule, and that it was what they thought it was all along. In fact, the rule was "three ascending numbers." The subjects would have discovered that their hypothesis was wrong if only they had given certain sequences that did not conform to the condition of their rule, such as 1 3 7, but most

subjects failed to do this. Many other investigators have discovered analogous errors in analogous tasks (e.g., Mynatt, Doherty, & Tweney, 1977; see Tweney, Doherty, & Mynatt, 1981, for additional examples). The phenomenon has come to be called "confirmation bias." Subjects are said to try to confirm their hypothesis rather than to falsify it, or to seek confirmatory evidence rather than disconfirmatory evidence.

Such a description is often related to two arguments made by Popper (e.g., 1962). First, confirmation of a prediction of a hypothesis does not imply that the hypothesis is true, but disconfirming a prediction does imply that the hypothesis is false. The hypothesis that Andrea has appendicitis implies that she will have lower-right abdominal pain (let's say), but the presence of such pain does not demonstrate appendicitis, because other disorders could cause the same pain. However, if her pain is on the left, we can rule out appendicitis (given the assumption as stated). Second, one should choose experiments capable of yielding results that are incompatible with the theory one is testing, and likely to yield them if the theory is false. If the likely alternative to appendicitis is food poisoning, we might ask whether Andrea has fever (which, we assume, would be present in appendicitis but absent in food poisoning). Both of these arguments stress the importance of falsification. Neither, however, is directly relevant to the experiment at hand.

I have no quarrel with the claim that Wason's subjects made an error. I would like to question the description of this error as a bias to confirm one's favored hypothesis. To put my case as simply as I can, we cannot tell from the subject's behavior whether he is trying to falsify his hypothesis or not. He may well be trying to find a series that conforms to his hypothesis yet does not follow the experimenter's rule. Such a series would falsify the subject's hypothesis. For example, when the subject says 2.5 4.5 6.5, he might think it is possible that the experimenter will tell him that this sequence does not follow the rule. The subject would then revise his rule, perhaps to include only sequences of integers. Of course, if the subject thinks his hypothesis is likely to be correct, he will not think it is very likely that his sequence violates the rule. But so far as we know, the subject may think it *very* likely that this sequence would falsify the rule in the unlikely case that the rule is false — for example, he might regard the integer rule as the most likely alternative. If asked, the subject might say that the sequence 1 3 7 would probably not falsify the rule, even if the rule were false, because it would probably yield a "no" answer (and hence not falsify) whether the original rule was correct or not. (The only case in which it is impossible to tell a story like this is the case in which the subject gives a sequence he has given before; only such a sequence

cannot possibly falsify the current rule.) With each sequence, the subject's confidence in his rule may grow, as potential alternatives are eliminated. Eventually, the subject might run out of ideas and announce that he has found the rule. Such an announcement would, of course, be incorrect. But the subject may actually have tried as hard as he could to do exactly what Wason says he is not trying to do at all, that is, to falsify his rule.

It is, in fact, possible that Wason's account is correct — although it has not been shown to be correct, and it is in fact a somewhat more tortuous account than it first seems to be. The subject might believe (or behave as if he believes) two contradictory propositions: first, that he can predict with certainty (or near certainty) what the answer to a question will be; second, that despite the predictability of the answer, when the expected answer is given, he is justified in increasing his confidence in his favored possibility. The error here is this: If the subject is correct that the answer is (nearly) predictable, then he is not justified in changing his confidence, for the evidence he gets is (nearly) useless, as good as no question at all. If this is what the subject is doing, it might be called a bias, but the bias is not in the choice of questions but in the interpretation of their answers, the use of the evidence. The bias is in fact a kind of belief perseverance (chapter 3).

Another kind of bias that might be involved is a simple bias toward questions whose answer is likely to be "yes." We might be inclined to say that this was what Wason had in mind, but if so, it is not clear that the subjects expect confirmation, so the term "confirmation bias" would be inappropriate. However, yes-bias, as I shall call it, is a true bias in the evidence-search phase, for the subject would ask a question likely to yield a yes answer even when it is not optimal to do so.

Another possible source of the subject's error could be in premature cessation of the search for possibilities: The subject could simply fail to think of possible explanations of the data other than the first one to occur to him. The subject may consider some alternative possibilities, but may not search hard enough so as to find those that might include a larger set of sequences than his rule includes. Of course, the experimenter in this case happened to choose a rule that few subjects consider, but this does not necessarily excuse the subjects from failing to consider it, just as the scientist should not be excused for failing to consider alternative explanations of his results. Once again, the error here is not in the evidence-search phase but in the possibility-search phase.

The last two explanations — yes-bias and insufficient search for possibilities — are consistent with a deeper explanation (pointed out to me by

D. Billman): The subject may have conflicting goals. One goal is to be correct in his original hypothesis, and the other is to learn which hypothesis is true. In the case of yes-bias, the "yes" may (mistakenly) satisfy the first goal; the subject may confuse "yes, your example fits the rule" with "yes, your rule is correct." In the case of insufficient search, the goal of being correct in his original guess weakens the subject's motive to discover the truth — if the truth is different from what he thought — and thus lowers the expected utility of searching for possibilities. (It ought to lower the expected utility of evidence as well, and, indeed, some subjects seem satisfied with asking very few questions.) If this is the correct account, it exemplifies the motive to be right in one's initial hunches, which may often be a cause of insufficient thinking.

It should also be noted that the error made in this task may be something more like an error than a bias. The subject may think that the goal is to discover a likely hypothesis or one consistent with all the evidence he creates, or he may think that the last two numbers must be determined once the first is given. Such misunderstandings or "bad mental models" (a term suggested by D. Perkins) do not seem sufficient to explain errors of this type however, as the same kind of error has been found in situations that do not seem to be open to this sort of question (Wason & Johnson-Laird, 1972; Mynatt et al., 1977).

In sum, to explain Wason's results, we do not need to assume any error in the choice of evidence itself. But subjects may be making such an error. To evaluate the subject's behavior, we may begin by considering a normative model for choice of evidence. Such a model should allow us to measure the informativeness of a particular number sequence, or, more generally, a particular question in situations like Wason's experiment. A subject is nonnormative to the extent to which the question he asks is less informative than the most informative question he could ask, according to the model. We may then consider whether such nonnormative behavior may result from particular heuristics that subjects use, and whether there are other heuristics for choice of evidence that bring behavior closer to the normative model.

A normative model

In this section, I first present and illustrate a normative model for choice of evidence. Although the model itself is widely accepted (appearing in textbooks such as Raiffa, 1968), its application to laboratory tasks has only recently been suggested (Baron, 1981b; Fischhoff & Beyth-Marom, 1983). This application is of interest because it is such experiments that

bear most directly on the question of whether people left to their own devices choose evidence rationally or not. Second, I elaborate the point already made that the model allows us to conceive of different kinds of explanations of the error, in terms of different phases. Third, I deal with extensions of the model to situations involving multiple questions (as did Wason's task) and to situations in which the subject is too ignorant to assign prior probabilities meaningfully. Finally, I compare the model to one reasonable alternative, information theory, and I discuss its application to the conduct of scientific investigation itself.

The model, based on utility theory, has been proposed by Savage (1954, especially ch. 6; see also Marschak, 1974). I begin with a form of this model, which, although simple, is adequate for most of the experiments I shall discuss. The model is stated most easily as an expression for the value of a single question, for example, the value of a diagnostic test in medicine. Different questions (tests) may be compared in terms of this value. The model assumes a finite set of mutually exclusive possibilities (diseases), each with a prior probability assigned to it, and a finite set of possible answers (test results) to the question under consideration. The subject (diagnostician) may be viewed as in a gambling situation. He may either make his best guess about which possibility is true, without asking the question, or he may ask the question, get the answer, use the answer to revise his beliefs, and then make his best guess. If we assume some sort of payoff for the subject's guess, the value of the question is simply the difference between the expected payoff before getting the answer and the expected payoff after getting it.

Let us make the simplifying assumption that the subject cares only about being correct, so that being correct may be assigned a utility of 1 regardless of which possibility is true. I shall usually assume that being incorrect has a utility of zero, although I shall sometimes assume that it has a constant negative utility. These assumptions are simplifying because, in the real world, some incorrect decisions may be worse than others, and some correct ones may be better than others. For example, a good physician need not always treat the most likely disease, for the costs of an error may be lower if she treats another one. There may also be cases in which the goal of thinking is not simply to choose (or bet on) the most likely possibility, but rather to bring our degrees of belief in line with the evidence; I shall return to this question later.

To state this more formally, let H_i indicate the possibilities (indexed by i), and let D_j indicate the possible answers (indexed by j) to a question under consideration. (The letters H and D are traditionally used in presentations of Bayesian statistics to indicate hypotheses and data, which

are equivalent to possibilities and evidence — or answers — respectively.)
Before asking the question, a person who is forced to make a guess will
choose the possibility that maximizes expected utility, which we assume
to be equivalent to the probability of being correct. If we assume that
utility is 1 if the H_i is the correct possibility and 0 otherwise, then the
expected utility of the gamble is max $p(H_i)$, where $p(H_i)$ is the probability
that H_i is correct.

After the question is asked, the best guess made may depend on its
answer. However, our model must allow the subject to determine the
value of a question before he knows its answer. Thus, it must compute
the expectation of the expected utility over the different possible
answers. In order to determine this, the subject must have a representation of the probability of the various answers, D_j. For each possible
answer D_j, the prior probabilities $p(H_i)$ are replaced by conditional
probabilities, $p(H_i/D_j)$, which represent the subject's new beliefs, given
D_j. The utility v (probability of being correct) after asking the question
(but before the answer is known) is thus the sum of these maxima, each
multiplied by the probability of its corresponding answer; hence:

(1) $v = \sum_j [p(D_j) \cdot \max_i p(H_i/D_j)] - \max_i p(H_i)$

The rightmost term is the probability of being correct without asking the
question, and the summation term is the expected probability of being
correct after asking the question, computed before the answer is known.
When one is considering a number of possible questions, the best one to
ask is the one for which v is maximum.

Another form of (1) will also be useful. If we assume that $p(H_i/D_j) =$
$p(D_j/H_i) \cdot p(H_i)/p(D_j)$ — from the definition of conditional probability —
then (1) simplifies to:

(2) $v = \sum_j [\max_i p(D_j/H_i) \cdot p(H_i)] - \max_i p(H_i)$

In the medical interpretation, $p(D_j/H_i) \cdot p(H_i)$ is just the proportion of all
patients who have both disease H_i and result D_j (when given the test).
The maximum of these values thus corresponds to the most likely disease,
given the test result, and the sum of these maxima across different
answers corresponds to the number of patients who are correctly treated
after testing.

The main justification for this model is its derivation from utility theory. However, the model should also fit our intuitions in its own right.
Given sufficient time to make calculations, we should prefer to follow the
model rather than not follow it. It should account for our intuitions, on
reflection, about the value of different questions.

For the kind of normative model we seek, in which unlimited calcula-tion time is the only unrealistic assumption, the model should take into account only what its user can know. The model thus determines the value of a question, given a person's beliefs, but without assuming he can know the answer to the question in advance. There is no rule a person could follow that would allow him to do better than the best he can do, given his beliefs.

To show how the model works normatively, let us apply it to a hypo-thetical example. Suppose that a subject in Wason's experiment is con-sidering three possible rules: H_1, numbers ascending by 2; H_2, integers ascending by 2; H_3, all other possibilities. Based on his beliefs about the the experimenter's lack of guile, he assigns a probability of .7 to rule H_1, .2 to H_2, and .1 to H_3. Before any questions at all, his expected gain is thus .7, for he would choose H_1 if he had to announce a rule. What would be the value of the question 2.5 4.5 6.5? The probability of a yes answer to this question is 1 given H_1, 0 given H_2, and, let us assume, .5 given H_3; hence, $p(D_{yes}/H_1) = 1$, $p(D_{yes}/H_2) = 0$, and $p(D_{yes}/H_3) = .5$. If the answer is yes, $p(D_{yes}/H_i)$ would be maximum for H_1, and $p(D_{yes}/H_1) \cdot p(H_i)$ would be $(1) \cdot (.7)$ or .7. If the answer is no, the maximum would occur for H_2, and $p(D_{no}/H_2) \cdot p(H_2)$ would be $(1) \cdot (.2)$ or .2. Thus, the value of the gamble after the question is asked would be .7+.2, or .9, a gain of .2. (If the question is answered affirmatively, the subject will have eliminated rule H_2. He would revise the probabilities of the other rules accordingly and start again. If the rule that was most probable to begin with is repeatedly supported, whereas other rules are eliminated, his confidence in his rule would justifiably increase, to the point where the value of an additional question may seem too low to be worth the effort.)

Another set of examples may help to make the model clear. Suppose that an urn contains 100 balls, each of which is either red, green, or blue, and each of which has a dot on it or not. Table 1 shows the distribution of balls of each color, according to whether they have dots or not. A ball is drawn from the urn, and you earn 100 points if you correctly guess its color. You are shown the table corresponding to the chosen urn. Note that in each table, the sum of each column corresponds to $p(H_i)$ for each of the three possible hypotheses (red, blue, green), the sum of each row corresponds to $p(D_j)$ for each of the two answers (dot, no dot), and the entry in each cell corresponds to the joint probability of the hypothesis and the answer, $p(H_i$ and $D_j)$, which is equal to $p(D_j/H_i) \cdot p(H_i)$, a term in Equation 2. How many points should you be willing to give up to know whether the ball has a dot or not before you guess its color, assuming that your goal is to maximize the expected net number of points you earn?

Table 1. *Number of red, green, and blue balls,*
according to whether each ball has a dot or not,
in each of five hypothetical urns

	Red	Blue	Green
Urn 1			
Dot	13	8	4
No dot	39	24	12
Urn 2			
Dot	0	12	6
No dot	52	20	10
Urn 3			
Dot	13	0	12
No dot	39	32	4
Urn 4			
Dot	0	28	14
No dot	52	4	2
Urn 5			
Dot	31	12	6
No dot	21	20	10

Note: There are 52 red balls, 32 blue balls, and 16 green balls,
for a total of 100 balls, in each urn.

(You might try to estimate these values, without calculating, before reading on.) Note that for each urn, in the absence of evidence (about dottedness), red is the best guess, because red is the hypothesis with the maximum value of $p(H_i)$. Thus, the expected payoff from guessing without
evidence is 52 points, which is 100 times the maximum $p(H_i)$. The value
of asking whether there is a dot or not is determined from the rows of
each table. The best guess, given each answer, is the highest value in each
row, which is 100 times the maximum of $p(D_j/H_i) \cdot p(H_i)$. The expected
value of the gamble after the question is answered is thus the number of
balls corresponding to the best guess in the top row plus the number
corresponding to the best guess in the bottom row. For example, for Urn
2, the expected value is 12 + 52; thus, the expected value of the question
for this urn is 64 (the value after) − 52 (the value before) = 12.

Table 1 illustrates three general principles that follow from the normative model. First, there is no value to a question whose answer cannot
affect the probabilities of the H_i's, as in Urn 1. Second, if the answer
cannot change one's best guess, the question is likewise worthless, as in

Urns 3 and 5. Of course, this principle implies the first. This principle holds because the maximum values in each row are in the same column, and must therefore sum to 52, which is exactly the value of guessing without asking the question. There are two subcases here, illustrated by Urns 3 and 5, respectively. The first subcase is that a question is worthless if all it does is to affect the relative probabilities of alternatives that one would not choose in any case (Urn 3). The second subcase is that a question is worthless if all it does is to affect the probability of the alternative that remains best in any case (Urn 5); we might call this "increasing one's confidence without affecting one's best guess." Subjects in studies I have run (to be reported elsewhere) seem to regard the question about dottedness as worth asking in these cases. Possibly, they confuse value with some more general notion of information, of a sort I shall describe later. The third general principle is that the value of a question ordinarily depends on the probability of the answers to it. In the extreme, if a question has only one possible answer, it is worthless. As I noted above, this difficulty could be part of the problem in the 2 4 6 task. A fourth general principle, not shown in Table 1, is that the $p(H_i)$ matter as well as do the $p(D_j)$. Evidence cannot be very valuable if one of the H_i's is extremely probable in any case.

In these examples, probabilities rarely reach 0 or 1, no matter what answer is obtained. Later, I shall consider examples in which answers normally rule out certain possibilities completely, as in the 2 4 6 problem. We shall see that the model accords with our intuitions in these cases just as well as in the present ones.

A prescriptive model: proper heuristics

A thinker cannot be expected to follow the normative model of Equations 1 and 2 exactly (except in unusual cases in which it is worth the time to calculate). Rather, in most cases, a thinker should find a question on the basis of a *proper* heuristic for choosing questions, one designed to choose questions as close as possible to what the normative model would choose, but without the effort of calculation. A proper heuristic might be (roughly): Seek a question that distinguishes likely hypotheses from one another, that is, a question whose answer will tend to differ depending on which of the more likely hypotheses is true. There are of course many ways of measuring the extent to which this condition is met, including the normative model just described. However, for prescriptive purposes, the form in which I have just stated the instructions the thinker gives himself may be sufficient. The effectiveness of this heuristic depends, of course,

on the prior specification of two or more hypotheses; if the thinker has failed to search for more than a single hypothesis, the heuristic is essentially useless. The search for several hypotheses, combined with the heuristic just given, is, of course, the "method of multiple hypotheses" of Chamberlain (1890/1965; see also Platt, 1964).

A second proper heuristic, similar to the first, might be to choose questions that will distinguish any hypotheses from one another, likely or not. This heuristic might be useful in the early stages of enquiry when several more questions will be asked after the one chosen, or in cases in which the thinking is motivated by some sort of curiosity rather than the need to decide on action. Both of these cases will be discussed in more detail later. This heuristic, when used in the wrong situation, will lead to a bias in favor of information that cannot affect one's actions.

A third method for deciding what questions to ask — which we might call "thinking ahead" - requires a subepisode of thinking. This is to consider questions themselves as possibilities, and to evaluate questions by considering possible answers to each question and the consequences of these answers for behavior. This heuristic is useful when utilities of different kinds of mistakes are not the same (as I have assumed they are). It will also help (as well as the first heuristic) to avoid the kind of error just referred to, in which the thinker seeks information for its own sake when his goals should actually be to discover only what will affect his behavior.

Types of biases in choosing evidence

The normative and prescriptive models just given allow us to specify several sources of irrationality, some of which have already been mentioned. One source of bias is that the subject's prior probabilities, the $p(H_i)$'s, might have been irrationally formed. For example, in the Wason 2 4 6 task, subjects might be overconfident in the first possibility that occurs to them (because it is present in the mind and others are not; see Fischhoff, Slovic, & Lichtenstein, 1978). This overconfidence could be both a cause and an effect of a failure to search for additional possibilities. Note that this bias is not actually in the choice of evidence, but in another phase of thinking, search for possibilities. It is very likely part of the problem that subjects have in Wason's 2 4 6 problem.

Other biases may result from *improper* heuristics for choosing questions. For example, the second heuristic (distinguishing hypotheses, likely or not) may be used in situations appropriate for the first (distinguishing likely hypotheses), leading to the seeking of useless information. Another

heuristic is the yes-bias already mentioned: The thinker chooses a question designed to get a yes answer. This heuristic can be used at the same time as a proper heuristic, so that the thinker tries to meet both criteria. In this case, the yes-bias will simply distort the results of the proper heuristic. Another improper heuristic is to ask the question most likely to give a yes answer if the most likely hypothesis is true (regardless of the probability of a yes answer given other potential hypotheses). Still another is to ask a question whose answers depend most heavily on the truth or falsity of the most likely hypothesis. All of these heuristics are modifications of the method of distinguishing likely hypotheses; all of them can be seen as distortions of that method; and all of them will often lead to the same question as that method. The fact that they often lead to the same question might be used to justify their use, if their use were (sufficiently) easier than that of the more proper method. However, there is no reason to think that the improper heuristics are any easier than the proper ones, so I shall assume that their use is irrational.

Evidence for yes-bias

Several results from the literature are consistent with existence of the sort of yes-bias (or one of the other related biases) suggested above. In Shaklee and Fischhoff (1982), subjects were given a situation, such as "Jim was arrested for speeding," along with several possible causes, such as "He had a penchant for fast driving. He was late. He was framed." They were then given a fact implicating one of the causes, such as "He has a sports car." Subjects were then asked (in one experiment) to choose one of several questions, related to one of the hypothesized causes, such as "What's Jim's past speeding record? Was the arresting officer short on the number of citations he'd given that night? When was Jim supposed to be at his destination?" Subjects tended strongly to choose the question corresponding to the hypothesis implicated by the original fact. Importantly, this occurred even when the subjects were told to assume that this hypothesis was true. This question was totally uninformative, because it has no bearing on the remaining possible causes. It was the only question where subjects could be reasonably sure they would get a "yes" answer. The yes-bias may have prevented subjects from asking a more informative question. (This experiment, by the way, is the only one of its kind in which the subjects' behavior is clearly irrational, given the beliefs they are supposed to have.)

Tweney and associates (1980) attempted to manipulate "confirmation bias" in the Wason 2 4 6 task. There were three main findings. First,

subjects would follow instructions to test their hypothesis with negative examples (e.g., 10 9 8, when their hypothesis was "ascending by 2"), but the use of negative examples did not lead to faster discovery of the correct rule. Second, subjects instructed to think of two hypotheses on each trial instead of one did not discover the rule any faster as a result. Third, subjects did discover the rule more quickly when they were told that the rule specified two complementary and exhaustive categories called "med" and "dax," rather than one category and its complement.

The first result suggests that subjects simply had a hard time thinking of the correct hypothesis even when the evidence contradicted their original one. In addition, it is likely that the negative examples chosen (e.g., 10 9 8) did not often disconfirm the original hypothesis, possibly because they were not chosen with some specific alternative hypothesis in mind.

The second result was the ineffectiveness of the instructions to think of multiple hypotheses. Apparently, subjects did follow the instructions, but their hypotheses were always too restricted. One protocol given, for example, lists such hypotheses as 3 even numbers, and 3 even numbers in consecutive order; 3 even numbers in ascending order, and 3 even numbers in consecutive order less than 20; etc. (In some cases, the subjects also apparently made other errors, such as drawing false conclusions from the outcome of tests, or returning to hypotheses already rejected, but the frequency of these errors is not reported.) Once again, we are led to the suggestion that the difficulty in the 2 4 6 problem has to do largely with the low prior probability (possibly zero) that subjects assign to the correct hypothesis or any set (e.g., "other") that contains it. Carol Smith and I have (in as yet unpublished work) found that instructions like those of Tweney et al. are beneficial in a task in which the subjects may be more prone to think of the correct hypothesis than they are in the 2 4 6 problem. (Our instructions also emphasized the need to think of two hypotheses together with a test item that would distinguish them; the instructions of Tweney et al. may not have cautioned subjects sufficiently against choosing tests that would give the same outcome for both hypotheses.)

The third result is that asking the subject to discover two categories rather than one did help. This manipulation may have led the subject to think of the task as involving a rule for two sets rather than a rule for a sequence of numbers, thus increasing the subjective probability of the correct hypothesis. More likely, the use of "med" and "dax" instead of "yes" and "no" could have removed a bias toward "yes" answers, because "med" is not as rewarding as "yes." Subjects may have been more prone to use an appropriate balance of positive and negative examples.

Tschirgi (1980) both illustrates once again the possible harmlessness of

"confirmation bias" and argues for a kind of yes-bias as its cause. A typical problem, given to children and adults, was the following:

John decided to bake a cake. But he ran out of some ingredients. So: he used margarine instead of butter for the shortening, he used honey instead of sugar for the sweetening, and he used brown wholewheat flour instead of regular white flour. The cake turned out great (just terrible); it was so moist (runny). John thought the reason the cake was so great (terrible) was the honey. He thought that the type of shortening or the type of flour really didn't matter. What should he do to prove his point?

The subject was then given three choices, one of which involved changing only from honey to sugar (VOTAT—vary one thing at a time), one of which involved changing everything but the sugar (HOTAT— hold one thing at a time), and one in which all three variables were changed (CA—change all). Most subjects, at all ages, used HOTAT when the outcome was good (moist), that is, they tried to keep the good outcome by keeping the honey that was likely to have caused it and changing everything else. A plurality at all ages used VOTAT when the outcome was bad (runny), that is, they tried to change the bad outcome to a good one by changing the likely bad ingredient. Thus, both strategies aim to wind up with a good cake, in addition to the information they provide.

Tschirgi argues that VOTAT and HOTAT are equally informative, and this is consistent with the present model. To see how this might be, consider first a simplification of the situation in which the critical ingredient is either honey, with probability .6, or margarine (.2), or flour (.2), but not some combination. If a subject simply guesses which hypothesis is true without doing an experiment, his probability of being correct is .6, which is also the expected utility. If a subject gets a good cake and uses a HOTAT strategy (holding the honey constant), he has a .6 probability of getting a good cake, and if he does, the probability of "honey" will increase to 1.0. The probability of a bad cake is .4, and if he gets a bad cake, he will have to guess between "margarine" and "flour," so his probability of being correct will be .5. In sum, the expected utility of guessing after the experiment is done (calculated before the result is known, by the method of Equation 1) is $(.6)(1.0) + (.4)(.5)$, which equals .8. The value of the experiment is thus $.8 - .6$, or .2. Notice that the same argument applies, exactly, if the subject starts out with a bad cake and uses the VOTAT strategy; now changing just the honey will yield a good cake with probability .6, just as before. Hence, the two experiments are of equal value. (The same sort of argument, on the basis of symmetry, can extend to the more general case, even if we allow conjunctive and disjunctive hypotheses.)

Now Tschirgi points out that the HOTAT strategy is equivalent to "confirmation bias." In this strategy, the subject makes a test that his hypothesis predicts will yield a positive outcome. This is just what Wason's subjects do. Use of the HOTAT strategy may be optimal in both experiments, given the subject's $p(H_i)$, his prior beliefs. (In Wason's experiment, subjects seem to assign a very low probability to the correct hypothesis, but this need not be irrational, given how little they are told.)

This experiment once again suggests that there is a bias to get favorable answers. In this case, the answer is in the form of a moist or nonrunny (hypothetical) cake, rather than a "yes" from the experimenter. Here, the bias is harmless. Elsewhere, as in the 2 4 6 problem, the bias might prevent people from asking the most informative question. We might describe such cases by saying that people are confused about their task: They are supposed to be seeking information, but they are also seeking favorable outcomes at the same time.

Some of Schwartz's (1982) experiments are based on this very idea. In one, one group of subjects is told that their goal is to get rewards by pressing two buttons (L and R) in a certain pattern. Another group is told to figure out the rule for how to get the reward, under otherwise identical conditions. The rule actually specifies a fairly large class of patterns, e.g., any sequence of exactly four L's and four R's starting with LL leads to reward. However, the subjects in the first, reward, group usually discover a single pattern, such as LLLLRRRR. At the end of the experiment, when asked to give the rule, these subjects state exactly the pattern they have been using, and they often feel that their pattern is necessary, the only one that will work. The second, rule discovery, group does discover the rule. When the reward group is given a second task under discovery instructions, they are less likely to discover the rule than are subjects exposed to the task for the first time. Apparently, their ability to discover the rule was inhibited by their set to work for reward. This kind of experiment, where reward contingencies may be manipulated independently of requirements to seek information, provides a good way to simulate many real situations in which people must choose between repetition of behavior that has worked (imperfectly, but well enough) in the past and experimentation with new behavior in hopes of finding general rules or of finding new behavior that works better.

Note that the problem of mixed motives occurred in another possible explanation of errors in gathering evidence, in which the goal of finding the truth conflicted with the goal of having been right all along. If the subject counts "yes" as satisfaction of that goal, these two sources of error might be essentially the same.

Multiple questions

In many, if not most, situations in which we choose evidence, we are allowed to ask more than a single question. In this section, I show that the choice of the first question is not necessarily the same when the subject is allowed several questions as it is when he is allowed only one. In particular, the criterion "do not ask a question unless the answer can change your best guess" no longer applies. My presentation here is abstract, and may be skipped without loss of continuity.

The choice facing the subject may be conceived as a choice of strategy. A strategy, once chosen, is a rule for deciding what question to ask at each point in the sequence, as a function of the answer to prior questions. The value of a strategy can be determined in the same way as the value of a single question. To do this, we treat a series of answers as if it were a single answer consisting of the conjunction of the answers to the separate questions. Of course, each separate answer must contain a representation of its question; thus, "yes" is only a shorthand for "yes, 10 12 14 is a member of the category." Instead of a set of answers to a single question, indexed by D_j, we have a set of series of answers, which we might index as D_{j1}, D_{j2}, D_{j3}, and so on. The j indexes the different possible series of answers and the 1, 2, etc., index the first, second, etc., answer in each series. The value of a strategy (assuming that one cares only about being correct or not) is thus determined analogously to (2):

$$(3) \qquad v = \sum_j [\max_i p(D_{j1}, D_{j2}, \ldots /H_i) \cdot p(H_i)] - \max_i p(H_i)$$

Here, the first maximum is over all possible series of answers resulting from a given strategy, and the conditional probability is that of each series given each possibility under consideration. The possible sequences of questions may be constrained by a strategy that chooses a question on the basis of previous answers and questions. We evaluate a strategy, a rule for asking questions, according to the answer sequences it can possibly yield under the various possibilities, H_i. We may easily modify (3) to take into account the possible cost of asking a question; we simply subtract a term representing this cost. Note that a strategy might have positive value by (3) even if the first question alone would have no value by (1) or (2); the remaining questions in the sequence might change the H_i for which v is maximum.

If the joint probability $p(D_{jk} \& D_{jl}/H_i) = p(D_{jk}/H_i) \cdot p(D_{jl}/H_i)$ for all $i, j, k,$ and l, that is, if the conditional probability of each answer given each hypothesis is independent of other answers, then (3) becomes:

(4) $v = \sum_{j} [\max_{i} p(D_{j1}/H_i) \cdot p(D_{j2}/H_i) \cdot \ldots \cdot p(H_i)] - \max_{i} p(H_i)$

One conclusion that follows from (4) concerns those cases in which the strategies we are considering consist only of the possible orderings (permutations) of a given set of questions and in which answers are conditionally independent in the sense required for (4). In this case, it is clear from (4) that the order is irrelevant.

We are now in a position to say something about what is perhaps the most prototypical case of choice of evidence, the game of twenty questions. This game will serve as an example to show that the first question of the best strategy is not necessarily the best question if only one question is allowed. In this game, the subject is allowed to ask up to 20 questions, each of which can be answered only yes or no, with the goal of trying to guess when the experimenter has in mind. Let us assume that a guess must be made after the last question. It is usually thought that the optimal strategy is to ask a series of questions each of which will be answered yes only if one of about half of the remaining possibilities is true. Each question thus eliminates about half of the remaining possibilities.

In what sense is this strategy optimal? Interestingly, not in the sense that its first question is the best if only one question is allowed. Consider the alternative strategy of simply guessing the various possibilities one at a time. Suppose there are N possibilities. The value of a wild guess is $1/N + 1/N - 1/N = 1/N$ (from Eq. 2). The value of a "good question," namely one whose answer is yes if the answer is contained in one of $N/2$ of the possibilities, is exactly the same.

When we look at a sequence of two questions, things begin to look different. Two good questions together have a value $4/N - 1/N = 3/N$. Two guesses together have a value $3/N - 1/N = 2/N$. This is because there are only three series of answers that can occur with the guessing strategy: yes no no, no yes no, and no no yes. More than one "yes" is impossible. The maximum of $p(D_{j1}, D_{j2} \ldots /H_i) \cdot p(H_i)$ is always $1/N$, so the number of allowable sequences determines the value of the strategy, according to (3). (I am assuming that the subject continues to make different guesses even if he guesses correctly on the first or second trial. I could also assume that he repeats a correct guess, once it is confirmed, or that he stops guessing. In any case, there are still only three possible sequences.) In general, the value of the guessing strategy, for M trials, is M/N, and the value of the correct strategy is $(2 - 1)/N$.

In sum, in the game of twenty questions, the best question to start with is not necessarily the same as the best question to ask if only one question is allowed. In general, it may make a difference how many questions a

subject is allowed. It seems advisable for experimenters to make clear to their subjects which case is involved.

The representation of ignorance in probability assignments

Suppose you volunteer for a psychology experiment, and the experimenter shows you an urn and asks you to state the probability that the first ball drawn from the urn will be black. Is it reasonable to assume that the probability of drawing a black ball is .5, just because there are two possibilities (black or not black)? It may be, but this assumption is of a different sort than the assumption that the probability of heads for a fair coin is .5. You might just as well reason that there are about five different colors for balls, and that any one of these is as likely as any other, so the probability of a black ball should be .2. In either case, you are basing your probability judgments on the "principle of insufficient reason" (Savage, 1954): Probabilities of different events should be equal unless there is some reason for them to not to be. For another example, consider the position of the scientist about to do an experiment to distinguish two hypotheses. How can he assign prior probabilities to these hypotheses? In some cases, it seems that there is simply no evidence one way or the other. The principle of insufficient reason does not help, because one hypothesis may be divided into many hypotheses, thus increasing its total probability according to this principle.

Shafer (1976, 1981; Shafer & Tversky, 1984) has described a system of probability theory in which ignorance can be represented in a reasonable way. In his system, degrees of belief in mutually exclusive possibilities do not have to sum to 1. Shafer allows a certain amount of belief to be free — assigned to a set of possibilities but to no particular possibility within it. Thus, he might represent the case of the black ball as one in which it would be appropriate to have zero belief in the ball being black and zero belief in it being not black; the belief that it is either black or not black will still be 1. In this case, the total belief will be uncommitted between the two possibilities. In other cases, there may be some evidence in favor of one alternative or the other, but still some reason to keep some belief uncomitted. When a single possibility can be subdivided (e.g., black with or without stripes), the belief in the subpossibilities (black with stripes, black without stripes) need not sum to the belief assigned to the possibility itself (black). One interpretation of the idea of uncommitted belief is this: When belief is uncommitted among several alternatives, there is no uniquely correct way to subdivide it among them. Any subdivision of belief among the alternatives (including the one in

Table 2. *A basic probability assignment for an urn,*
analogous to Urn 2 in Table 1

	Red	Blue	Green
Dot	0	20 2	6
No dot	30 42	0	0

Note: The number of balls indicated in the upper left corner of
each rectangle can fall in any cell contained in the rectangle. If
balls are distributed evenly Urn 2 results.

which belief is divided equally) is as good as any other. (Note that from
the point of view of utility theory, as described in chapter 2, this interpretation implies that there is no unique expected utility for an action, and in
some cases there may be no single optimal action. This is no difficulty
here, however, for we have already allowed as much, even for the idealized creatures for whom probability theory is intended.)

Mathematically, Shafer holds that we divide our belief up among sets of
events that may overlap or include one another. For example, one set
might be "the ball is blue"; in this case, it may still be "blue and dotted"
or "blue and not dotted." The *basic probability number* of a set A, $m(A)$,
is the proportion of one's belief that one commits exactly to A, not to any
of its subsets or supersets. Concretely, suppose our evidence consisted of
a coded message, but we are not sure which code to use for decoding it.
By one code, which has probability p of being the correct code, the
message means "the truth is in A" (e.g., the ball is blue), but by any
other code, the message tells us nothing new. In this case, $m(A)$ would be
equal to p, and m(all possibilities) would be $1-p$. Table 2 shows a basic
probability assignment for a situation analogous to that shown in Table 1.
In practice, one does not estimate a whole basic probability assignment
all at once. Shafer recommends decomposing one's total evidence into
parts, each of which supports a single set. The resulting belief functions
can be combined to yield a total belief function based on one's evidence.

How do we evaluate a question in such a case? One way might be to
divide the belief that is held in reserve equally among the relevant alternatives. By this method, the information in Table 2 would be converted

into Urn 2 of Table 1, and the value of the question about dottedness would be exactly what it was for that question. However, this method ignores the fact that uncommitted belief may (by assumption) be divided freely among the alternatives.

A more acceptable method involves *conditioning* our beliefs on the different answers (Shafer, 1981, p. 24) and then asking what we would do in each case. Conditioning involves finding out what our basic probability assignment would be if we began with a certain assignment (e.g., that in Table 2) and then discovered that the truth was in a certain set (e.g., dotted). Conditioning will lead to a new assignment in which no belief will be assigned outside the set in question. In Table 2, conditioning on "no dot" leads to assignments of about .46, .24, and .07 for red, blue, and green, respectively. This leaves .23 held in reserve among the three possibilities. If all of the .23 went into "green," the "probability" of green would be sufficiently high so that it would be the best guess (.47). Hence, the best guess in this case is indeterminate, and therefore it is also indeterminate whether asking the question about dottedness has any value at all. Clearly, by an extension of this reasoning, we could calculate an upper and lower bound on the utility of a question. Such calculations would leave many cases in which there was no uniquely best question to ask. In such cases, the proper heuristics given above would be even more likely to yield a question that was in the set of possible best questions, which would now be a larger set.

Another interpretation of Shafer's system involves interpreting uncommitted belief as evidence that is available yet not obtained. This interpretation corresponds to the idea of upper and lower probabilities (Shafer 1976, 1981). The upper probability of a subset is the belief that we would have if all possible uncommitted belief were committed to that subset, and the lower probability is the belief we would have if no uncommitted belief were counted. From this point of view, the point of seeking information is to change uncommitted belief into committed belief. An appropriate measure might be the absolute reduction in the gap between upper and lower probabilities, summed across subsets. To use this as a normative model, we might assume that the subject knew exactly what questions could be asked, and that the upper probability assigned to a possibility is the highest that could result from answers to the remaining questions, and the lower probability is the lowest. This model might be of value in situations such as medical diagnosis, in which there are few possible questions, and in which (to a first approximation) all probabilities are relevant, rather than that of the most likely possibility only.

Other approaches to the value of information

When our goal is the satisfaction of curiosity rather than the making of a decision, it is more difficult to specify a normative model for the value of a question, for our goal is not so clear. One measure that is often considered relevant in such cases is that provided by the mathematical theory of information (e.g., Theil, 1967, particularly p. 27). This theory defines the information in a message in terms of the number of bits, where a bit is a just the information required to say which of two equally likely possibilities is true. For example, if I am thinking of an integer between 0 and 7 (inclusive), you can find what it is by asking three yes-no questions, each subdividing the remaining numbers in half (is it less that 4? etc.). The answer to each question supplies one bit of information.

Although information theory is sometimes recommended as a measure of the utility of questions, I have never seen (nor can I think of) a justification of this recommendation. In fact, as Marschak (1974) points out, information theory is intended for a different purpose, the measurement of the cost of information under ideal conditions. The number of bits of information (rounded upward) is precisely the number of on-off signals that must be used to transmit that information, and if each signal has a fixed cost, the number of bits is a measure of transmission cost, e.g., how many milliseconds a telephone line must be used, assuming that the information is encoded with the smallest number of signals possible. Marschak points out, as well, that there is simply no reason to expect the value of information to be equal to the cost of transmitting it.

The standard that the information measures, tries, and fails to capture may be the value of information for unanticipated decisions after unanticipated additional information. Since we cannot anticipate the decisions, we have no idea about utilities, so even information about very low probability hypotheses might be of value. We also have no idea which hypotheses will be ruled out by subsequent evidence, or which will have their probabilities raised so that they become serious contenders. One way to capture this idea formally is to imagine a situation in which we are faced with several possibilities, e.g., possible diagnoses, and we want to assign probabilities to them. The reason for assigning probabilities is not (as assumed earlier) to decide which is most likely, but rather to compare these probabilities to those we shall assign in the future to other possibilities we have not yet thought of (or that have not yet been presented to us). This corresponds to our intuition that we sometimes seek information because we might need it in the future.

Now consider first a single possibility with initial probability P_i, which

might be changed (assume, for simplicity, raised) to Q_{ij} by a certain datum (D_j). What is the value of that datum? One reasonable way to estimate the value might be to imagine that we will be presented with some other possibility that has a probability of R and then asked which is more probable. We then calculate value in the usual way, namely, in terms of increased probability of choosing correctly. Thus, if R is less than P_i or greater than Q_{ij}, the datum has no value because it will not change our decision (again, assuming $P_i < Q_{ij}$). If R is between P_i and Q_{ij}, the value of the datum will be $Q_{ij} - R$, for the datum will change our decision to Q_{ij}, and we shall be that much more likely to be correct. Now let us assume that R has a uniform distribution, that is, R is equally likely to have any value between 0 and 1. With this assumption, the expected value of the datum, given P_i and Q_{ij}, is just

(5) $$\int_{P_i}^{Q_{ij}} Q_{ij} - R \, dR = \frac{(Q_{ij} - P_i)^2}{2}$$

Considering all possibilities (H_i) and all possible answers (D_j) to the question we ask, then, and eliminating the constant 2, we see that the equation for the expected value of a question (v) is

(6) $$v = \sum_{i,j} (Q_{ij} - P_i)^2$$

If there are two answers to the question, 0 and 1, and if $Q_{i0} - P_i = P_i - Q_{i1}$ for all i, then this measure is equivalent to chi-square, calculated from the same table used above for information theory.

Although (6) must be seen as a kind of approximation, its general point is that it is possible to extend the present pragmatic framework to the idea that information has a value that is independent of any immediate action we shall base on it. Note that the analysis of multiple questions provides another way of making this extension, since the value of a question as part of a series may be positive, even when its value alone is nil.

Scientific method and the value of information

The methods I have advocated for evaluating evidence before it is collected can be applied to the scientific enterprise itself. Science is, after all, a type of thinking, and scientists spend a great deal of time evaluating each other's thinking very explicitly. The framework I have presented so far may be used to determine the value of a scientific experiment, a kind of question. This determination may be made either before the experiment is done — as in the cases discussed so far in this chapter — or after the result is in (with $p(D_j)$ now given a value of 1).

It is worthwhile to distinguish several kinds of cases. In one case, common in applied research, expected utility may be positive even if the guess made is wrong, depending on what the truth actually is. For example, Semmelweis did a critical experiment to test his hypothesis that childbed fever was transmitted by "cadaveric matter." He had the interns who delivered babies wash their hands in chlorinated lime beforehand, and the incidence of the fever declined markedly. There is in fact an alternative explanation, as we now know, namely "germs," and the experiment did not distinguish the two. However, the utility of the wrong decision in this case was quite high, as many people's lives were saved. (Its utility was not quite as high as that of the correct decision would have been. Semmelweis himself succumbed to the disease, presumably because germs were transmitted from a wound rather than a cadaver. Further, if the truth had been discovered at the time, the causes of other diseases might have been discovered more quickly.) This is a typical situation for experiments involving a manipulation such as a cure for a disease, a kind of training or therapy, or a social invention. There is often more than one explanation of the success of the manipulation, but for some purposes the explanation does not matter much.

Another type of experiment is one designed to affect the probability assigned to a certain hypothesis, without ruling out the alternative completely, even though only the first hypothesis is of interest. This is typically the case when we are interested in a "best guess," because we must act one way or the other, and we feel we would rather have some evidence than none. For example, we are interested in correlations between diet and heart disease, even though such correlations do not always indicate an effect of diet on disease. (There may be other factors that affect both, so that a change in diet will not necessarily change one's chance of getting heart disease.) If we want to determine the value of this kind of experiment, it is important to estimate accurately the relevant probabilities. These estimates may well vary from person to person. Consequently, it may be hard to agree about whether funds should be spent on such experiments, or about whether one should act on them once the results are in. The present analysis provides a way of locating sources of disagreement, but it does not otherwise help resolve such disagreements.

As we get further from direct application, we get less satisfied with anything less than the truth itself. We may conceive such cases as being characterized by large costs (negative payoffs) for wrong decisions, and by an option not to decide at all, in which case the payoff is zero. It is in fact the option not to decide that characterizes "basic" research, simply because there is no immediate need for a decision among competing

hypotheses. In such a case, a line of experiments that can only change probabilities, without eliminating any hypotheses and without confirming any conclusively (to the extent that this is possible) has no value. Further, arguments for a hypothesis that are based on analogy, parsimony, or simplicity are out of place, for these arguments never establish certainty.

Another consequence of this stance — that a decision need not be made and that the cost for an error is very high — is that we need not assign prior probabilities to hypotheses. The only kind of result that will lead to a decision is one that establishes (or refutes) a hypothesis with certainty, and such a result will do this practically without regard to what the priors — the $p(H_i)$ — are.

Is there any justification in basic research for an experiment that can only increase the probability of a hypothesis, without establishing that hypothesis with virtual certainty? When we use correlational methods — with all their uncertainties — to test hypotheses about diet and disease, our need to know is sufficient to require a decision, so we are interested in any relevant evidence. But are we justified in using the same methods to test hypotheses, for example, in personality theory? I think there are two kinds of justifications. First, there may be a kind of applied relevance to experiments that affect probabilities without leading to certainty. There may be people who are very curious about the question at issue, and they may be interested in any information even if it is inconclusive. These people may even apply the results of such experiments in their daily lives (or their work, e.g., if they are clinical psychologists). To the extent that there are such people, these experiments may be evaluated as if they were applied experiments, other things (like the reputation of science) equal. Second, probabilistic knowledge about truth may affect our willingness ot undertake more expensive experiments. This is also a kind of applied relevance, but the application is to the decision about further research. In sum, even research that appears to be basic in the sense of not demanding immediate decisions might be more applied than it seems to be at first, and, as a result, there might be some value to indecisive experiments.

A common type of experiment concerns the use of descriptive models, as is now fashionable in much of the study of memory and learning. A model may be viewed is a single possibility. When someone shows that a model fits a set of data, he shows that an answer, D_j has been obtained for which $p(D_j/H_i)$ is near 1. But what we really want to know is $p(H_i/D_j)$, and if there is another model, or, more seriously, another type of model, that would give as high a value of $p(D_j/H_i)$, $p(H_i/D_j)$ might be no higher than it was before the experiment was done. The typical situation is one

in which we are ignorant about whether the alternative exists and, if it does, about its prior probability, because the modeler has taken the attitude that the burden of proof is on others to show he is wrong. The situation is closely analogous to the 2 4 6 task, in fact, and many of the explanations that we considered there may apply here. Because sufficient models are indecisive, they are hard to justify in pure research. In applied research they may be more useful (e.g., models for predicting the economy), but even here they have the danger of distorting the prior probabilities — and thus the posterior probabilities — held by the consumers of the research, because they do not call alternatives to the attention of these consumers. In sum, the present analysis provides a rationale for Platt's (1964) recommendation that scientists should attempt to specify the set of possibilities before an experiment is done, and thus for the proper heuristics described earlier. (Eells, 1982, p. 52 ff., discusses further the general Bayesian approach to scientific method, which is fully consistent with the approach I take here.) It may be possible to discover biases and improper heuristics in the actual work of scientists as well as in psychological experiments.

Interim summary

I have argued (following Savage, 1954) that the expected value of evidence, the answer to a question, may be conceived as the expected value of a gamble with the evidence, minus the expected value of the gamble without it. When trying to decide which of a set of questions to ask, a person interested in maximizing utility would ask the question with the highest value. This rule may be used to evaluate cases in which people's choice of evidence is at issue, in particular, a number of experiments that claim to show "confirmation bias." Because we do not know many of the relevant personal probabilities, we cannot say whether people in these experiments were choosing evidence rationally or not. The value measure I have provided may be used as a basis for the design of new experiments, however. These experiments may reveal other kinds of biases, some of which I have listed. The present approach may be extended to deal with ignorance, and to the seeking of information for its own sake, although there is much room here for further work. It may also provide an argument for rules of scientific method such as strong inference in pure research, or, in applied research, at least trying to think of alternatives, and trying to do the most informative experiment rather than the one most relevant to one's favored hypothesis.

Optimal stopping and impulsiveness

A special case of the general model proposed here is the case in which there are two possibilities being considered and two possible data. One datum favors one possibility, and the other favors the other. The thinker can sample as many data as he likes, but he must pay some cost for each (i.e., the cost of thinking). As usual, we assume there is some payoff for choosing the correct possibility after data collection has ceased. The question is when to stop sampling data. Consideration of this question will lead us to a more precise definition of optimal stopping for evidence search than was possible in the last chapter. Although this definition is applicable only in experiments in which the stated assumptions hold and the subject understands the task, such situations can be devised, and they allow us to study the determinants of impulsiveness (or overcautiousness).

Edwards's model

This question has been treated from a normative point of view by Edwards (1965; following Wald, 1947), from a point of view very similar to the one presented in this chapter. Edwards's normative model can be applied in the following sort of situation: The subject is in a position to observe data from a well-defined data-generating machine. He knows that the machine is one of two types. For example, one machine can be an urn filled with 70% red balls and 30% blue ones, the other machine an urn with 30% red and 70% blue, and each datum could be drawing a ball from an urn (and replacing the ball). It is his task to decide which type of machine he is observing. He is paid some amount for being correct, but he must pay a fixed cost for each ball he draws. Thus at each point in time, the subject must choose between asserting that it is a type 1 machine (hypothesis H_1), asserting that it is a type 2 machine (hypothesis H_2), or observing another datum from the machine.

A normative subject—one who maximizes the expected value of his decisions —will choose on the basis of the values (payoffs) associated with choosing correct or incorrect hypotheses, the cost of sampling data, and his current probability for the most likely, or favored, hypothesis. This probability is revised after each ball is drawn (see Phillips & Edwards, 1966, for a simple exposition of how this should be done). The amount of revision depends on the *diagnosticity* of the evidence. In our example, the diagnosticity of a red ball would be .7/.3, because .7 is the probability of drawing a red ball from the first urn, and .3, from the

second. If the probabilities differed more, the diagnosticity of a single draw would be higher.

One essential insight behind Edwards's model is that the optimal stopping point can be defined in terms of the current (posterior) probability of the favored hypothesis alone, for any given task. Before this cutoff value of the probability of the favored hypothesis is reached, one should continue sampling data. The number of balls drawn so far is irrelevant, except insofar as this affects the current probability of the favored hypothesis. This is because the diagnosticity of the data is fixed, so the change in probability of the favored hypothesis to be expected from drawing another ball is determined only by the probability of that hypothesis before the ball is drawn. This aspect of the model is counterintuitive, and its neglect is similar to a common mistake of naive poker players who, when deciding whether or not to fold, consider how much money they have already put in the pot rather than the amount that might be gained or lost as a result of continued play (Fried & Peterson, 1969).

Edwards also shows that for a given set of payoffs and costs, the amount of data (balls) we would expect a normative subject to purchase is an inverted U function of diagnosticity. To get an intuitive sense of why this is true, consider the two extreme cases. When the data are worthless, that is, when the proportion of balls of each color is the same in urn 1 as in urn 2, there is no point in drawing any balls at all. At the other extreme, for example, when one urn has all red balls and the other, all blue, it will suffice to purchase only one datum. At intermediate levels of diagnosticity, each datum is valuable but not definitive. Here, one will have to purchase many data.

A number of studies have asked about optimal stopping, as defined by Edwards's model, in bookbag and pokerchip experiments. In such experiments, subjects sample pokerchips from bookbags in order to decide which of two bags they have been presented with. The bags contain red and blue chips, and the distribution of red and blue chips in each bag is known to the subjects, but the particular bags sampled from is a matter of chance. For example, Snapper and Peterson (1971) examined the amount of information required as a function of the diagnosticity of the data. He found that subjects bought more information than they should have when diagnosticity was low, but less than they should have when it was high. In general, it appeared that subjects did show an inverted U curve for amount of evidence sampled as function of diagnosticity, but the peak was shifted to the left (and was also lower than it should have been, in one experiment). In another study, Edwards and Slovic (1965) presented subjects with a complex task in which both payoffs and diagnosticity

varied from trial to trial. Some subjects were overcautious, buying more information than they should have, and others were impulsive, buying less than they should have; these individual differences were consistent across different tasks. These experiments must be interpreted with caution because of the nature of the bookbag-and-pokerchip task, which calls attention to the numerosities of different kinds of events as evidence. For example, Kahneman and Tversky (1972) found that subjects based probability of the favored hypothesis on what amounts to the ratio of red to blue balls they had drawn so far, where what is actually relevant is the difference. The ratio might be simply a salient property of numerical evidence. In this case, the subjects seem to be using incorrect formulas more consciously than they might in more naturalistic situations.

Possible determinants of impulsiveness

In the last chapter, I suggested that there might be a general bias to stop too soon when collecting evidence. We may call this bias impulsiveness. (I reserve the term "impulsivity" for the related concept from individual differences research, which denotes a person's willingness to give up accuracy for the sake of speed, relative to other individuals.)

In order to study impulsiveness in the laboratory, we need to use tasks that are more realistic than bookbag-and-pokerchip tasks, for the reasons just described. Baron, Badgio, and Gaskins (in press) describe some tasks that can be used for this purpose (and we shall be reporting results of their use in subsequent papers). In one task, on each trial, subjects are asked to examine a series of pairs of random patterns for 4 seconds per pair. They are told that each series is generated by a different machine, and each pair in each series is different from every other pair. However, if the machine is a "good" one, then it always produces pairs in which the two patterns are identical, and if it is a bad one, it always produces pairs in which the two are different. Subjects are informed that the probability on any trial that the machine is good is .5. Their job is to determine, on each trial, whether the machine is good or bad. They do so by looking at as many pairs produced by that machine as they wish. Each pair is exposed for only four seconds, and subjects must pay four points for every pair they choose to look at. When a subject decides not to purchase a look at any more pairs, he must decide if the machine is good or bad. If he is correct, the subject gains 50 points; if incorrect, he loses 50. Subjects are told to maximize points in a given number of trials.

It is assumed that a subject proceeds by looking for a difference. If, after looking at a number of pairs, no difference is found, then the

subject responds "good." Since the differences are quite subtle, and the pairs are exposed for brief intervals, "good" responses cannot be made without some degree of uncertainty. The interesting dependent variable is the average number of pairs each subject chooses to look at before responding "good." In order to assess impulsiveness, this number will be compared to the optimal number of pairs they ought to look at according to a normative model.

According to the normative model for this task, the optimum depends on the payoffs, costs, prior probabilites of each hypothesis (that the machine is good or bad), and the diagnosticity of the evidence. The payoffs and costs are set, in terms of points, by the experimenter, and the prior probabilities of each hypothesis were set at .5. Thus the optimum stopping point varied across subjects as a function of diagnosticity. Since subjects respond "good" unless a difference is found, and since they rarely err by seeing a difference when there is none, the diagnosticity of each pair is the probability of finding a difference, given that there is one, in each 4-second look. This probability can be computed for each subject by simply dividing the number of times that he found a difference by the number of pairs that he looked at in which there was a difference. The diagnosticity of each stimulus pair is also a measure of subjects' efficacy at the task. (Note that the dependence of "diagnosticity" on ability is characteristic of thinking tasks in general, but not the bookbag-and-pokerchip tasks described earlier.) As in the case of Edwards's model, it is possible to calculate the optimum number of looks by asking how many looks are required — given the subject's efficacy — until the next look has negative expected value.

In a second task, the subject solves real problems such as anagrams. (Here, the optimal stopping is determined by search for possibilities rather than evidence, but the model is the same.) He is told that there is some probability that each anagram is insoluble, that he will get some number of points for finding an answer when there is one, and that he will lose some (much smaller) number of points per second until he either gives up on the problem or solves it. The "diagnosticity" here, which is essentially the probability of solving the problem in the next second, given that it has not been solved so far and that it is soluble, changes as a function of time since the problem was presented. Before the optimum stopping-time can be computed, the function relating diagnosticity to time must be estimated. Again, further details are given by Baron, Badgio, and Gaskins (in press) and in subsequent papers.

With these methods in mind, we can now discuss the possible determinants of impulsiveness, defined as stopping when the value of further thinking is still greater than the cost.

Values and costs. The optimal amount of thinking (active search) for a given task depends in part on the values (utilities) of correct and incorrect responses and the cost of searching (see Shugan, 1980; Russo & Dosher, 1983). Individuals may behave as if they differ in relevant values, so that these differences in values determine differences in the time spent thinking. The value a student places on being correct in a homework assignment, for example, might depend on whether the homework will be graded, but not on the effect of understanding his homework on his final grade or its value for his life beyond the course in question. Similar failures could occur in comsumer purchases, personal decisions, professional decisions, or decisions concerning the proper stance to take toward issues of public concern. In all of these cases, a person may place too low a value on making the best decision, relative to the cost of the thinking involved. Undervaluation of thinking may occur from either the student's perspective or the educator's (chapter 2), but it is especially likely to occur from the educator's, since this perspective is sure to include the moral value of thinking. In sum, one likely source of irrationally premature stopping is reliance on the values of the moment, the pain of thinking, the fear of failure, and so on, without adequately considering the long-term values that one would ideally want to apply.

Undervaluation is not at issue in the experimental procedures we have used, for the benefits of thinking are immediate. However, it is possible to modify the laboratory task so as to simulate one kind of long-term value. On certain anagram problems, we have told a subject that he will get the problem again, under conditions of high cost for time. Thus, solving the problem the first time is like solving a problem that one knows one will get on a later examination (under time pressure), so that solving it the first time will guarantee later success (and more points in the task). Despite the extra value of solving a to-be-repeated problem, subjects in one experiment spent no more time on these problems (before giving up) than they did on control problems that were not to be repeated. Thus, the underweighing of the future value of thinking is something that seems to occur.

Probabilities. In addition to the values and cost parameters, estimates of various probabilities are necessary to determine the optimal amount of time one should spend thinking in a given situation. There are two biases in the estimation of probabilities that can lead to impulsiveness: overconfidence in one's favored hypothesis, and underconfidence in the effectiveness of one's thinking.

If one overestimates the probability that his favored hypothesis is cor-

rect (overconfidence), then he is likely to overestimate the value of responding without further thought. In the extreme, if one is certain that
his favored hypothesis is correct, then he will make his decision without
any further thought. (Note that we are not assuming that subjects have
numerical probabilities in their heads. Rather, we assume that it is possible for the subject to behave as if he were affected by some internal
parameter analogous to such numerical probabilities.) In fact, a number
of studies indicate that people's confidence judgments are generally inaccurate. For example, if we consider cases in which subjects claim to be
100% certain of their answer to a factual question, they may actually be
correct 70% of the time or less (see Lichtenstein, Fischhoff, & Phillips,
1982, for a review). In the tasks described by Baron et al. (in press),
overconfidence may be measured by asking subjects to state the confidence that they are correct (in thinking that the machine is good, or that
the anagram is insoluble) at the time they give up. Preliminary results
suggest that overconfidence correlates with impulsiveness across subjects.

The second way in which subjects' biased estimates of probabilities can
lead to impulsiveness is underconfidence in the efficacy of further thought
(as suggested by Bandura, 1977, in a related context). In terms of Edwards's model, a subject might act as if the diagnosticity of further evidence were low, even if the same person assigned a high probability to his
favored hypothesis. This factor may be assessed by asking subjects to
estimate their probability of success with some amount of further work.
When this was done in the anagram task, the extent to which subjects
gave up too soon was correlated with the extent to which the efficacy of
further thinking was underestimated (with true efficacy determined by
extrapolation from data).

It may seem somewhat paradoxical that one possible determinant of
impulsiveness is overconfidence while another is underconfidence. This
apparent paradox is resolved when we notice that the confidence applies
to different places in the two cases. The overconfidence is in the thinking
that one has done so far; the underconfidence is in the thinking one
would do if one were to continue. Both biases lead to low expectations
concerning the value of further thought.

Note that failure experiences may affect either subjective confidence or
subjective diagnosticity, or both. Individuals may differ in what is affected. For some, failure may lower their confidence without lowering
their diagnosticity, which would make them work harder the next time;
for others, the effect of failure would be the reverse. The same could be
said, mutatis mutandis, for success. In fact, Diener and Dweck (1978,
1980) have found individual differences among children in subjective re-

sponses to success and failure. Of interest is the question of how these subjective responses affect the parameters of our model.

Insensitivity and misweighing. A final source of impulsiveness is the failure to weigh correctly the expected value of thinking against its cost, or to weigh confidence against efficacy in estimating the usefulness of further thinking. Such misweighing can occur in two ways: First, a person might be insensitive to variations in some factor (e.g., confidence, future utility) that ought to affect the amount of time he spends; second, a person may be sensitive to such variations, but might consistently overweigh one factor relative to others, thus stopping too soon or too late, depending on which factor it is. For example, if a person overweighs cost relative to expectation, that is, if his stopping point is more affected by costs than expected values, then other things equal, he will stop too soon. Note that misweighing is indistinguishable from certain other biases, such as misestimating expected payoffs by a constant proportion of their actual value. However, there is no reason that misweighing and insensitivity should make a person think too little rather than too much, and both sorts of deviations might be expected. (This is not to suggest that these factors are unworthy of investigation.)

Generality

Impulsiveness as defined here might be general across tasks, or it might not. It might be general across tasks within a certain domain. The extent to which impulsiveness is a general trait depends on the source of the impulsiveness. For example, if impulsiveness results from low subjective efficacy, and if this in turn results from certain failure experiences, a person's interpretation of the failure experiences will affect the generality of the impulsiveness. Given the same grade of D in a math course, one person might conclude he is bad at calculus, another that he is bad at school, a third that he is bad at everything. The resulting impulsiveness would generalize accordingly (Alloy et al., 1984).

There are many idiosyncratic kinds of personal histories that would lead to impulsiveness in different situations for different reasons. In general, then, I see no reason to expect any orderly principle to govern the domain over which impulsiveness, or any other style, is general. However, because some reasons for impulsiveness will have some generality, on the average, there will be some correlaton between impulsiveness in one situation and impulsiveness in another. This is consistent with the evidence available (see Messer, 1976; Baron et al., in press). The more

similar the situations from the perspective of the determinants of individual differences, the higher the correlation. The whole question of generality of traits is less important than the question of how people might be taught to be unbiased or optimal in a way that will apply across situations. This question is answered most directly by studies of training. General training may be possible even when there is, at present, little generality of individual differences. (I do not mean to suggest that training in cognitive styles is useless if it turns out to be specific to certain classes of situations, such as schoolwork.)

Confirmation bias in choice of evidence from memory

So far, I have discussed the selection of evidence when the answer is not controlled by the thinker, but by the state of the outside world. The general view of this chapter is also relevant to the somewhat different case in which evidence is sought in memory itself. I include cases in which we rely on the memories of other people (or computers) and cases in which we construct evidence, as when we make up examples in philosophical thinking. Although invention is surely different from recall in many ways, the causes and effects of biases in the two cases may be much the same.

When we ask questions of memory, for the purpose of evaluating one or more possibilities, we can show a true "confirmation bias." We can seek evidence that will tend to support our most favored hypothesis or possibility. We can do this because traces in memory can usually be recalled with a variety of different kinds of cues, among them conjunctive cues, such as "cases of such and such a form with such and such an attribute." (To see this, first try to recall words to support the claim that all words ending in *-ia* are names of countries, and then try to recall words to refute it. The role of memory processes is discussed more extensively in the next chapter.)

The person who shows this bias is asking his memory, "Give me a case that supports my position," not, "Give me a case that is informative one way or the other (or uninformative)." For example, in thinking about a social question such as whether violence on television should be reduced, a person's initial reaction might be that it should. He then searches memory for evidence in support of this possibility, such as a news item we recall in which some crime had apparently been modeled after a crime recently shown on television. When asked such questions, many people stop when they recall a single piece of supporting evidence, rather than continuing to look for counterevidence or counterarguments as well (Per-

kins, Allen, & Hafner 1983). This sort of bias is a true confirmation bias, that is, a bias to seek evidence that tends to confirm a favored possibility, usually in fact the only possibility under consideration. Of course, for the bias to lead to overconfidence in the original possibility, the thinker must not take the bias into account when using the evidence to revise belief; if he does, he will weigh the evidence according to its true value — very little — and he will have lost only the time spent finding it.

Many results can be explained in terms of the existence of confirmation bias (chapter 6), but I know of only one study that seeks direct evidence for its existence. Specifically, Jane Beattie and I, in unpublished work, told subjects that a deck of cards had a letter and a number on each card. The subject was asked which cards he would want the experimenter to look for in order to find out whether a rule — such as "If there's an A, then there's a 3" — was true of the deck. (The subject used the experimenter as an extension of his own memory in this case, and was thus forced to give an explicit instruction for search.) Many subjects asked to see only positive examples, e.g., cards with both A and 3, thus failing to put the rule in danger of falsification. Other experiments are planned in which the subject searches his own memory.

Belief perseverance, or insensitivity to evidence

As described in chapter 3, belief perseverance is the overweighing of evidence that favors the strongest possibility or the underweighing of evidence against it. Often, the "strongest" possibility is in fact the only one being explicitly considered. In the most extreme form of this bias, beliefs are held almost without regard to evidence against them.

There are several sources of evidence for the existence of this sort of belief perseverance. One is the work of Bruner and Potter (1964), who presented pictures of common objects, first out of focus, and then, on each repeated presentation of the same picture, more and more in focus. When the first presentation was very much out of focus, recognition of the picture was delayed far beyond the degree of focus that was sufficient for other subjects (who started at that degree of focus) to recognize the picture. It appears that early, incorrect hypotheses inhibited the use of good evidence in favor of the correct hypothesis. What is unclear from this study is whether this bias is a property of perception, as opposed to thinking. If it is not remediable or under control, it is not irrational.

Another source of evidence for belief perseverance is the work of Pitz (1969, and other papers cited therein). In a typical experiment, balls are drawn from an urn one at a time (and put back after each draw). The

subject must predict whether the next draw will be red or blue, and he must give a confidence rating. The urn has either a majority (e.g., 60%) of red balls or a majority of blue ones. Suppose that after a few draws, the subject begins to think that the urn is majority blue. Each blue ball will support this hypothesis, but each red should weigh against it. Normatively, from a Bayesian point of view, a red and a blue ball should exactly cancel each other. This is because the true support for "majority blue" depends (surprisingly) exactly on the difference between the number of red and blue balls drawn (Phillips & Edwards, 1966). However, it was found, in general, that a sequence of mixed evidence, e.g., a red ball followed by a blue ball, or vice versa, led to increased confidence in the hypothesis that had initially been favored. It thus appears that subjects overweigh the positive evidence and/or underweigh the negative evidence, so that mixed evidence leads to increased belief.

Lord, Ross, and Lepper (1979) tried to show belief perseverance in a more realistic context. Subjects were selected who either favored capital punishment or opposed it. Each subject was then presented with two purportedly authentic studies, one claiming to show that capital punishment acted as a deterrent to serious crime and the other claiming to show that it did not. One was a comparison of crime rates in several states before and after capital punishment was instituted; the other was a comparison of pairs of adjacent states with and without capital punishment. Subjects were more likely to criticize the study going against their position, whichever study it was. They revised their belief very little in the face of opposing evidence, but increased their belief in the face of supporting evidence. In the end, both groups of subjects had stronger, and hence even more divergent, beliefs than they had at the beginning.

Although this result appears to show a simple bias in the use of evidence, we must note that the subject has a chance to look for flaws in each piece of evidence before he uses it. Suppose that the subject rationally decides (from a prescriptive point of view) that it not worthwhile to look for flaws in evidence favoring his side. Finding, or not finding, such a flaw would not affect the direction of his belief. However, evidence for the other side might really change his belief, if it is valid, so it is worthwhile to look for flaws in that. Further, suppose that the subject does look for a flaw in the evidence favoring the other side, and finds one. Finding such a flaw would legitimately undermine the evidence for the other side so long as he believed that he would be unlikely to find a flaw in that evidence if the other side were correct. This belief about the probability of finding a flaw in evidence for the other side if the other side were correct might itself be erroneous, but it need not be irrational to

have such a belief or to use it. Hence, this form of the polarization effect need not be irrational from a prescriptive point of view.

Another source of evidence is from the work of C. A. Anderson, Lepper, and Ross (1980; also Anderson, 1982, 1983). In these experiments, subjects were given descriptions of two firefighters, one rated as good at his job, the other as not so good. Included among the descriptions were the firefighters' responses to items on a test of "risk taking." For some subjects, the good firefighter tended to be more prone to take risks; for other subjects, the not-so-good one. Subjects were first asked to say what they thought the relationship would be between risk taking and firefighting, and they seemed to have been convinced somewhat by whatever evidence they were given. Finally, the subjects were told that the evidence was totally fabricated, and they were asked once again to say what they thought the true relationship was between risk taking and firefighting. Subjects turned out to be still influenced by the evidence they had been given. This experiment seems to show belief perseverance in a situation in which prior belief was not involved, since the relevant belief was created during the experiment. However, several lines of evidence indicate that subjects had constructed justifications of the relationship they found when reading the original evidence, and that the experimenter's total discrediting of the evidence did not eliminate these justifications from the subject's memory. Thus, the effect might have to do with the subject's lack of control over his memory, and with his inability to tell whether his beliefs came from the experiment itself as opposed to prior experiences, rather than from a true bias.

A better experiment would combine the advantages of the Lord et al. approach with those of the Anderson approach. Subjects might be given three unambiguous pieces of evidence with respect to some question (e.g., evidence about a student's grades, etc., with the question being whether she had won a scholarship). The first piece of evidence would lean the subject one way or the other, and the second and third pieces would conflict. The subject's belief could be measured after each piece of evidence. At issue is the question of whether the second and third pieces of evidence caused the belief to move further in the direction indicated by the first piece, whatever that was. Such experiments are now underway in my laboratory.

If true belief perseverance can be found, there might be several different sources of it. First, when beliefs are integrated with each other, so that each provides support (evidence) for the others, a change in one belief might weaken others as well. If we are also motivated to have consistent beliefs, such a change might require the reevaluation of other

beliefs than the one under attack at the moment. Such reevaluaton will require thinking, which has a cost. Thus, revision of a single belief might lead either to inconsistency or to further thinking, both undesirable consequences, although perhaps not equally undesirable for all people.

Another source of motivation is social. We might believe (perhaps truthfully) that others consider it bad to change one's beliefs. Thus, sticking to one's belief in the face of opposing evidence might be taken as a sign of integrity, trustworthiness, and so on. Perhaps there is also a general belief that adults should have well-supported beliefs to begin with, so that a tendency to change one's beliefs is a sign that one was not fully mature to begin with. Of course, from the point of view of the present theory, such social beliefs are misguided and damaging. There is no good reason I can think of for placing a social value on stubbornness rather than open-mindedness, and, indeed, the fact that the second of these words has good connotations and the first, bad connotations suggests that such social norms exist alongside the others. It seems likely that some circles place a greater value on open-mindedness than others, as well.

Another possible motive for belief perseverance (pointed out to me by John Sabini) comes from confusions about the relations of beliefs to one another, in particular, a false belief that one belief is crucial evidence for another. For example, in the Lord et al. study, a subject who favors capital punishment might do so on purely moral grounds. He might feel that certain crimes fundamentally deserve such punishment, whether the punishment deters or not. Similarly, a subject opposed to capital punishment might feel that it is barbaric and fundamentally immoral, no matter how good a deterrent it might be. However, these subjects might be unaware that their beliefs are purely moral, so they might mistakenly think that the deterrence question is relevant to their beliefs. They would then resist changing their beliefs about deterrence, for all the reasons given above for people who want to maintain consistent beliefs. However, they will be mistaken in their belief that consistency would be threatened by a change in their belief about deterrence. Thus, what they fear, the need to reexamine their belief in the overall goodness or badness of capital punishment, might be nothing to fear at all. They fail to realize this because they fail to ask themselves whether they would need to change their belief about capital punishment if they changed their belief about deterrence. (Another example of this sort of motivation might occur in people who resist the idea that intelligence is partially inherited, because they fear they will have to reexamine their belief that races are essentially equal in intelligence. In fact, they won't, since higher heritability in general does not imply that racial differences are genetic.)

Another explanation of belief perseverance is that the thinker behaves as if he is confused between two goals: making up a (one-sided) defense to convince someone else (or himself) of a position he already "knows" is true; and discovering what position he ought to hold. This confusion may be encouraged by a social emphasis on debating and advocacy, in and out of school, in contrast to individual or cooperative problem solving.

A final cause of belief perseverance might involve the use of a single schema (as discussed in chapter 5) to keep track of the effect of evidence. The schema corresponding to the favored hypothesis might lead to several types of expectations, and when one of these is confirmed, the schema is strengthened. When evidence for the other side of an issue is found, the thinker has no way to use that evidence; it is as if the evidence were simply irrelevant. If, on the other hand, the thinker simultaneously maintains schemata for both sides, evidence for the other side can be used to strengthen the schema on that side. Thus, irrational belief perseverance might result from failure to consider the effect of evidence on alternative hypotheses, and this failure may sometimes result from failure to search for alternatives. This explanation of belief perseverance suggests a simple cure: Consider how the other side would evaluate the evidence.

In this chapter, I have suggested that a number of different biases can be described in terms of a decision–theoretic model based on utility. The principle of utility maximization may be applied directly to the choice of evidence in hypothesis testing and to the optimal duration of search for evidence. In the case of confirmation bias in search for evidence from memory, and the case of belief perseverance in the use of evidence, I have assumed (as argued in chapter 3) that utility maximization is essentially equivalent to a kind of evenhandedness in the treatment of strong and weak possibilities. I hope that the suggestions made here will lead to further experimental work in all areas, based on the general idea of applying normative models to the process of thinking itself, and to the evaluation of heuristics used in thinking, rather than to its outcomes.

5   Conditions of effective thinking

In the last two chapters, I outlined a theory of the rational conduct of thinking. In this theory, rationality is defined in terms of the setting of certain parameters. It is not defined as intelligence is usually defined, namely in terms of effectiveness or success. The factors that make thinking effective or ineffective in a given case include many abilities, knowledge, and luck, as well as rationality in the conduct of thinking. These other factors have so far been treated as extraneous to the theory, as factors that need to be taken into account in setting parameters, but not as determinants of rationality itself. (For example, the expectation of the value of further thinking reasonably depends on one's ability.) In the present chapter, I address the role of these factors in determining the success of thinking. I shall assume here that parameters are set optimally, so that rationality is not a factor. This chapter thus fleshes out some of the claims of chapter 1 concerning the relation between intelligence and narrow intelligence.

Limits on cognitive processes

I begin with what I take to be a textbook analysis of the major limits on cognitive processes. The major limits I consider are speed, selective attention, limited capacity, primary memory, and secondary memory. I try to show how each of these limits could affect thinking itself. I also discuss the problems involved in empirical study of these limits. It will turn out to be difficult to separate these limits from one another, and that this difficulty extends to other investigations of individual differences as well, since any other types of limits that may be described (e.g., speed of certain general processes such as encoding or comparison) may be affected by several of the limits I discuss.

I make no special claims for the particular list of limits I have chosen, except that its members are traditional divisions within cognitive psychol-

ogy itself. Moreover, with the exception of primary memory, we can discuss any of the processes involved in thinking in terms of these limits. (Primary memory may be seen as a quick method of storage and retrieval, thus bypassing the need for secondary memory in many tasks.) I also do not intend to claim that these limits are general across many different kinds of thinking tasks, so that a person who is slow in choosing words, for example, is also slow in manipulating mental images. This is an empirical matter.

Speed

A major source of individual differences in mental tasks is the speed of doing the tasks. Such differences can be seen in complex tasks such as reading (Jackson & McClelland, 1979) or in simple tasks such as pushing a button when a light goes on (Jensen, 1982). Speed differences could clearly affect differences in the success of thinking, in particular, by increasing the expected benefit of the various search processes relative to their cost in time. A person who searches more quickly will find more possibilities, evidence, and goals in a given time than a person who searches slowly. (A rational fast thinker might end up spending more time thinking than a rational slow thinker. For example, there are tasks for which the expected payoff per unit time is so low that a slow thinker would do best by not undertaking them at all.) More generally, a person who is slow, like a person who needs a lot of sleep, must expect to accomplish less in a day, and he therefore must form more modest plans, other things being equal, or reduce his expectations about their completion.

It is tempting to conclude that the speed of mental operations is a basic source of individual differences, perhaps even one that is general across different kinds of operations. However, there are many other reasons why people can differ in the speed of performing a task. For one, people may differ in the way they do a task, either because they have learned to do it in different ways from the outset or because one person discovered more shortcuts in the course of practice than another. People may also differ in their tolerance for errors. Even if people try to maintain a constant error rate in a task, one person may have to go more slowly than another in order to compensate for some sort of increased variability in his mental processes, which would lead to an increased error rate in the absence of such compensation. People may also differ in the amount of practice they have had at the task or in similar tasks, and they may differ in the effect of such practice on their speed (although Baron, Freyd, & Stewart, 1980, suggest that such differences in benefit from practice, if they exist, are

unrelated to intelligence). However, even in tasks in which such extraneous factors are not apparent, substantial individual differences in speed remain, and these differences are correlated with performance in intellectual tasks, in schoolwork, and so on (e.g., Spearman, 1904; Hunt, 1978, 1982; Nettlebeck & Lally, 1979; Baron, Freyd, & Stewart, 1980; Smith & Baron, 1981; Jensen, 1982; Chi & Gallagher, 1982). Speed differences distinguish older and younger children, young adults from older adults, normals from retardates, and those with very high IQs from those with moderate IQs. These results hold for a variety of measures of speed: reaction time; perceptual accuracy following exposure to a stimulus, such as a letter or word for a fraction of a second; or differences in reaction time between two different conditions. In the last case, when the two conditions differ in the complexity (or in the presence versus absence) of a particular stage of information processing, the effect of the manipulation can be taken as an index of the speed of the affected stage.

It would be reasonable to think that there is some sort of mental clock — the alpha rhythm of the brain has even been suggested (Kristofferson, 1967) — and that individuals differ in the speed of this clock. A given task might take a given number of ticks of the clock, regardless of who did the task, provided that differences in extraneous factors were controlled. If this were the only source of individual differences, we might expect that speed of performance in the simplest tasks could be taken as a measure of the speed of the clock. Individuals should then differ by a constant proportion in such tasks. If subject A took 20% longer than subject B in task 1, then the 20% difference should also be found in task 2, even if task 2 requires many more ticks of the clock, thus taking longer for both subjects. Such results are sometimes found (Kristofferson, 1967), but more typically, this simple view does not provide a full account of individual or age differences in reaction time (e.g., Keating & Bobbitt, 1978; Chi & Gallagher, 1982). Thus, the results supporting the simple model could be coincidental, which is likely, given that any theory would hold that this model would be a reasonable first approximation. (All that is required for a crude fit of the simple model is that more difficult tasks show larger absolute differences in reaction time.) On the other hand, there are many things that could obscure the essential correctness of the simple model, and therefore the mental clock might really exist even though it is hard to discover. For example, carefulness might be affected by the nature of the task or by manipulations of a single task. (We cannot eliminate effects of carefulness simply by ensuring that error rate is held constant across conditions being compared — although even this minimal precaution is rarely taken — because a given level of carefulness — de-

fined, for example, as we defined impulsiveness in chapter 4 — may express itself as different error rates in different tasks.) In fact, there is evidence that high-IQ subjects are more careful in some components of some tasks, so that these components show disproportionately small effects of IQ on speed (Jensen, 1982), or even reversed effects in which high-IQ subjects or older children take more time on the component in question (Sternberg, 1984).

Other factors that might obscure the existence of simple differences in clock speed are some of the other limits, such as "capacity" or total effort available, or the ability to prepare for a task. Another factor is the effort actually expended, which might not depend all that heavily on the total effort or capacity available. Johanson (1922) has shown that reward, punishment, and feedback about performance can shorten reaction time without increasing error rate. This might be more true for some tasks than others. If high-IQ subjects tend to try harder, both in laboratory tasks and in tasks outside the laboratory, we might observe larger effects of IQ on reaction time than the clock model would predict. (Apparent demonstrations that more able subjects actually try less hard in some tasks, such as Ahern & Beatty, 1979, might be the result of these tasks being better practiced in the more able subjects, so that little effort was required even for performance at maximum speed and accuracy for these subjects. It would be helpful in such studies to equate the tasks for sensitivity to changes in effort.)

Note that the possibility of such extraneous factors as effort and knowledge about the task obscure the issue in two ways. First, they make it difficult to test the clock model fairly; any failure of the model can be attributed to such factors as these. Second, they raise the possibility that true individual differences in mental speed are simply absent in any given case, or even in general. Although it seems likely that speed differences (between high- and low-IQ subjects, for example) are real, I know of no studies that have controlled for more than one of these extraneous factors. In fact, Chi and Gallagher (1982) review a number of studies suggesting that there are no effects of age on speed of processing in children after about age 6. Speed differences do tend to be found in complex tasks, and especially in tasks with a complex decision component, for example, a multiple-choice reaction-time task as compared to a simple reaction-time task. However, the cases in which age differences are found are just those in which we might expect a greater dependence of reaction time on effort or practice. If individual differences in speed are to be found, we shall have to show that the tasks in question are insensitive to practice and effort.

Selective attention and set

The term "selective attention" is used in descriptions of several different phenomena. For example, when a subject must respond to one spoken message, e.g., by shadowing it or reporting it after a delay, the presence of another spoken message disrupts performance in the attended task. Schizophrenics are especially disrupted by this sort of interference unless they are given antipsychotic drugs (Oltmanns, Ohayon, & Neale, 1978). Smith, Kemler, and Aronfreed (1975) have found that young children show impairments in similar tasks. (These two studies are unusual in this literature because they deal with the problem of showing that the individual differences are due to interference itself rather than to the fact that group differences in performance are likely to be exaggerated by more difficult tasks, whatever the nature of the tasks; see Baron & Treiman, 1980.) Still another difficulty attributed to attention is the interference effect investigated by Stroop (1935) and many others, in which a subject is asked to name the colors in which words are printed when the words are the names of other colors. The subject tends to read the words instead of naming their colors, and he must slow down to avoid doing this. Finally, when a subject is asked to judge whether a rod is vertical, a tilted frame around the rod distorts the judgment.

These different kinds of interference might have different explanations (Reisberg, 1980). Some (for example, the effect of an irrelevant spoken message) may be due partly or wholly to perceptual factors such as masking. (Masking may be hard to distinguish from other factors, except by their exclusion; the idea is that masking occurs before any intention of the subject takes effect.) The Stroop effect might result from response competition from responses that tend to be made automatically to the words (Egeth, Blecker, & Kamlet, 1969). Such competition might occur in auditory shadowing tasks as well. There might also be an effect of familiar material on the direction of attention itself, that is, on the subject's set to do the task he is supposed to do. For example, Schneider and Shiffrin (1977) gave subjects extensive practice at searching for a small set of letters in visual displays consisting of other letters. When subjects were subsequently instructed to search only the top half of the display, the presentation of a target letter in the bottom half would disrupt the subject's ability to detect a target presented just afterwards in the top half.

One possible determinant of interference has to do with the subject's set for a task. We may assume that when a subject does a laboratory task or a real one, he behaves as if he has given himself an instruction, set, or rule to follow for a certain period of time. For example, "shadow the

woman's voice but not the man's" or "name the colors but do not read the words." This set must be maintained in mind over the period, and it must be used to govern performance. Both maintenance and use might be more difficult for complex sets than for simple ones. (By complexity, I mean whatever is increased by the addition of more contingencies.) Further, the presence of irrelevant stimuli in a task may create a need for a more complex set or rule. For example, when there is only one message present, the subject might use the rule "repeat anything you hear," but when there is an irrelevant message, he might use the rule "repeat what is on the right," and the latter rule might be more complex. In the Stroop task, a subject naming color patches might instruct himself to name anything to which he can assign a color name, but to name the colors of words, he would have to instruct himself to name colors only. The existence of such differences in set can be seen in this task by presenting the subject a list which he thinks contains only X's in different colors; when a single color word appears unexpectedly, subjects tend to read it instead of naming its color. In the case of irrelevant variation, the set might be stated in terms of the stimuli themselves when the variation is absent, but in terms of attributes when it is present. In general, we may test for an effect of instructional complexity by giving different instructions but holding constant the material, i.e., using the only the simpler material. (To make sure that the subject is actually maintaining the complex set, we must insert some stimuli from the complex task as catch trials, as in the Stroop example just described.) The maintenance and use of sets is also related to the positive effects of preparation for a task (LaBerge, 1975; Posner, 1978).

Individual differences in the effect of rule complexity may account for differences in the ability to ignore distraction of various sorts. (Persons and Baron, 1983, suggest a difficulty in following a set as an explanation of schizophrenic thought disorder; Shakow, 1962, has proposed a theory that is superficially similar.) Of course, changes in rule complexity with different tasks do not preclude other explanations of interference.

The effect of instructional complexity seems important to me not only because it can account (potentially) for many phenomena of selective attention but also because it seems more closely related to the effectiveness of thinking than many of the other sources of interference I have mentioned. The other sources of interference are present only when there is actual interference present, but the effect of instructional complexity is present in any *task* at all. Any attempt to learn a strategy, or to control one's mental processes, requires sets in the sense I have discussed. All instructions have some degree of complexity, so it is likely that those who

find it difficult (relative to others) to follow complex instruction actually have difficulty following any instructions. Thinking, in particular, involves the use of sets. The search for possibilities, for evidence, and for goals must be under the control of some sort of self-instruction about the nature of the search. A person who cannot maintain and use such an instruction, such as (perhaps) a florid schizophrenic, a young infant, or a lower animal, literally cannot think.

Thus, individual differences in the effectiveness of thinking might result in part from the ability to maintain and use a set for search. Apparent lack of "planfulness" in the retarded (Brown, 1974) might result from such difficulty. If a person has great difficulty maintaining and using a set for search, he will have a justifiably low expectation for the value of further search, i.e., he will have low efficacy. Given this, he may simply give up the effort; this may happen in schizophrenics.

The ability to maintain and use a set might be a fundamental mental ability, or it might be a consequence of other abilities such as the deployment of effort in general. Even in the latter case, however, it would be an important consequence.

I know of no good studies relating set maintenance to IQ or other measures of intelligence. However, Jensen (1982) reports an interesting result that might be related. Specifically, low-IQ subjects show greater variability in reaction time, and this increased variability cannot be easily explained in terms of longer times alone. (See also Grim, Kohlberg, & White, 1968, for a similar result.) The increased variability may result from a lower ability to maintain a set for the task consistently.

Limited capacity

The idea that there is a basic limit on capacity (effort, resources, one's sense of "attention") is both widespread and controversial. I shall present the "standard theory" first, and its implications for intelligence, and then some of the criticisms.

According to the standard theory (Bryan & Harter, 1899; Kahneman, 1973; LaBerge & Samuels, 1974; Norman & Bobrow, 1975), each task may be said to use a certain amount of effort. Total effort is limited, so that what is used in one task cannot be used for a concurrent task. Hence, there is a limit on our ability to do two tasks at once. The explanation of this limit is the main role of the concept of effort, but it is supposed to correspond to our everyday concept as well. If we think of a task as composed of a number of subtasks, stages, or steps, then each of these subtasks may be thought of as using a certain amount of effort as well.

The total effort used by the task is the sum of the efforts used by the subtasks.

If effort is thought of as something that can vary over time, we might define a concept of "resources" as the sum of effort over time, so that effort would be defined as resources per unit time. (The relation I have stated between effort and resources is my idea; the terms are used more loosely in the literature.) The subject may control the amount of effort put into a task or subtask at a given time, and he may divide effort among two or more concurrent tasks. The speed at which each task gets done, or its quality (in case the task is time limited), is an increasing function of the effort put into it. As Norman and Bobrow (1975) point out, the form of this function may vary considerably from task to task. Some tasks may increase steadily in speed as effort is increased. Other tasks may reach maximum speed when only a small amount of effort is used. Some tasks may require a fair amount of effort to get done at all, that is, for their speed to rise above zero. Others may have some positive speed even when no effort is put into them. This may be true of well-practiced tasks, such as reading words. In the Stroop color-word interference task described above, the color words may be read despite the absence of any effort to read them. Tasks done in this way are said to be automatic, in one sense of the term.

Assuming that this standard view is correct, it is clear that resources and effort have quite a bit to do with thinking. The effectiveness of a search for possibilities, evidence, or goals may depend on the effort put into it. Individual differences in effort might affect observed differences in processing speed, ability to maintain a set, or in other components to be described later. The cost of thinking may depend in some complex way on effort and resources, and the expected cost of thinking may depend on expected effort and resources. It seems reasonable to assume that the cost of thinking increases with effort, once effort exceeds a certain point. The maximum effort that can be expended without subjective cost may decrease as a function of the amount of time spent working on a given task. The cost of effort at a given point in time might also depend on the cost incurred so far, etc.

Individuals may differ either in the maximum effort they can deploy or in the level of effort they can sustain over an extended period. The latter parameter, sustainable effort, seems more relevant to the study of intelligence, because it affects most tasks. It may also largely determine maximum effort, the other parameter. There have been a few attempts to test such an idea. For example, Pascual-Leone (1970) taught children of different ages to make a different response (e.g., a cough, raising the right

hand, raising the left hand, shutting the eyes) to each of several signals. The signals could be perceived simultaneously and the responses were compatible with one another. Older children could respond correctly to a greater number of simultaneous signals than could younger children. Although Pascual-Leone's description was different from mine in detail, such a result suggests that older children have greater sustainable effort. If we assume that each association requires a certain minimum effort to be used, the more effort there is to divide among the associations, the more that can be used at once. However, studies of this sort are difficult to interpret for several reasons. As I shall discuss, the older and younger children might differ in sensitivity to practice of the different associations, in memory for the signals (if the signals are withdrawn), or in perseverance at making sure that all signals are responded to. (Perseverance might not show itself as increased time to make all the responses, because the older children could be faster as well.)

It is widely assumed that practice at a task or subtask decreases the effort required to reach a given speed. If we consider a curve in which speed is plotted as an increasing function of effort, in general, practice would move this curve to the left, or perhaps upwards. Either of these movements of the curve could account for automaticity, the fact that well-practiced tasks, such as reading words, seem to get done at some speed even with no effort at all. Specifically, some tasks will get done to some extent with essentially no effort at all, so long as the stimulus is presented. If we also assume that performance has some absolute upper bound, this idea can account for another phenomenon: The effect of a concurrent task (such as holding in memory a list of six digits) on the speed of a given task (such as a choice reaction-time task) is reduced with practice, in some cases essentially to zero (Logan, 1979). After practice, maximum speed at the given task is reached with only the effort left over from the concurrent task.

The relationship between practice and effort creates methodological problems for any attempt to measure individual differences in sustainable effort. To measure effort, it is necessary to equate tasks used by different subjects in effective degree of practice. However, this does not mean simply giving the same number of practice trials, because people may differ in their sensitivity to practice. Nor is it easy to measure the sensitivity to practice without at the same time worrying about individual differences in sustainable effort. A person with more sustainable effort might show a different kind of practice curve; in particular, he would reach maximum speed more quickly. I do not mean to imply that these problems are insoluble, but to solve them will require more knowledge than

we now have. For example, if it turns out that the effects of practice on required effort approach a limit for some tasks (and that these tasks still require some effort), we can distinguish a concept of sustainable effort from a concept of benefit from practice by measuring the former at the asymptote. Alternatively, we could simply give up trying to distinguish the two concepts and seek some measure of sustainable effort that is independent of the actual number of practice trials given. (This has not been shown for any measures now in use.)

However problematic the relation between practice and effort may be for the researcher, it seems to be a great boon for the rest of the species. Performance of complex tasks seems to require the automatization, through practice, of lower level processes, thus freeing effort for higher-level processes (Bryan & Harter, 1899; LaBerge & Samuels, 1974; Baron, 1977). This claim accords with the introspections of pianists, tennis players, drivers, typists, readers, and speakers of second languages. In all these activities, with skill, one attends only to the highest levels, the level of strategy, expression, or meaning, as the case may be. At the beginning of learning, however, the lower levels—pressing keys, turning wheels, speaking words, and so on—require great effort, with little remaining for higher levels. This may be true for common accomplishments, such as reading or speaking a language, and uncommon ones, such as piano or chess playing. (The same principle may apply to the learning of a first language, although the early age of learning makes introspection difficult. However, we can infer only from the two-year-old's furrowed brow and her deliberate manner that she is putting as much effort into the production of words as does the beginning typist.) As Bryan and Harter put is, "Automatism is not genius. It is the hands and feet of genius." I think that this can be said for our species, compared to other species, as well as for some members of our species, compared to others. Animals cannot learn to talk or read with the fluency of most humans, but neither can they learn to play tennis, play the piano, and so on, it seems. The acrobatic feats they can perform seem to require relatively little automatization, since these feats are based largely on specific reflexes or fixed action patterns.

In the case of thinking, the effect of practice on effort allows us to master complex kinds of thinking involving a particular knowledge base, such as chess. The experienced chess player need not think about whether a move is legal, and the master chess player often need not think about whether a move will lead to immediate trouble. Automatization does not relieve the expert chess player of thinking, but it allows him to think in terms of possibilities, evidence, and goals different from those the novice must use. Automatization also lowers the cost of thinking, insofar as cost

depends on effort and effort is reduced by automatization. Finally, automatization of various search processes allows several searches to go on simultaneously with greater efficiency than would otherwise be possible. These may include searches for evidence, possibilities, and goals, or two different kinds of evidence, etc.

However, one property of automatization is that it appears to be highly specific (see Baron, 1985, for a review). Because of this, automatization can help us to learn specific skills, and it can help us to learn to think effectively in a particular domain (such as chess), but it cannot help us to learn to think in general. It is important to distinguish here between automatization and habit. The former concerns the need for effort; the latter, a tendency to perform a certain action under certain conditions, regardless of one's goals or expectations concerning its effects (see chapter 7 for more discussion). Although the effect of practice on effort may be situation specific, I know of no research concerning the generality of the effects of practice on habits, and it is conceivable that habits that promote good thinking could be learned in general.

It is worth considering in more detail how the ability to do complex tasks is related to the effect of practice on the curve relating speed and effort. Three parts of this effect are important. First, practice reduces the minimum amount of effort needed for a subtask to be done at all (with speed above zero). Second, practice reduces the effort needed to attain maximum speed. Third, practice increases the speed that can be attained with a given level of effort. The first of these effects is what allows subtasks to be done simultaneously at all. The second effect may allow whole tasks to be done simultaneously. For example, in typing, the limits on the motor system may set a maximum rate of about 10 keys per second. Expert typists seem to require far less than full effort to reach this rate. This allows them to do other tasks while typing, such as sing, or even shadow a spoken message unrelated to the text they are typing (Shaffer, 1975). In reading easy texts, the limit on speed may be set by the need to control eye movements so as to bring all the words into a part of the visual field that allows them to be seen with sufficient clarity. Fluent readers might therefore have some spare effort to devote to other tasks (Hirst et al., 1980; Broadbent, 1982, makes a similar point). The third relevant effect of practice, the effect on the speed that can be attained with a given level of effort is important when there is some sort of time limit on a task. The time limit might be part of the task itself, as when listening to someone speak a language one does not know well. In such cases, thinking may be needed to make sense of what is being said, but there may be no effort left over to do it. A time limit might be

imposed by the subject as well. I have noticed that dyslexic readers, even after they learn to read most words, tend to rush through a passage and make many errors when reading aloud. It is as if they feel that reading must be done at a certain rate. Possibly they are correct. If they were to read slowly enough to read all the words correctly, they might forget the beginning of a sentence by the time they reached the end, and thus have to go back and read the sentence over. Their probability of understanding the sentence even with a few words missed may be sufficiently high that this risk is not worth taking. Alternatively, the extra time required to be more accurate might be (or be seen as) too costly. In sum, a time limit may be caused by time limits on memory or by a high subjective cost for time, as well as by external task demands.

It is of possible interest that the ability to automatize tasks with practice may be somewhat independent of other limitations on effective intelligence. Many retardates, unable to function outside of institutions, manage to master quite complex skills, such as mental calculations, especially calendar calculations. Some of these people can tell quite quickly and accurately the day of the week on which a very distant date will fall. Others master other skills or crafts. A general characteristic of these "savants" seems to be that they devote practically all their time to the mastery of their particular skill (Hill, 1978). They seem to be distinctive simply in their failure to be bored by doing the same thing much of the time (a characteristic they would share with virtuoso musical performers). However, they do seem capable of the kind of automatization I have discussed. What is not known is whether these are statistical flukes, or whether the capacity to automatize is really independent of other limits on intelligence.

As I mentioned at the beginning of this section, the standard theory I have presented is controversial. The main topic of controversy concerns the question of whether effort exists as a single dimension. One alternative to this is that there are many different kinds of effort. Another alternative is that there is no such thing as effort at all.

There is pretty clear evidence that there are different kinds of effort. The general form of the evidence is the finding that tasks (or subtasks) v1 and v2 interfere greatly with each other when a subject tries to do them concurrently, and so do tasks (or subtasks) s1 and s2. However, v1 can easily be combined with s2, and s1 with v2. Typically, v1 and v2 are verbal and s1 and s2 are spatial. The inference is that there are separate kinds of effort for the two types of tasks or subtasks, e.g., spatial effort and verbal effort. For example, Brooks (1968) found that classifying successive words in a sentence as nouns or not was easy when the

response was made by pointing to Y's and N's but hard when the response was made by saying "yes" or "no" for each word. However, classifying the corners of an imagined block letter as on the top or bottom line, versus neither, was hard with pointing and easy with speaking. Imagining the block letters seems to draw on the same kind of effort as pointing, and holding the sentences in memory seems to draw on the same kind of effort as speaking. Treisman and Davies (1973) provide a similar demonstration. Most dramatically, perhaps, Reisberg, Rappaport, and O'Shaughnessy (1984) have found that people can be taught to increase their digit spans by up to 50% by rehearsing some of the digits with their fingers while rehearsing others verbally.

We do not know how many different kinds of effort there might be. If there are many different kinds, perhaps there is no such thing as general effort in addition. Any two tasks are likely to interfere with each other because they draw on one or more of the specific kinds of effort. In principle, if there is no general effort, it ought to be possible to find two tasks that do not interfere with each other at all, even though each one could be said (on other grounds) to require effort.

More generally, we might imagine that there are so many different kinds of effort that the concept becomes useless (roughly the view of Neisser, 1976). By this view, interference among tasks might be better described in terms of the use of common machinery — common perceptual systems that are subject to mutual masking, common motor systems that are incompatible, and so on.

Against this view, it must be noted that general effort has both subjective and physiological manifestations. We all know what it means to put effort into a task. When we do so, we show certain physiological changes: Our pupils widen, our palms sweat, the amplitude of our EEG decreases and its frequency goes up. Stimulant drugs seem to affect available effort, and depressants seem to decrease it; stimulants have been found to improve performance on mental tests, particularly those that seem more sensitive to effort than to knowledge, i.e., those whose scores decline after adolescence (Gupta, 1977). Mathematicians sometimes describe their science as "the black art of turning coffee into theorems" (although the cognitive effects of caffeine, in fact, are difficult to demonstrate). What remains to be shown is that this kind of effort has something to do with the kind of effort that is depleted by a concurrent task. However, even if the effect of concurrent tasks cannot be explained in terms of general effort, the concept may still be useful in a theory of intelligence, for it is the kind of effort that is affected by drugs, sleep loss, etc., that might be involved in intellectual performance.

If there are different kinds of effort, we can make the same argument about the relation between each kind and effective thinking that I have already made. However, the cost of thinking would be more difficult to determine. In the simplest case, the cost would be a weighted sum of the different kinds of resources used. Also, the more kinds there are, the harder it is to define and measure individual differences in sustainable effort of the different kinds. However, it does not seem difficult for me to order tasks in terms of effortfulness, subjectively, so I suspect that a common scale is possible, from which the effort component of the cost of thinking may be taken.

Primary memory

At least since the time of James (1890), most theories of memory have made some sort of distinction between primary memory (or working memory) and secondary memory. The terms of the distinction have varied from theory to theory. The distinction I prefer is one that has been stated most clearly by Norman (1968), Craik and Lockhart (1972), and Baddeley and Hitch (1974; see also Baddeley, 1976). By this view, primary memory is the use of effort to maintain a memory over a period of time. The most common instance of this is rehearsal of a telephone number. Between the time we look up a number and dial it, we repeat the number to ourselves, or use effort in some other way (such as forming an image of the number, if we are so inclined) to maintain the number over the interval. (This concept of primary memory as involving effort by definition differs substantially from other conceptions, particularly that of James, 1890.)

By this definition, primary memory is not exactly the same as short-term memory, because such maintenance could, in principle, be used for quite a long period of time. Nor does primary memory include the more passive kinds of "echoic" and "iconic" memories described by Neisser (1967; these would be included in James's view). In these cases, the memory of an event could be continuously available over a short period even though no effort is put into its maintenance. (Nor is primary memory, in my sense, appropriately measured by the recency effect in recall; see Baddeley, 1976, for a critique of this view.)

The closest I can come to an experimental measure of primary memory is the phenomenon of directed forgetting (Reitman, Malin, Bjork, & Higman, 1973). The subject is given a short list of items, say, words or paired associates, and then, immediately, another short list. On some trials, the subject is told to forget the first list immediately after receiving

it. On the other trials, (usually) the two lists are just run together, so that the subject is effectively given one, longer list. The memory of the second list is improved by having been told to forget the first. Further, when the subjects are told to continue to forget the first, even after they know they might be tested on it, memory of the first list is poor as a result of the forget signal. The most likely explanation of these effects, I think, is that telling a subject to forget makes him stop expending effort on remembering. Presumably, these results are found only under conditions in which effort is used to maintain both lists. In particular, we cannot (I assume) voluntarily forget something in secondary memory, so that it ceases to interfere with later learning.

The possible importance of primary memory in thinking has been stated clearly by Baddeley and Hitch (1974). They use the term "working memory" to refer to essentially what I call primary memory. Their term points to the fact that this sort of memory can be used as a kind of workbench during thinking itself. The contents of primary memory need not be simply telephone numbers or short lists of paired associates; they may also be the intermediate products of one's own thinking. In the terms of chapter 3, working memory can be used to hold possibilities, evidence, and goals, as well as the instructions that one has given oneself to search for these (i.e., one's set). Under certain conditions, strengths, weights, and expectations may also be held in working memory, particularly when these are the results of subordinate episodes of thinking rather than when they are directly available from secondary memory. Simon (1978b) has pointed out that the demands on working memory become very severe in search problems such as chess. In these problems, ordinarily, one must evaluate possibilities (e.g., moves) by searching ahead (see chapter 3). To do this, one must remember one's path of search, so that it can be retraced. Because of the use of primary memory in almost all kinds of thinking, it has been considered to be an extremely important limit on the effectiveness of thinking. Simon (1978b) goes so far as to suggest that this sort of memory limit is, to a first approximation, the only general limit on effectiveness other than specific knowledge relevant to the problem at hand. (However, he does not deny that individual differences in learning ability, in secondary memory, might account in part for differences in relevant knowledge.)

Primary memory is useful in thinking because it is easier to store possibilities, evidence, goals, subgoals, etc. in primary memory than to store them in secondary memory (which does not require continuous effort) and recall them as needed. In planning a chess move, without primary memory, we might repeatedly go over the same sequence of moves, the

need for repetition resulting from forgetting—for example, forgetting where the various pieces were after each move. Several attempts to do this will eventually succeed, because we shall eventually memorize the sequence in question, and all the positions of the pieces. Thus, time spent trying to overcome the limits of primary memory may be of lower value than time spent in some other activity. (We can also write things down, but this takes time as well, and, in some cases, is impossible, or socially unacceptable.) More generally, we can imagine a function relating the effectiveness of thinking to the time spent (as discussed in chapter 4). As time increases, effectiveness increases rapidly up to a point, and then less rapidly. There may be a sudden decrease in the slope of the curve at the point at which extra time is used to overcome limits on primary memory. But the size of the decrease in slope might not be all that great. For example, it might be worthwhile to search for more possibilities, even though the list is already so long that secondary memory will have to be relied upon. Thus, some failures in thinking that are laid at the doorstep of primary memory limits might more justifiably be laid at the doorstep of impulsiveness.

An interesting finding, to which these questions are relevant, is that of Borys, Spitz, and Dorans (1982). This study compared retarded adolescents to controls matched in "mental age," that is, on the raw score of the IQ test. Of course, the controls were younger. These researchers gave both groups a set of search problems such as a three-disk version of the Towers of Hanoi, in which the subject must move a stack of disks from one of three pegs to another without ever putting a larger disk over a smaller one. The retardates performed much worse than the controls on these problems. Thus, the ability to do search problems is a more sensitive index of retardation than the IQ test itself. Put another way, performance on search problems is relatively less affected by age than is the score on the IQ test, and relatively more affected by individual differences that are independent of age, in particular, those individual differences that cause a person to do less well than their age mates on IQ tests and to be classified as retarded.

In principle, such results might be due to retardates having smaller primary memory capacity or to their being more impulsive. It is hard to tell. In fact, Borys and Spitz (1978) found that the retardates were not more impulsive on another test (the Matching Familiar Figures test), but the measure of impulsiveness on this test is known to be affected by age (Messer, 1976). An appropriate measure of impulsiveness in the search problems themselves might not be as much affected by age. Likewise, although a measure of primary memory (the digit span) did not seem to

account fully for the results, it might be that primary material for the actual sequence of moves in the problem would account for them.

It appears that there are individual differences in primary memory capacity, but it is not clear whether such differences represent a basic limitation. Alternatively, they might be the result of other sources of individual differences, such as differences in speed, in sustainable effort, or in effective practice with the material to be retained. To see the difficulty, consider the most commonly used test of primary memory, the digit span. In this task, the subject is given a list of digits at the rate of one digit per second (typically), and is asked to report them back immediately in order. The span is the longest list the subject can report without error. (The subject can get partial credit for reporting lists of a given length only some of the time.) Average span is seven. From the subject's point of view, the task is done almost entirely through use of primary memory; no effort is made to memorize the list for future recall.

There are objections to the view that individual differences in memory span are caused by differences in primary memory. Some objections have to do with details of the span task itself. For one thing, various recoding strategies seem to be used in the memory span task; for example, the number 1492, embedded in a sequence to be recalled, might stand out, and this sort of effect might occur more for some subjects than others. [However, Huttenlocher and Burke (1976) and Lyon (1977) present evidence that recoding differences do not account for span differences. In particular, span differences are unaffected by variations in the opportunity to use recoding strategies.] For another, maintenance of digits in memory seems to involve the use of an "articulatory loop" (Baddeley, 1976), and other similar systems (Reisberg et al., 1984), which do not seem to require effort and which therefore should not be counted as part of primary memory. Individuals may differ in the effectiveness of these loops. Finally, the span task may involve some use of secondary memory (Craik, 1976; again, however, evidence against this is that span does not seem to be affected by brain lesions that seriously disrupt secondary memory: see Baddeley, 1976).

Putting these objections aside, a different sort of difficulty comes from the possible effect of speed on primary memory. The relation between speed and span performance has received some attention. Baddeley, Thomson, and Buchanan (1975) have examined the effect of word length on the span for words, finding that this effect is best accounted for by the time taken to vocalize the words, a factor that can be unconfounded from other possible influences such as number of phonemes or number of syllables. Standing, Bond, Smith, and Isely (1980) followed up this work

by looking at speed of vocalization as a determinant of individual differences in span, and the effect of different kinds of materials (digits, letters, words) on span. Both effects were almost completely predicted by the speed of vocalization. To a first approximation, the span for a given individual, or for a given type of material, is determined entirely by the speed of vocalization. Roughly, the number of items that can be recalled is the number that can be vocalized in 2 seconds. There is, in addition, an apparent small effect of the size of the vocabulary used (10 for digits, 26 for letters, etc.).

The implication of these findings — if they are supported by subsequent research — is that it is speed, not effort, that accounts for the ability to use primary memory successfully. This would mean either that primary memory as I defined it does not exist — which seems unlikely because of the "directed forgetting" experiments I described — or that there are no consequential differences in sustainable effort that affect memory. By the definition I have given, differences in primary memory ought to result from differences in sustainable effort, so there may be no differences in that either. (Alternatively, the kind of effort involved in span tasks may differ from the kind of effort involved elsewhere.)

Secondary memory

The "ability to learn" has often been taken as roughly equivalent to intelligence itself, especially when "learn" is replaced with a more evaluative term such as "adapt." In my theory, the ability to learn plays several roles. First, it allows people to learn the rules of rational thinking, in particular, the setting of parameters in specific classes of situations. Thus, rationality in thinking is itself affected by (but, importantly, not determined by) the capacities involved in learning. Second, learning is needed to develop a stock of possibilities that serve as potential solutions to any problem in thinking, the knowledge of relationships between possibilities and evidence, and the general rules of inference required for using evidence. The more of these kinds of knowledge a person has, the more likely he is to complete an episode of thinking successfully and the more effective his thinking will be. Finally, many episodes of thinking are extended over time, or they involve the consideration of more elements than can be held in working memory; good thinking sometimes requires the ability to learn and recall the intermediate products of thinking itself. (Of course, external aids such as pencil and paper may be helpful as well.)

As I discussed in chapter 1, the ability to learn is not uniform or simple.

To a large extent, differences in the ability to learn seem to be the result of differences in use of strategies, rather than differences in biological limits. This is shown by two sorts of experiments. In one type, memory in a deficient group (e.g., young children, retardates) is improved by giving instructions in some useful strategy, such as rehearsal, or elaboration of the material to be learned. In another type, strategy use is held constant across different groups by presenting the material to be learned under incidental conditions, in which the subject does not know that memory will be tested. To make sure that subjects do the same things under these conditions, they are given an orienting task, something to do with the material. For example, if the material is a list of words, the subjects might be asked to read the words aloud as the orienting task, or to make some sort of decision about each word, such as whether it rhymes with "rain," or whether it is an animal. When different groups of subjects, which otherwise differ in learning ability, are given the same orienting task, group differences in recall are greatly reduced (Craik, 1976). Other strategies (less well identified) seem to be used at the time of retrieval. Although incidental retrieval tasks (such as free association to a stimulus that might evoke the to-be-remembered item) are rarely used, it has been found that some retrieval tasks are more sensitive than others to group differences. In particular, recognition, in which the subject indicates whether an item has been presented or not in the experiment, is less sensitive than recall, in which the subject must produce the item. When the use of an orienting task is combined with recognition measures, group differences in memory ability essentially disappear. Craik (1976) showed this for differences between young and old adults; Baron et al. (1980) found the same thing for differences in intelligence among adults of the same age. (In fact, in the latter study, the less intelligent adults performed better, but this difference disappeared when differences in effective word frequency were taken into account.)

These results suggest the following principle: There are no individual differences in limits concerned with secondary memory in its purest form; all individual differences in learning are the result of the use of strategies for learning or retrieval. This principle is consistent with other evidence (Ellis, 1970) that individual differences in rate of forgetting do not exist either. If there were differences in rate of forgetting, such differences would lead to differences in recall at least in experiments with long retention intervals. This is not to say that there are no biological limits that affect secondary memory. The ability to do the orienting tasks, to carry out the learning strategies quickly or easily might be affected by such

limits as those I have already discussed, such as speed or effort. But the limits on the tasks are not limits on secondary memory itself.

Probably this principle goes too far. For example, there is evidence that alcohol intoxication results in a secondary memory deficit even when the orienting task is held constant (Hartley, Birnbaum, & Parker, 1978). It is hard to imagine that there are not individual differences along the same dimension.

Another reason that the principle might be wrong is that there might be individual differences in abilities used only in more difficult tasks. One such ability, which might be very important, is one I have called "weak-cue retrieval." The usual test stimulus in a recognition experiment is a copy of the stimulus presented during learning, and the subject need only recall whether that stimulus was presented during an experiment. This copy is the strongest possible cue for the memory of its prior presentation. There might be special abilities that come into play during retrieval when the cue is less effective, when it is weaker. Paired-associate experiments may be thought of as using one type of weaker cue. As analyzed by Asch (1969) and others, a paired associate is essentially a single item or trace with two parts. When the first term of the item is presented, this evokes, or fails to evoke, the memory of the whole, which is then completed or not in order for the rest of it to be recalled. At the time of learning, different parts of the trace may acquire different salience as retrieval cues; in general, when the subject expects one word to be the cue, he will do something (the nature of which is unknown) to make that a more salient part of the trace. Individual differences typically occur in paired-associate retrieval even if they do not appear in recognition. Thus, there might be special abilities involved in evocation of a whole by a part, or in completing the whole. (The former ability would be tested simply by asking the subject whether there was an item in the list containing a given part, without asking what the other parts of that item were.) On the other hand, apparent individual differences in retrieval in such situations might be the result of differences in strategies rather than biological limits.

A type of weak cue that is of some interest is one that is not a natural part of a stimulus as perceived at the time of learning. Such cues are provided routinely in crossword puzzles. For example, a word might be some of its letters, or the completion of a compound word of which the target word is a part. Baron et al. (1980) showed that the ability to use such cues correlated with intelligence, even when learning occurred under incidental instructions. In the task used, the subject was given only the

first and last couple of letters of the target words (e.g., C-------A for California), and was asked whether a word that fit this frame had occurred in the list of words presented earlier. This procedure, like the usual recognition procedure, did not require the subject to fill in the word; however, subjects were also asked to fill in any words they could, and the more intelligent subjects were differentially prone to fill in words that had been presented as opposed to words that had not.

If there is an ability to use weak cues, it is especially useful in the phase of thinking concerned with generation of possibilities. This phase is an important limit on performance in insight problems, as well as other kinds of thinking. This kind of limit may affect thinking even when the possibilities to be considered are not simply memory traces, but rather something more like constructions or inventions. Constructions are never completely new (Fodor, 1975), but must be composed, in some way, out of elements already available, which are memory traces in the most general sense of that term. (Innate beliefs, if they exist, must be available in the way that memory traces are available if they are useful in thinking; I thus use the term "trace" to include innately held propositions.) Bregman (1977) discusses the way in which "ideals" may be composed in cognitive processes and perception. Bregman's principles of composition and transformation may be applied to the generation of possibilities out of traces. Thus, a possibility, as represented in thinking, is sometimes a composition of several traces, which are transformed before being composed together; some transformations involve being put into relationships with other traces. For example, a melody, when thought of by a composer, is a composition of certain intervals, rhythmic and melodic patterns, and harmonic sequences, each transposed (or instantiated) so as to fit in with the attributes of the other traces. In such cases, the retrieval cue for each trace is just the requirement that it, in composition with other traces, serve as a possibility in the situation at hand. When the composition arrives in consciousness all at once, this process is rather mysterious.

The ability to retrieve traces with such weak cues as these might not be a basic ability. Apparent individual differences in such an ability might be the result of differences in knowledge. Those who are better at weak-cue retrieval might have different kinds of traces, perhaps more general ones, or ones that are more finely articulated into parts, or ones with some other property that makes them more retrievable with weak cues. Or, even if there are individual differences in weak-cue retrieval with the nature of the traces held constant, this ability might require effort, and the apparent differences might be a consequence of differences in effort. These possibilities are open to empirical investigation.

General comments on the separation of limits

The limits involved in the storage and retrieval of memories have not yet been distinguished from other limits, such as speed and sustainable effort. This has two implications for current work concerning the relation between intelligence and the parameters of information processing (e.g., Keating & Bobbitt, 1978; Hunt, 1982; Sternberg & Gardner, 1983). First, those studies that have directly investigated the kinds of limits discussed here cannot be taken as conclusive in showing individual differences in these limits (in specific tasks or in general), for apparent differences may be explained in terms of other limits that are not controlled (or even, quite often, in terms of measurement artifacts of the sort discussed by Baron & Treiman, 1980). Second, there are several studies in this tradition that concern themselves with several different speed parameters, such as speed of encoding, speed of memory search, speed of comparison in induction problems, and speed of memory access. These parameters are assumed to characterize specific stages of information-processing tasks. It is assumed that these parameters will show substantial cross-task generality, whereas other classifications of speed measures (e.g., by content) will not. (This assumption is practically never tested directly; Chiang & Atkinson, 1976, come closest.) The implication of the current analysis for these studies is that these speed measures, too, may be affected by other variables, such as effort, and benefit from practice. Even cross-task consistencies in the apparent speed of a processing stage could be the result of consistencies in the effort requirements of that stage.

A sensible goal for an information-processing theory of capacities would be a classification of basic abilities, of the sort the factor analysts tried to develop. This seems to be what Sternberg and Gardner (1983) are after, for example, when they propose that performance on inductive tasks can be accounted for in terms of speed parameters for the processing stages of those tasks: encoding, inference, mapping, etc. However, achievement of this goal will be difficult until the problems I have raised here have been solved (see also Neisser, 1983). Aside from these problems, there is little reason to be optimistic about the achievement of this goal. What reason is there to think, for example, that speed of encoding would be a general parameter showing cross-task consistency? Encoding of different stimuli involves different sensory and perceptual systems and draws on different kinds of perceptual learning. Nor do processing stages seem to correspond to subdivisions of the nervous system, or anything else that might lead to discrete subdivisions of mental processes. It is conceivable that the search for orderliness in the study of intelligence will

be more successful in the study of the dispositions of thinking—however messy that investigation might appear to be—than in the study of basic capacities and limits.

Abstracting and using rules and schemata

The theory described in this book is not intended as a complete theory of thinking. Rather, as I have emphasized, it is a theory concerned with the rational control of thinking, and deviations from optimal control, taking knowledge and capacities as given. If the theory were to be made into a more complete theory, it is obvious that a tremendous explanatory burden would be placed on knowledge. A complete theory of intelligence as effective rationality would also draw heavily on knowledge as an explanation. This is especially true if we are trying to account for the difference between obviously great thinkers, such as Einstein, and the rest of humanity. Based on present evidence, it seems unlikely that such geniuses differ from other people in the kinds of capacities or biological limits that I have been discussing so far in this chapter. Surely, Shakespeare, Newton, and Einstein had above average speed, primary memory capacity, mental energy, ability to store things in secondary memory, and so on, to the extent each of these is meaningful to talk about. (Even this might not be true: Handel and Pasteur did some of their best work after suffering strokes, a condition likely to affect many of the limits I have discussed.) But there are many people who have apparently even more unusual mental capacities who are not geniuses except in the sense of having unusual capacity. The most astounding example is Luria's (1965/1968) mnemonist, who despite his incredible memory seems to have lived a very limited life. A mnemonist studied by Hunt and Love (1972) also lived a rather ordinary life, although he was an excellent chess player. (One exception is the mathematician A. C. Aitken, whose contributions to his field were substantial, and who had both an unusual memory and an unusual ability to do mental calculation; see Hunter, 1977; also Neisser, 1982, for other cases). But basically, it seems clear that if we are looking for the "secret of genius," we must look elsewhere than in biological limits.

Nor should we expect to find the secret in the kind of rational thinking I have described, for several reasons. First, I have defined good thinking in a way that will be independent of capacities and specific knowledge. There ought to be many relatively rational thinkers whose capacities and limited knowledge prevent them from achieving much in intellectual domains, although they may be appreciated for their "common sense."

Also, great intellectual achievement may require rational thinking only in a very limited domain. (Recall that I never insisted that rational thinking need be general, unless it is effectively taught that way.) In other cases, achievements in arts and even in sciences may require something more like luck and blind persistence than good thinking. The public pronouncements of Nobel Prize winners on matters outside their fields seem to vary enormously in the extent to which rational thinking was involved, insofar as one can judge this.

It might be said that the secret is in motivation, and this makes a certain amount of sense. Indeed, Perkins (1981) has argued that the motivation to do creative work is the major determinant of creative accomplishment and that there is no special *kind* of thinking that should be called creative. But the will to be effective in one's intellectual work is not enough, as any novice will tell you. Motivation is important in part because it leads to knowledge, and without extensive knowledge, the most rational and highly motivated thinking is usually ineffective. Knowledge is also very likely a powerful determinant of effectiveness in more mundane situations, such as deciding what kind of car to buy or which candidate to vote for. But what sort of knowledge? How should we speak about knowledge in a way that makes our discussion relevant to the present analysis?

There are several ways in which the structure of knowledge may be analyzed: memory traces, associations, labeled associations, concepts, schemata, and surely others. Traces and associations are simple records of experience, the sorts of units we need when discussing the kinds of capacities I have just described. The other kinds of units are more derived, more oriented toward function rather than toward a theory of basic mental capacities. It is no coincidence that the study of these more derived units has been inspired by the study of artificial intelligence. If one is trying to get a computer to think in some useful way, one does not get far with associations or traces, unless one is willing to try to organize these lower-level units into higher-level ones. I regard these as different kinds of descriptions, different methods of analysis, rather than as mutually exclusive theories (as does Estes, 1976). A major task of cognitive psychology, ultimately, is to show how the higher-level descriptions are derived from the lower-level ones, what sorts of rules and constraints are involved, and so on. Fortunately, this is not my problem here, and I need not await its solution to proceed on the assumption that it will eventually be solved.

Of the higher-level descriptions, one of the most useful is the idea of the schema, which I take to be essentially identical to what is called a "frame" (Minsky, 1975) or a mental model (Stevens & Collins, 1980).

Although this idea has a long history (see Bartlett, 1932), I take the essence of it to be as follows. A schema is something like an abstract description of a class of situations. It can have "structure," in the sense that it need not be a simple list of attributes or properties. For example, it can describe the situations in question in terms of parts and subparts, temporal relations, causal connections, and so on. In principle, there is no reason to exclude from our definition of a schema any sort of relationship that can be used in any description that can be given in language. (In practice, it may turn out that there are limits of some sort.) A schema is usually incomplete as a description of any particular situation. (In this way, a schema differs from a prototype, which is a complete description of a typical member of a class of situations.) It contains "slots" to be filled in, in order to make the description complete. Other parts of the schema may be removable or replaceable in the course of making the description specific. A replaceable part may be called a "default value," or an implicit assumption.

The most common example of a schema in the literature is that for "going to a restaurant." It is a series of subevents in temporal order: being seated, ordering, eating, paying. Each of these is subdivided in turn; for example, eating is subdivided into courses, as is ordering. The description of a particular trip to a particular restaurant would have to have a number of slots filled in: the dishes ordered, the prices paid, and so on. Also, parts of the schema may be optional; for example, being seated and ordering may be omitted when the restaurant is a cafeteria.

Collins, Brown, and Larkin (1980) provide an example of the use of schemata in reading comprehension. As you read the following passage, stop and think after each sentence: "He plunked down $5 at the window. She tried to give him $2.50 but he refused to take it. So when they got inside she bought him a large bag of popcorn." According to Collins et al., the process of understanding is a matter of finding a schema that applies and filling in the slots. The first sentence, for most readers, triggers the schema of a racetrack, a store, or a bank. The second sentence must then be fit into that schema. The first clause is easy enough, for it may be thought of as "change," part of the schema of buying something or placing a bet. But the second cannot be easily fit. By the third sentence, the whole schema is replaced with a more suitable one, the schema of a date.

In terms of my analysis, schemata are possibilities that may be accepted or rejected by thinking, as in this example. Subepisodes of thinking are also involved in filling slots of a given schema, or in eliminating unnecessary parts; these activities may be seen as revisions of a single schema.

Schemata can direct the search for evidence in two ways. First, the schema is usually suggested by a single part, so one kind of question is whether another part is present. There are of course many parts one could look for, at first, and the search might be focused more effectively if there are two schemata under consideraton. Second, a thinker could search for evidence about the contents of an empty slot. This kind of question can lead to modificaton of the possibility as well as its acceptance or rejection. Different parts of a schema might be differentially relevant to its adequacy as a possibility. For example, acceptance of change is nearly essential for the schema of paying for something. (Subsidiary schemata may be invoked to reconcile inconsistencies, for example, the schema of an error, which is still inconsistent with simple refusal.) The relevance of a part would yield a weight of evidence, and would thus permit revision of the strength assigned to the possibility as a whole. Filling in of slots would also lead to a very simple sort of revision.

The essential point of the schema for my purposes is that it removes (or at least moves) the mystery of "how does the thinker know what questions to ask and how to use the evidence he gets?" The answer is that the possibility itself, in the form of a schema, supplies this knowledge.

In some cases, a thinker may need special strategies for the use of schemata as guides to thinking. That is, in a particular domain, there may be some general principles that can be applied to particular schemata so that the schemata can be used effectively as guides to asking questons and revising strengths. There are also likely to be general strategies, which apply across domains, for the use of schemata to formulate questions. Possible examples are: Ask about critical parts first; ask about parts that distinguish two schemata under consideration; and so on. Teaching such strategies might be one way to make people think more rationally and more effectively (chapter 7).

The use of schemata in the way I have suggested points out some parallels between the present theory and some other theories in cognitive psychology, particularly those of Bruner (1957), Rumelhart (1977), and Adams and Collins (1979). (Bruner used a somewhat different terminology, but his theory is equivalent to the others for present purposes.) By these accounts, such processes as recognition of words or construction of meanings in reading or listening proceed through activation of schemata by parts of the text (e.g., letters) and by evaluation of these schemata through directed search for evidence concerning slots whose content is not yet known with certainty. This search may be directed by a single possibility or by several possibilities.

One difference between these theories and mine is that most other the-

ories do not concern themselves with prescriptive questions. A second difference is that they make no distinction between processes that are conscious and intentional, on the one hand, and those that are unconscious and automatic, on the other. My own theory is specifically about the former, which are the ones most under a person's control, and hence those most easily affected (I assume) by instruction. The tradition I refer to, especially as expounded by Rumelhart, tends to support the view that unconscious processes of recognition, such as those used to recognize printed words, involve what is essentially thinking except for its automaticity. I have argued (Baron, 1977) that it is quite hard to obtain evidence for such a view, and I still know of none. However, if this view is correct, then we might go on to ask whether these unconscious processes are in fact the residues of what were once actual episodes of conscious thinking, practiced so often that they have become fast and automatic.

Acquisition of schemata

If schemata are so important in thinking, then the ability to acquire them must be an important determinant of effective rationality. Schemata may be acquired through thinking, in a self-conscious way. The learner may set about evaluation of possible schemata for a certain kind of situation. This may, for example, occur in school learning, when a student is trying to understand a new "concept," which often takes the form of a schema. Thinking may be used either to abstract the schema from a series of instances, as one might do for the concept of a "proof" in mathematics, or to understand a definition provided by a teacher or text. In such cases of conscious acquisition, schema acquisition is a particular form of thinking, and nothing special need be said here about the abilities required for this kind of thinking as opposed to other kinds.

More interestingly, schemata may, apparently, be acquired "tacitly" (Polanyi, 1958) or "implicitly" (Reber, 1976). In such cases, there is no special effort directed at the formaton of the schema. Although the learner may be trying to achieve other ends while being exposed to instances of a schema, any schema acquisition that occurs is incidental to his other goals. Yet, the learner behaves as if a schema were formed, for he can respond to novel stimuli in a way that conforms to the schema the experimenter has tried to teach (Evans, 1967; Posner & Keele, 1968; Reber, 1976). For example, Reber found that subjects asked to memorize, or simply scan, consonant strings that followed certain rules about which letters could follow other letters could subsequently classify new strings as following the rule or not.

Recently, it has been suggested that this behavior need not require a memory representation of the schema itself (Brooks, 1978; Baron, 1977; Medin & Schaffer, 1978). Rather, transfer to new instances occurs by generalizing from the memory of specific examples. This may occur consciously at the time the subject responds to new stimuli. For example, a new letter string might remind the subject of a string he remembers, and the subject might therefore conclude that the new string follows the rule. A number of different kinds of support for this view have been provided in the papers cited, and to my knowledge there is no convincing evidence of any other mechanism for implicit learning of schemata or rules.

Note that transfer on the basis of similarity to memories of examples can occur in principle even when the subject is unaware of the precise item to which a new item is similar. Further, transfer may be based on several items rather than just one (Baron & Hodge, 1978). These are arguments in principle; as yet, there is no direct evidence for this sort of basis of transfer.

If apparent implicit learning never involves a representation of the schema itself (as opposed to specific instances or fragments of instances), this does not imply that it is useless to speak of schemata. Even by this account, transfer to new instances occurs, and this is the essential role of schemata in our theory. We simply need to be on our guard against assuming that schemata actually exist in the head, in the same way that memory traces are thought to exist there.

However, this analysis does suggest that there are no special abilities involved in implicit schema abstraction, beyond those we have already discussed, in particular, the capacity to store traces in secondary memory, the capacity to retrieve those traces, and, perhaps most crucially, the capacity to retrieve the traces on the basis of relatively weak cues. In this case, the weak cues are just the new items, which must evoke somewhat dissimilar traces in order to be classified correctly, that is, in order to do what we would call "evoking the relevant schema."

The memory system required for thinking

In chapter 3, I have suggested three search processes and one inference process that constitute thinking. The search processes involve search for possibilities, evidence, and goals. The inference process involves use of evidence to change the strengths of possibilities. In this section, I ask what sort of memory system is required for these processes to operate. In the next section, I ask what sort of memory system would permit these processes to work most effectively. These sections might thus be con-

sidered as a sketch of a theory of the memory substrate of successful thinking, and the relation of successful thinking to knowledge in general.

By "memory system" I mean a type of organization of information, plus a set of methods for retrieving or accessing that information when it is needed. Information may, of course, be represented in many ways, e.g., photographic records, associations, feature lists, feature sets, complex descriptions (including schemata), or even procedures. Many of these types may be required for different kinds of thinking, and it is therefore probably fruitless at this point to try to propose limits on the kinds of information used. Thus, I shall adopt the most neutral term I know for units of information, "knowlege structures," or KSs, for short (following Davis & Lenat, 1982). I adopt this term for continuity with past literature, despite its implicit and unwarranted assumption that all information in memory is knowledge (an assumption that would seem to disallow false beliefs). I shall also speak of retrieval cues, which are other units of information used to retrieve, activate, or access KSs, that is, to bring KSs to bear on a particular task.

What sort of retrieval cues are used for each process of thinking? Let us begin with search for possibilities. In general, when we search for possibilities, we use some or all of the following cues:

1. Goals — the possibility must be a candidate to satisfy the goals in operation.
2. Evidence — the possibility should, if possible, be consistent with available evidence.
3. Other possibilities — the possibility retrieved must be new, and, in some cases, we may want it to be like or unlike some possibility already retrieved.

Of interest here (and elsewhere) is the fact that we search for possibilities with several different cues. There are three ways we can use multiple cues.

First, our memory could be organized so that there are direct associations between KSs and *sets* of multiple cues. For example, we might have a rule of the sort, "When you have already thought of ulcers and gallstones, and when there is no association of pain with eating, think about cancer." If we relied entirely on such rules, we would have to know a tremendous number of them, and a great burden would be placed on our ability to learn them and to construct them from information we have learned.

Second, we could use a single cue as a basis for search, and we could use the other cues as ways of evaluating each KS retrieved. For example, we could search for diseases consistent with stomach pain, and then ask, for each disease retrieved, whether we had thought of it already, whether

it is consistent with the evidence we have, and so on. Of course, we could use this method as a backup for the first.

Third, we could have a memory system that allows us to use all cues simultaneously, even when no prior association exists between the set of cues we have and the relevant KSs. Instead, all we would require is that each retrieval cue be capable of increasing the chance that a relevant KS would be retrieved, regardless of whatever other cues were present. Later, I shall argue that this third method makes the whole system most effective.

The following retrieval cues are used to retrieve evidence from memory:

1. Other evidence — we do not want to think of the same evidence over and over, and we may want to retrieve evidence that is consistent with evidence already at hand
2. Possibilities
3. Goals

The last two factors may operate in complex ways. In simple cases, each possibility under consideration may evoke evidence consistent with itself. However, in some cases, we may want to search for evidence that is inconsistent with a possibility, as in searching for counterexamples. Or we may want to retrieve evidence that distinguishes various possibilities from one another, so that the evidence is consistent with one possibility and inconsistent with another. For example, we may want to ask a patient a question such that one answer would be most consistent with ulcers and another answer most consistent with gallstones. The same three retrieval mechanisms seem to be possible here as in the case of search for possibilities.

The relation between goals and evidence is complex in a different way. The goal does not act directly as a cue, but only through possibilities. Thus, we often seek evidence that will bear on the suitability of a particular possibility for a particular goal. In making decisions about courses of action, for example, we try to imagine whether a given plan will achieve a certain goal. I find myself unable to think of a case in which we do this with complete flexibility, so I am inclined to think that the mechanisms for use of goals are limited to the following. First, possibilities might be represented differently depending on the goal in effect. Second, the retrieval of evidence might occur through a subepisode of thinking, in which the thinker constructs a model (mental or otherwise) of the situation and runs the model through. For example, in trying to determine whether a certain plan will reach a certain goal, the thinker imagines the plan being carried through, and observes what happens.

The following retrieval cues are used to search for goals:

1. Possibilities. A possibility can activate goals that it achieves.
2. Goals. A goal can act as a retrieval cue for subgoals or superordinate goals (e.g., other parts of a plan).

In both of these cases, the link is fairly direct, and no use of multiple cues need be assumed. However, it is worthy of note that the first type of retrieval cue works exactly backward from the use of goals to retrieve possibilities, as described above. If we learn one-directional associations between possibilities and goals, we would have to use different associations to retrieve goals (given possibilities) and to retrieve possibilities (given goals). If, on the other hand, we can use associations bidirectionally, once they are learned, the same learning would serve both functions. Asch and Ebenholz (1962) have in fact claimed that such backward associations are normally available, although Waugh (1970) has shown that the effect of practice on speed of retrieval may be in one direction only. The fact that retardates are somewhat deficient in backward association (Baumeister, Kellas, & Gordon, 1970) suggests that the issue is not fully resolved; some of the effect found by Asch and Ebenholz may be the result of search strategies. However this issue is resolved, use of backward associations between goals and possibilities puts a smaller burden on learning, and makes the whole system more effective.

The fourth process of thinking is the use of evidence to modify the strength of possibilities. I suspect that retrieval is not an issue here. Typically, the impact of evidence may be assessed directly, by reading off from the KS that is the possibility. For example, if "ulcers" is a KS, this KS will have attached to it a list of symptoms and test results associated with ulcers. If one of these symptoms is found, the strength of this possibility is increased; if it is sought and not found, the strength is decreased. In other cases, more complex inference rules may be needed, but these are stored as general inference-making procedures (see chapter 3), which are retrieved automatically as part of the thinking episode. It is noteworthy that the possibility KSs must sometimes—by this account—contain information about evidence consistent or inconsistent with the possibility. This places constraints on the form of these KSs; for example, unitary images or even simple associations will not do. (In other cases, as in artistic work, this does not apply. As noted in chapter 3, the possibility is identical to the evidence for or against it, in many cases.)

There is one further complication. I have spoken so far as if possibilities, evidence, and goals were all unitary KSs that could be retrieved and used intact. However, as I have noted earlier in this chapter, it is often the case that one of these elements is a combination or composition of two or more KSs. Poets do not seek individual words or previously used

phrases, but, rather, combinations of words. And they do not seek single goals, but rather complex themes that the words of a poem are supposed to express. Likewise, in philosophical argument, a piece of evidence is rarely a single fact, but it is usually a complex argument put together out of several individual KSs.

How are these complexes created? One possibility is that they are constructed by subepisodes of thinking involving trial and error. For example, in reflective thinking, we typically modify a weakened possibility by changing it rather than by replacing it completely (although we do that too). Additions may actually be retrieved as individual KSs, even though the modified possibility that results was never previously stored as a single KS. Another possibility is that we retrieve complexes in one step. For example, we could ask our memory for a pair of household objects that could be used to make a pencil sharpener, and both objects could enter our mind at once. Such retrieval, like retrieval with multiple cues, may be unreliable. (If it were completely reliable, creative tasks would not be so difficult.) However, it may be a useful mechanism nonetheless. My hunch is that it does not occur, for my introspection tells me that such retrieval occurs either by rule (as when we pick a set of words to express an idea in everyday speech) or in steps. For example, in the case of the pencil sharpener, I first thought of a knife as a blade, and then thought of a clamp to hold the knife. Introspection, however, is probably not a good method for finding out what retrieval mechanisms are used, and it would seem that further experimental work is needed here.

The memory system it would be nice to have

I have already hinted at the additional power that may be obtained from some retrieval mechanisms. In this section, I elaborate these suggestions in the form of a proposal about the kind of memory system that would make thinking most effective. Any elements of this proposal that are correct may suggest individual differences, but I shall not concentrate on these here.

In making this proposal, I shall assume that KSs have at least certain properties. These are essentially the properties of what are called records in computer programs and database systems. An example of a record is all the information about a single person in a personnel file. A record is usually divided into fields, such as the person's name, ID number, etc. Some of these fields may function as pointers to other records; for example, if the person is an employee, one field might contain the name of his supervisor, and another field might contain a list of his subordinates

(or a pointer to such a list). The function of each field is easily identified. For example, the supervisor field might be written as "Supervisor: Bill Jones."

Note that this outline is simply to set up a language for discussing certain issues. It places very few constraints on anything else. A simple association may be stored as a record with two fields, e.g., stimulus and response. This outline is also compatible with much more specific systems, such as the sort of production system used in a great deal of recent work on problem solving and skill (Newell & Simon, 1972; Anderson, 1981). In a production system, each record has two subdivisions, called condition and action. The action usually involves adding or removing some symbol from a structure called working memory. In the simplest production systems, a test is made to find out whether the condition of a production matches the contents of working memory, and if it does, the action is taken. A production is thus a type of rule that can be used in tasks of different kinds.

One issue in memory structure concerns the necessity of *key fields* in retrieval. If key fields are necessary, then only certain fields of the record can be used to retrieve the record directly, and these fields are somehow specified at the time that memories are acquired. For example, in a card catalog in a library, the (equivalent of) key fields are book title, author, and, in some files, subject. If you want a book with a certain number of pages or a certain publication date, you have to search through the records until you find one; there is no key field for this information, no catalog organized by size or date. However, size and date are parts of every record, and they may be read off immediately once a record is found.

When I say that a record may be accessed directly by its key field, I am somewhat oversimplifying the actual situation, in computers and probably in human memory as well. What actually occurs is a very fast search process, one that is largely independent of the number of items in the file and hence essentially "parallel." Analogously, when we know the author and title of a book we want, this allows us to use a simplified search procedure based on our knowledge of the alphabet. This procedure is much faster than searching through a randomly arranged card catalog would be. Thus, what is crucial is not that access is "immediate" but rather that a special method of access may be used if the key field is known.

Furthermore, it is also reasonable to assume that key fields may differ in their speed and reliability. For example (and perhaps extending the library analogy too far), it may take longer to search by author than by

title, and books might not be listed at all under the appropriate subject heading. Thus, whether key fields are required or not, some cues will be better than others. The question of whether key fields are necessary comes down to the question of whether we must fall back on some sort of blind search when a key field of some utility (however small) has not been created at the time of acquisition. Thus, when I say that "key fields are not necessary," I mean that *any* field of a record may be used to retrieve that record directly (i.e., without blind search based on other fields) with some positive probability of success.

Note that production systems, in their simplest form, do assume the necessity of key fields. Typically, the entire condition serves as a key field; it must match some of the contents of working memory exactly for the production to be evoked. Many writers on human memory, particularly Tulving (1974), seem to be advocating something like the view that key fields are used in human memory. In particular, Tulving suggests that a memory trace cannot be retrieved unless the retrieval cue matches a cue that has been specified at the time of encoding (acquisition). This is one interpretation of his "principle of encoding specificity."

The work of Asch and Ebenholz, cited above, seems inconsistent with Tulving's view. When subjects are taught a list of paired associates with the expectation that they will be given the stimulus term and asked for the response term of each, they do just as well at recalling the stimulus, given the response, provided that the stimuli and responses have been equally well learned as sets. The simplest interpretation of the principle of encoding specificity would seem to hold that the stimulus term would function as a key field, so that backward recall without search would be impossible. (The issue is still open, however, because use of backward associations could involve the use of special search strategies, as noted above. Further, the conditions of learning in the experiments might serve to create two key fields for each stimulus — although here we would be led to ask whether there were any conditions that would not do this, in which case the issue would be essentially decided in favor of the view that key fields are unnecessary.)

A second issue concerns summation of activation. If a record has more than one key field, or if it can be evoked by fields not previously designated as key fields (as we assume), we can ask what happens when two fields are used instead of one at the time of retrieval. Is the probability (or speed) of direct retrieval greater when we know the size and the date of a book than when we know one or the other? If so, how much greater? Is the probability of retrieval (by a given time) simply what would be expected if two independent records were involved, or is there some

summation of activation from different cues? To address this question, McLeod, Williams, and Broadbent (1971) had subjects learn two paired-associate lists with the same responses, but different stimuli. When both stimuli associated with a given response were presented together, recall was more likely than would be predicted on the basis of independent traces. Thus, it seems plausible that summation of activation occurs. Note once again that it does not occur in simple production systems, for the simple reason that the full condition is required for any activation at all. (However, summation is used freely in many expert computer systems, such as that of Weiss, Kulikowski, Amarel, & Safir, 1978.)

A third issue concerns spreading activation, or indirect activation of KSs. Suppose that KS-1 has a pointer to KS-2. If we present cue A, which corresponds to a field of KS-1 but not to any field of KS-2, will the activation spread to KS-2? As argued by Collins and Loftus (1975), it is hard to account for many of the things we can do without assuming spreading activation. However, to my knowledge, nobody has shown that such an assumption is required to account for our memory abilities.

A fourth issue concerns the ability of the system to carry on two searches in parallel. For example, when searching for evidence, can it search for symptoms consistent with ulcers and inconsistent with gallstones, and symptoms inconsistent with ulcers and consistent with gallstones, both at the same time? Or, if it tries to do so, will it behave as if there were one single set of retrieval cues, so that it retrieves symptoms consistent with both or inconsistent with both as well? In another case, suppose an artist is searching for possibilities and goals at the same time. If this could be done, each possibility activated by this search might also activate—by spreading activation—goals it was consistent with. Because there is a simultaneous search for goals, these goals might also be activated by this search, and the summation of activation would help bring them into awareness. The goals, in turn, would also activate the possibilities that achieved them. In this way, with spreading activation, summation of activation, and parallel search, a person could direct retrieval, with some success, at *combinations* of possibilities and goals, which, to an artist, are the essential bright ideas.

Note that the present question of parallel search is distinct from the question of whether records can be searched in parallel. I have already noted that, by definition, the latter sort of parallel search is possible with key fields, and (possibly fallible) parallel search is also possible with other fields, if key fields are not required. What is at issue here is whether two search instructions can be obeyed in parallel.

I know of no evidence concerning whether parallel search is possible.

In sum, a charitable set of assumptions about our memory is that it does not require key fields (i.e., a KS may be accessed directly by any field with some probability), it can use summation of activation, it can use spreading activation, and it can carry on separate searches in parallel. I now move on to consider and review the advantages of such a system, given the assumptions about thinking made in the last section.

The main advantage of the type of system proposed is that it will allow the use of multiple simultaneous cues, without involving any special learning process relevant to those cues. For example, in thinking of possible diseases, a system like this need have only a record for each disease, containing its symptoms as fields. Given any set of symptoms, the diseases likely to produce those symptoms will be (probabilistically) retrieved. Because of summation of activation, the more relevant symptoms there are, the more likely a disease will be retrieved. Because key fields are not required, this system will work (to some extent) even if the learning was all in the other direction; it is as if the system were a "student" who learned to respond with symptoms when given the name of a disease. (If Asch and Ebenholz are correct about backward associations, it should work as well this way as the reverse, provided the diseases are themselves well learned as possible responses.) Without these properties, the student might have to learn to think of a disease given any good-sized subset of its symptoms. (This need not require separate learning trials. We could imagine a device that would build new records, or create key fields, during the time of learning. But this device would have to display some intelligence in anticipating what cues would later be used. Note also that there might be intermediate systems. For example, we might imagine that the entire set of symptoms functions as a single key field, but partial matches create partial activation. In this case, different symptoms would have to be learned together as a unit. The idea of activation from partial matches would then play the same role as summation of activation.)

Furthermore, suppose that our "student" learned about diseases only in terms of their underlying symptoms as distinct from their observed ones. For example, he might learn that certain heart diseases cause insufficient blood flow to the extremities. Later, in a separate lesson, he might learn the signs of insufficient blood flow. Spreading activation will then allow him to use these signs as cues for the disease itself. A sign or set of signs will activate the record for the underlying symptom, which will, in turn, activate the record for the disease. Of course, this might occur as a two-step process even without spreading activation. The need for spreading activation could also be circumvented if the student anticipated such

cases, and added observed-symptom fields to his disease records at the time of learning. But there may well be cases in which neither of these ways of bypassing spreading activation is practical.

All of these mechanisms may also be of use for the other two search proceses, search for evidence and goals. I have already pointed out the advantage of parallel search in retrieving evidence, and in the simultaneous discovery of possibilities and goals.

A final example of the advantages of the system proposed concerns its ability to learn from exemplars. Suppose our hypothetical medical student is never taught which symptoms are associated with which diseases, etc., but rather learns on the job from individual cases. (Some of this surely happens, if not in medicine, then elsewhere.) The records stored in memory are thus records of individual cases. Nothing corresponds to rules of the sort, "If these symptoms, consider this disease," or, "If this disease, expect these symptoms." However, each record does have a field for the disease and one for each symptom. We might further assume that there is a record for the disease name itself, and the disease field for each patient is in fact a pointer to that record. Now suppose we are given a new patient with certain symptoms. This patient will "remind" us of other patients with similar symptoms. That is, their records will be activated. By spreading activation, these records, in turn, will activate the diseases that these patients have had. The strength of activation of each disease will be affected by the similarity between the present case and patients with that disease, and by the number of patients with similar symptom sets. Possible diseases will then come to mind that actually do correspond to the given symptoms, even though no direct rules have been learned corresponding to those symptoms. Brooks (1978) and Medin and Shaffer (1978) have shown that something like this kind of retrieval does occur in a number of categorization tasks, and Brooks has argued convincingly that retrieval of this sort plays a large role in expert knowledge.

Once again in this case, we see a tradeoff between the power of the retrieval system and the burden placed on the learning system. In the absence of summation of cues (symptoms) and spreading activation, rules must be induced from exemplars at the time of learning. As noted, Brooks and others have shown that this does not occur in some cases, and this provides some evidence for the system suggested here.

I have tried in these last two sections to provide a general framework for asking questions about the relation between memory and thinking tasks. I have also suggested that thinking would work best with a very powerful retrieval system, which does not require key fields, which can use summation of activation and spreading activation, and which can

carry out simultaneous searches. Thinking, in general, allows us to compensate somewhat for incompleteness of learning (a state we must live with, for we cannot learn to anticipate every situation we shall encounter), and when the retrieval system it uses is powerful, the burden placed on learning is even lighter. Furthermore, whatever retrieval mechanisms are available, it seems likely that individual differences in their operation will lead to individual differences in the effectiveness of thinking. The study of retrieval mechanisms, and individual differences in them, seems to be a prime candidate for further work.

6 Effects of rational thinking on the individual and society

I have argued that intelligence consists in part of a disposition to follow the rules of good thinking and to avoid the biases that often interfere with such conduct. In this chapter, I ask, what is the good of being rational in this way? This question is necessary as a justification of any attempt to teach people to think more rationally (chapter 7). There are three answers. First, rationality is good because it can be expected to increase individual happiness or fulfillment. Second, rationality makes for effectiveness, in the sense of chapter 1, that is, success at achieving rationally chosen goals. This must be shown in order to complete the argument that rationality is part of intelligence. Third, I argue that rationality has a kind of external justification, in particular, a moral one, of the same sort that other moral traits such as honesty might have.

Rationality and happiness

People who are healthy, wealthy, and wise are not necessarily happy as well, but it helps; few would trade their wealth and learning for the supposed bliss of the ignorant and poor. Health, wealth, and knowledge can be thought of as "primary goods" (Rawls, 1971), which would help anyone achieve his goals, no matter what those goals might be. The relation between rationality and happiness is of a similar sort. In particular, rationality in making decisions and plans can be defined as the following of rules that are likely to lead to consequences that would be desired on reflection (chapter 1). A good definition of happiness, in turn, is the achievement of just these consequences, or, more precisely, the successful pursuit of a plan that is expected to lead to them (chapter 2). If the world is at all predictable, rational plans and decisions will, on the average, lead to better outcomes in this sense than will irrational ones. Luck, of course, may still intervene; a person might make the best decisions possible, but still be unhappy because things turned out badly (or because

she was born in an unfortunate time or place, or with a handicap). The very idea that luck is a determinant of happiness in life, which it surely is, is in part a way of accounting for the lack of complete correspondence between rationality of decisions and goodness of outcomes.

We all know people who seem to ruin their lives, to varying degrees, by making the wrong decisions or plans, or by being reliably poor decision makers in general. We hesitate to say that such people are irrational, because we know of the danger of making judgments in hindsight, and we know of the effect of luck on the outcomes of perfectly rational decisions. However, the fact that any particular outcome can be ascribed to bad luck (or good luck) does not imply that rationality is everywhere irrelevant. Whatever skepticism we might have about the *extent* to which rational thinking matters, it would be extremely radical to claim that it has no effect at all.

Rationality concerns beliefs as well as decisions. Rational beliefs are those whose strength is in proportion to the evidence available. One way of arguing for the relation between happiness and rationality of belief is to argue (as in chapter 2) that rationally held beliefs are required for effective decisions. Indeed (as pointed out to me by John Sabini), a creature that did not act on its beliefs could not be properly said to have beliefs at all. We can, of course, judge the rationality of a decision, given the beliefs the decision maker holds. From this perspective, a decision may be rational even if it is based on irrationally held beliefs. However, if such a decision turns out well, it seems appropriate to attribute it to luck rather than rationality. If the decision had been based on rationally held beliefs, it might have been different. Other things equal, if we are in control of our beliefs, we would surely want them to be rational rather than related to the evidence in an arbitrary way. Although there are surely cases in which we would prefer false beliefs to true ones (e.g., cases where knowing the truth would by itself make us irretrievably unhappy), it is reasonable to assume that such cases are rare enough so that we would not want to take them into account in deciding what methods of thinking to adopt for general purposes.

Beliefs may also be of intrinsic value. We might want to have rational beliefs even if we were sure that no decisions would ever be based on them. This might be a natural condition of human happiness. Although this might be true, it not necessary here, and I have trouble making a case for it.

It is of interest to contrast rationality (which I take to cover the dispositional components of intelligence) with capacities (as defined in chapter 1) as determinants of happiness. In general, people who have more ca-

pacity, when they are rational, tend to choose richer and more complex plans. However, the pursuit of more complex plans, by definition, makes these plans less likely to be achieved, other things equal. Put simply, the ambitions of a high-capacity person might be, on the average, only a little more likely to be achieved than the ambitions of an average person. The dispositional aspect of intelligence does not have this property. Thus, capacity is a mixed blessing, but rationality is a pure one, guaranteed to promote happiness, except for the possibility of bad luck.

Effects of rationality on effectiveness

To show that rationality in the conduct of thinking is part of intelligence, it is necessary to show that it increases the effectiveness of thinking. In chapters 3 and 4, I tried to show in some detail how this would happen. In particular, the biases that lead to too little thinking, including confirmation bias and belief persistence, would cause errors that could be corrected by more thinking or by thinking in a less biased way. (The opposite kind of error, thinking too much or being too open minded, would lead to indecisiveness or to paralysis of action for no good reason.) In this section, I shall suggest the possible scope of such effects by discussing the possible effects of impulsivenss, or premature cessation of search, relative to the optimum amount. In the sections to follow, I shall show how biased thinking may contribute to errors or poor performance in a number of situations studied in the psychological literature. (The chapter then concludes with a discussion of rationality and morality, the resistance to rationality, and suggestions for research.)

It is important to contrast this definition of impulsiveness with the traditional one. Most studies of impulsiveness grew out of the work of Kagan and his associates (Kagan et al., 1964, 1978). In most tasks that require thinking, if not all, an individual may trade off speed and accuracy. Up to a point, by taking more time, by being more careful, errors may be avoided. Kagan and others have found that children differ in their position on the speed–accuracy tradeoff function. Some children tend to be fast and inaccurate on certain tasks, and others tend to be slow and accurate; the former are called impulsive, the latter, reflective. Children who are both fast and accurate relative to other children, or slow and inaccurate, are in the middle of the reflection–impulsivity dimension, along with those children who are simply average in all respects. In many tasks, there is a strong negative correlation between speed and accuracy, so that there are in fact very few fast accurate, or slow inaccurate, children. One task that usually shows is the Matching Familiar Figures task

(Kagan et al., 1964). In this task, the child is shown one detailed line drawing as a standard and six other drawings that look identical at first glance. The child is told truthfully that only one of the six is an exact match to the standard, and he is asked to find it. Subjects seem to differ greatly in their tendency to trust their inability to find a difference between a given drawing and the standard. Thus, the more impulsive subjects will choose a drawing after only a few seconds of examination, and without looking through all the alternative drawings to see if any appear to be just as close. Although this definition of impulsiv*ity* is different from the present definition of impulsive*ness* in that no prescriptive standard is invoked, the results from the study of impulsivity may hint at the importance of impulsiveness. This is because we should expect the two traits to be correlated; those who are fast relative to their optimum will tend to be fast relative to other subjects as well.

Reflectivity tends to be stable over several years (Kagan et al., 1978). Children are also consistent across tasks in their position on the dimension (see Messer, 1976, for a review of the extensive literature on this point). For example, Kagan (1965) found that impulsive children made more uncorrected nonsensical errors when reading aloud. Baron et al. (in press) found fairly high correlations in reflection–impulsivity across tasks involving arithmetic problems, logic problems, and visual matching. There must be some limit to this consistency, but I know of no research that systematically addresses the question of where that limit is.

Impulsivity also correlates with various measures of school performance and intellectual success. Impulsive children tend to have more difficulty in school, even when IQ is held constant (Messer, 1976). Even IQ scores themselves are affected by impulsivity, depending on the test. Some IQ tests, more than others, use fairly difficult problems, and do not weigh heavily the time taken to do them. (The most outstanding test in this regard is Raven's Progressive Matrices, which is often given with no time limit.) Scores on these tests correlate negatively with impulsivity; that is, there is a strong negative correlation between IQ and the error rate in the task used to measure impulsivity, but only a very weak negative correlation, or even a positive correlation, between IQ and latency in that task. Findings of positive correlations between IQ and some measure of latency are of interest, especially since long latency is typically treated as a negative factor in the scoring of the IQ test itself. Yet such findings are not all that rare (see Sternberg, 1984; Baron et al., in press). These findings suggest that many people do not perform as well as they could, in intellectual tasks, if they were to take more time.

It is also of interest that impulsivity may be modified in a way that

transfers to other tasks (e.g., Egeland, 1974; Meichenbaum, 1977; Baron et al., in press). I shall discuss this in chapter 7. For now, the important point is that reflection–impulsivity is at least to some extent dispositional. If people stop too soon, it is not because they have no choice in the matter.

The fact that impulsives are less successful in school and on IQ tests suggests that people are, on the average, too impulsive; they would do better if they spent more time. Would this be true if values were taken into account? Would the extra time be worthwhile? The arguments made in chapter 3 would imply that people indeed tend to be impulsive rather than overcautious. Thus, it is plausible that the results from impulsivity research should be taken at face value.

Let us consider the fact that impulsivity usually correlates with school performance even when IQ is held constant (Messer, 1976). To begin, note that accuracy and speed are both involved in IQ tests and in schoolwork. In the case of IQ tests, speed is often measured and taken into account according to some sort of formula. In the case of schoolwork, speed is relevant for several reasons: tests are often time limited; a "slow thinker" will have trouble keeping up with what a teacher says; and the time available for homework may in fact be limited both by motivational and practical considerations. In essence, any measure of IQ or school performance reflects a combination of accuracy and speed. At issue is the relative weight of these two in each measure. From this point of view, the simplest interpretation of the evidence is that the relative weight of accuracy and speed is different in schoolwork and in IQ tests. It ought to be possible to improve the power of IQ tests to predict school performance by weighing speed less heavily in their scoring. (And, other things equal, current IQ tests that do not stress speed should be better predictors than those that do.)

One reason that speed may be less important than test designers think is that speed may not be as stable a property of performance of a given task (e.g., reading) as impulsiveness. Most of the tasks done in school, or in work, will ultimately be practiced quite a bit. Practice, as we know, increases speed. Because people may differ in their sensitivity to practice and in the amount of practice they have, a person's ultimate speed on a task may be very hard to predict from speed at an early stage of practice. However, impulsiveness at an early stage of practice might be much more predictive of later performance. First, impulsiveness might be largely unaffected by practice, so that an impulsive person will continue to make many errors even as his speed increases. Second, low accuracy in the early stages of learning may be particularly harmful when this learning is

a component of some more advanced skill. For example, errors in under-standing the basis of addition and subtraction (e.g., the place system) will become more and more harmful as more advanced subjects are learned. Thus, a student with initially low accuracy in understanding principles may fall further and further behind, whereas a student who is initially careful will acquire a firm basis for later learning, and her speed will improve with practice. In sum, then, it would seem that test designers underestimate the benefits of thinking, and thus design tests that tend to penalize those students who have an appropriate appreciation of how great these benefits can be relative to costs in the long run.

Other results suggest that impulsivity in school children declines with age. In particular, in the Matching Familiar Figures test, the test most commonly used to measure impulsivity, latency increases slightly with age and error rate decreases substantially (Messer, 1976). We would expect latency to decrease, given the evidence that mental speed itself increases with age (Chi & Gallagher, 1982). Thus, the fact that latency increases at all, even if only a little, is impressive evidence of a decrease in impulsiv-ity. (However, here especially, an increase in latency may result from an increase in the true effectiveness of extra thinking, so that age changes in impulsivity, traditionally measured, need not reflect age changes in im-pulsiveness.) Whatever the reason for this developmental change in im-pulsivity, its effects on performance of various tasks might be substantial. We simply do not know how much of the literature on intellectual devel-opment can be accounted for in terms of impulsivity alone.

For example, many of the tasks studied by Piaget and his followers (see Flavell, 1977) might be affected by impulsiveness. Klahr and Wallace (1970) in fact provided this sort of account of a number of Piagetian classification tasks. They developed a computer model of performance of these tasks. Some of the tasks required many more steps than others. After each step, the model used a parameter called MOTIVE to decide whether to continue. (The name of the parameter seems to reflect a particular account of impulsiveness; however, Klahr and Wallace make no explicit commitment to this account.) Younger and older children are assumed to differ primarily in the strength of MOTIVE. The model ac-counts for the developmental sequence of the tasks, that is, the order in which the various tasks are first "passed." (Of course, as in the case of most models, there are alternative accounts. For example, the more com-plex tasks might place more burden on working memory.)

More generally, it is conceivable that a great many of the tasks mastered in childhood are affected by impulsiveness. Barstis and Ford (1977) found that impulsive kindergarteners performed less well than

reflectives in Piaget's tests of conservation of number and quantity. Many conservation tasks, for an adult, seem to be "tricks." We are tempted to give the wrong answer, but we stop ourselves. A child, however, might give the first answer that comes to mind.

Baron et al. (in press) found that children's accuracy in solving syllogisms, an ability not taught in school, is positively correlated with latency. Recently, Galotti, Baron, and Sabini (1984) have found further evidence that individual differences in college students' performance at categorical syllogisms can be accounted for in terms of impulsiveness. In one experiment, good and poor reasoners were selected by a test of performance on such syllogisms as "All French books are large. Some large books are blue. What can you conclude about the relation between subject and color?" They were then asked once again to solve such syllogisms, first giving an initial answer wihin 20 seconds and then proceeding to give a final, considered answer. Although the good reasoners were faster than the poor reasoners in giving the initial answer, they were slower in giving the final one, and the interaction was significant. The good reasoners thus spent more time evaluating their answers. They were also more likely to correct errors made in the initial answers. (They were also more likely to be correct to start, it turned out, so that impulsiveness was not the only factor at work.)

In sum, there is reason to investigate the possibility that developmental trends and individual differences in intellectual tasks can be accounted for in part by changes in impulsivity, in the old sense, and perhaps also by changes in impulsiveness, in the new sense. This holds for tasks that are taught in school as well as those mastered naturally. For school tasks, impulsiveness may play a particularly important role, given the fact that impulsiveness in the early stages of learning can have cumulative negative effects, whereas the effects of overcautiousness on latency in the early stages may be largely overcome through practice. Baron et al. (in press) provide further discussion of the role of impulsiveness in accounting for task performance and for correlations between task performance and other style measures, such as the analytic dimension of Kagan, Moss, and Sigel (1963), the holistic–analytic continuum of Smith and Kemler (1977), and the Phonecian–Chinese dimension of Baron (e.g., 1977).

Availability

When subjects (or real people) are asked to judge probability, relative frequency, or strength of belief, they often gather evidence — in the form of examples, arguments, or reasons — from memory. Often, the

examples (or reasons) available for recall are unrepresentative of the true population of examples, so the subjects make errors. For example, when asked whether the letter *K* is more frequent in the third position or the first position of English words, subjects generally say the first position, although the third is correct (Tversky & Kahneman, 1973). Examples of words beginning with *K* are easier to think of, that is, more available, than examples of words with *K* in the third position. These effects have been attributed to an "availability heuristic" (Kahneman & Tversky, 1972) — although the term "heuristic" may be inappropriate, for there is little else a subject may do besides recalling evidence. (The real issue is how this search is carried out, what sort of evidence is sought.) The distorting effect of availability has been called a bias, but it need not be irrational. It is surely an irrational bias if it is an example of confirmation bias in the recall of evidence, that is, the bias to seek evidence that favors strong possibilities (chapter 3). In other cases, it seems more appropriate to call it a error, perhaps a correctable error, resulting from lack of knowledge about how one's memory works or failure to use this knowledge to correct one's thinking. Let us consider these cases first.

As Tversky and Kahneman point out, the reliance on what is available is usually benign. In general, the easier it is to think of examples of a category, the larger the category is; and the easier it is to think of arguments in favor of a proposition, the more likely that the proposition is correct. However, there are several factors that can distort the process and lead to error. One is the organization of memory. For example, the fact that it is easy to recall words beginning with *K* is surely due to this factor; our card catalog for words is organized by initial letter, not by third letter. Another cause of error is selective exposure due to forces beyond our control. Slovic, Fischhoff, and Lichtenstein (1982) found that beliefs about the frequency of different causes of death were distorted by the overreporting of certain causes in the new media. Likewise, vividness surely affects what we are likely to recall (Nisbett & Ross, 1980; see also Ross & Sicoly, 1979). Errors of this sort are not necessarily irrational. At issue is whether it would be worthwhile to correct them by thinking about methods for doing the tasks. The same may be said for other errors in probabilistic reasoning, such as the use of representativeness and the neglect of base rates (Kahneman & Tversky, 1972).

The idea of availability has been used to explain a number of phenomena. We have already seen (chapter 4) how it explains certain phenomena related to belief perseverance: For example, when the evidence for a belief is totally discredited, the belief may survive because the

subject had enriched the evidence he was given with evidence from his own memory, and even after the given evidence was removed, the re-called evidence remained available. Another phenomenon that seems to work the same way is "hindsight bias." For example, Fischhoff (1975) gave subjects case histories, or excerpts from history books, to read. "Hindsight" subjects were told which of several outcomes had occurred (e.g., who won the battle, whether the patient recovered) and were asked to estimate the probability they would have assigned to that outcome if they had not known it. Control subjects were not told the outcome, but were asked to assign probabilities to each possible outcome. The hind-sight subjects assigned higher probabilities than the control subjects. At least part of the explanation for this effect (and related effects) seems to be that hindsight subjects, when they are told the actual outcome, think of reasons why this outcome might have occurred (see several papers in Kahneman et al., 1982). When they are asked to judge what probability they (or someone else) would have assigned without knowing the out-come, these reasons are available, and influence their judgment. Slovic and Fischhoff (1977) found that subjects were less susceptible to this sort of bias when they were asked to think of reasons why they might be wrong.

Although these various "hindsight" biases are of interest, it is hard to conclude from the evidence we have that the subjects are irrational. By encouraging the subjects to think of reasons to justify one of the choices, the experiments make these reasons more available when the subjects are asked to make later judgments. But there is nothing irrational about thinking of reasons to support a conclusion you are told is true, and there is nothing irrational about recalling such reasons in preference to other reasons at a later time, unless you know about the very psychological mechanism at work and have a means to avoid it.

In sum, all the factors described so far are inevitable, so it is not irrational to be affected by them unless one has an easy way of avoiding their influence. The issue here is not one of fundamental bias but of the costs and benefits of whatever strategies might be required to overcome the error. It is surely not worth the effort for a subject in a laboratory experiment to sample words from a text in order to estimate the true frequencies of letters in different positions, even if the subject were aware of the differential availability of different types of words from memory. Likewise, it might not be worthwhile to do whatever is necessary to compensate for the effect of recency on the recall of reasons (in hindsight and debriefing experiments).

Overconfidence

One situation in which confirmation bias may be involved is in the "over-confidence" phenomenon (Kahneman et al., 1982). When subjects are asked to state their confidence in a judgment by stating a probability that the judgment is correct, high confidence is usually inappropriate. Judgments made with 100% confidence may be correct only 75% of the time, and judgments made with 90% confidence may be correct only 70% of the time, for example. These results are found for a variety of judgments, including such things as answers to factual questions (Is Bogota the capital of Colombia?) or examination questions. The inappropriateness of extreme-confidence judgments seems not to be fully explained as an artifact of subjects' lack of undertanding of the task or the probability scale (Fischhoff, Slovic, & Lichtenstein, 1977). (Although extreme high-confidence judgments are generally overconfident, extreme low-confidence judgments are underconfident; that is, when people think they are guessing, they actually do considerably better than chance.)

There are several likely determinants of this phenomenon of overconfidence for high-confidence judgments. One is that feelings of confidence are affected by irrelevant factors (noise) that do not really affect the probability of being correct, but subjects do not compensate for the noisiness of their feelings. Thus, subjects take extreme feelings at face value, even though it would be wise to move toward more moderate judgments (Ferrell & McGoey, 1980). (In the limit, if subjects' feelings about particular items were totally useless, the confidence assigned to each item in a test should be the same for every item, and should equal the expected percent correct on the test.) There is also some evidence (Lichtenstein & Fischhoff, 1977) that subjects are insensitive to factors that affect overall difficulty of a set of items. Thus, the overconfidence effect is larger for difficult items than for items that are easy for the subject in question. In general, subjects tend to assume they will get about 75% of a set of items correct, regardless of the actual difficulty of the items for the subject in question (Ferrell & McGoey, 1980). All of these determinants are artifactual for our purposes, for they tell us nothing about the rationality of the subjects' thinking; they tell us only about the subjects' ignorance with respect to the particular task. Such ignorance might, but need not, result from irrational lack of thinking about methods for making judgments.

There is, however, one additional likely determinant that is quite relevant. Koriat, Lichtenstein, and Fischhoff (1980) asked subjects in one

condition of a typical experiment (using general information questions) to try to think of reasons why their answer might be incorrect. Confidence judgments were lower in this condition, although confidence judgments were unaffected by instructions to think of reasons why the answer might be correct. It thus seems likely — and this is supported by examination of actual reasons given by subjects — that subjects typically think of an initial answer and then search for reasons to support it. They do not look for reasons against it, and when they are asked to do so, confidence becomes appropriately lower. This seems to be a clear case in which the availability of evidence is affected by a bias to search for evidence in favor of an initial possibility. (It is possible that an underweighing of negative evidence is also involved, but this has not been examined in this context.) Thus, overconfidence in general may often result from such a bias. This is of interest beyond the phenomenon itself, because overconfidence may be a determinant of premature cessation of thinking. Thus, people might stop thinking too soon because they are biased in their search for evidence in a way that tends to produce unrealistically high confidence in the first possibility that comes to mind. Such high confidence reduces the expected value of further thinking.

Illusory correlation

A second phenomenon that seems most easily explained in terms of biases in search for evidence — and possibly also biases in the interpretation of evidence — is called illusory correlation (Chapman & Chapman, 1967). In one exemplary study, clinical psychologists were given brief case descriptions together with test results and were asked to discover what correlations existed in the sample between diagnoses and results. The test used was the "Draw a person" test, which had been shown objectively to be uncorrelated with any of the diagnoses used in the study. Nonetheless, the subjects tended to "discover" that drawings with large eyes were correlated with paranoia, drawings with big shoulders indicated concern with masculinity, and so on. In general, people report perceiving correlations that they expect to find. A likely explanation of this (although one not yet demonstrated) is that subjects selectively recall those cases that support their initial beliefs when reviewing relevant data. It is also possible that another bias is involved, the tendency to write off evidence inconsistent with one's favored belief. The former explanation (confirmation bias) puts the source of the problem at the time the correlation is estimated, after the data have been seen. The latter (belief persistence)

puts the explanation at the time the evidence is presented. Of course, both explanations could be true.

Illusory correlation seems to manifest in a number of other phenomena. One concerns correlations between personality traits. Shweder (1977; see also Shweder & D'Andrade, 1979) reanalyzed data in which summer camp counselors made daily ratings of campers' behavior as well as overall ratings at the end of the summer. Some traits tended to correlate in the daily ratings but not in the end-of-summer ratings, and others showed the reverse pattern. A group of students was then asked to make judgments of conceptual relatedness of the traits. Traits judged to be related, such as "gives loud and spontaneous expressions of delight or disapproval" and "talks more than his share of the time at the table," were those that showed high judged correlations in the end-of-summer ratings, but not necessarily in the daily ratings. In sum, judgments of traits at the end of the summer seem to have been influenced by prior beliefs about which traits ought to correlate, as inferred from the ratings of relatedness. Again, a distortion of the search for evidence in memory, at the time of the end-of-summer ratings, might be implicated.

Other possibly related phenomena are those observed by Ward and Jenkins (1965) and Jenkins and Ward (1965). In these experiments, subjects were asked to estimate the extent to which one event was contingent on another. For example, the subject was given a choice of two buttons on each trial, and he was asked whether his choice of buttons affected whether or not a light came on, or the subject was shown the results of a series of trials in a cloud-seeding experiment and was asked whether the seeding affected the occurrence of rain. In general, subjects perceived a contingency (a correlation) in situations in which it was reasonable to think there might be one, e.g., in button pressing but not cloud seeding, even when there was no correlation, so long as the critical event (light) occurred frequently. Although the literature surrounding these phenomena is complex (Alloy & Abramson, 1979; Schwartz, 1981; Abramson & Alloy, 1981; Allan & Jenkins, 1980 — in addition to the papers cited), the general point is that some people might tend to believe that there is a correlation between what they do and what happens to them, and they might continue to believe this even when the data do not support it — for whatever reasons cause illusory correlation in general. Other phenomena, such as those involved in personality judgment, may be explained the same way. The sources of illusory correlation in general might include both confirmation bias and belief persistence. Thus, the illustrations of illusory correlation also illustrate some possible effects of biases in thinking.

Meaningful learning

One very important distinction between good and poor students is that the former seem to understand what they learn while the latter tend to learn blindly, without understanding. This has been the universal observation of teachers and scholars in education, not to mention the students themselves, who often regard memorizing, when used as a substitute for understanding, as a kind of dishonest ploy. The distinction between the two types of learning has been drawn most clearly by Katona (1940) and Wertheimer (1945/1959). (Katona acknowledges Wertheimer's primacy; Wertheimer took a long time to decide to publish his book.) Katona used largely artificial materials, but Wertheimer's most impressive examples were from the learning of mathematical procedures, where the issue seems to arise most clearly. In this section, I want to suggest that meaningful learning is a consequence of good thinking as I have defined it.

Wertheimer and Katona provided us with, at minimum, a list of properties of learning with understanding, and with some illustrations of what it is not. First, meaningful learning can form the basis of appropriate transfer. Wertheimer showed this by observing the behavior of schoolchildren who had just been taught how to find the area of a parallelogram. He then gave them several figures of two types, A figures, which, like parallelograms, could be transformed into rectangles by moving congruent parts, and B figures, which could not. Most children either transferred the base-times-height formula to all problems or to none. Learning with understanding would have been indicated by use of the formula for the A problems only. (Although use of the formula on all problems is probably an indication of senseless learning, reluctance to try at all is consistent with meaningful learning combined with inability to see the analogy between the new figures and the parallelogram.)

Meaningful learning often results from solving a problem on one's own; when a child has figured out how to find the area of the parallelogram, the solution is usually understood. A child who learned this way could understand that the reason for thinking about moving a triangle to fill a gap was to make the parallelogram into a rectangle, whose area could be found in the usual way. However, meaningful learning is not the same as learning by "discovery" or "induction," for Wertheimer found that children would "discover" the rule that the area of a parallelogram is the sum of the two sides, if they were presented with a number of examples that happened to fit this rule. On the other hand, a child who learns with understanding resists being taught a rule that is false, despite the seductiveness of the examples a demonic teacher might provide.

Katona showed that meaningful learning is more resistant to forgetting. When a rule is learned meaningfully, it increases the probability of solution of problems that can be solved by the same rule. He also showed that meaningful learning should be distinguished from learning with "meaning" in the usual sense. When subjects were asked to memorize a number such as 1,214,172,126, they were not helped by being told that its meaning was the annual tonnage shipped through the port of New York, but they were helped by being told that it was actually a number sequence that followed a rule (12, 14, 17, 21, 26).

Wertheimer tried to explain the distinction between the two types of learning in terms of concepts of "inner necessity" and "rho relations." His theory requires explication. My own best statement about the nature of meaningful learning for mathematical procedures (at least) is that such learning involves the perception and representation of relationships of *purpose* between each element of the procedure and the goal or subgoal it is designed to satisfy. For every mathematical procedure, there is usually a treelike structure of such goals and subgoals. (This view is similar to that of VanLehn & Brown, 1980, and Greeno, Riley, & Gelman, 1984.)

For example, a student might come to understand the formula for the area of a parallelogram by first setting the goal of making the parallelogram into a rectangle (a figure she already knows how to find the area of). By searching for possible ways to achieve this goal, she discovers that it can be achieved by moving a triangle. Then she has to find the area of the rectangle. Its height is unchanged, but it may take more thought to discover that its base is also unchanged; again, a search for possible ways for achieving the subgoal of finding the base may be required. When the formula is learned in this way, the student knows the purpose (goal or subgoal) served by each step in its derivation. In principle, a student might acquire such knowledge without solving the problem herself: A teacher might simply tell her the purpose of each step. (In practice, the student might not pay sufficient attention so as to allow the same representation to be formed as would be formed if she solved the problem herself.)

This idea accounts for the demonstrations of Wertheimer and Katona. Memory is aided by meaningful learning because knowledge of purposes can be used to rederive parts of the procedure in case they are partially or fully forgotten. Meaningful learning results from problem solving because the structure of subgoals in solving the problem corresponds closely to the structure of purposes in the final procedure. A child can see that the reason for moving the triangle is to make the parallelogram into a rectan-

gle, because the child started out with this very goal. A meaningful learner resists learning what is false because he cannot see the purpose of the steps. (Of course, if we insisted on learning everything meaningfully or not at all, most of us would never get through introductory statistics.) And learning by induction is indeed "blind" because induction need give no clue about purpose.

By this criterion, much of our learning is only partially meaningful. For example, when reading VanLehn and Brown (1980), I found that I did not fully understand the purpose of borrowing and carrying in arithmetic. Why, for example, do not we write the sum of 47 and 18 as something like "5,15," where the 15 is the sum of the 7 and 8. The answer is that one of the constraints on arithmetic procedures is "canonicity," which is that every quantity must have exactly one representation in the number system.

Now how might a person ever come to *know* that a procedure achieves a purpose? Something like reflective thinking might be invoked here, at least as a last resort. (In simpler cases, the conclusion might be an immediate inference from well-known facts.) In principle, we might engage in an episode of thinking in which the goal was to discover a procedure to achieve a certain goal. We would propose procedures and test them by looking for evidence. The evidence would take the form of imagined examples in which the procedure either did or did not serve its purpose. The latter would constitute counterexamples, which would be particularly relevant. A concrete example of this is the development of a computer program, which is the conscious invention of a procedure. For example, in trying to modify my word-processor program so that it would underline all letters between two marks, I failed to consider various possibilities. My first working version printed the marks themselves and underlined them. The next version did not print the marks, but it did underline them (which amounted to underlining the space before each underlined word). If I had designed the procedure by reflection instead of trial-and-error experimentation, I would have anticipated these counterexamples to my procedure in advance.

In sum, good thinking might contribute to meaningful learning in two ways: First, meaningful learning may be achieved by thinking—by searching for possible ways of achieving goals and subgoals. A learner who does this has in a sense "thought through" the derivation of the procedure by the kind of problem solving illustrated in Duncker's protocol of the tumor problem (chapter 3), so that the subgoal structure is apparent. This may occur either when the learner solves the problem for himself, or when he is led through the solution in a way that ensures

knowledge of the relations between procedure and constraints. Second, the relationship between a part of a procedure and the purpose it serves may be discovered by a kind of reflective thinking with particular attention to counterexamples. Possibly, this account may be extended to the meaningful learning of material other than mathematical procedures, and, if it is, I suggest that these principles will again be at work.

Problem solving

The effect of good thinking on learning with understanding is one way among many in which rational thinking can increase effectiveness in those domains traditionally associated with the study of intelligence. Let me review some of the others. To focus the discussion, it may help to bear in mind the kinds of problems that are often included in IQ tests, namely, puzzles, mazes, and analogies of various sorts. In focusing on these things, I do not mean to grant any special status to them; given the arguments I have made, effectiveness on such problems is no more important, and probably less important, than effectiveness in understanding, moral reasoning, planning, and everyday decision making. (Of course, these things are hard to quantify, so they have been excluded from IQ tests, and — as I argued in chapter 1 — from the official concept of intelligence.) First, impulsiveness can hinder problem solving, as noted. For example, an impulsive person may fail to "check" his answers by seeking additional evidence of their correctness; he may respond with the first possibility that comes to mind.

Much of the thinking in problem solving concerns finding a method, either in the broad sense of an overall approach or the narrow sense of — for example — a method for calculating the last item in a number-series problem. The search for either type of method may be affected by biases in search for evidence and in use of evidence so as to favor the current best possibility. These biases would lead to rigid attachments to wrong approaches, for example, undertaking a tedious calculation when a simple shortcut will do. These effects, and the effect of impulsiveness, could accumulate over a series of problems, because the effort spent in considering alternative approaches on early problems, and evaluating them, could be more than paid back in terms of increased speed on later problems. This can occur over a series of tests taken over years as well as within a single test. Thus, faster performance on some components of problem solving (Sternberg, 1977) could result from better thinking at an earlier time, when the person learned how to solve the type of problem in question. It is worthy of note that most of the models of problem solving

proposed in the literature (e.g., Sternberg, 1977; Mulholland, Pellegrino, & Glaser, 1980) map easily into the present scheme; they all involve stages that could be classified as search for possibilities, search for evidence, and use of evidence. For example, in solving an analogy problem, a possibility is a relation between the first two terms, and the search for evidence consists of asking whether this relation applies to the third and fourth terms as well. Errors could result from insufficient search for possibilities or evidence, or for failure to criticize a general possibility (or approach). In informal studies, I have observed such failure to give up unproductive approaches in verbal protocols of people solving problems from Raven's Progressive Matrices. Of course, it is as yet unknown whether performance would improve if subjects were taught only to be more self-critical.

Finally, as Sternberg (1984) points out, the learning of vocabulary and other bits of knowledge tested on IQ tests often involve the solving of problems, such as deducing a word's meaning from context, or, one might add, reflecting on the meaning of the word when trying to use it in writing. Good thinking at an early stage of learning could lead to knowledge that would make learning easier later on; hence, the quality of thinking can have cumulative effects, which might not be cured easily by later improvements in thinking alone.

Reflective thinking and morality

One of the more straightforward areas in which good thinking pays off is in reflective thinking of the sort described in chapter 3. When we think in this way, we use intuitions or beliefs as evidence to test various principles, modifying the principles and sometimes the intuitions as well until we achieve a good fit. Such a method is rational not because it explains observations, but rather because we have good reasons for the conclusions we draw and the changes we make. I have already noted that this method is the main one used in the development of the theory of rationality in general, and in this book in particular.

Reflective thinking is not restricted to the airy realm of the philosopher. To take a mundane example, the tennis instructor Vic Brayden is distinguished not only by his sense of humor, but also by his ability to explain things in terms of simple principles, which, despite their simplicity, appear to be absolutely correct. He — or whoever taught him — did not arrive at these principles by magic. Most likely, they went through the same kinds of refinements and questionings that I have discussed. The process also occurs in schoolwork of all sorts. Even such a simple task as

summarizing what someone else said—a task often described as "regurgitating" - may take several attempts, each involving criticism of a proposed summary by looking for evidence from memory or from a text. It is conceivable that the vast majority of people are capable of useful reflective thinking in such contexts, if it were encouraged throughout their education and if they were familiar with fields they thought about.

I know of no studies of the adequacy of reflective thinking except for some very preliminary work of Baron et al. (1980) and Baron (1985). It is clear, however, that there are several opportunities for bias to operate, and it would be surprising if biases were absent. Probably the most serious bias is the simple failure to initiate reflective thinking, or continue it for very long, resulting from an underestimation of its value. Other relevant biases, of course, are confirmatory search for evidence and insensitivity to evidence against a favored principle.

The kind of reflective thinking that has received the most attention is moral thinking, for example, thinking about everyday dilemmas (such as that of our executive in chapter 3) or questions about public policy. At issue here is whether moral thinking can be usefully done.

What is moral thinking? It has been pointed out by many (perhaps most persuasively by Hare, 1952) that moral principles cannot logically be derived from statements of fact alone, even though statements of fact alone may be relevant. (Hare's argument, greatly simplified, is that moral principles are prescriptive statements, which are imperatives, and an imperative conclusion cannot be derived from declarative premises alone.) This leaves us with the method of reflection as about the only possible one for the derivation of moral principles. Rawls (1971, ch. 9, particularly pp. 48-49) called the result of such reflection a state of "reflective equilibrium," a kind of analogue of scientific "truth." (In both cases, these ends are approached but probably never fully attained.) Rawls argued that we ought to use all kinds of intuitions as evidence in such reflection, including intuitions about moral principles or rules that might be consistent with the higher-order principles we consider. When we do this, we must remain open to changing the intuitions themselves on the basis of stronger principles. An analogy is found in grammar: When we discover (or learn) the rule of subject-verb agreement, we may change our intuition about the grammaticality of "A few of the books are here," despite the fact that it is from just such linguistic intuitions that the rules of grammar are derived.

Later workers have amended Rawls's original statement. Putnam (1981, pp. 104-105) points out that the reflective process is not normally one that occurs in a single individual, but rather occurs through history.

Although the individual philosopher — or ordinary person trying to work out his own principles — is thus part of a larger, social thinking process, the quality of his thinking is no less at issue, for the quality of social thinking doubtless depends on the quality of thinking in individuals (a topic that is, I admit, neglected in this book).

Daniels (1979) points out that although we cannot assume that a consensus reached in reflective equilibrium is identical to truth, we do have reason to think that such a consensus might be true. Namely, the truth (if there is any) might play a role in bringing the consensus about. This sort of argument seems to lie at the basis of scientific method as well as other methods of inquiry, and, indeed, most skeptical doubts that can be raised about the conclusions of prescriptive philosophy have their parallels in science.

Finally, Hare (1981) has advanced a more radical claim that we should not use moral intuitions in moral thinking. Hare suggests (extending the arguments of Hare, 1952 and 1963) that the nature of moral thinking may be deduced logically by reflecting on what moral judgments are. (This involves our intuitions about the meanings of moral terms and the like, but not about substantive moral issues.) From such considerations, it follows that the essential method of moral thinking involves putting oneself in the position of all whose interests are affected by a moral decision, and weighing the interests against each other as if they were simultaneously one's own. Such thinking could, in principle, be used to make decisions about specific cases, but it is more appropriately used to criticize the maxims and principles that we live by from day to day, which, in turn, are used to decide cases. In this kind of thinking, no intuitions about morals themselves are involved, only intuitions about the interests of self and others. Although Hare's arguments would seem to require some modification of Rawls's original arguments, they do not affect much the conception of good moral thinking advanced here. For in thinking about principles, we still must consider alternative principles, and we still must use our best guesses about interests as evidence bearing on these principles. What Hare's argument implies is that we should not use our intuitions about moral rules directly, unless they can be restated in terms of interests. This amounts to a restriction on the kind of evidence that is relevant. (In fact, even Rawls — Hare's target — obeys this restriction much of the time in his own writing, and appeals to intuitions largely to show that the principles he derives do not seriously fly in their face.)

A possibility of interest is that reflective thinking is relevant not only to the work of moral philosophers but also to the moral behavior of people in general. One relevant question here concerns the relation between ration-

ality and morality, a topic of heated discussion in current philosophy. If it is not rational to behave morally, then, even in principle, let alone fact, a theory of rational thinking cannot help much in bringing about more moral behavior. Provisionally, I shall assume that this debate will be resolved in such a way that morality can be brought within the scope of rationality in some way. The weakest sort of argument for this view is probably that of Williams (1981, chs. 8, 9). This is the argument that moral obligations are rational only for people with moral motives. If a person has a general motive to behave morally, then the whole system of moral thought is relevant to him, because he could subvert his own goals by failing to behave morally. Further, it is not irrational to have such a moral motive. This is consistent with the broader, nonhedonistic conception of rationality sketched in chapter 2 here. Williams stops short here, and is unwilling to say that it is irrational not to have such a motive. However, Williams does grant that it is rational for "society" to bring people up to have moral motives, especially on the likely assumption that members of society already have such motives. That is, those of us who have moral motives (probably everyone, however distorted these motives might sometimes get) are rational to want to maintain them, and would probably be irrational not to want to do so. In particular, the "educator" whose perspective I have adopted will want his students to have moral motives.

Others (e.g., Putnam, 1981; Gewirth, 1983, and citations therein) go to considerable lengths to argue that it *is* irrational not to have moral motives, given that one has egoistic motives. In general, such arguments hold that there are certain things that people want (such as fair treatment), such that there is no good reason to want those things for oneself and not for someone else as well. One may still choose to be selfish, but if one does so, one is being inconsistent, unreasonable, and therefore (to the extent that thinking is involved) irrational. The most basic sort of Golden Rule argument (of the sort we use to teach children morality) may thus be firmly embedded in good thinking itself. If so, my case for the relevance of rational thinking to morality is strengthened considerably.

A second question concerns the relation between moral thinking and moral behavior. This is actually part of a more general question about the relation between any thinking and behavior. However, in the moral realm, the question is particularly acute, because of the frequent occurrence of conflict between morality and self-interest. If morality never wins in this conflict, the question of whether it is rational to be moral seems to be moot.

First, it is important to note that very often the relevance of self-interest to moral decisions is trivial. An important example consists of the

decisions one makes about how to raise one's child, or what to teach one's students. Most of the things we teach our children or our students have little effect on our own interests. Other cases where self-interest plays a negligible role are those where efforts are made to protect a judgment from the claims of self-interest. Many institutions do this as a matter of course. Even the apparatus of anonymous voting and many of the laws about fair campaign practices serve to protect the voter from direct considerations of self-interest. Of course, a voter, as a moral thinker, may find it easier to see the point of view of people like himself than of other people, but this is not the same thing as voting purely for personal gain. If voting were entirely for personal gain, it would hardly be worthwhile, given the improbability that one vote could really affect one's own interests.

Note that these are all important cases. They are the very cases where the arguments about why we want each other to think well morally apply most directly. In these cases, the moral quality of behavior—to the extent to which it is meaningful to judge this at all—is dependent on little else than the quality of moral thinking. This is not to say that a decision cannot be difficult to execute—for example, a decision about goals in child rearing—but that even if it fails, its failure is not a moral failure. It is the moral thinking—or the lack of it—that accounts almost entirely for the morality of such decisions.

Second, it seems practically undeniable that we are sometimes able to resist the demands of self-interest in favor of morality. By self-interest here, I mean what our interest would be except for moral considerations. In a sense, once we have adopted moral motives, morality becomes as much a part of our interest as any other interests we have. On the other hand, sometimes, our (narrow) self-interest wins, so that we have specifically moral regrets (Williams, 1981). It seems to me that the general question of "which wins most often when consistency with moral beliefs conflicts with consistency with self-interest" is practically unanswerable. There is no way to define the population of cases we want to sample from. Those of us who think that self-interest either loses or is irrelevant in a fair number of important cases will be the ones who are more interested in the kind of theory I am trying to develop here. Of course, how often morality wins, and how often people even engage in moral thinking, are things we might try to affect through a different sort of educational enterprise than that under discussion here.

We may still wonder whether enough moral thinking can occur for the effects of good moral thinking to be felt. This is a question that is difficult to settle by evidence; each of us has a view of history and society that

leads to a different answer about it, and it is easy to dismiss the evidence on the other side (because the evidence is indeed poor). The parts of history that make me answer this question affirmatively are those in which moral arguments — made first by a few but then evaluated critically by many and finally accepted — appear to have changed the course of history. The abolition of slavery and the emancipation of women are possible cases. Of course, many ideas are vying for current attention — those concerning human rights, nuclear war, the Third World, etc. The quality of people's thinking about these issues — on a large scale — might just have some effect on the way they are resolved.

Development of identity and moral reasoning

There is a tradition of research concerned with the development of moral reasoning and personal identity. A number of different theories share the assumption that there are stages of development of thinking about ethics, social relationships, knowledge, and personal commitment. Major influences on this tradition are Piaget (1932), Erikson (1950, 1959), and Maslow (1954, 1962). Although Piaget and Erikson proposed stages that everyone, by and large, is supposed to go through, the theories I shall discuss assume, following Maslow, that most people do not go through the full sequence. Because of this, these theories become theories of individual differences among adults as well as of developmental differences. These theories also posit broad dispositions of thinking that cut across all the domains of the life of a person, including the formation of life plans. I shall suggest that many of the facts that support these theories can be accounted for as well by a theory based on the application of thinking, as I have defined it, to these domains. If this interpretation is true, these facts provide further evidence for the effects of rational thinking, and the importance of training such thinking. (A similar argument was made by Baron, 1975.) I have also noted (chapter 1) that these theories share — if only implicitly — my concern with the difference between what people do and what we should do (which, for these theories, is equivalent to performing at the highest stage possible).

Loevinger, Wessler, and Redmore (1970) discuss the general concept of ego development and show how its stages may be measured in a sentence completion test. The test is taken as a projective measure of impulse control, interpersonal style, conscious preoccupations, and cognitive style. There are six levels, and the highest two are rarely reached. Here are some examples for each stage, with the subject's completion to the right of each dash:

Stage 2: impulsive — "tends to dichotomize the world . . . ."
"A good mother — is nice."
"Usually she felt that sex — is good to me because I get hot."
"Being with other people — gives me the creeps."

Stage 3: conformist — "Formulas . . . tend to be stated in absolute terms, without contingencies or exceptions."
"A good mother — always understands her children."
"Being with other people — makes you feel like you belong."
"When people are helpless — I feel sorry for them."

Stage 4: conscientious — "will often combine alternatives that are polar opposites."
"A good mother — conceals the fact."
"A woman should always — be a lady in the parlor and a whore in the bedroom."
"Being with other people — is one way of finding you're not the only one with problems."

Stage 5: autonomous — "construes conflicting alternatives as aspects of many-faceted life situations."
"Usually she felt that sex — was delightful, intriguing, and very, very boring."
"I feel sorry — for those who do not appreciate the beauty of nature."
"Sometimes she wished that — she had things she would not be happy with if she had them."

Stage 6: integrated — "responses combine separate thoughts that would otherwise be rated [stage] 5."
"A good mother — is kind, consistent, tender, sensitive, and always aware a child is master of its own soul."
"The worst thing about being a woman — cannot be generalized, as one woman makes an asset of the same situation decried by another."
"My main problem is — I am afraid, I lack courage to be what I want to because it is different from what my parents feel I should be."

There is a general movement from simplistic, one-sided statements, to statements that recognize apparent contradictions, to statements that recognize other kinds of complexity. There is also a widening of concerns, from immediate feelings to life plans and identity.

Although some of this scale concerns content, e.g., the widening concerns, some of it (naturally, the part I have emphasized) concerns thought as well. It is likely that the more mature responses to the test items result from more thinking or better thinking according to the model described in chapter 3. For example, statements about complexity may result from the discovery of counterevidence against an initial possibility (for an answer to the item). Early stages may result from impulsive responding, with little thinking at all after an initial possibility has been thought of. Of course, differences in the quality of thinking might reflect differences in the value of high-quality answers to the subject. However, a general

disposition to disregard the value of the outcome of thinking (as it would be on reflection) might well express itself in the responses to a test like this. The items would seem to be at least moderately worth thinking about for their own sake.

Kohlberg (1970; Colby et al., 1983) proposes a sequence of stages for moral development in particular, based on Piaget's and Loevinger's, and he argues that these stages are actually manifestations of more general developmental patterns. Kohlberg is concerned only with moral "reasoning," although he argues (on the basis of some empirical evidence) that the stage of thinking can influence behavior when the situation is unambiguous and when different kinds of reasoning naturally lead to different substantive conclusions. Kohlberg measures the stage of moral reasoning by giving people dilemmas that can be argued either way by almost any stage. For example, one is based on a man who has a chance to steal a drug, which he cannot afford to buy, and which might save his wife's life. The subject is interviewed, and his statements on various issues are scored, such as the value of life, the authority of government, and the motives for engaging in moral action. The scores are based on the *type* of underlying principle appealed to. In the lowest, "preconventional," stages, morality is confused with self-interest or avoidance of punishment, for example, the reason for not stealing the drug would be to avoid jail. (Note that it is not the subject's self-interest, but that of the character in the dilemma; thus, this sort of response reflects a principle of reasoning rather than the distortion of reasoning by the subject's self-interest.) In the "conventional" stages, morality is confused with conventions, with emotions or feelings, or with societal norms or laws. The reason for not stealing might be to avoid disapproval or to support the system of society. In the "postconventional" stages, morality is based on principles that transcend conventions, principles such as maximizing utility, or justice based on an implicit social contract. A reason not to steal would be that doing so would be to violate a social contract that, in the long run, saves more than a single life.

Kohlberg's dilemmas, despite the stated emphasis on reasoning, may actually elicit less reasoning than the sentence-completion items. People are frequently faced with moral questions, and most people have developed a stock of principles that are simply retrieved and applied. Most people, when faced initially with Kohlberg's dilemmas, feel little doubt or perplexity because they do not question the first principle that comes to mind as an answer to the question. (Of course, it may be that they *should* question it, but my point is that we rarely get to see what would happen if they did.) It may be that different principles result statistically from think-

ing of different kinds, but this need not be the case. A person who applies a "high-stage" principle may have learned that principle from someone else, and a person who applies a low-stage principle may have figured it out for himself after considerable thought of a high quality (but limited, perhaps, by lack of relevant experiences or inability to recall them).

Miriam Glassman and I (in pilot work) have found it possible to score moral reasoning according to a scheme akin to that described in chapter 3 (as illustrated in the example of moral thinking given there). Of particular interest are the thinker's attempts to criticize his initial principles by looking for counterexamples, and then to use those counterexamples to revise a principle. It turns out that those who use high-stage principles, in Kohlberg's sense, *are* also more likely to report counterevidence they think of spontaneously and to change, in response to evidence they think of, the first statement they offer. However, this does not need to be the case.

In a third relevant project, Perry (1971) interviewed Harvard students each year for several years about general issues in their studies and their lives. He found he could classify their responses accoding to a developmental scheme based on a student's attitude toward truth, in his studies, and the development of his life goals and commitments concerning religion, morality, politics, personal relationships, and work. The attitudes of each student were generally consistent across these different domains. Students moved through the stages as they stayed in college, although some began at a fairly high stage, and many never completed the progression. At the earliest stages, truth was defined by authority, and professors who argued both sides of an issue were seen as obstructive. Commitments, as well, were defined by one's own past history, one's family, and so on. In the middle stages, students became aware of relativism and the possibility of making a good argument against almost any possibility, whether it concerned an issue in a course or a decision about life. These stages often began when students realized what some of their professors were doing (thinking out loud?) and discovered that they could get better grades by arguing this way in their papers. They then realized that this sort of "complex thinking" could be extended to matters beyond the classroom, to problems not previously thought to be problems; hence the "freshman identity crisis," which, of course, often occurs in the junior year. Finally, students became aware of the need to make a commitment in spite of the possibility of counterevidence. These final commitments were often identical in content to those the student entered with (medical school, Judaism, etc.), but the new commitments were consistent with better understanding of the paths not chosen.

One interpretation of Perry's findings is that students' thinking actually improved, in the sense of becoming closer to the optimum, as a result of the example of their professors and the tasks they were required to do. They might have become more self-critical, that is, less insensitive to evidence against favored possibilities, and less prone to seek only confirming evidence. They might also have become more prone to "question," that is, to seek evidence, and less impulsive in completing their thinking once it had begun. This might have occurred in all domains. Alternatively, the students might have already been capable of good thinking in some domains, and the changes might have involved the extension of this sort of thinking to new domains, particularly those concerned with the formation of life plans, or, more concretely, commitments to work and to ideologies.

In sum, much of the evidence that supports developmental-stage theories of personality may be accounted for by changes in the quality of thinking (including the amount of thinking, which may have been too little before the changes). What is highly suggestive about these theories is their claim that thinking may influence the aspects of a person's life that are most important for him and for others, such as his personal commitments and his morality.

Thinking and pathology

It is possible that some of what we call neurosis and psychosis is in part the result of irrationality in thinking. In some cases, such pathology might consist of biased thinking and little else, but more normally, biases might serve as predisposing conditions for certain kinds of pathology. In contrast to generally deficient thinking, in which all biases characteristic of normal people are exaggerated, some pathologies may result from imbalances, that is, extreme values on some parameters but not others. I shall discuss a few pathologies classified according to traditional diagnostic criteria; however, I should note that pathological biases, in their own right, might ultimately require new diagnostic categories. These suggestions draw heavily on the suggestions made by Shapiro (1965), but I should note that Beck (1976) and others have also called attention to distorted forms of thinking characteristic of different types of neurotic pathology.

The clearest example may be paranoia, in particular, the tendency of paranoid patients to form delusions. We must be careful in defining a delusion, for we would not want to include just any manifestly false belief. It might even be too broad to define a delusion as a *strong* belief

that is objectively false. Such a definition would include false beliefs formed in a supportive social context or in a physical environment that provided limited evidence (e.g., belief in the world's flatness). A definition of delusions in terms of the way beliefs are formed would not have these problems. Thus, it makes sense to say that the strength of a delusional belief is way out of proportion to that warranted by the evidence, as the evidence would be perceived by the subject without the distorting effect of the belief itself. In other words, a delusion may be considered as a belief whose strength is wildly greater than is justified by the evidence that would be available assuming unbiased — i.e., good — thinking. Real delusions also involve beliefs that are so important to a person that considerable thinking has actually been devoted to them. Small "delusions" due to impulsiveness or lack of thinking are, for our purposes, not real delusions at all.

Because delusional beliefs are found even when a person has reason to do a great deal of thinking, it seems unlikely that such beliefs are due to impulsiveness or to failure to search for evidence. Indeed, some delusional patients are people who think a great deal, and delusional people may be found among those who think for a living, e.g., academics.

Some biases that *can* account for delusions are failure to search for possibilities (other than the favored one), confirmation bias in the choice of evidence from memory, and insensitivity to evidence against a favored possibility, in this case the delusion itself. Of course, it is not a new idea that delusional people do these things to maintain their delusions. All I have added that is new is to place this description of delusions in the context of the present theory; this allows delusional thinking to be seen as one of many kinds of biased thinking. I have thus pointed out that there are biases that delusionals do not have, yet others probably do have.

An interesting research question is whether the biases of delusional people are found only in their thinking about their delusions, or in other areas as well. If the biases are somewhat general, this will suggest that general biases play a causal role in the formation of delusions. This is consistent with the findings of Gillis and Blevens (1978), who found that paranoid schizophrenics, as compared to nonparanoids and normals, were prone to discover incorrect rules in a learning task in which the value of one criterion variable could be predicted probabilistically from the values of three others. If such results hold up, they would support the view that delusions, as a "choice" of symptom, are supported by a style of thinking that exists before the delusion. Alternatively, delusional thinking may be a reaction to some other kind of cause, and may be found only within a limited area (which would make it much harder to study systematically).

Note that delusional people need not be found just in mental hospitals. The extent to which delusions impair functioning may depend on their content. Thus, delusions of persecution and grandeur might make a person particularly bothersome to others, whereas delusions about politics, medicine, the supernatural, etc., might be tolerated and in some circles even encouraged. In addition, other kinds of delusions may contribute to other pathologies in which the delusions are not the primary problem. In depressive patients, for example, the belief in the worthlessness of the self is often maintained in the way I have described for delusional beliefs.

Delusional thinking may increase in certain emotional states. (In the middle of a temper tantrum, otherwise reasonable three-year-olds are remarkably insensitive to evidence!) Such states may involve the adoptions of impossible goals, for example, the goal of wanting something false to be true, and hence refusing to accept evidence against it. Strong emotion (e.g., grief) may impel the adoption of such goals. Such emotion-induced bias need not be truly irrational. If a person cannot help himself, the charge of irrationality is otiose.

The obsessive style characterized by Shapiro (1965) may also be interpreted in my framework. Obsessives cannot get certain ideas out of their heads. They return to the house repeatedly to make sure they really turned off the gas; they wash their hands 50 times a day to rid themselves of germs; and they worry about everything. Obsessives do not seem to exhibit the "typical" biases of insufficient search for evidence and possibilities. If anything, they are biased in a direction opposite from the normal: They seem to think too often and too much. However, their most basic problem may be insensitivity to evidence. The fact that they remember turning off the gas is not enough; they must check. In the worst cases, the belief that the gas is on takes on a life of its own, separate from the patient's consciously stated belief. Here, biased thinking is not the immediate problem, because the patient (says he) knows that the gas is not really on. However, even this kind of automatic recurrent thinking might be a residue of earlier problems resulting from biases alone.

The obsessive seems to be unlike the delusional in a couple of ways. First, the obsessive does consider alternatives. Second, he shows no confirmation bias; he does not look for evidence that the gas is on, because he really wants it to be off. His problem may be that he cannot use the negative evidence once he finds it, so he must return to get more.

The hysterical personality described by Shapiro (1965) is characterized by quickness and spontaneity, but an apparent incapacity for sustained thinking. Hysterics typically do not form and carry out realistic long-term plans. What they call "planning" is what the rest of us call "fantasy."

They have a poor memory for details, and seem to fail to distinguish what they know from what they make up. "Repression" is a favored defense mechanism. Hysterics are thus prone to such symptoms as multiple personalities, as well as the more classic (but now rare) conversion reactions (false sysmptoms of physical diseases). Hysterics seem to be classic impulsives, even in areas of importance to them. An interesting research question is the relation between hysterical disorders and other manifestations of impulsiveness.

Hyperactivity is characterized both by impulsiveness in mental tasks and inability to sustain attention in vigilance tasks, as well as by overactive behavior. Conceivably, the impulse to get up and run around may cause all of the other symptoms. However, it is also possible that the distortions of thinking are separate and that they survive the effect of maturation on the motor behavior itself (Weiss & Hechtman, 1979). The simplest interpretation of these distortions is again that hyperactives are impulsive. Hyperactivity is a clear case in which biological factors are likely to contribute to stylistic distortion, although this contribution would not imply that the style was unmalleable through training (as Meichenbaum, 1977, argues it is).

In sum, various pathological symptoms may be in part the result of disorders of thinking. These disorders might be characterizable in terms of extreme values of the parameters of thinking I have listed. Ordinarily, biases in thinking would not be the major cause of pathology, but they may (as suggested by Shapiro) determine the form than a pathology takes. (However, thinking disorders might also be pathological in their own right.) It ought to be possible to apply the framework I have outlined to the study of the nature, diagnosis, and treatment of these distortions (in the tradition of Beck, 1976). Failure to treat the biases might account for some of the failures of treatment of the more specific pathologies they help to produce.

Rational thinking as a moral trait

To some extent, rationality in thinking is, and should be, a moral character trait of the same sort as courage or honesty. Likewise, irrationality is a manifestation of poor character, just as is cowardice or dishonesty. I chose honesty and courage because being honest or courageous is not quite the same as being moral. Honesty and courage, like rationality, are traits that we would want to encourage for moral reasons, but being honest or courageous in a given occasion may be morally neutral (e.g., courage on a solo mountain-climbing trip). In contrast, generosity or

greed are always direct manifestations of morality or immorality, what-ever else they say about character.

This moral aspect of rationality is more closely bound up with our concept of intelligence than we often realize. When we disapprovingly call a person "stupid" because of some action, for example, a political leader, we do not often mean that the action was done too slowly, or that it would not have been done if the doer had a larger working memory capacity. Nor do we mean that it was just erroneous, for there many errors where the term is simply inappropriate. We hardly use the term in the case where it might be expected to apply most directly on its most literal interpretation, the case of the behavior of retardates. When we call someone stupid, we are really saying he is irrational, not that he is re-tarded. Being retarded is a state to be pitied, but being irrational is a state to be condemned. I grant that this is somewhat of an overstatement, for in fact some of us (especially children) use the term "stupid" in much the same way as they use "ugly," not as a moral condemnation but as a simpler sort of derogation. Although the connotations of this usage still affect the moral usage, this is not the sense I am concerned with here.

It is because intelligence is in part a moral quality that my view of it is more in accord with common usage than is the view of those who regard intelligence as purely a matter of capacity. Lack of capacity is undesirable to be sure, as is lack of natural beauty, but it is not justifiably a matter of moral censure. Rationality, like courage, is something potentially under control. The efforts of the moral community to uphold rationality, or courage, as a moral ideal can have some effect, whereas it will do no good at all to uphold a standard of capacity.

Further, the fact that "intelligence" refers to capacity as well as rational-ity may account in part for the tremendous emotion often aroused by discussions of the inheritance of intelligence. The proponents of the idea that intelligence is inherited have what I take to be is a narrow and rather benign concept of what intelligence is, namely, capacity. They often fail to understand the passions they arouse (e.g., Herrnstein, 1982). Yet their audience takes them to be talking about intelligence in all its manifesta-tions, including the part I call rationality of thinking. Since this is a moral quality, the claim that intelligence is inherited is like the claim that any other moral virtue or defect of character is inherited. The claim implies that there is no point in maintaining standards of this kind of morality, for our individual fates are determined at birth. This is a disturbing picture to those who value rationality as a trait. Perhaps this is why the strongest opposition to hereditarianism comes from teachers and others concerned with education, for it is in part their business to uphold just such standards.

Having made the distinction between the capacity and dispositional components of intelligence, I am not particularly disturbed by the hereditarians, for I take them to be talking about capacities only, where their case is quite plausible. Although dispositions may be influenced by capacities, dispositions have other influences as well. Thus, there is room for an effect of our efforts to uphold rationality as a virtue of character. The only thing that bothers me about the hereditarians I know is that they tend to avoid any discussion of what they think intelligence really is, thus doing nothing to reduce the kind of confusion I just mentioned.

There are many reasons why rationality of thinking should be a moral trait. One is the political idea, stemming from the early social-contract theorists and embodied in the U. S. Declaration of Independence (and elsewhere), that people are in fact responsible for their own government and have only themselves, collectively, to blame if they do not like it. Although some of us take this idea more seriously than others — some even extending it to the world as a society — I suspect that it is generally part of our system of values. It is a small step from this idea to the conclusion that we can blame people individually as well as collectively, for poor citizenship, for actions that hurt the whole society or the absence of actions that help it. This, in turn, implies that we must value to some extent the traits of character that make for good citizenship, and we must censure those traits that lead to poor citizenship. Rationality in thinking is one of these traits. Morality and concern for the welfare of society are others. If rationality helps us hold true beliefs and make good decisions, and if we concern ourselves with beliefs and decisions relevant to society, then rationality will help society make good collective decisions on the basis of the best available beliefs. Rationality also makes a person well suited to group participation at any level of self-government, for a rational person will be sensitive to evidence provided by others, even when that evidence conflicts with his initial beliefs. He will also accept possibilities from other people and add them to the list of those he is considering, and he will seek evidence that might contradict his own favorite possibility and support someone else's. Without these manifestations of flexibility, productive group discussion is impossible, and political argument is reduced to mere manipulation. This is not to say that everyone must be fully rational for democracy to work; rather, there must be enough rationality to provide a force for progress. (Other forces, such as fashion, the whims of authorities, and so on, may be much more unpredictable in their effects than is commonly supposed, and may thus amount to noise rather than systematic error.)

Other reasons for the value we place on rationality are analogous to the

reasons given for rationality as a standard of citizenship. Families and friendships may be considered as tiny communities, and being a good husband or a good friend is like being a good citizen of that community. To that extent, one's wife or one's friend will value one's rationality for the same reason she values her own. It will help to achieve the ends that she will desire on reflection for this small community. In this sense, rationality is as much of value as an interpersonal trait, like sincerity, as it is as a trait of citizenship.

Rationality is as relevant to "world citizenship" as it is to citizenship of any other social unit. Arguments for loyalty to a particular group (an ethnic group, a union, a nation) are vulnerable to counterarguments that are exactly analogous to the arguments against selfishness: How can you want this for yourself but not someone else (or some other group)? Thus, the narrow morality of group loyalty may be a result of failing to think of counterevidence to one's principles (e.g., nationalism, racism). (Of course, there may be elaborate moral defenses of nationalism, but these must go beyond the simple counterargument I have pointed to.)

A comment is in order about cases in which we censure a person for irrationality that is utterly unrelated to citizenship or to personal relationships. (It is hard to think of such cases. Even intellectual arguments are often part of some community enterprise. But let us assume they exist.) Really, we ought to be concerned with the trait only when it matters. But in fact, we value courage nearly as much on the football field as on a dangerous expedition where everyone's life is dependent on the willingness of others to risk their own lives for the sake of the group. This suggests that we believe that traits are somewhat general, or at least that people cannot deal with the inconsistency that would result from encouraging a trait only in certain domains. This may not be the case. However, it would seem very risky to act as if it were not the case. For example, it seems ill advised to tell a schoolchild, "Well, your thinking was really sloppy on this assignment. But there's no need to worry about it, because it has no real consequence. I'm sure that when it's really important, you'll do fine."

The attack on rationality

I have argued that rational thinking helps us to think more effectively in a number of ways: It helps us avoid impulsiveness and other biases, it helps us learn with understanding, and it helps us think well about moral issues. If rationality is so good, why is it so frequently attacked? These attacks take many forms. In popular psychology, there is much discussion of the

merits of intuitive or holistic thinking (often thought to be carried out in the right hemisphere of the brain), as distinct from linear or analytic thinking. Similar sentiments are found in the general (but, of course, not universal) distrust of intellectuals in many domains. Last but not least, a reader of an early draft of this book (up to here) said, "I'm not sure there is no such thing as being too rational. If people were as rational as you want them to be, I think they would be very unhappy. I know I would be."

I think that there are many reasons for these kinds of attacks. First, some of them are based on a false conception of rationality, one that I have tried to remedy. In the minds of many, the idea of rationality is associated with a kind of cold calculation based on a single kind of value: the quarterly report in the business world, the Gross National Product in economics, the body count in war, or the advancement of socialism. The extreme of this conception is surely the character of Dr. Strangelove in the Stanley Kubrick film, a character who was not particularly bothered by the destruction of most of humanity in nuclear war, provided only that a genetically superior strain could be preserved for posterity. (Of course, such simplistic thinking is found at all ends of the political spectrum.)

It seems to me that the critics are often right, but not because Strangelove thinking is too rational, but rather because it is rational in the service of goals that are too simple and one-dimensional. It is its single-mindedness that is most disturbing. Thus, those who criticize others for not considering morality, sentiment, the disruption of people's lives by rapid change, and so on, are in fact making a criticism about values, which guide the process of thinking. In fact, the view presented in chapter 3 suggests that there will be a general bias toward oversimplified goals, because of premature cessation of the search for goals. Hence, single-mindedness of the sort at issue is a prime example of one of the biases implied by the present theory.

More difficult is the question of why thinking with simple goals has come to be called "rational" in the first place. Sometimes, it may be because such simplification often allows decisions to be made by a kind of technical calculation, such as cost–benefit analysis. In other cases, some sort of abstract theory is involved. Further, the thinkers who are being criticized, the Strangeloves and the radicals, like to think of themselves as rational, and they call their opponents irrational or overly sentimental. Sentiment, it is thought, is the enemy of reason.

However, sentiment is not necessarily the enemy of reason, only certain sentiments, namely, those that encourage an unwillingness to think, to consider alternatives, to evaluate evidence correctly, and so on. Other

sentiments are among the very values that give us any reason to think at all: moral sentiments, sentiments of personal loyalty and attachment, desires for a better life, and sentiments favoring rationality itself. These sentiments are usually rational components of our life plans.

In this class of objections to rationality we should put two others. One is the argument that rational people do not fight hard enough (e.g., against communism) because they are too prone to see the other side. Another is that rational people are not moral enough, because they are too concerned with their self-interest. In both cases, the disagreement is really, once again, about goals. Given the flexible view of rational life plans presented in chapter 2, a rational person can be a totally committed fighter for a cause, or altruistically devoted to the service of others.

A second kind of criticism of "overly rational" thinking is that it is too reflective and too little concerned with action. We hesitate to place intellectuals in positions of responsibility because we fear that they will think too much and never be able to make the decisions required of them. From the point of view of my theory, the critics might once again be correct. It is possible to be irrational by thinking too much, beyond the point at which the expected benefits of thinking are greater than its costs. Thus, to criticize a person for thinking too much is not to say that he is "too rational," but to say that he is not rational enough. Once we take into account the cost of thinking, there is no such thing as being "too rational," unless it can be said that one's behavior is too much in accord with the goals one would have on reflection (including moral ones).

A third source of attack on rationality is the opposition to those who don the mantle of rationality and then claim to speak for the interests of others. Often, those who claim to know better are just those who are privileged by education, wealth, or positions of authority — a possible example is the support of the use of tax money to aid "high-brow" arts.

It must be acknowledged that there are serious questions here. There are surely cases in which true paternalism is justified; we assume that children, retardates, and the insane are not, in fact, rational enough to make their own decisions. (If we were to switch places with them, we too would want help in defining and defending our interests.) Conceivably, even some governmental paternalism on behalf of the average citizen — e.g., subsidies for adult education, laws requiring seat belts — may be justified. Of course, there are many difficult cases, and the line between benevolent paternalism and violation of basic rights is hard to draw. But the fact that there are difficult cases in using superior rationality as a justification of paternalism does not require us to abandon the concept of justified paternalism, let alone the concept of rationality. To do so would

be to argue that children should be allowed to make all their own decisions as if they were adults, for example, and this seems wrong even from the child's own (long-term) point of view. If we are concerned about the false claim of rationality as a defense of self-interest or abuse of authority, let us attack the falsity.

It is important to point out here that rationality is not restricted to those privileged by education or high intellectual capacity. A person without these things can in fact be rational in pursuing his interests, taking his limitations into account. Part of the rational course for such a person will often involve finding others, with more effectiveness, whom he can trust to defend his interests. Indeed, this is what politics is largely about, and even the well-educated person is not an expert in every matter affecting his interests.

Fourth, some of the attacks on rationality have been attacks on particular models of rationality. The work of Simon (1957), March (1978), and others has often been intepreted as an attack on the importance of rationality, when it really was only an attack on particular normative models — albeit the major models available. Such attacks are, I think, part of a constructive effort to develop better models, perhaps even models that are better by virtue of imposing fewer constraints on what can be called rational. The present theory is in large part an effort to respond to this kind of constructive criticism, by taking the cost of thinking and other problems into account. Once again, the problem is not with the goodness of rationality itself, but with the goodness of a particular conception of rationality. Criticisms such as these need not, and do not, detract from the fundamental idea that some methods of thinking are better than others, and we should strive to use the former.

A fifth kind of attack comes from adherents of religions (and other ideologies), who fear that adoption of rational methods of thinking will turn people (such as themselves) away from the religion in question. Such people are in a difficult position, for they claim to have a true belief, yet a belief that might not withstand the kind of criticism that these people would find valuable in other domains. This would seem to imply that their belief is not really as certain as they would like to think. When such people oppose the teaching of rational thinking to others, we can also make a moral argument against them: From their point of view, prevention of such teaching is analogous to preventing them from teaching their own religion.

In sum, I see some of the attacks on rationality as attacks on the values of thinkers who claim to think rationally in the service of those values. Others are attacks on particular conceptions of rational thinking, concep-

tions that are in fact seriously flawed. Although the present theory is a response to some of these attacks, it can undoubtedly be attacked the same way. Some of the attacks on rationality are based on appropriate fears of domination by those claiming to be more rational. But these attacks are misdirected, for they should be focused on the abuses of this claim, not on rationality itself. By attacking rationality, they involve antagonism to ways of thinking that ultimately would serve the considered interests of the attackers themselves. Finally, the fear of rationality by the purveyors of religious doctrines and other ideologies is, in a way, an admission of defeat; if the doctrines were indeed true, they would stand the scrutiny of rational inquiry.

Directions for research

I shall close this chapter with some suggestions for research within the framework I have outlined. Such research is in the tradition of research concerned with the effects of intelligence on economic success, on school performance, and so on. Often, such research has shown rather small effects. For example, the Terman Study (Terman & Oden, 1959; Sears, 1977) selected children with very high IQs and followed them into old age. Compared to the general population, these subjects were only a little better off in such things as mental health, divorce rate, and so on. There is precious little evidence that intelligence, as usually measured, at least, leads to happiness.

I have argued here that rationality does lead to happiness. If so, it ought to be possible to show that this is true. We could do this by showing that some good test of rationality (perhaps in a certain domain, such as home economics) correlates with happiness (perhaps in that domain — see Kourilsky & Murray, 1981). Or, we could attempt to increase the rationality of a group of people, and ask how this affects them. A beginning in this direction has been made by Duckworth (1983), who trained a group of students to "apply general problem-solving techniques to their personal problems" with apparent positive results of a very general sort. The latter kind of study is analogous to the studies of preschool interventions designed to raise intellectual abilities and to improve attitudes (Lazar et al., 1982).

To carry out such studies, we shall need some good measures of both rationality of thinking and goodness of the outcomes of thinking. There are several approaches to the development of such measures. One approach is to assume that the disposition to think rationally is somewhat general. In this case, we can deveop abstract laboratory tasks to measure

rationality, and we can ask whether performance on these tests correlates with the success of individuals in various aspects of their lives, or whether it is affected by training. For example, Steinlauf (1979) showed that a measure of "problem-solving skills" (as well as a measure of beliefs about locus of control) correlated the number of unwanted pregnancies in young women. Of course, the measure of problem-solving skills was not based on the present theory, but its spirit seems somewhat similar. If the present theory were used as a basis for development of tests, these tests would be more direct measures of biases.

Studies may be done of rationality within specific domains as well as in general. For example, the overconfidence phenomenon discussed earlier has been studied in a variety of domains (Lichtenstein et al., 1982). Here, little can be said in general, for the methods used must be tailored to the domain, and the obstacles and opportunities it provides.

In the next chapter, I discuss methods that might be used to train rational thinking. Training studies, like correlational studies, are inconclusive, but in a different way. The training may have unintended side effects, and these, rather than its effect on rational thinking, might account for any effects it has on outcome measures. However, for practical purposes, a successful training study gives us reason to go ahead and institute a type of training on a larger scale. A successful clinical trial with a new drug usually leads to the use of the drug for the disease in queston, even if the best theory about why the drug works may be wrong. Of course, further analysis may lead to clarification of the reasons for positive effects, and this understanding may be useful in the development of new treatments.

In correlational studies and in training studies, good outcome measures, as distinct from measures of thinking itself, are needed. The clearest kind of outcome for the study of the effects of irrationality is one that is undesirable from the point of view of the thinker himself. An unwanted pregnancy, in a woman who wants an abortion, is a clear example; a pregnancy in an unmarried adolescent, however undesirable in the eyes of some, is not. Now I do not mean to say that such outcomes necessarily result from irrational thinking. As I argued in chapter 1, bad outcomes can come about even when thinking is as rational as it can be, for rational thinking cannot anticipate the future very well, and bad luck is always possible. The question of whether irrational thinking leads to bad outcomes in a particular kind of situation is an empirical one. The problem in answering it is to find outcomes that are unambiguously bad, and this is why the clearest cases are those in which the thinker himself regards them as bad.

Some possible areas, other than birth planning, in which it might be feasible to look at outcomes in this way are home economics and management of personal finances, decisions about marriage and divorce (or getting together and breaking up before marriage), decisions about taking or refusing jobs or educational opportunities, decisions about selection of people for jobs or opportunities, and, of course, business decisions.

The effect of rationality on political behavior and citizenship is perhaps the most important effect rationality might have. However, this is also the most difficult area in which to evaluate the effect of rationality on outcomes, for good outcome measures are hard to come by. One approach is to examine measures that might reasonably affect real outcomes, e.g., the extent to which individual citizens can justify their political behavior or the lack of it. I have in mind such measures as those used by Perkins et al. (1983) to measure the quality of arguments made about whether or not television violence should be restricted. In essence, Perkins looked for fallacies in arguments such as generalizing from a single case, ignoring obvious counterarguments, and so on. Perkins asked whether such measures correlated with, for example, level of education (finding only tiny effects here). A similar approach is that of Tetlock (1983, 1984). The general problem with this approach is that it begs the question about what is "better," so that additional measures are needed.

One possible outcome measure is disagreement itself. Most major political conflicts involve the drawing of different conclusions from the same evidence; in such cases, one side or the other is likely to be irrational. If some method of thinking reduces disagreement, we cannot be sure that the new consensus is correct, but it is certain that people who disagree cannot both be correct. This method has been used by Gardiner and Edwards (1975) for the evaluation of a multi-attribute utility scheme.

In general, there is good reason to believe that the sum of the rationality or irrationality of individual citizens has a profound effect on the extent to which future generations will regard our governmental decisions as correct. (I choose future generations because I take them to be the ones most affected by our most difficult decisions.) Although some may not be convinced of the relevance of rationality to politics, the burden of proof in this case is not on those who are concerned with the promotion of rationality. The benefits of rational thinking in personal matters are probably enough reason to go ahead with our efforts to study rationality and try to teach it. If the hope that there will also be a political effect is further encouragement for some of us, there is little harm in this, even if we are wrong.

7   The teaching of rational thinking

I take teaching to be most narrowly what is done or could be done by teachers and professors. More broadly, it is what is done by parents and peers as well. Still more broadly, we can learn things from anything we do. So, if we are concerned with the promotion of certain kinds of knowledge, dispositions, or abilities, we can take teaching to include any attempt to arrange our environment to promote these things. I take the broadest view in this chapter, although it seems likely that discussion of the issues I raise will have its greatest effect on schools.

My purpose here is to show how the theory I have outlined (particularly in chapter 3) is relevant to the teaching of good thinking. In essence, this theory suggests that teaching should direct itself at the removal and prevention of the major biases: insufficient search (and its total absence), belief perseverance, and confirmatory bias in the search for evidence. I shall first discuss some basic issues: the question of equal opportunity, the question of generality of teaching, the question of developmental readiness. Then I shall sketch an analysis of the various objectives of instruction and the methods used to achieve them. I shall argue that only some of these objectives — principally the inculcation of beliefs and goals — are relevant to the teaching of thinking. This leads to a discussion of the relevance of beliefs and goals in a bit more detail. Then, I shall review various methods that have been used to teach rational thinking. Finally, I shall discuss the relation between the promotion of rationality and some of our other cultural institutions, taking the broad perspective I just described.

Equal educational opportunity

It might be argued that the teaching of good thinking to the privileged could only increase the inequalities that exist. Surely, this is true, but such an outcome is by no means a consequence of my theory. In fact, it

244

may be argued that the disadvantaged are those who have the most to gain from the least extra effort. Increased rationality of planning and decision making can help the disadvantaged manage their personal affairs more effectively — a task all of us can probably do better than we do, but one of particular importance to the poor. (The very rich, of course, do not need to be rational in these things, for they may hire lawyers and accountants to to the job for them!) Increased learning, which requires good thinking, may help to provide several paths out of poverty, from job skills in a technological society, to effective political organization, to new agricultural methods. In sum, although reduction of inequality is not a primary goal of the present effort, there is no reason to think that widespread education along the lines I propose will increase inequality, and some reason to think it might help to decrease it.

Generality

Should we try to teach thinking in general, or in specific domains such as citizenship, home economics, mathematics, and so on? This is a question that has occasioned considerable debate. On one side are those who argue that we can do little to anticipate the domains in which good thinking will be required, and that domain specific knowledge is rarely of any use after the final exam is over. On this side are some of the designers of programs designed to teach thinking in general (reviewed in Segal, Chipman, & Glaser, 1984) and some theoretical writers such as Baron (1985). On the other side are those, such as Hayes (1985), who argue that attempts to teach thinking in general or to raise intelligence have been disappointing, and, in any case, it is specific knowledge and skill that really count for the things most important in life. Education should not waste time trying to do what it cannot do, at the expense of what it can do, namely, impart specific knowledge and skill.

I do not regard the empirical evidence on the effectiveness of general teaching as very convincing either way. Common observation argues both ways. On the one hand, there are striking examples of people who think well only in limited domains. On the other, there are people who carry general attitudes about the value of thinking (for or against it) into most areas of their lives, and there are people who carry ways of thinking into new and unfamiliar areas, e.g., mathematicians whose "mathematical sophistication" extends to new branches of mathematics and artists who attempt to work in new media. There are also research studies showing apparent general transfer (reviewed by Baron, 1978, 1985), and others that fail to show it, although it might be argued that some of the

failures—particularly those that tried to teach memory skills (chapter 1)—were naively undertaken to begin with, because they required the subjects to discover for themselves what the general strategy actually was. However, even the best studies of the effects of general training can be interpreted in terms of specific effects, if one works at it. The question of the effectiveness of general training is probably unanswerable if our criterion is scientific certainty. However, if the question turns out to be important, we shall have to make a best guess. I shall argue here that some of the objectives of the teaching of good thinking may be accomplished quite generally, particularly the inculcation of "attitudes" (beliefs and goals), but other objectives, such as the learning of habits and heuristics, although relevant, might have to be taught more specifically, that is, within specific subjects or within areas of the taxonomy of chapter 3. When teaching must be specific, it is still possible that we can anticipate to a large extent the domains and areas in which good thinking will be important in our students' futures. Thus, even if our teaching does not transfer broadly, we might be able to teach good thinking where it is most important. Note that such areas need not be restricted to academic subjects, but could also include citizenship (including the ability to make and criticize arguments about matters of public concern, from both a practical and moral point of view) and personal decision making (including decisions about finances, careers, interpersonal commitments, and the bearing and raising of children).

If general teaching is ineffective, and if we also fail to anticipate the domains in which good thinking is needed, all is not lost. There are many social institutions that might be seen as ways of picking up the pieces of such failures (assuming they are failures at all). Among these are remedial programs in schools (for reading, writing, and general approaches to mathematics), clinical psychology, counseling, and psychiatry, family planning counseling, marriage counseling, personal financial advising, special training programs for business managers, and so on. Much can be done to promote rational decision making in these areas. A way to begin is for the professionals who provide these services to become well educated in rational thinking themselves. They then can—as many now do—take it is their mission not just to treat the immediate problem of their clients but also to teach their clients how to deal more effectively with similar problems that arise in the future (Schön, 1983). Part of this mission might involve the teaching of rational thinking in the domain in question.

In sum, the burden of maintaining rationality of thinking need not be seen as falling entirely on teachers, whose job would be to immunize their

students against irrationality forever. Rather, rational thinking is most easily maintained by a high respect for it among all members of society, especially those who are in a position to do any teaching at all, at any age level. In this way, generality of teaching becomes less important, and rational thinking can be maintained within domains themselves.

On the other hand, the idea of respect for rational thinking in general implies at least some appreciation of the common standards of rational thinking, of the sort I have tried to develop here. The theory of rational thinking thus needs to exist as a domain independent theory. Some people need to think in these terms, so that the standards of thinking in different domains can fertilize each other. It would be best if everyone had some understanding of the common basis of rational thinking. But such universality is not necessary for the kind of teaching I propose to be of value.

Developmental questions

What age is best for general teaching?

If we are to attempt any general teaching of rational thinking, or if we are to expect domain-specific teaching to transfer broadly, what age is best? There is an argument for starting early teaching and an argument for late teaching.

In favor of early teaching, it seems to be the case that young children have relatively few distinct domains of activity. For a toddler, for example, life seems to be divided up into work/play, hilarious play, and dealing with distress (mostly by complaining). By this I mean that toddlers will (I suspect) be highly consistent in their behavioral style within each of these classes. Later, the work/play category will differentiate into schoolwork, fantasy play with friends, and so on. If it were possible to influence a child's style of thinking before a great deal of differentiation took place, the style might carry through to all the various domains that grew out of the one where the training occurred.

It might be said in objection that there is very little thinking done at such early ages, and what is done is hard to influence. Karmiloff-Smith and Inhelder (1974/5) have documented this thinking in children's attempts to make blocks balance. Some literature (e.g., Rosen & D'Andrade, 1959) suggests that persistence in thinking can be taught even at an early age by arranging the environment so that it includes problems that are solvable with some persistence, but not so much that children will give up, and by encouraging children to keep working on

their own. Anyone who observes toddlers at play will find it hard to deny that thinking occurs.

Another reason for early teaching of thinking is that many of the traits that encourage or discourage good thinking are matters of personal commitment to values, such as "getting to the bottom of things," or "never admitting that you're wrong." Such values as these become part of a person's identity, whether they help rational thinking or hinder it (as I shall presently discuss). Now most theorists and observers agree that many such fundamental values are most easily inculcated relatively early, as soon as the child is capable of understanding them. Once a child begins to develop its own identity in a way that defines other conceptions as foreign, the child will simply refuse to listen to anyone who does not seem to agree with him on fundamental values. The young child, however, seems to be biased to admire its parents and teachers and to absorb their values whatever they might be.

There is also an argument for later teaching. One reason is that the student may be taught a number of formal tools that are useful in thinking, such as decision theory, the use of the decisional balance sheet (Janis & Mann, 1977), or the methods of philosophical argument. Another reason for later teaching is that the student may become more aware of his own thinking, more capable of analyzing it in terms such as those used in the present theory. The student can understand the reasons for good thinking, and can undertake explicit efforts to learn to do it in a variety of domains. Because the student does this out of understanding of the value of rational thinking, coercion is not required. The teacher's role is less one of inculcation and indoctrination, and more one of an assistant to a student who wants to improve himself.

On the other hand, if the student lacks the values that would cause him to seek such training and to try to learn from it, there is little that can be done. It thus seems that training in rational thinking should ideally occur throughout the course of education, to the extent that any generality is desired.

When is it possible to teach thinking in different areas?

If we would plan to teach general thinking in each of the areas of the taxonomy of chapter 3, it is worthwhile to know when it is appropriate to begin to emphasize each of these areas. The findings of developmental psychology can help us somewhat in this regard, but they must be tempered for two reasons. First, there is no single "age of acquisition" of each kind of relevant knowledge. Rather, things like scientific thinking, arithmetical thinking, or logical thinking are acquired gradually over a

long period, and the apparent age of acquisition will depend on the severity of the criterion we use to say that some piece of knowledge has been "acquired" (Flavell, 1971; Baron, 1978; Baron & Treiman, 1980; Gelman, 1982; Gelman & Baillargeon, 1983). Second, even if we could determine the natural age of acquisition, this is not necessarily the age at which a concept or type of reasoning is best taught. The development of reasoning in children may be much more influenced by culture — including education — than many developmentalists seem to assume. Thus, widespread innovations in education or in cultural emphasis could change the ages at which certain ways of thinking are acquired. Put radically, developmental psychology may be, to a larger extent than admitted, a catalog of educational deficiencies.

As an example, consider the appropriate age for the teaching of reflective thinking (in the sense of chapter 3). Many have interpreted Piaget's work to imply that reflective thinking is largely impossible to teach before adolescence. In this regard, it seems important to cite the work of Lipman (1985), who has developed a packaged program for elementary school children called *Philosophy for children*. In its essence, it seeks to teach elementary school children to reflect in just the way that philosophers do. It does this by example, by classroom discussion, and by homework assignments. The "example" consists largely of a series of story books concerning the adventures of "Harry Stottlemeyer," a child who is unusually interested in problems of logic, ethics, and the precise meaning of words such as beauty and truth. In his first adventure, Harry discovers that sentences like "All oaks are trees" become false when reversed (All trees are oaks), and he concludes that all sentences have this property. His friend Lisa provides a counterexample, "No eagles are lions." They experiment with different sentences and discover that the first word is crucial. Classroom discussion goes through several other sentence frames of this sort. As homework, the students are told to work through a few more on their own.

According to Lipman (1985), the program is highly successful in getting students interested in academic pursuits, and it improves their grades and test scores. This is at least first-blush evidence that the claim of the Piagetians is wrong. It looks as if reflective thinking can be taught at the elementary school level. If it can, it would seem advisable to do so, for at this age, identity has not yet hardened, and the teaching might well inculcate values as well, values such as respect for good arguments, and, more generally, good thinking.

My own informal observations of my son David suggest that elements of reflection and scientific thinking might be taught even earlier. At age

2 1/2, he noted that women cannot whistle; luckily, a counterexample was readily available in his great-grandmother, and David gave up his belief. Later, just before his third birthday, he corrected a similar overgeneralization, namely, that all men have beards, on the basis of memory alone: when I asked whether he could think of any men who did not have beards, he recalled that Andrea's dad did not, and he then agreed that some men had beards, and would not agree that all men did. At 3 1/2, he was able to tell me what we would need to look for to test his assertion that all Cadillacs were hatchbacks, namely, a Cadillac that was not a hatchback (which we soon found). Of course, biases may also be present in young children's reflective or scientific thinking. At age 2, David had decided that the numbers written on the bottoms of some blocks corresponded to the number of sides of each block, as indeed they did for the figures between triangle and hexagon. When he told me that the circle had one side because it had the number 1, I first thought that he had attained a deep insight. However, he then went on to tell me that the Greek cross had 10 sides, and he counted them, stopping at ten. When I counted them correctly, he said I was wrong. (The nature of biases in young children would seem to be an interesting research topic.) If thinking of this sort is present, and if it shows biases, it seems likely that there is room for teaching; this is the goal of the preschool program developed by Blank (1973), which I shall discuss.

The objectives of teaching and the teaching of thinking

What does it mean to teach thinking? We may think of education as having several different kinds of objectives, each of which demands certain methods. Let me classify these objectives, somewhat loosely, as methods, skills, habits, facts, beliefs, and goals. These kinds of objectives play different roles in the theory of knowledge, where there is considerable debate about their meaning and their significance for education (see Scheffler, 1965, for a review). I shall put aside much of this debate by ignoring the question of how we know whether a person has acquired a skill, knowledge of a fact, a belief, etc., and by discussing the objectives in terms of the methods used to attain them. I shall argue that the teaching of good thinking involves some of these objectives — hence some teaching methods — but not others.

Methods are ways of doing something. We teach methods by telling people what to *do* to achieve a certain goal, which we assume they have, and we may then observe them and provide corrective feedback. We teach methods when we teach people how to do long division, how to

drive, or how to memorize lists. Methods are taught most directly by making imperative statements, usually with a condition, e.g., "If you want to add a list of numbers, first add the right column, then . . ." As discussed in chapter 6, methods may be taught with the goal of having the student understand them, or with the goal of the student simply learning them "by rote." In the former case, part of the teaching of methods involves the teaching of facts. If thinking itself is a method, it is one that everyone already knows and therefore does not need to be taught. Of course, knowing how to think, or how to drive, does not guarantee that one thinks well or drives well.

Most heuristics are methods for making thinking more effective in particular domains (chapter 3). Some heuristics, such as those mentioned at the end of chapter 3, are methods for avoiding biases in thinking. For these heuristics, and only these, we may say that the teaching of thinking involves the teaching of methods. However, this sort of instruction presupposes that the student has the goal of thinking well.

Use of a schema (chapter 5) is also a method, to the extent to which it is useful to instruct a person in *how* to use it, but it may also be a fact or a belief. [Schemata are often said to involve mental representations that are neither facts, beliefs, nor methods (procedures). One way to think about such representations is that they are parts of methods. The student is assumed to know a general method for using representations of a certain sort, so that when we teach him a new method, we need only fill in the parts of it that are new, and these parts do not mention actions as such.] Use of schemata is not thinking (in my sense) unless they are used to resolve doubt. Schemata are usually best seen as specific, and the teaching of schemata is therefore part of the teaching of specific subject matters, not the teaching of thinking. (General schemata, if any, may be considered as general heuristics.)

Skills, in the narrow sense in which I use the term, are distinguished by the goal of effortless fluency, accuracy, or speed in their performance. When we teach a skill, such as piano playing, driving, or wine tasting, we are concerned not only with teaching someone how to do something (methods) but also with getting the student to do it well. This involves a period of practice designed to build speed, accuracy, or effortlessness, independently of the student's actually knowing how to perform the skill. During this period, the student need do nothing qualitatively new; he just does the same thing better and better. By this, I mean that the practice itself is the crucial element of instruction, and any advice we give along the way (typically in the early stages of learning) is part of teaching a method, not a skill.

Although thinking is often referred to as a skill (Bartlett, 1958), it is probably unproductive to teach it this way. This is because thinking involves, by definition, situations in which the thinker does not know what to do, and therefore cannot have practiced doing it in that situation. We might think that thinking itself would be a practiceable skill, which could be practiced in some situations and transferred to novel ones, but empirical evidence suggests that this teaching method is weak at best. A large body of empirical evidence supports the findings of Thorndike and Woodworth (1901) that transfer of skills occurs only when there are common components (Baron, 1985). For thinking, it seems hard to specify what those components might be, in such a way that provision of practice might help. Simply searching for possibilities, evidence, and goals is surely done enough by everyone that a little more practice would not help—even if the practice would result in transfer. The setting of parameters for thinking in specific kinds of situations may have an aspect of skill, for accuracy is at issue, but it seems most likely that biases in the setting of parameters are not easily corrected by practice alone, given the sources of these biases (see chapter 3: underweighing of future value, asymmetry in learning from feedback).

There are of course skills involved in the teaching of specific subject matter such as reading or arithmetic. And the availability of skills undoubtedly makes thinking in these domains more effective. But the teaching of these skills is not the same as the teaching of thinking in these areas.

When we teach a *habit*, our objective is to make a student do a certain action in a certain situation. Habits are distinguished from methods in that the external situation, rather than the student's goal, is crucial for their occurrence. The goal is either assumed to be present in the situation, or it is irrelevant. Thus, when asked, "How are you?" most of us answer, "Fine, how are you?" regardless of whether we are fine or not, whether we want to convey information or not, and whether we care about the questioner or not. Many of the heuristics for avoiding biases (consider alternatives, look for evidence against my view, etc.) can be taught as habits, provided the teacher knows enough about the situations the student will encounter. In many situations, thinking is not worth it, so that it would be counterproductive to teach a student to *always* check his initial hunches, etc. Thus, if these heuristics are to be taught as habits, the situations in which they are to be used must be specified. Doing this is not out of the question; for example, in many types of schoolwork, thinking is always worthwhile. However, the teaching of thinking through the teaching of habits is somewhat limited, because we cannot anticipate all situations in which the heuristics of good thinking will be useful.

Facts consist of objectives that we teach most directly by making declarative statements, e.g., "Harrisburg is the capital of Pennsylvania." In many cases, when we say that a student knows a fact or has learned that a fact is true, we require something more than that the student simply memorize what she is told. Specifically, we require that the student came to believe the fact in an appropriate way, roughly, through a rational method; this requirement stems from the view that knowledge is *justified* true belief (Scheffler, 1965).

Knowledge of facts, like methods, skills, and habits, is part of what it means to be an expert in a specific subject. Thus, it is not surprising that experts in particular subjects are found to know more facts about those subjects (and have more appropriate methods, etc.) than novices (see Glaser, 1984). (These facts may include facts about the organization of other facts, such as taxonomies.) Moreover, it seems useful to characterize the course of development as the acquisition of expertise about a variety of domains; adults are at least as expert as children about almost everything. We might be tempted to conclude, then, that the teaching of good thinking amounts to the teaching of expertise, through the teaching of facts, specific methods, specific habits, and skills. (Glaser, 1984, argues for this view, and then inexplicably backs off from it.) By this view, intelligence is roughly the sum of a person's expertise, and the teaching of intelligence is just the teaching of everything.

I have argued throughout this book that it is possible to have a conception of good thinking that is essentially orthogonal to expertise. A good thinker is good at managing her skills and knowledge, whatever they might be. A novice can be a good thinker if she uses the knowledge she has to solve problems that look soluble, and gives up when the problem looks impossible (when effort will not pay off). She can be a poor thinker if she always gives up too soon; in this case she will also be a poor learner and is unlikely to become an expert. An expert can be a good thinker if she thinks well about problems that are truly difficult, or a poor thinker if she refuses all these problems, preferring the routine ones that can be solved without thinking. The main difference between an expert and a novice from the present point of view is that the expert can often be effective without thinking, but the novice rarely can do so.

The main implication of the present theory is that the teaching of intelligence is not, in principle, limited to the teaching of expertise. The fact that expertise must be taught by teaching specific content does not, then, imply that good thinking must be taught the same way.

I use the term *beliefs* in a narrow sense, which refers to beliefs of a general sort, other than facts, which form a basis of action. Religious

beliefs are a prototypical example. These are (in most cases, I assume) not facts, for they are not fully justified. A person who holds these beliefs acts as if they were true, and is thus "committed" to them. Yet, beliefs are not simply goals, for beliefs do not determine goals: A person who believes in God may still decide to take the side of Satan. Many things that we call "values" are beliefs in this sense, although some are more properly thought of as goals.

Beliefs may be taught as if they were facts (and are surely often taught this way), but such teaching is a kind of deception (however justified it might sometimes be). Otherwise, the teaching of beliefs usually involves the giving of arguments for them and the rebutting of arguments against them. It often involves modeling, demonstrating by personal example that one can hold the beliefs, act on them, and be satisfied as a result.

There are many beliefs that make for good thinking in general, and many beliefs that tend to prevent it. Among the former are the belief that thinking often leads to better results, that difficulties can often be overcome through thinking (rather than, say, through luck), that good thinkers are open to new possibilities and to evidence against possibilities they favor, and that there is nothing wrong (per se) with being undecided or uncertain for a while. Among the latter are beliefs that changing one's mind is a sign of weakness, that being open to alternatives leads to confusion and despair, that quick decision-making is a sign of strength or wisdom, that truth is determined by authority, that we cannot influence what happens to us by trying to understand things and weigh them, and that intuition is the best guide to the making of decisions. The former beliefs act to oppose the natural biases I have described, and the latter act to support them (whatever germ of truth they might otherwise contain). (In the next section, I shall discuss these beliefs and others at greater length.)

It seems likely that the teaching of beliefs of the former sort, and the opposition to beliefs of the second sort, are an important part of any effort to teach good thinking. Sometimes this kind of teaching is implicit. For example, when we teach students to suspend judgment, consider alternatives, and so on, we are implicitly conveying the message that it is a good thing to do these things (or else why would we teach them?). Sometimes the teaching of beliefs may be quite explicit. For example, when students object to my own arguments for open-mindedness by arguing that too much is bad for one's mental health, I present myself as an example of an open-minded person (I hope) who does not have ulcers as a result. An important property of beliefs is that they can be taught in full generality, and — in contrast to the teaching of habits or methods — there

is no reason to think they will be any less effective when taught in general than in connection with specific domains of thinking.

The importance of beliefs in thinking is consistent with the suggestion of Perkins et al. (1983) that poor thinking often results from a "makes-sense epistemology," in which the thinker believes that the way to evaluate conclusions is by asking whether they "make sense" at first blush. It is also consistent with the claim of Dweck and Elliott (1983) that children's beliefs about intelligence affect their response to failure. According to Dweck and Elliott, children who believe that intelligence is a fixed "entity" tend to attribute their failures to their stupidity (or to the difficulty of the task) and thus reduce their effort after a failure. Children who believe that intelligence is a "process," a way of dealing with difficulties, tend to attribute their failures to lack of sufficient effort and thus increase their effort after a failure. Although the latter children — in the extreme — hold a somewhat oversimplified belief, it is one that tends to encourage thinking. Both the belief that error or failure is due to stupidity and the belief that success is due to effort may become self-fulfilling in the long run.

The belief that good thinking helps to discover the truth and to make good decisions, and all the associated beliefs of the sort just listed, are useless unless a student has the *goal* of discovering the truth and making good decisions. Richards (1971) points out the parallel between rationality and morality: Unless one wants to be rational, or good, all the knowledge (and belief) in the world about what makes for rationality and goodness is useless. Surely, just about everyone wants to know the truth and to make good decisions (and to be moral) to some extent, but the real issue is the strength of these goals relative to others. For example, a student who is a good thinker, who values good thinking, and who wants to do it, may find himself at odds with his peers. He may find himself reaching conclusions they disagree with and are unwilling to discuss, and so on.

Goals may be taught by deriving them from other goals, by showing the student that the goal in question will help him achieve some goal he already has. Such demonstration can be done in many ways: by argument, by example, or by inducing the student to adopt the new goal (or to increase its weight) as an experiment. It should not be hard to teach the goals associated with good thinking by this method, for good thinking is supposed to help people achieve other rational goals, regardless of what those goals might be (chapter 1). Goals can also be taught by modeling. A student may come to want something because someone he likes or admires wants it. Goals cannot by taught directly by imperative

statements: We can tell a person to *do* something, but it does not make sense to tell him to *want* something. (Nor can goals be taught as if they were facts, even with deception — in contrast to beliefs.)

Many goals, at many levels of the hierarchy of goals and subgoals, make for good thinking: the goal of thinking well (as something one can take pride in); the goal of knowing the truth, of getting to the bottom of things; the goal of making good decisions; the goal of being reasonable in the sense of being likable for one's open-mindedness and receptivity to the suggestions of others; the goal of being moral or doing the right thing (since it often requires good thinking to decide what the right thing is); the goal of being a good citizen; or the goal of thinking for its own sake, as something that is enjoyable as an activity (socially or alone). There are also goals that discourage good thinking: the goal of being steadfast (in sticking to one's conclusions despite counterevidence); the goal of reaching conclusions quickly; the goal of being authoritative (powerful in some sense); and the goal of honoring authority (despite counterevidence). Like beliefs, many of these goals can be taught (or inculcated) in general, and there is no reason to think they are any less effective this way than when taught specifically. In general, but not always, beliefs and goals come in pairs: people who want to do (or avoid) X tend to believe that it is *good* to do (or avoid) X. Surely, beliefs and goals affect each other, although much anguish may result from the imperfection of this linkage.

Goals, beliefs, and expectations

The considerations just mentioned should call our attention to the immense literature on goals (motives) and expectations (see, e.g., Feather, 1982, and Dweck & Elliott, 1983, for recent reviews). Although it should not be ignored by the student of intelligence, this literature is flawed, from our point of view, by lack of concern with normative theory (with some exceptions, such as Janoff-Bulman & Brickman, 1982; see also Baron, in press). It fails to make distinctions that from a normative point of view would seem crucial. For example, much of the literature on achievement motivation ignores the distinction between the desire to do one's best and the desire to do better than others (if necessary, by making sure they do worse). In addition to this literature, we can get many useful suggestions from other literature on cognitive style, cognitive consistency, and other issues in personality and social psychology. However, much of the personality literature is concerned with particular measures rather than the underlying dispositions being measured, and the other relevant literature is not usually directly concerned with the issues relevant here.

Thus, from all this literature, we can at best get some hints about the causes and prevention of irrational thinking.

Let us begin by asking what goals might cause the various biases discussed in chapter 3, the main ones being insufficient search and biases in the search for evidence and use of evidence. One negative goal is a distaste for thinking, a simple sort of mental laziness or sluggishness completely analogous to physical laziness. Laziness could lead directly to premature cessation of search, and it could also lead to the development of other biases — such as biased use of evidence — that eliminate the need for thinking by (falsely) strengthening possibilities that are initially only moderately strong. The question here is when laziness is irrational. I would suggest that mental or physical activity is in part an acquired taste, or at least our tolerance for it, and our enjoyment of it is influenced by experience. Children should thus have the opportunity to learn to enjoy mental (and physical) activity when possible, and to tolerate it when they cannot enjoy it. Such an overall increase in the utility for mental work is rational because it serves the student's other long-term ends, whatever they might be. More generally, learning to enjoy thinking — through games or real problem-solving — may be one of the best ways to learn to think well.

Mental work on a given task might start out being enjoyable but quickly become aversive. Such buildups of aversiveness are common in motivational systems, and they may happen more quickly in some people than others. This buildup could lead to premature cessation of search. But it need not always do this, for thinking tasks may often be interrupted and resumed, if the thinker is willing to leave a task with his doubt still unresolved.

Many have spoken of some sort of intolerance of doubt (Dewey, 1933), ambiguity (Rokeach, 1960), or lack of closure (Wollman, Eylon, & Lawson, 1979) as a source of poor thinking. (The specific instruments used to measure these properties are beside the point here.) Since doubt (unlike effort) is a ubiquitous property of thinking, intolerance of doubt can function as a general goal not to think. However, things are not this simple, for the function of thinking is sometimes to resolve doubt that is already present, and if intolerance of doubt is to function as a goal against thinking, there must be some way of removing the doubt. What may occur is that a person who dislikes doubt discovers thinking methods that remove subjective doubt very quickly, but without really removing it from the point of view of an external observer. These methods may include biased search for evidence and biased use of evidence, so that possibilities that are initially fairly strong attain high strength quickly. Of

course, this is like dealing with a cold house by holding a match under the thermostat and declaring the house to be warm when the thermostat reaches 70. Although there may be a natural goal to avoid effort, it is harder to imagine a natural goal to avoid doubt. Hence, it seems more likely that intolerance of doubt is socially transmitted.

We might avoid thinking because we are afraid of failing in a task that is important to us (Feather, 1982). If we don't try, we cannot properly be said to fail, and we can maintain a belief in our ability to have succeeded. Thus, we satisfy our fear of failure, because we do not really fail. This sort of goal seems irrational in two ways: First, pure fear of failure (as distinct from desire for success) serves no purpose in advancing our other plans; for this purpose, the only problem with trying and failing is the lost time taken away from plans more likely to succeed, not the failure itself. Second, a person who behaves this way may be basing his self-esteem on an image of what he might have done, rather than one of what he habitually does. Once again, this serves no general purpose of advancing other plans, especially in children — although it might be an appropriate feeling for adult victims of injustice or bad luck.

Another goal against thinking is a desire not to reconsider a decision already made (Janis & Mann, 1977) or a belief already formed (as dealt with in the literature on cognitive consistency, e.g., Abelson et al., 1968). This goal would cause us to avoid in particular those episodes of thinking that might lead to conclusions inconsistent with those already drawn. Of course, this goal is rational up to a point, for it is rational not to think too much in general. However, the same reasons that make us avoid thinking in general can make us avoid — more than we ought to — situations that would cause doubt and thus give us reason to think. Further, it might be best to learn to live with certain conflicts unresolved, so that we are not inhibited from thinking in general by the fear that we shall be compelled to resolve every doubt we encounter. Again, intolerance of doubt may play a role.

There are also positive goals that encourage rational thinking. Among these are curiosity (a positive value attached to search for evidence in particular), and the desire for competence (White, 1959). For at least some people, thinking can be fun. These goals are surely natural ones, but they are evidently also affected by culture and child rearing (McClelland, 1960). These goals do not in themselves promote rational thinking, but they work against the common biases that would cause too little thinking. In some cases, these goals might cause too much thinking by themselves, except that they are reasonable parts of any person's plan, so

that their satisfaction cannot be called irrational. It also seems reasonable that some people also have goals to think rationally and to abide by the conclusions of their own thinking, but I know of no studies of such goals.

Another kind of positive goal is moral. Because — as I argued in chapter 6 — rational thinking has moral value, a person with moral goals, such as being a good citizen, can want to think well as a way of satisfying these goals. This is not a trivial reason to think rationally. It is in the domain of public debate, where charges of irrationality are most frequently made, that the desire to avoid such charges may be a powerful goal in those who participate at all.

All of the goals I have listed may be affected by culture, and some are very likely due entirely to cultural beliefs about how people ought to run their intellectual lives. Cultures that encourage rational thinking are those that value questioning, inquiry, the satisfaction of curiosity, and intellectual challenge. Cultures that oppose such thinking are those that value authority, quick decision-making, correctness (even from guessing) rather than good thinking, and constancy of opinion to the point of rejecting new evidence. Such values are transmitted in a variety of ways, by expressions of admiration for people who embody them, by the tasks children are given to do at home and in school, and so on. Of course, most cultures are not purely positive or negative from this point of view; rather, they teach conflicting beliefs, which lead to conflicting goals.

Expectations are as important as goals, and may, in fact, interact with goals in various ways. If people do not believe that thinking is useful, they will not think. This is perhaps the major argument one hears against thinking about things like nuclear war, religion, or morals: "These matters are beyond me. They are best left to experts who are capable of thinking about them — if anyone."

On a more mundane level, the effort that children put into their school work may be in large part a function of how much good they think effort will do. There is a substantial literature on this question, much of it related to the study of "helplessness" (Seligman, 1975). The basic finding is that when subjects are made to fail on one task (e.g., an insoluble problem), they are more likely than other subjects to fail on similar tasks in the future (or even on very difficult tasks in the immediate future). One explanation of this effect is that the initial failure experience lowers the expectation for success, and the amount of thinking (or other work) in subsequent tasks thus decreases. (Another explanation is that the emotional response to failure has a direct effect on performance.) This explanation is supported by several findings showing relations between the effect of failure experi-

ence and the subject's explanation of the failure. For example, Diener and Dweck (1978) asked children to do a series of arithmetic problems, with every fifth problem being beyond the child's level and hence insoluble. Some children tended to fail on immediately subsequent problems, despite being able to solve similar problems not preceded by failure, but other children, if anything, did better on subsequent problems. Subjects were asked to talk aloud as they worked. The first, "helpless" group tended to blame their failures on such factors as stupidity, which would persist into subsequent problems and hence provide a reason (if true) for lower expectations. The second, "mastery-oriented" group did not spontaneously explain their failures at all, but tended to remark that they would have to try harder on the next problem, thus implicitly attributing their failure to lack of effort, an attribution that would give them no reason to lower their expectation about the value of thinking. Other evidence supporting the role of expectations comes from the training studies I shall describe. As yet, however, there has been no attempt to examine directly the effect of induced helplessness on impulsiveness.

In sum, the teaching of good thinking might ideally require inculcation of positive goals and expectations throughout the course of development. Although it may seem wrong to give high expectations to a low-capacity child, even here there is an argument for erring on the high side rather than the low side. High expectations in children are to some extent self-fulfilling, for they encourage a child to work harder and thus benefit from practice. Further, even children of low general capacity can probably learn to think well in a few areas, with sufficient practice, so that high expectations coupled with relatively early specialization might not be unrealistic at all.

I have argued so far that the teaching of thinking is best done at all ages. It may involve the teaching of methods and habits, but it must involve the inculcation of beliefs and goals. This requirement implies that such teaching cannot be divorced from an ideological commitment to good thinking among all those who influence the young.

Methods of teaching

In this section I review some of the methods that have been and that might be used for teaching good thinking in general or in specific areas. I shall try to show how whatever success these methods might have can be understood in terms of the theory I have presented. At present, the developers of each method use their own idiosyncratic theoretical language, and it is hard to see the underlying thread.

Tutorial method

The goal of the tutorial method is to make the student internalize the values and some of the rules of good thinking. The method in its basic form requires one-to-one interaction between a tutor and a student. The tutor must be an expert in the domain being discussed, in the goals of instruction, and in the methods of teaching.

The most fully worked out example of the tutorial method is the technique presented by Blank (1973) for teaching preschool children, particularly those whose background makes it likely that they will have later trouble in school. The teaching is integrated into a preschool program with a low ratio of children to teachers, so that the teacher can spend a few periods a day with each child. Thus, the method is expensive, yet the data available suggest that it is well worth the cost. Blank (1973) reports gains of 14 IQ points, relative to control groups with no special training or with an equal amount of one-to-one interaction not of a tutorial character (these two control groups not differing from each other). However, Blank correctly points out that the IQ test ought to be less sensitive than other measures to the quality of the child's thinking, so these results may well underestimate the effects of the program. Lazar et al. (1982), reviewing the results of a number of preschool programs (not including Blank's), finds that effects on IQ are generally small, if present at all, yet effects on school success, defined as not dropping out, not being put in a special class, and not staying back a year, are substantial. Since Blank's program does seem to affect IQ, even though it is no more directed at this goal than are any other programs, we might expect even greater effects on school performance.

In Blank's method, the tutor gives the child instructions to follow or questions to answer. The tutor looks for a level of difficulty of questions and instructions that is great enough to produce occasional errors yet not so great as to induce total frustration. The heart of the method is the tutor's response to errors. As Blank puts it (pp. 88-89):

The confrontation of error has value which goes beyond helping the child recognize why a particular response is incorrect. The need to examine the "wrong" response not only solidifies the "right" response, but it also leads the child to gradually internalize the "rules" used by the teacher to demonstrate the appropriate response. As a result, even when the adult is not present, the child has techniques by which to evaluate his thinking (e.g., if he has an appropriate idea, he may try it out to see if it works because this is the pattern that has been set by the teacher).

Here are some of the techniques the tutor uses to respond to the child's errors.

Delay. This should be used when the "child is capable of performing the response demanded although he has not done so before because of his impulsivity." For example, if the child starts to follow a command before the teacher has finished giving it, the teacher says, "Wait a minute, listen to . . ." This may induce the child to search for possibilities or evidence before responding, thus working against impulsiveness.

Introduce a cue to restructure the situation. As an example, Blank gives the following (p. 93): "Teacher — 'Why do you think we couldn't get this sponge into the (small) cup and we could fit the marble?' Child — 'Because it's a sponge.' Teacher — 'Okay, I'LL CUT THIS SPONGE IN TWO. Now it's still a sponge. Why does it go into the cup now?' " It seems to me that this is actually the construction of a counterexample to a principle implied by the child's explanation, namely, the principle that sponges do not fit in cups. Thus, the point of this technique (if the example is a good one) is to teach the child to seek counterevidence (or potential counterevidence) when testing a general proposition.

Relating unknown to the known. For example, a child who fails to answer a question about how the spaghetti will feel after it is cooked is asked if he can recall how the potatoes felt after *they* were cooked. This seems to encourage the child to make the generation of a possibility into a subepisode, in which the goal is to recall a similar case. This may be a very generally useful heuristic for generating possibilities (see Baron, 1978).

Other techniques take the form of hints, which are essentially ways of simplifying the problem to bring it within a suitable range of difficulty without at the same time eliminating the need for the child to think. One way to do this is to isolate components of the task. For example, "The teacher presents a group of blocks in a pattern and then says, 'Now you make this pattern over here with these blocks.' " If the child does nothing, the teacher says, "Show me the block at the bottom. Get one like it." (pp. 92-93) Another simplification technique is to make the question asked more specific ("How did the stove feel?" instead of "Why did you remove your hand from the stove?"). Such techniques do not include the common ploy of simply giving the answer in the form of a question ("Was it because the stove was hot?"), which might encourage an unthinking "yes" from the child. In contrast, Blank's simplification techniques (of which there are many) might have the effect of encouraging thinking, and discouraging premature cessation. These effects would come about through increases in the child's expectation of the value of thinking. If the

child cannot answer the question asked, or if the teacher makes the question so easy that the child need not think, the child may learn that thinking is not a very effective way to deal with questions and instructions. These techniques thus encourage thinking, and discourage premature cessation, by increasing efficacy or self-confidence. At the same time, Blank never recommends simply "encouraging" the child by saying "very good" regardless of the child's answer. The question should always be simplified so that the child figures out the answer on his own. The avoidance of such blind encouragement prevents the child from developing overconfidence (in the thinking done so far), a different kind of "self-confidence" that might increase the bias to stop thinking prematurely (chapter 4).

A second recent approach to the tutorial method is that of Collins (1977). Collins is concerned with the use of the "Socratic" method of teaching at the high school and college levels. He proposes no new techniques, because he assumes (correctly, I think) that the method has been in more or less continuous use since the time of Socrates himself. (Blank cites her own experience with the method when she was a graduate student at Cambridge University as one of the major influences on her own work.) Rather, Collins tries to state a theory of tutorial dialogue at this level. The theory takes the form of a set of rules thought to be used by good Socratic tutors. Collins worked on the theory by examining a set of actual (and imagined) tutorial dialogues; thus, his own work is an example of reflective thinking.

Collins suggests that tutorial dialogue can be used for several purposes: to teach specific content, to teach how to use knowledge in a specific domain, and to teach general methods of reasoning. The second purpose, the use of knowledge within the domain, presumably occurs in part through the creation of what I have called schemata. Collins make no commitment on the question of whether the general methods will transfer to other domains. In fact, this may depend on whether such transfer is encouraged during the teaching. Even if such transfer does not occur, however, the general methods are useful to the extent that thinking in the domain itself is useful. The tutorial method seems especially useful for teaching reflective thinking (as in my taxonomy). Although the method can surely be adapted to other purposes, most of Collins's examples are from this domain.

The main example in Collins (1977) concerns a geography student's discovery, using his own knowledge, of a general rule for the conditions required for the growing of rice. Here are some of the rules that tutors use, according to the theory, with illustrations from this example; note

that each rule specifies conditions for its use (from Collins, 1977, pp. 342-350):

Rule 1: Ask about a known case. If (1) it is the start of a dialogue, or (2) there is no other strategy to invoke, then (3) pick a well-known case and ask what the value of the dependent variable is for that case, or (4) ask the student if he knows a case with a particular value of the dependent variable. Example: Ask the student "Do they grow rice in China?" or "Do you know any place where rice is grown?"

Rule 5: Form a general rule for an insufficient factor. If (1) the student gives as an explanation one or more factors that are not sufficient, then (2) formulate a general rule asserting that the factor given is sufficient and ask the student if the rule is true. Example: If the student gives water as the reason they grow rice in China, ask him "Do you think any place with enough water can grow rice?"

Rule 6: Pick a counterexample for an insufficient factor. If (1) the student gives as an explanation one or more factors that are not sufficient, or (2) agrees to the general rule in Rule 5, then (3) pick a counterexample that has the right value of the factor(s) given, but the wrong value of the dependent variable, and (4) ask what the value of the dependent variable is for that case, or (5) ask why the causal dependence does not hold for that case. Example: If a student gives water as the reason they grow rice in China or agrees that any place with enough water can grow rice, pick a place like Ireland where there is enough water and ask "Do they grow rice in Ireland?" or "Why don't they grow rice in Ireland?"

Rule 15: Request a test of the hypothesis about a factor. If (1) the student has formulated a hypothesis about how the dependent variable is related to a particular factor, then (2) ask him how it could be tested.

Rule 24: Trace the consequences of a general rule. If (1) a student agrees to a general rule such as Rule 5 . . . then (2) ask if he agrees with the consequences of that rule in a particular case. Example: If the student states that it is necessary to have flat terrain to grow rice, then point out that since they do not have flat terrain in Japan, they must not grow much rice and so must import most of the rice they eat.

The theory of chapter 3 can suggest reasons why most of these techniques (and others not presented) can be effective in teaching thinking, in much the same way it did in the case of Blank's techniques. Rule 1 is a way of suggesting a possibility, when the goal is to come up with necessary and sufficient factors for some dependent variable, such as growing rice. It thus acts as a heuristic for generating possibilities; it is a way to encourage the initation of a subepisode of thinking with a possible factor as its goal. If this technique — and each of the others — is to be effective in teaching good thinking, the student must learn to ask himself the same kind of question in the tutor's absence. These tutorial devices come to function as heuristics to overcome biases if the student internalizes the tutor's role. Specifically, the student's anticipation of what the tutor might say serves as a goad to carry out the request the tutor might make, even in the absence of the request itself.

Rule 5 asks the student to state a general principle. (Baron, 1978, called this the strategy of principle stating.) In terms of the present theory, the goal of the entire process here is a principle, so that an explanation of a single case is not a real possibility. For an explanation of a single case to become a possibility, it must be stated in the correct form, which in this case is the form of a general principle. Only when the possibility is represented in this way can the appropriate kinds of evidence — examples and counterexamples — be brought to bear. There are thus two different ways of saying what Rule 5 does in terms of the present theory. First, it might simply encourage the student to form a representation of a possibility. On this account, the explanation given by the student is not a possibility at all, but rather something that can suggest a possibility. The explanation might be the outcome of a subepisode of thinking (of the sort encouraged by Rule 1), but the student may simply fail to use the result of the subepisode as part of the main episode. This heuristic might be particularly useful in reflective thinking, where the failure to generate appropriate possibilities may be a common error. We thus see an example of how a certan heuristic may be useful in avoiding a certain bias only in a particular domain of the taxonomy of chapter 3, in this case reflective thinking.

Alternatively, Rule 5 might be seen as a way of gathering evidence against a possibility, so that a new possibility may be generated by improving the original one. In this case, the explanation of the specific case *is* seen as a possibility, but not a good possibility, because it is not a general rule. By this interpretation, Rule 5 encourages a general heuristic of asking whether a possibility is the *sort* of possibility one wants, even before one begins to gather the usual kind of evidence for or against it.

Rules 6, 15, and 24 might encourage the choice of relevant evidence from memory or imagination. In particular, they might encourage the search for counterexamples as evidence against general principles. This would overcome any bias in favor of confirming rather than disconfirming evidence in reflective thinking. This may be the most important bias in this sort of thinking. Other rules proposed by Collins may have the same effect as I suggested for Blank's simplification rules. They essentially simplify the problem so as to keep the student thinking about it. They also provide ways for the student to do this for himself, in the same way that Rule 1 does. (These ways may tend to be more specific to the content used.) Thus, they may have the effect, among other effects, of increasing the student's expectation for the value of thinking.

The effectiveness of the tutorial technique at any level may depend on the willingness of the student to internalize, to take over for himself, the role of the tutor. The technique itself may promote the goals of good

thinking, through a process of personal identification, and it may promote as well the belief in the effectiveness of good thinking, through demonstration. To use the method most effectively, then, the tutor must be aware of the several "levels" of message being conveyed to the tutee, both the instruction in heuristics and habits and the inculcation of beliefs and goals. In addition, all the literature on identification (e.g., Kohlberg, 1969; Aronfreed, 1968) becomes relevant when we inquire about what makes for the method's success.

Pair problem-solving

Whimbey and Lochhead (1980) have developed another approach to the teaching of good thinking. The domain is the solution of insight and search problems of the sort encountered in school mathematics and on aptitude tests. The basic technique is to have students work together in pairs. One student solves a problem, talking aloud as he does so, and the other acts as a listener and critic. The students take turns in these roles. The obvious advantages over the tutorial method are first, that it is less expensive, and second, that, the student may be helped to internalize the tutor's role by actually performing that role when someone else is doing the thinking. The obvious disadvantage is that the "tutor" (the listener) is not an expert either in the subject matter or in tutorial methods. These constraints will surely limit the domain of application as well as the effectiveness of the method. So far, the technique has been used mainly at the college level.

Only one evaluation has been done to my knowledge. Physics students did much better with the method than in a control condition (Lochhead, 1985), but Lochhead suggests that the magnitude of the effect may be as much related to the low quality of the control condition as to the real effectiveness of the training. In general, it is difficult to evaluate methods of this sort, because of the difficulty of making sure that one has both a good instantiation of the method and an equally good instantiation of the control condition. (This applies to Blank's outcome study as well.) Unless there is some sort of natural control condition — which seems not to be the case here — it seems to me that we should consider other factors than outcome studies in making decisions about whether to implement a given program. Outcome studies may succeed or fail for spurious reasons, and often our understanding of the technique and our firsthand experience with it are equally good as sources of evidence about effectiveness, especially when we have equally good understanding of, and experience with, other techniques as well.

Whimbey and Lochhead begin with a general orientation, in which the techniques of pair problem-solving are described. More importantly, perhaps, the students are given some general guidelines about the kinds of errors that are typically made in problem solving. These include (pp. 20-22) (1) inaccuracy in reading, e.g., reading "too rapidly, at the expense of full comprehension," or reading without concentrating fully on the meaning of what is being read; (2) inaccuracy in thinking, e.g., failure to "place accuracy above all other considerations such as speed or ease of obtaining an answer"; (3) weakness in problem analysis, such as failing to break a complex problem into parts, failure to draw on relevant knowledge or experience, failure to use the dictionary when relevant, failure to "evaluate a solution or representation in terms of its reasonableness"; and (4) lack of perseverance, e.g., failure to think enough because of lack of confidence, or jumping to a conclusion without completing one's train of thought. On the positive side, Whimbey and Lochhead list the following as attributes of good problem solvers (pp. 28-29): "a strong belief that academic reasoning problems can be solved through careful, persistent analysis," in contrast to the attitude that "you either know the answer or you don't"; concern for accuracy, including the checking of each step; breaking the problem into parts; avoiding guessing; and, more generally, the tendency to "do more things as they try to understand and answer difficult questions." Clearly, Whimbey and Lochhead feel (as I do) that the major general stumbling block to good problem-solving is insufficient thinking (which is not necessarily the same as insufficient time spent staring at the page). They also feel (consistently with the writing of Polya, 1945, Wickelgren 1974, and others) that thinking in problem solving must be directed at the formation of an appropriate representation of the problem as well as at finding a solution. Part of forming a representation is simply the comprehension of the problem as stated. Thus, thinking in problem solving includes thinking in reading comprehension (as described in chapter 3).

In pair problem-solving itself, the listener must first of all continually check accuracy at every step. The listener must not let the solver get ahead, so that the listener may frequently have to ask the listener to stop so that the listener can check a step. However, the listener should not work through the problem himself. When the listener catches an error, he should point it out without suggesting the correct answer, even if he knows it. Since this is done step by step, it is hoped that the solver can usually recover from the error on his own. The second major role of the listener is to demand constant vocalization from the solver. The listener must demand explanations for what seem to be missing steps in the solu-

tion. Constant vocalization not only ensures that the method can be used, but also makes it easier for the solver to monitor his own thinking. Whimbey and Lochhead recommend that vocalization be used even in the absence of a listener. For the same reasons, they also recommend the use of other "crutches" such as drawing, counting on fingers, and so on. (It should be no surprise that Whimbey and Whimbey, 1975, express strong reservations about speed-reading courses and the philosophy behind them!)

From my point of view, the main value of this technique is, once again, to eliminate insufficient thinking, especially thinking directed at the goal of representing the problem. In addition, it may teach the student specific methods for evaluation, for selecting and using evidence about the success of an approach to a problem, in the domain in which the teaching is done. Finally, it would seem likely to increase efficacy (expectation for success of thinking) without at the same time increasing overconfidence. It does this only to the extent to which the technique actually leads the student to solve problems he could not otherwise solve. The extent to which this happens depends heavily, I would think, on the choice of problems. In particular, they must be difficult, yet they must not require knowledge that the student does not have. Such problems can probably be chosen within the context of a specific course. If problems of general usefulness are required, Whimbey and Lochhead present a great many, typically puzzle problems and problems of the sort used on aptitude tests, e.g., verbal analogies and number series problems. Problems in logic, and problems used on IQ tests such as Raven's Progressive Matrices, might also be useful.

Cognitive behavior modification

Behavior modification is a set of techniques for therapy and management that grew out of the attempt to apply behavioristic learning theory to the problems of clinics and schools. The emphasis is on the use of reward, punishment, or the principles of conditioning. *Cognitive* behavior modification is a more recent attempt to take mental states and processes into account in such methods, paralleling the attempts of various learning theorists (e.g., Rotter, 1966; Bandura, 1968; Aronfreed, 1968) to do the same. The applications that grew out of these theories were characterized by attempts to manipulate relevant beliefs, expectations, and self-instructions directly rather than by rewarding or punishing the behavior they were thought to produce. The work of Russian theorists, particularly Luria

(1961), has also influenced this tradition. At present, this tradition is thriving, with several journals of its own and several other successful new techniques (Beck, 1976; Meichenbaum, 1977).

Explicit attempts are now being made to apply the methods of this tradition to the teaching of good thinking, both in the case of clinical patients whose disorders are thought to be related to poor thinking (Beck, 1976) and in the case of children with problems in school (Meichenbaum, 1977). However, the field now seems to be more of a historical tradition than a body of practice held together by coherent theory. The incorporation of cognitive concepts has now become so extensive that the anchoring in the principles of learning theory has, apparently, been lost, except for the emphasis on simple techniques that are easy to study replicably.

Meichenbaum's (1977) technique involves teaching children to talk to themselves. The underlying theory, derived from Luria, is that inner speech plays a regulative function. If we want to teach self-control, we must teach the child to give himself instructions. For example, if we want the child to be careful, we teach him to remind himself to be careful. Teaching is done in several steps. First, an adult model performs a task while talking to himself out loud. For example, he says to himself (Meichenbaum & Goodman, 1971, p. 117):

Okay, what is it I have to do? I have to copy the picture with the different lines. I have to go slowly and carefully. Okay, draw the line down, down, good; and then to the right, that's it; now down some more and to the left. Good, I'm doing fine so far. Remember, go slowly. Now back up again. No, I was supposed to go down. That's okay. Just erase the line carefully . . . Good. Even if I make an error I can go on slowly and carefully. I have to go down now. Finished. I did it!

Next, the child tries to do what the model did, first under the model's guidance and then on his own. Finally, the child moves from talking aloud to whispering and then to "inaudible or private speech." Typically, the method is applied first to a simple task, such as copying line drawings or coloring within boundaries; this may require several sessions. Then, more difficult tasks are used, up to the level of difficulty of problems from Raven's matrices, mazes, and problems from the Matching Familiar Figures test. Typically, as in this example, the goal of Meichenbaum's technique is the elimination of impulsiveness, but similar techniques have also been used to teach creative problem-solving to college students, or to eliminate inappropriate behavior in psychotics, with apparent success (Meichenbaum, 1977).

In some ways, the theory behind this method seems naive. If a child

cannot remember to check his answer, how is it that he can remember to remind himself to check his answer (see Flavell, 1977, pp. 69-70)? Must he be taught to remind himself to remind himself? Possibly, the self-instruction is not as important an aspect of the training as Meichenbaum suggests. Its function may serve mainly as a device for ensuring that the child is making an effort to change his behavior during the training itself, to slow down, be more careful, and so on. Effects of training may result from changes in habits, beliefs in the effectiveness of extra thinking, and the goal of accuracy, rather than from changes in inner speech. The effective part of the training may be that it induces the child to experiment with extra thinking and thereby discover its value.

Another technique of some interest is the attribution retraining technique of Dweck (1975). The experimenter sits next to the child as the child works through a series of problems, some of which are designed to be too difficult for the child to solve correctly (or to meet a criterion of performance). After each such programed failure, the trainer says, "You needed _____ [to reach the criterion of success] and you only got _____. That means you should have tried harder." As a result, subjects begin to attribute their failures to lack of effort rather than such factors as stupidity, and their tendency to become helpless as a result of failure is reduced. Helplessness in this case is defined as a detrimental effect in which failure on one problem impairs performance on the next problem. Because this effect is reduced, overall performance improves as well, as a result of the training (Dweck, 1975).

The effect of the training is probably to increase the expectation of success given further thinking. The training would thus decrease premature cessation by increasing the expectation that further thinking will lead to success. One problem with this interpretation is that the training causes latency to decrease (on problems following failure) as well as errors. Possibly, children who are helpless on a given problem may stop thinking prematurely, yet still sit and stare at the problem, perhaps out of a desire to put off having to do the next problem.

Dweck's technique is of special interest here because it appears to work for the reasons given to explain it, namely, changed attributions for failure. (Dweck's explanation has survived quite a bit of scrutiny: see Andrews & Debus, 1978; Chapin & Dyck, 1976; and Schunk, 1982.) It is thus an example of the use of a theory, such as the theory proposed here (which incorporates Dweck's theoretical perspective), to derive simple training techniques, in the tradition of cognitive behavior modification.

In some schools and preschools, children are given perceptual tasks of

various sorts in order to improve "perceptual skills." The evidence I discussed earlier, however, suggests that such skills will not improve in general. However, any task might be useful in reducing impulsiveness, and here is where the value of these tasks may lie.

Organized environments

Another long tradition in the teaching of thinking involves the effort to create total learning environments (as suggested by Montessori, 1912). The well-designed environment, by this view, contains opportunities for thoughtful exploration, puzzles, blocks, and so on, as well as opportunities for learning of specific subjects in a natural way.

A recent expression of this point of view has received considerable attention. Papert (1980, and in his earlier writings) has argued that this approach can be much more effective when coupled with the technology of the computer. Papert advocates the use of computers, particularly those equipped with LOGO, an interpreter language he and his associates have developed, as part of an environment designed to stimulate intellectual growth and exploration. In Papert's demonstration projects, children program the computer to draw simple pictures, to write poems, and so on. For example, pictures are drawn by a "turtle," which is either a mechanical device that moves on paper, or a point that moves on a video display. A simple instruction to the turtle is to go forward a short distance and then turn to the right a small amount. Another instruction specifies that the first instruction be repeated a certain number of times. This can create a polygon, an approximation to a circle, or part of a circle. A routine to draw part of a circle, once created, can then be used to create other drawings. For example, two circle parts can become the petals of a flower, and another routine can draw an entire flower. The LOGO language allows a set of instructions, once written, to be named and used as if it were a basic instruction. Thus, the list of instructions to make a flower is:

```
TO FLOWER
  PETAL
  RIGHT 90
  PETAL
  RIGHT 90
  etc.
```

The instruction RIGHT 90 means "turn right 90 degrees"; this is a basic instruction. The instruction PETAL is itself defined as follows:

```
TO PETAL
   QCIRCLE 50
   RIGHT 90
   QCIRCLE 50
   RIGHT 90
   END
```

The instruction QCIRCLE n means "draw a quarter of a circle, size n," and it has been defined elsewhere in terms of basic lines and turns. The children learn this language easily, and play with it, discovering what complex figures they can draw. They are also led into the discovery of rules concerning the systems they have invented, such as the Total Turtle Trip Theorem: "If a Turtle takes a trip around the boundary of any area and ends up in the state in which it started, then the sum of all turns will be 360 degrees." (Papert, 1980, p. 76) Papert argues that the experience with the process of discovering such theorems is much more important than the learning of any particular body of mathematical theorems, such as those of Euclidian geometry.

Papert would agree with Dweck that a great deal of failure in school is the result of some sort of helplessness, for example, the feeling that "I cannot learn math because I'm dumb." The environment he recommends is designed to circumvent such problems in several ways. First, there are no grades or externally imposed criteria of success, so the child need never feel that an irrevocable failure has occurred. In particular, the child always has the opportunity to improve any project with which he feels dissatisfied. Thus, the child has no basis in reality for coming to think that he is "dumb." Second, the child cannot help but be impressed with what he is able to accomplish through step-by-step construction. Finally, Papert's system provides a vocabulary for talking about knowledge itself. Much of what we know, Papert argues, consists of routines that are analogous to computer routines. Just as we "debug" a computer program, we can also make corrections in our own procedures. To my knowledge, the method has not been systematically evaluated.

From the present point of view, Papert's methods have the effect of encouraging thinking. The kinds of projects the students do fall mostly into what I have called creative thinking, in which the goal is continually redefined by the student himself. The use of LOGO can thus allow students to learn the value of search for goals in a way that is practically unique. The advantage of the computer is that it provides a medium of creativity that is more flexible and easier to learn to use well than all the alternatives I can imagine, such as oil paints.

Papert himself warns against the obvious danger. The computer must

not be seen as a teacher-proof device for teaching thinking. It is a tool for the teacher even more than for the student. To be used most effectively, the teacher must be as skilled in his own work as is any teacher of a creative enterprise.

Incorporation of rational thinking into the teaching of content

In this section, I discuss how rational thinking may be taught as part of the teaching of specific content. True to its origins, the present theory provides a rationale for a type of "progressive" education. Such education is not to be confused with license. It involves forcing the student to think, to reexamine comfortable conclusions, and to respect accuracy and thoroughness. For some students, this will be liberating, as it will be seen as having more purpose than alternative approaches and as challenging arbitrary authority. But to most students, true progressive education may be somewhat painful, at least on the first exposure to it. (Perry, 1971, documents some of the pain in the case of college students exposed to "different points of view" in the same course for the first time.) The implications of the present theory concern both the teacher's conception of what is taught and the methods used to evaluate students.

The main consequence for the conception of what is taught is that the teacher should consider how the knowledge taught will eventually be used as part of a process of thinking. In this thinking, what will be the possibilities? What sort of evidence will be relevant? How will the evidence be weighed? How will the goals of thinking be defined? Given that the answers to these questions are available, what kinds of schemata will unite possibilities, evidence, and goals? Finally, what kinds of heuristics (or more formal methods) will eliminate biases in thinking in this domain?

The answers to these questions will, of course, vary from subject to subject. Many subjects are already taught in a way that focuses on the thought process characteristic of the domain, for example, the case method in law and business schools, the research seminar in graduate school, the course in studio art, literature and history courses that encourage scholarly analysis rather than "regurgitation" of facts, and so on. In other cases — particularly large lecture courses in colleges and high school courses in general — the emphasis tends to be on memorizing and accepting the view of various authorities without question. Of course, there are practical considerations here, such as the difficulty of grading large numbers of essays (and meeting with students to discuss them), and in some fields, such as biology or chemistry, there may be so many facts to learn before any serious thinking can be done that it is inefficient to do any-

thing but teach them directly. However, the argument that this is the case can sometimes be questioned, as it has been in medical education with apparent success (Neufeld & Barrows, 1974).

A desire to teach good thinking in a content domain ought to affect the standards by which students are evaluated as well as the organization and content of the teaching itself. For one thing, the present theory argues against the use of "speed" examinations, that is, examinations in which the speed of working, rather than the effectiveness of thinking, has a strong influence on the grade. If examinations can be used to encourage good thinking, failure to use them this way is a missed opportunity. Use of speed tests may give some students the idea that the ability to think does not matter much, and that they need not try to cultivate it.

When possible, examinations and other assignments ought to require actual thinking rather than "rote recall." In many college courses, for example, it is possible to require essays, even on examinations, that require a display of original reflective thinking. That is, the student must try to arrive at some principle to account for knowledge acquired in a course of study. Often, a professor's lectures will be of this form in any case. It may not be a bad idea to begin by requiring simple "regurgitation" of such lectures, provided that the students understand that the point of this exercise is not for them to display their ability to memorize but rather for them to learn what an episode of reflective thinking is, so that they can learn to do it on their own. It is important that such assignments be within the students' capacity, lest the students get discouraged.

In some science courses, it might also be possible to require students to do actual scientific thinking, that is, to do what amounts to writing a grant proposal, a plan of experiments designed to understand a given phenomenon. This may sound like an ambitious goal, but it seems less ambitious to me if the teacher actually tries to teach how to do this, first by giving examples of doing it himself. The task can be made easier by choosing easy phenomena. Computer simulations might also help in that they might allow students to carry out the experiments they have designed with relative ease.

There are disadvantages to these methods. For one, they might be expensive (e.g., in requiring extra teaching assistants). The answer to this is that they might be worth the extra cost.

The emphasis on thinking and the use of course content in making arguments, etc., also can detract from the amount of content actually taught. In some courses, such as gross anatomy for medical students, this is a serious problem. In other courses, teachers may overvalue the content itself. They underestimate the amount of it that will never be used,

or rendered useless or trivial by new advances in the discipline or new ideas the student encounters later. Such overvaluation of the content of a course allows a teacher to continue use of the more "objective" methods of examination, which turn out to require less work to grade.

Finally, the heavy use of thinking tasks as homework assignments and projects for evaluation of students seems to be less fair than the use of in-class exams. With the former, there is more opportunity for seeking help from others, and the quality of the work is more heavily influenced by idiosyncratic opportunities of one sort or another. My answer to this objection is that we might be overvaluing evaluation itself. Grades do not predict much except other grades, and future level of education (Wallach, 1976; Jencks et al., 1972). The correlation between grades and the level of education may even be spurious to the extent to which grades themselves are used as criteria for admission to higher levels.

Teaching thinking by teaching about thinking

Another way to teach good thinking, aside from doing this in connection with the teaching of other content, is to set up a course in thinking itself (under the rubric of psychology, philosophy, or both). This is most easily done at the college level, and much of what I say here is based on experience with the course I teach at this level. We would expect that such a course would be most effective in an environment that otherwise encouraged good thinking. On first exposure to such an environment, students may feel confused by the absence of authoritative statements and by the need to figure things out for themselves (Perry, 1971). One benefit of a course in thinking would be to prevent such confusion by teaching the students quite explicitly what academic work of this sort is about and how it is different from memorizing. However, the main benefit of the course would be in essence to present the argument for good thinking, and thus to convince students — fairly and without neglecting alternative views — that good thinking is effective, that it will help them achieve their rational goals, and that many of the arguments made against it do not survive scrutiny. Thus, the effect of such a course would be largely on students' beliefs and goals.

There are many possible choices for the content of such a course. A brief introduction to logic could introduce the general argument for consideration of the rationality of our thinking, for in the study of logic, there is a clear separation between the truth of an argument and its form. Students can learn to reflect on the form of arguments in much the way that Harry Stottlemeyer did (Lipman, 1985; described earlier). Logic is

often taught with the idea of teaching good thinking directly. As documented by Finocchiaro (1981) the use of logic for this purpose may be an empty exercise, since it is nearly impossible to find good examples of logical fallacies in daily life. Thus, the practical importance of logic should not be overemphasized, lest students come to see the whole course as an artificial exercise. In this respect, logic contrasts with probabilistic reasoning, where fallacies may be found in realistic or real situations (Lichtenstein et al., 1982; Eddy, 1982).

Instruction concerning the common errors made in probabilistic reasoning and decison making (Nisbett & Ross, 1980; Kahneman et al., 1982; Kahneman & Tversky, 1984) could be useful. Many of the biases in probability assignment can be explained in terms of more general biases, such as failure to consider alternative possibilities or failure to think of evidence against one's favored possibility (in the case of overconfidence). Learning about the probability biases would provide an example of the detrimental effect of the general biases. Learning about the overconfidence bias itself may serve to reduce this cause of insufficient search (in combination with other training). In addition, the idea of probability as an appropriate representation for degree of belief can provide an alternative to the view that only certainty is of value, a view that may discourage good thinking.

An introduction to utility theory would be appropriate, especially some of the simplied forms of multi-attribute utility theory, the simplest being the decisional balance sheet of Janis and Mann (1977). Such methods may be of practical use in many decisions in which there is time for thinking. They also show the value of considering alternatives, carrying out a thorough search for evidence, and weighing evidence on both sides equally. It may be helpful to ask students to use these methods in real decisions, such as deciding where to live, where to go to college, or what courses to take.

It may be appropriate to discuss the theory of life plans as I presented it in chapter 2. The idea of life plans itself is an important area for the application of thinking, and it can be liberating for a student to begin to think of a life plan as a set of policy decisions to be made. The idea here is to illustrate the value of careful thinking in a domain in which many students had not thought much, despite its importance to them.

Likewise, it may be helpful to teach students that it is possible to think effectively about moral questions. Many students seem to believe various doctrines that imply that moral arguments cannot be made, for example, the doctrine that moral beliefs are a matter of taste. Such students do not seem to discover for themselves the technique of the "Golden Rule argument" described in chapter 6, in which moral principles are evaluated by

considering their acceptability to different people involved in situations where the principles might apply. This type of argument can be taught as a technique, even without giving it a philosophical justification. Often, demonstration of the effectiveness of the techniques is sufficient to make the point that thinking may help. Of course, it may also be helpful to discuss some of the philosophical questions concerning the justification of this technique.

It may also be helpful to teach students to do protocol analysis of the sort illustrated in chapter 3, especially in combination with later criticism of the thinking in the protocols. This can also help them to become aware of the value of thinking, and it can help them to monitor their own thinking and thus to improve it through experience in specific types of situations. Protocol analysis may be especially useful in a course that combines instruction about thinking with exercises in thinking itself.

Social conditions for the encouragement of rational thinking

Throughout this chapter, I have suggested that the battle for good thinking must be fought on many fronts. A course or a set of exercises cannot be expected to have much impact unless it is embedded in a supportive environment, where the methods and habits it teaches can be used and where the goals and beliefs it inculcates will be appropriate. Because of this, fair evaluation of an attempt to teach good thinking is difficult, since no one component is likely to be responsible for the success of an educational environment designed to teach good thinking. On the other hand, there is reason to think that such an environment would succeed as a whole. There is no reason to think that the teaching of good thinking is any more or less difficult than the teaching of good conduct in other domains. And it seems clear that good conduct is largely the result of a total environment that encourages it, from the home a person is raised in, to the school he attends, to the social circles he travels in. Thus, it seems reasonable to move beyond the role of the parent and teacher and to ask what kind of society encourages good thinking. Without at least some social support, even the best educational institutions will be largely powerless in this regard. To return to the conduct analogy, in a land of criminals, the teaching of virtue to a few is an empty exercise.

First, educational institutions themselves should serve as bastions of rational thinking not just in the conduct of their courses but also in their self-government and their relations with their constituents, including the public. For one thing, their internal policies ought to be justifiable by argument and open to challenge. This does not mean that the policies

must be decided by majority vote, for such a policy need not be the most rational one, all things considered. It does mean that those responsible for policy ought to be personally willing to explain the reasons for their decisions and to listen to criticism. This is a simple extension of the attitude of any teacher who tries to teach rational thinking. Such a teacher is simply inconsistent if he asks his students to think critically and reasonably, yet resorts to "because I say so" as a defense of any of his claims or requests. The same principles extend to the roles of educational institutions as members of society. Educational institutions should not readily tolerate the kind of public debate in which people are manipulated by the well meaning. To assume that people cannot understand the real issues is to make this assumption self-fulfilling, and thus to discourage thorough inquiry.

The standards of public discourse itself are not only a major consequence of support for rational thinking but also one of its causes. For example, consider the conduct of political campaigns in the United States. Most campaigns are conducted at the level of simplistic slogans, with little opportunity for argument, criticism, or counterargument. The press provides us mostly with analysis of campaign tactics and of our own uninformed opinions as reflected by polls. One is hard put to find such a simple thing as a list of the positions of each candidate on each of a series of major issues, let alone a critical analysis of the coherence of these positions, the evidence supporting them, their likelihood of success, and their goals. In general, politicians and journalists should, I think, see themselves as having in part the role of educators, and thus having some obligation to set an example of high standards of thinking.

Another area where rational thinking can be encouraged is in the family. Support for good thinking at home is required if students are to be taught it in school. The best efforts of a teacher can be sabotaged by an anti-intellectual parent. But the family is not just a means of supporting the school but an important source of education in its own right. The family is in many ways the chief means of transmission of more general cultural norms, values, and habits. For example, one thing a family can do is to tolerate argument and criticism. Rather than simply saying "no" to a request, the parent may ask why, and then criticize the answer. Eventually, the parent decides who has won the argument, but sometimes he decides that the child has won by making a good case, or perhaps an acceptable compromise is reached. More generally, in some households or groups (e.g., people who do a lot of joint problem-solving), it is acceptable to challenge a statement without implying that the person who made the statement is stupid or otherwise inferior.

There are other aspects of culture that promote or discourage rational thinking. These correspond to some of the attitudes or beliefs I described earlier in this chapter. For example, there is the belief that nobody's opinion should be challenged, because in a democracy everyone is entitled to his own view; the belief that it is a sign of bad character to change one's mind, because it admits that the old opinion was wrong; the belief that a challenge to an assertion made by another amounts to an assertion of the superiority of the challenger; and the belief that important matters must be decided by authority and that individuals do not have the power or ability to decide for themselves. The last belief prevents questioning and challenge, because any challenge is a challenge to the authority behind the original statement. (Research on the nature of such beliefs and their effects is surely in order.)

I see no reason to think that these beliefs are necessary parts of human culture, nor any reason to think that the opposite beliefs create any harm or any imbalance, such that it would be difficult for other groups to adopt them. Many of the positive beliefs are at least nominally accepted in the culture of intellectuals. In sum, good thinking will be most encouraged by an ideology in which belief and planning, of the individual and group, are seen as a fluid process, constantly subject to correction, in which the search for truth and for the best path to take is seen as a common enterprise, and in which the self-esteem of the individual is based on his ability to participate in this collective search rather than on his ability to be right on his own and to assert his authority. As I have argued throughout this chapter, it is such sources of beliefs and goals that might turn out to be more important, in the long run, than any special courses or tinkering with educational methods.

References

Abelson, R. P., Aronson, E., McGuire, W. J., Newcomb, T. M., Rosenberg, M. J., Tannenbaum, P. H. (Eds.) *Theories of cognitive consistency: a sourcebook*. Chicago: Rand McNally, 1968.

Abramson, L. Y., & Alloy, L. B. Depression, nondepression, and cognitive illusions: Reply to Schwartz. *Journal of Experimental Psychology: General* 1981, *110*, 436-447.

Adams, M., & Collins, A. A schema-theoretic view of reading. In *Discourse processes: advances in research and theory* (Vol. 2): *Multidisciplinary approaches*. Norwood, N. J.: Ablex, 1979.

Ahern, S., & Beatty, J. Pupillary responses during information processing vary with Scholastic Aptitude Test scores. *Science*, 1979, *205*, 1289-1292.

Ainslie, G. Specious reward: a behavioral theory of impulsiveness and impulse control. *Psychological Bulletin*, 1975, *82*, 463-496.

Allais, M. Le comportement de l'homme rationnel devant le risque: critique les postulats et axiomes de l'école americaine. *Econometrica*, 1953, *21*, 503-546.

Allan, L. G., & Jenkins, H. M. The judgment of contingency and the nature of the response alternatives. *Canadian Journal of Psychology,*, 1980, *34*, 1-11.

Alloy, L. B., & Abramson, L. Y. Judgment of contingency in depressed and nondepressed students: sadder but wiser? *Journal of Experimental Psychology: General*, 1979, *108*, 441-485.

Alloy, L. B., Peterson, C., Abramson, L. Y., & Seligman, M. E. P. attributional style and the generality of learned helplessness. *Journal of Personality and Social Psychology*, 1984, *46*, 681-687.

Anderson, C. A. Inoculation and counterexplanation: debiasing techniques in the perseverance of social theories. *Social Cognition*, 1982, *1*, 126-139.

Anderson, C. A. Abstract and concrete data in the perseverance of social theories: when weak data lead to unshakable beliefs. *Journal of Experimental Social Psychology*, 1983, *19*, 93-108.

Anderson, C. A., Lepper, M. R., & Ross, L. Perseverance of social theories: the role of explanation in the persistence of discredited information. *Journal of Personality and Social Psychology*, 1980, *39*, 1037-1049.

Anderson, J. R. (Ed.). *Cognitive skills and their acquisition*. Hillsdale, N. J.: Erlbaum, 1981.

Andrews, G. R., & Debus, R. L. Persistence and the causal perception of failure: modifying cognitive attributions. *Journal of Educational Psychology*, 1978, *70*, 154-166.

Aronfreed, J. *Conduct and conscience: the socialization of internalized control over behavior*. New York: Academic Press, 1968.

Asch, S. E. A reformulation of the problem of associations. *American Psychologist*, 1969, *24*, 92-102.

Asch, S. E., & Ebenholz, S. M. The principle of associative symmetry. *Proceedings of the American Philosophical Society*, 1962, *106*, 135-163.

Baddeley, A. D. *The psychology of memory*. New York: Basic Books, 1976.

Baddeley, A. D., & Hitch, G. Working memory. In G. H. Bower (Ed.), *The Psychology of learning and motivation* (Vol. 8). New York: Academic Press, 1974.

Baddeley, A. D., Thomson, N., & Buchanan, M. Word length and the structure of short-term memory. *Journal of Verbal Learning and Verbal Behavior*, 1975, *14*, 575-589.

Bandura, A. Social-learning theory of identificatory processes. In D. A. Goslin (Ed.), *Handbook of socialization theory and research*. Chicago: Rand McNally, 1968.

Bandura, A. Self-efficacy: toward a unifying theory of behavioral change. *Psychological Review*, 1977, *84*, 191-215.

Baron, J. Is experimental psychology relevant? *American Psychologist*, 971, *26*, 713-716.

Baron, J. Semantic components and conceptual development. *Cognition*, 1973, *2*, 189-207.

Baron, J. Some theories of college instruction. *Higher Education*, 1975, *4*, 149-172.

Baron, J. Mechanisms for pronouncing printed words: use and acquisition. In D. LaBerge & S. J. Samuels (Eds.), *Basic processes in reading: perception and comprehension*. Hillsdale, N. J.: Erlbaum, 1977.

Baron, J. Intelligence and general strategies. In G. Underwood (Ed.), *Strategies of information processing*. London: Academic Press, 1978.

Baron, J. Reflective thinking as a goal of education. *Intelligence*, 1981a, 5, 291-309.

Baron, J. An analysis of confirmation bias. Paper presented to the Psychonomic Society, Philadelphia, November, 1981b.

Baron, J. What kinds of intelligence components are fundamental? In J. Segal, S. Chipman, & R. Glaser (Eds.). *Thinking and learning skills* (Vol. 2): *Current research and open questions*. Hillsdale, N. J.: Erlbaum, 1985.

Baron, J. Rational plans, achievement, and education. In M. Frese & J. Sabini (Eds.), *Goal directed behavior: the concept of action in psychology*. Hillsdale, N. J.: Erlbaum, in press.

Baron, J., & Hodge, J. Using spelling-sound correspondences without trying to learn them. *Visible Language*, 1978, *12*, 55-70.

Baron, J., & Treiman, R. Some problems in the study of differences in cognitive processes. *Memory and Cognition*, 1980, *8*, 313-321.

Baron, J., Freyd, J., & Stewart, J. Individual differences in general abilities useful in solving problems. In R. S. Nickerson (Ed.), *Attention and Performance VIII*. Hillsdale, N. J.: Erlbaum, 1980.

Baron, J., Badgio, P., & Gaskins, I. W. Cognitive style and its improvement: a normative approach. In R. J. Sternberg (Ed.), *Advances in the psychology of human intelligence* (Vol. 3). Hillsdale, N. J.: Erlbaum, in press.

Barstis, S. W., and Ford, L. H., Jr. Reflection-impulsivity, conservation, and the development of ability to control cognitive tempo. *Child Development*, 1977, *48*, 953-959.

Bartlett, F. C. *Remembering: A study in experimental and social psychology*. Cambridge University Press, 1932.

Bartlett, F. C. *Thinking*. London: Allen & Unwin, 1958.

Baumeister, A. A., Kellas, G., & Gordon, D. Backward association in paired-associate learning of retardates and normal children. *Child Development*, 1970, *41*, 355-364.

Beach, B. H., & Beach, L. R. Expectancy-based decision schemes: sidesteps toward applications. In Feather, N. T. (Ed.), *Expectations and actions: expectancy-value models in psychology*. Hillsdale, N. J.: Erlbaum, 1982.

Beach, L. R., & Mitchell, T. R. A contingency model for selection of decision strategies. *Academy of Management Review*, 1978, *3*, 439-449.

Beck, A. T. *Cognitive therapy and the emotional disorders*. New York: International Universities Press, 1976.

Becker, G. S. *A treatise on the family*. Cambridge, Mass.: Harvard University Press, 1981.

Bell, D. E. Regret in decision making under uncertainty. *Operations Research*, 1982, *30*, 961-981.

Bernoulli, D. Expositions of a new theory on the measurement of risk. (1738) Trans. by L. Sommer. *Econometrica*, 1954, *22*, 23-36.

Binet, A., & Simon, T. Methodes nouvelles pour le diagnostic du niveau intellectuel des anormaux. *L'Année Psychologique*, 1905, *11*, 191-244

Blank, M. *Teaching learning in the preschool*. Columbus, Ohio: Merrill, 973.

Block, N. J., & Dworkin, G. *The IQ controversy: critical readings*. New York: Pantheon, 1976.

Borch, H. K. *The economics of uncertainty*. Princeton, N. J.: Princeton University Press, 1968.

Borys, S. V., & Spitz, H. H. Reflection-impulsivity in retarded adolescents and nonretarded children of equal MA. *American Journal of Mental Deficiency*, 1978, *82*, 601-604.

Borys, S. V., Spitz, H. H., & Dorans, B.A. Tower of Hanoi performance of retarded young adults as a function of solution length and goal state. *Journal of Experimental Child Psychology*, 1982, *33*, 87-110.

Braine, M. D. S., & Rumain, B. Logical reasoning. In P. H. Mussen (Ed.), *Handbook of Child Psychology* (Vol. 3). New York: Wiley, 1983.

Bregman, A. S. Perception and behavior as compositions of ideals. *Cognitive Psychology*, 1977, *9*, 250-292.

Brim, O. G., Glass, D. C., Lavin, D. E., & Goodman, N. *Personality and Decision processes*. Stanford, Calif.: Stanford University Press, 1962.

Broadbent, D. E. Task combination and the selective intake of information. *Acta Psychologica*, 1982, *50*, 253-290.

Brooks, L. R. Spatial and verbal components of the act of recall. *Canadian Journal of Psychology*, 1968, *22*, 349-368.

Brooks, L. R. Nonanalytic concept formation and memory for instances. In E. Rosch & B. B. Lloyd (Eds.), *Cognition and categorization*. New York: Wiley, 1978.

Brown, A. L. The role of strategic behavior in retardate memory. In N. R. Ellis (Ed.), *International Review of Research in Mental Retardation* (Vol. 7). New York: Academic Press, 1974.

Brown, A. L. The development of memory: knowing, knowing about knowing, and knowing how to know. In H. W. Reese (Ed.), *Advances in Child Development and Behavior* (Vol. 10). New York: Academic Press, 1975.

Brown, W., & Thomson, G. *The essentials of mental measurement*. Cambridge University Press, 1921.

Bruner, J. On perceptual readiness. *Psychological Review*, 1957, *64*, 123-152.

Bruner, J. S., & Potter, M. C. Interference in visual recognition. Science, 1964, *144*, 424-425.

Bruner, J. S., Goodnow, J. J., & Austin, G. A. *A study of thinking*. New York: Wiley, 1956.

Bruner, J. S., Olver, R., & Greenfield, P. *Studies in cognitive growth*. New York: Wiley, 1966.

Bryan, W. L., & Harter, N. Studies on the telegraphic language. *Psychological Review*, 1899, *6*, 345-375.

Campione, J. C., Brown, A. L., & Ferrara, R. A. Mental retardation and intelligence. In

R. J. Sternberg (Ed.), *Handbook of human intelligence*. Cambridge University Press, 1982.

Carey, S. Are children fundamentally different kinds of thinkers and learners than adults? In J. Segal, S. Chipman, and R. Glaser (Eds.), *Thinking and learning skills* (Vol. 2): *Current research and open questions*. Hillsdale, N. J.: Erlbaum, 1985.

Carroll, J. B. The measurement of intelligence. In R. J. Sternberg (Ed.), *Handbook of human intelligence*. Cambridge University Press, 1982.

Cattell, J. M. Mental tests and measurements. *Mind*, 1890, *15*, 373-381.

Cattell, R. B. Theory of fluid and crystallized intelligence: a critical experiment. *Journal of Educational Psychology*, 1963, *54*, 1-22.

Chamberlain, T. C. The method of multiple working hypotheses. (1890) Reprinted in *Science*, 1965, *148*, 754-759.

Chapin, M., & Dyck, D. G. Persistence in children's reading behavior as a function of N length and attribution retraining. *Journal of Abnormal Psychology*, 1976, *85*, 511-515.

Chapman, L. J., & Chapman, J. P. Genesis of popular but erroneous psychodiagnostic observations. *Journal of Abnormal Psychology*, 1967, *73*, 193-204.

Charness, N. Search in chess: age and skill differences. *Journal of Experimental Psychology: Human Perception and Performance*, 1981, *7*, 467-476.

Chase, W. G., & Simon, H. A. Perception in chess. *Cognitive Psychology*, 973, *4*, 55-81.

Chi, M. T. H., & Gallagher, J. D. Speed of processing: A developmental source of limitation. *Topics in Learning and Learning Disabilities*, 1982, *2*, 23-32.

Chiang, A., & Atkinson, R. C. Individual differences and inter-relationships among a select set of cognitive skills. *Memory and Cognition*, 1976, *4*, 661-672.

Christiansen-Szalanski, J. J. J. Problem solving strategies: a selection mechanism, some implications and some data. *Organizational Behavior and Human Performance*, 1978, *22*, 307-323.

Cohen, L. J. Can human irrationality be experimentally demonstrated? *The Behavioral and Brain Sciences*, 1981, *4*, 317-331.

Colby, A., Kohlberg, L., Gibbs, J., & Lieberman, M. A longitudinal study of moral development. *Monographs of the Society for Research in Child Development*, 1983, *48*, Serial No. 200.

Cole, M., Gay, J., Glick, J., & Sharp, D. *The cultural context of learning and thinking*. New York: Basic Books, 1971.

Collins, A. Processes in acquiring knowledge. In R. C. Anderson, R. J. Spiro, & W. E. Montague (Eds.), *Schooling and the acquisition of knowledge*. Hillsdale, N. J.: Erlbaum, 1977.

Collins, A., Brown, J. S., & Larkin, K. Inference in text understanding. In R. J. Spiro, B. C. Bruce, & W. F. Brewer (Eds.), *Theoretical issues in reading comprehension*. Hillsdale, N. J.: Erlbaum, 1980.

Collins, A., & Loftus, E. F. A spreading-activation theory of semantic processing. *Psychological Review*, 1975, *82*, 407-428.

Collins, A., & Michalski, R. The logic of plausible reasoning. Manuscript. Bolt Beranek & Newman, Inc., Cambridge, Mass., 1984.

Craik, F. I. M. Age differences in human memory. In J. E. Birren & K. W. Schaie (Eds.), *The handbook of the psychology of aging*. New York: Van Nostrand Reinhold, 1976.

Craik, F. I. M., & Lockhart, R. S. Levels of processing: a framework for memory research. *Journal of Verbal Learning and Verbal Behavior*, 1972, *11*, 671-684.

Cronbach, L. J., & Snow, R. E. *Aptitudes and instructional methods: a handbook for research on interactions*. New York: Irvington, 1977.

Crow, J. F. Comment. In *Environment, heredity, and intelligence*. Harvard Educational Review, Reprint Series No. 2. Cambridge, Mass., 1969.

Daniels, N. Wide reflective equilibrium and theory acceptance in ethics. Journal of Philosophy, 1979, *76*, 256-282.

Daniels, N. On some methods of ethics and linguistics. *Philosophical Studies*, 1980, *37*, 21-36.

Davis, R., & Lenat, D. B. *Knowledge-based systems in artificial intelligence.* New York: McGraw-Hill, 1982.

de Bono, E. The cognitive research trust (CoRT) thinking program. In W. Maxwell (Ed.), *Thinking: the expanding frontier.* Philadelphia: Franklin Institute, 1983.

de Groot, A. D. *Thought and choice in chess.* The Hague: Mouton, 1965.

Dewey, J. *How we think: a restatement of the relation of reflective thinking to the educative process.* Boston: Heath, 1933.

Diener, C. I., & Dweck, C. S. An analysis of learned helplessness: continuous changes in performance, strategy, and achievement cognitions following failure. *Journal of Personality and Social Psychology*, 1978, *36*, 451-462.

Diener, C. I., & Dweck, C. S. An analysis of learned helplessness: II. The processing of success. *Journal of Personality and Social Psychology*, 1980, *5*, 940-952.

Dörner, D., & Kreutzig, H. W. On the relations between problem solving abilities and measures of intelligence. Manuscript, Psychologie, Universität Bamberg, 1980.

Duckworth, D. H. Evaluation of a programme for increasing the effectiveness of personal problem-solving. *British Journal of Psychology*, 1983, *74*, 119-127.

Duncker, K. On problem solving. (1935) Trans. by L. S. Lees. *Psychological Monographs*, 1945, No. 270.)

Dweck, C. S. The role of expectations and attributions in the alleviation of learned helplessness. *Journal of Personality and Social Psychology*, 1975, *31*, 674-685.

Dweck, C. S., & Elliott, E. S. Achievement motivation. In P. H. Mussen (Ed.), *Carmichael's manual of child psychology* (Vol. 2). New York: Wiley, 1983.

D'Zurilla, T., & Goldfried, M. Problem solving and behavior modification. *Journal of Abnormal Psychology*, 1971, *78*, 107-126.

Eddy, D.M. Probabilistic reasoning in clinical medicine: problems and opportunities. In D. Kahneman, P. Slovic, & A. Tversky (Eds.), *Judgment under uncertainty: heuristics and biases.* Cambridge University Press, 1982.

Edwards, W. Optimal strategies for seeking information: models for statistics, choice reaction time, and human information processing. *Journal of Mathematical Psychology*, 1965, *2*, 312-329.

Edwards, W., & Slovic, P. Seeking information to reduce the risk of decisions. *American Journal of Psychology*, 1965, *78*, 188-197.

Eells, E. *Rational decision and causality.* Cambridge University Press, 1982.

Egeland, B. Training impulsive children in the use of more efficient scanning techniques. *Child Development*, 1974, *45*, 165-171.

Egeth, H. E., Blecker, D. L., & Kamlet, A. S. Verbal interference in a perceptual comparison task. *Perception and Psychophysics*, 1969, *6*, 355-356.

Einhorn, H. J., & Hogarth, R. M. Confidence in judgment: persistence of the illusion of validity. *Psychological Review*, 1978, *85*, 395-416.

Ellis, N. R. Memory processes in retardates and normals. In N. R. Ellis (Ed.), *International review of research in mental retardation* (Vol. 4). New York: Academic Press, 1970.

Elstein, A. S., Shulman, L. S., & Sprafka, S. A. *Medical problem solving: an analysis of clinical reasoning.* Cambridge, Mass.: Harvard University Press, 1978.

Elster, J. *Ulysses and the Sirens: studies in rationality and irrationality.* Cambridge University Press, 1979.

Emler, N., Renwick, S., & Malone, B. The relationship between moral reasoning and political orientation. *Journal of Personality and Social Psychology*, 1983, *45*, 1073-1080.

Ericsson, K. A., & Simon, H. A. Verbal reports as data. *Psychological Review*, 1980, *87*, 215-251.

Ericsson, K. A., Chase, W. G., & Faloon, S. Acquisition of a memory skill. *Science*, 1980, *208*, 1181-1182.

Erikson, E. H. *Childhood and society*. New York: Norton, 1950.

Erikson, E. H. Identity and the life cycle. *Psychological Issues*, 1959, *1*, 1-171.

Estes, W. K. Structural aspects of associative models for memory. In C. N. Cofer (Ed.), *The structure of human memory*. San Francisco: Freeman, 1976.

Evans, S. H. A brief statement of schema theory. *Psychonomic Science*, 1967, *8*, 87-88.

Eysenck, H. J. *Biological basis of personality*. Springfield, Ill.: C. C. Thomas, 1967.

Feather, N. T. (Ed.), *Expectations and actions: expectancy-value models in psychology*. Hillsdale, N. J.: Erlbaum, 1982.

Ferrell, W. R., & McGoey, P. J. A model of calibration for subjective probabilities. *Organizational Behavior and Human Performance*, 1980, *26*, 32-53.

Finocchiaro, M. Fallacies and the evaluation of reasoning. *American Philosophical Quarterly*, 1981, *18*, 13-22.

Fischhoff, B. Hindsight ≠ foresight: the effect of outcome knowledge on judgment under uncertainty. *Journal of Experimental Psychology: Human Perception and Performance*, 1975, *1*, 288-299.

Fischhoff, B. Predicting frames. *Journal of Experimental Psychology: Learning, Memory, and Cognition*, 1983, *9*, 103-116.

Fischhoff, B., & Beyth-Marom, R. Hypothesis evaluation from a Bayesian perspective. *Psychological Review*, 1983, *90*, 239-260.

Fischhoff, B., Slovic, P., & Lichtenstein, S. Knowing with certainty: the appropriateness of extreme confidence. *Journal of Experimental Psychology: Human Perception and Performance*, 1977, *3*, 552-564.

Fischhoff, B., Slovic, P., & Lichtenstein, S. Fault trees: sensitivity of estimated failure probabilities to problem representation. *Journal of Experimental Psychology: Human Perception and Performance*, 1978, *4*, 330-334.

Flavell, J. H. *The developmental psychology of Jean Piaget*. Princeton, N. J.: Van Nostrand, 1963.

Flavell, J. H. Developmental studies of mediated memory. In H. W. Reese & L. P. Lipsett (Eds.), *Advances in Child Development and Behavior* (Vol. 5). New York: Academic Press, 1970.

Flavell, J. H. Stage-related properties of cognitive development. *Cognitive Psychology*, 1971, *2*, 421-453.

Flavell, J. H. *Cognitive development*. Englewood Cliffs, N. J.: Prentice-Hall, 1977.

Fodor, J. A. *The language of thought*. New York: Crowell, 1975.

Freedman, D. A., & Purves, R. A. Bayes' methods for bookies. *Annals of Mathematical Statistics*, 1969, *40*, 1177-1186.

Fried, L. S., and Peterson, C. R. Information seeking: optional versus fixed stopping. *Journal of Experimental Psychology*, 1969, *80*, 525-529.

Fullerton, S. K. Examining comprehension processes of third grade readers. Doctoral dissertation, School of Education, University of Pennsylvania, 1983.

Galotti, K. M., Baron, J., & Sabini, J. Individual differences in syllogistic reasoning. Manuscript. University of Pennsylvania, 1984.

Galton, F. *Inquiries into human faculty and its development*. London: Macmillan, 1883.

Gardiner, P. J., & Edwards, W. Public values: multiattribute-utility measurement for social decision making. In M. F. Kaplan & S. Schwartz (Eds.), *Human judgment and decision processes*. New York: Academic Press, 1975.

Gelman, R. Accessing one-to-one correspondence: Still another paper about conservation. *British Journal of Psychology*, 1982, *73*, 209-220.

Gelman, R., & Baillargeon, R. A review of some Piagetian concepts. In P. H. Mussen (Ed.), *Carmichael's Manual of Child Psychology* (Vol. 3). New York: Wiley, 1983.

Gewirth, A. The rationality of reasonableness. *Synthese*, 1983, *57*, 225-247.

Gillis, J. S., & Blevens, K. Sources of judgmental impairment in paranoid and nonparanoid schizophrenics. *Journal of Abnormal Psychology*, 1978, *87*, 587-596.

Gilovich, T. Biased evaluation and persistence in gambling. *Journal of Personality and Social Psychology*, 1983, *44*, 1110-1126.

Glaser, R. Education and thinking: the role of knowledge. *American Psychologist*, 1984, *39*, 93-104.

Goodnow, J. J. The nature of intelligent behavior: questions raised by cross-cultural studies. In L. B. Resnick (Ed.), *The nature of intelligence*. Hillsdale, N. J.: Erlbaum, 1976.

Gould, S. J. *The mismeasure of man*. New York: Norton, 1981.

Greenfield, P. M. Commentary and discussion. In Stevenson et al. (1978).

Greeno, J. G., Riley, M. S., & Gelman, R. Conceptual competence and children's counting. *Cognitive Psychology*, 1984, *16*, 94-143.

Grim, P., Kohlberg, L., & White, S. Some relationships between conscience and attentional processes. *Journal of Personality and Social Psychology*, 1968, *8*, 239-253.

Guilford, J. P. *The nature of human intelligence*. New York: McGraw-Hill, 1967.

Guilford, J. P. Cognitive psychology's ambiguities: some suggested remedies. *Psychological Review*, 1982, *89*, 48-59.

Gupta, B. S. Dextroamphetamine and measures of intelligence. *Intelligence*, 1977, *1*, 274-280.

Hare, R. M. *The language of morals*. London: Clarendon, 1952.

Hare, R. M. *Freedom and reason*. Oxford: Oxford University Press, 1963.

Hare, R. M. *Moral thinking*. Oxford: Oxford University Press, 1981.

Hartley, J. T., Birnbaum, I. M., & Parker, E. S. Alcohol and storage deficits: kind of processing? *Journal of Verbal Learning and Verbal Behavior*, 1978, *17*, 635-637.

Hausner, M. Multidimensional utilities. In R. M. Thrall, C. H. Coombs, & R. L. Davis (Eds.), *Decision processes*. New York: Wiley, 1954.

Hayes, J. R. Three problems in teaching general skills. In J. Segal, S. Chipman, & R. Glaser (Eds.), *Thinking and learning skills* (Vol. 2): *Current research and open questions*. Hillsdale, N. J.: Erlbaum, 1985.

Herrnstein, R. J. IQ testing and the media. *Atlantic Monthly*, 1982, *250*, 68-74.

Hill, A. L. Savants: mentally retarded individuals with special skills. In N. R. Ellis (Ed.), *International Review of Research in Mental Retardation* (Vol. 9). New York: Academic Press, 1978.

Hirst, W., Spelke, E. S., Reaves, C. C., Caharack, G., & Neisser, U. Dividing attention without alternation or automaticity. *Journal of Experimental Psychology: General*, 1980, *109*, 98-117.

Horn, J. L. The nature and development of intellectual abilities. In R. T. Osborne, C. E. Noble, & N. Weyl (Eds.), *Human variation: the biopsychology of age, race and sex*. New York: Academic Press, 1978.

Humphreys, L. G. The construct of general intelligence. *Intelligence*, 1979, *3*, 105-120.

Hunt, E. Mechanics of verbal ability. *Psychological Review*, 1978, *85*, 109-130.

Hunt, E. Intelligence as an information processing concept. *British Journal of Psychology*, 1982, *71*, 449-474.

Hunt, E., & Love, T. How good can memory be? In A. W. Melton & E. Martin (Eds.), *Coding processes in human memory*. Washington, D. C.: Winston, 1972.

Hunter, I. M. L. Mental calculation. In P. N. Johnson-Laird & P. C. Wason (Eds.), *Thinking: readings in cognitive science*. Cambridge University Press, 1977.

Huttenlocher, J., & Burke, D. Why does memory span increase with age? *Cognitive Psychology*, 1976, *8*, 1-31.

Inhelder, B., & Piaget, J. *The growth of logical thinking from childhood to adolescence*. New York: Basic Books, 1958.

Irwin, F. W. *Intentional behavior and motivation: a cognitive theory*. Philadelphia: Lippincott, 1971.

Jackson, M. D., & McClelland, J. L. Processing determinants of reading speed. *Journal of Experimental Psychology: General*, 1979, *108*, 151-181.

James, W. *The principles of psychology*. Boston: Holt, 1890.

Janis, I. L. (Ed.) *Counseling on personal decisions: theory and research on short-term helping relationships*. New Haven, Conn.: Yale University Press, 1982.

Janis, I. L., & Mann, L. *Decision making*. New York: Free Press, 1977.

Janoff-Bulman, R., & Brickman, P. Expectations and what people learn from failure. In N. T. Feather (Ed.), *Expectations and actions: expectancy-value models in psychology*. Hillsdale, N. J.: Erlbaum, 1982.

Jeffrey, R. C. *The logic of decision*. New York: McGraw Hill, 1965.

Jencks, C., Smith, M., Acland, H., Bane, M. J., Cohen, D., Gintis, H., Heyns, B., & Michelson, S. *Inequality: a reassessment of the effect of family and schooling in America*. New York: Basic Books, 1972.

Jenkins, H. M., & Ward, W. C. Judgment of contingency between responses and outcome. *Psychological Monographs*, 1965, *79*, No. 594.

Jensen, A. R. How much can we boost IQ and scholastic achievement? *Harvard Educational Review*, 1969, *39*, 1-123.

Jensen, A. R. *Bias in mental testing*. New York: Free Press, 1980.

Jensen, A. R. The chronometry of intelligence. In R. J. Sternberg (Ed.), *Advances in the psychology of human intelligence* (Vol. 1). Hillsdale, N. J.: Erlbaum, 1982.

Johanson, A. M. The influence of incentive and punishment upon reaction-time. *Archives of Psychology (New York)*, 1922, No. 54.

Johnson, D. M., Parrott, G. L., & Stratton, R. P. Production and judgment of solutions to five problems. *Journal of Educational Psychology Monograph Supplement*, 1968, *59*, No. 6, 1-21.

Kagan, J. Reflection-impulsivity and reading ability in primary grade children. *Child Development*, 1965, *36*, 609-628.

Kagan, J., Moss, H. A., & Sigel, I. Psychological significance of styles of conceptualization. *Monographs of the Society for Research in Child Development*, 1963, *28*, Serial No. 86, 73-112.

Kagan, J., Rosman, B. L., Day, D., Albert, J., and Phillips, W. Information processing in the child: significance of analytic and reflective attitudes. *Psychological Monographs*, 1964, *78*, Whole No. 578.

Kagan, J., Lapidus, D. R., & Moore, M. Infant antecedents of cognitive functioning: a longitudinal study. *Child Development*, 1978, *49*, 1005-1023.

Kahneman, D. *Attention and effort*. Englewood Cliffs, N. J.: Prentice Hall, 973.

Kahneman, D., & Tversky, A. Subjective probability: a judgment of representativeness. *Cognitive Psychology*, 1972, *3*, 430-454.

Kahneman, D., & Tversky, A. Prospect theory: an analysis of decision under risk. *Econometrica*, 1979, *47*, 263-291.

Kahneman, D., & Tversky, A. Choices, values, and frames. *American Psychologist*, 1984, *39*, 341-350.

Kahneman, D., Slovic, P., & Tversky, A. *Judgment under uncertainty: heuristics and biases*. Cambridge University Press, 1982.

Kamin, L. J. *The science and politics of IQ*. Potomac, Md.: Erlbaum, 1974.

Karmiloff-Smith, A., & Inhelder, B. "If you want to get ahead, get a theory." *Cognition*, 1974/5, *3*, 195-212.

Katona, G. *Organizing and memorizing: studies in the psychology of learning and teaching.* New York: Columbia University Press, 1940.

Keating, D. P., & Bobbitt, B. L. Individual and developmental differences in cognitive-processing components of mental ability. *Child Development*, 1978, *49*, 155-167.

Keeney, R. L. The art of assessing multiattribute utility functions. *Organizational Behavior and Human Performance*, 1977, *19*, 267-310.

Keeney, R. L., & Raiffa, H. *Decisions with multiple objectives.* New York: Wiley, 1976.

Keil, F. C. Constraints on knowledge and cognitive development. *Psychological Review*, 1981, *88*, 197-227.

Klahr, D., and Wallace, J. G. An information processing analysis of some Piagetian experimental tasks. *Cognitive Psychology*, 1970, *1*, 358-387.

Kogan, N. Stylistic variation in childhood and adolescence: creativity, metaphor, and cognitive styles. In P. H. Mussen (Ed.), *Handbook of child psychology* (Vol. 3). New York: Wiley, 1983.

Kohlberg, L. Stage and sequence: The cognitive-developmental approach to socialization. In D. A. Goslin (Ed.), *Handbook of Socialization Theory and Research*. Chicago: Rand McNally, 1969.

Kohlberg, L. Stages of moral development as a basis for moral education. In C. Beck & E. Sullivan (Eds.), *Moral education.* University of Toronto Press, 1970.

Köhler, W. *The mentality of apes.* London: Routledge & Kegan Paul, 1925.

Koriat, A., Lichtenstein, S., & Fischhoff, B. Reasons for confidence. *Journal of Experimental Psychology: Human Learning and Memory*, 1980, *6*, 107-118.

Kourilsky, M., & Murray, T. The use of economic reasoning to increase satisfaction with family decision making. *Journal of Consumer Research*, 1981, *8*, 183-188.

Krantz, D. H. Improvements in human reasoning and an error in L. J. Cohen's. The *Behavioral and Brain Sciences*, 1981, *4*, 340-341.

Krantz, D. H., Luce, R. D., Suppes, P., & Tversky, A. *Foundations of measurement* (Vol. 1). New York: Academic Press, 1971.

Kristofferson, A. B. Attention and psychophysical time. *Acta Psychologica*, 1967, *27*, 93-100.

Kruglanski, A. W., & Ajzen, I. Bias and error in human judgment. *European Journal of Social Psychology*, 1983, *13*, 1-44.

LaBerge, D. Acquisition of automatic processing in perceptual and associative learning. In P. M. A. Rabbitt & S. Dornic (Eds.), *Attention and Performance V*. London: Academic Press, 1975.

LaBerge, D. H., & Samuels, S.J. Toward a theory of automatic information processing in reading. *Cognitive Psychology*, 1974, *6*, 293-323.

Laboratory of Comparative Human Cognition. Culture and intelligence. In R. J. Sternberg (Ed.), *Handbook of human intelligence.* Cambridge University Press, 1982.

Larkin, J., McDermott, J., Simon, D. P., & Simon, H. A. Expert and novice performance in solving physics problems. *Science*, 1980, *208*, 1335-1342.

Lawson, G., Baron, J., & Siegel, L. S. The role of length and number cues in children's quantitative judgments. *Child Development*, 1974, *45*, 731-736.

Lazar, I., Darlington, R., et al. Lasting effects of early education: a report from the consortium for longitudinal studies. *Monographs of the Society for Research in Child Development*, 1982, *47*, Serial No. 195.

Lenat, D. B. Toward a theory of heuristics. In R. Groner, M. Groner, & W. F. Bischof (Eds.), *Methods of heuristics.* Hillsdale, N. J.: Erlbaum, 1983.

Lichtenstein, S., & Fischhoff, B. Do those who know more also know more about how

much they know? The calibration of probability judgments. *Organizational Behavior and Human Performance*, 1977, *20*, 159-183.

Lichtenstein, S., Fischhoff, B., & Phillips, L. D. Calibration of probabilities: the state of the art. In D. Kahneman, P. Slovic, & A. Tversky (Eds.), *Judgment under uncertainty: heuristics and biases*. Cambridge University Press, 1982.

Lipman, M. Thinking skills fostered by Philosophy for Children. In J. W. Segal, S. F. Chipman, & R. Glaser (Eds.), *Thinking and learning skills* (Vol. 1): *Relating instruction to research*. Hillsdale, N. J.: Erlbaum, 1985.

Lochhead, J. Teaching analytic reasoning skills through pair problem solving. In J. W. Segal, S. F. Chipman, & R. Glaser (Eds.), *Thinking and learning skills.* (Vol. 1): *Relating instruction to research*. Hillsdale, N. J.: Erlbaum, 1985.

Loevinger, J., Wessler, R., & Redmore, C. *Measuring ego development* (2 vols.). San Francisco: Jossey Bass, 1970.

Logan, G. D. On the use of a concurrent memory load to measure attention and automaticity. *Journal of Experimental Psychology: Human Perception and Performance*, 1979, *5*, 189-207.

Lord, C. G., Ross, L., & Lepper, M. R. Biased assimilation and attitude polarization: the effects of prior theories on subsequently considered evidence. *Journal of Personality and Social Psychology*, 1979, *37*, 2098-2109.

Luria, A. R. *The role of speech in the regulation of normal and abnormal behavior*. Elmsford, N. Y.: Pergamon Press, 1980.

Luria, A. R. *The mind of a mnemonist* (1965) Trans. by L. Solotaroff. New York: Basic Books, 1968.

Lyon, D. R. Individual differences in immeidiate serial recall: a matter of mnemonics? *Cognitive Psychology*, 1977, *9*, 403-411.

Lytle, S. L. Exploring comprehension style: a study of twelfth-grade readers' transactions with text. Ph.D. Thesis, School of Education, University of Pennsylvania, 1982.

Machado, L. A. *The right to be intelligent*. Oxford: Pergamon Press, 1980.

March, J. G. Bounded rationality, ambiguity, and the engineering of choice. *Bell Journal of Economics*, 1978, *9*, 587-608.

Marschak, J. *Economic information, decision, and prediction. Selected essays* (Vol. 2). Boston: Reidel, 1974.

Maslow, A. H. *Motivation and personality*. New York: Harper, 1954.

Maslow, A. H. *Toward a psychology of being*. New York: Van Nostrand, 1962.

McClelland, D. C. *The achieving society*. Princeton, N. J.: Van Nostrand, 1960.

McLeod, P. D., Williams, C. B., & Broadbent, D. E. Free recall with assistance from one and from two retrieval cues. *British Journal of Psychology*, 1971, *62*, 59-65.

Medin, D. C., & Schaffer, M. M. Context theory of classification learning. *Psychological Review*, 1978, *85*, 207-238.

Meichenbaum, D. *Cognitive behavior modification: an integrative approach*. New York: Plenum, 1977.

Meichenbaum, D., & Goodman, J. Training impulsive children to talk to themselves: a means of developing self-control. *Journal of Abnormal Psychology*, 1971, *77*, 115-126.

Messer, S. B. Reflection-impulsivity: a review. *Psychological Bulletin*, 1976, *83*, 1026-1052.

Miller, G. A., Galanter, E., & Pribram, K. H. *Plans and the structure of behavior*. New York: Holt, Rinehart and Winston, 1960.

Minsky, M. A framework for representing knowledge. In P. H. Winston (Ed.), *The psychology of computer vision*. New York: McGraw-Hill, 1975.

Montessori, M. *The Montessori method*. New York: F. A. Stokes, 1912.

Mulholland, T. M., Pellegrino, J. W., & Glaser, R. Components of geometric analogy solution. *Cognitive Psychology*, 1980, *12*, 252-284.

Mynatt, C. R., Doherty, M. E., & Tweney, R. D. Confirmation bias in a simulated research environment: an experimental study of scientific inference. *Quarterly Journal of Experimental Psychology*, 1977, *29*, 85-95.

Neisser, U. *Cognitive psychology*. Englewood Cliffs, N. J.: Prentice Hall, 1967.

Neisser, U. *Cognition and reality: principles and implications of cognitive psychology*. San Francisco: Freeman, 1976.

Neisser, U. (Ed.) *Memory observed: remembering in natural contexts*. San Francisco: W. H. Freeman, 1982.

Neisser, U. Components of intelligence or steps in routine procedures? *Cognition*, 1983, *15*, 189-197.

Nettlebeck, T., & Lally, M. Age, intelligence, and inspection time. *American Journal of Mental Deficiency*, 1979, *83*, 391-401.

Neufeld, V. R., & Barrows, H. A. The McMaster philosophy: an approach to medical education. *Journal of Medical Education*, 1974, *49*, 1040-1050.

Newell, A. The heuristic of George Polya and its relation to artificial intelligence. In R. Groner, M. Groner, & W. F. Bischof (Eds.), *Methods of heuristics*. Hillsdale, N. J.: Erlbaum, 1983.

Newell, A., & Simon, H. A. *Human problem solving*. Englewood Cliffs, N. J.: Prentice-Hall, 1972.

Nisbett, R, & Ross, L. *Human inference: strategies and shortcomings of social judgment*. Englewood Cliffs, N. J.: Prentice-Hall, 1980.

Norman, D. A. Toward a theory of memory and attention. *Psychological Review*, 1968, *75*, 522-536.

Norman, D. A., & Bobrow, D. G. On data-limited and resource-limited processes. *Cognitive Psychology*, 1975, *7*, 44-64.

Oltmanns, T. F., Ohayon, J., & Neale, J. M. The effects of anti-psychotic medication and diagnostic criteria on distractibility in schizophrenia. *Journal of Psychiatric Research*, 1978, *14*, 81-92.

Osborne, A. F. *Applied imagination*. New York: Scribner, 1953.

Osherson, D. N. *Logical abilities in children* (Vol. 2): *Logical inference: underlying operations*. Hillsdale, N. J.: Erlbaum, 1974.

Papert, S. *Mindstorms: children, computers, and powerful ideas*. New York: Basic Books, 1980.

Pascual-Leone, J. A mathematical model for the transition rule in Piaget's developmental stages. *Acta Psychologica*, 1970, *32*, 301-345.

Perkins, D. N. *The mind's best work*. Cambridge, Mass.: Harvard, 1981.

Perkins, D. N. Problem theory. Manuscript. Harvard Graduate School of Education, Cambridge, MA, 1983.

Perkins, D. N., Allen, R., & Hafner, J. Difficulties in everyday reasoning. In W. Maxwell (Ed.), *Thinking: the expanding frontier*. Philadelphia: The Franklin Institute, 1983.

Perry, W. G., Jr. *Forms of intellectual and ethical development in the college years: a scheme*. New York: Holt, Rinehart and Winston, 1971.

Persons, J., & Baron, J. Processes underlying clinical thought disorder in psychiatric patients. Manuscript, University of Pennsylvania, 1983.

Phillips, L., & Edwards, W. Conservatism in a simple probability inference task. *Journal of Experimental Psychology*, 1966, *72*, 346-354.

Piaget, J. *The moral judgment of the child*. New York: Free Press, 1932.

Piaget, J. Intellectual evolution from adolescence to adulthood. *Human Development*, 1972, *15*, 1-12.

Pinter, R. *Intelligence testing: methods and results* (2nd ed.). New York: Holt, 1931.

Pitz, G. F. An inertia effect (resistance to change) in the revision of opinion. *Canadian Journal of Psychology*, 1969, *23*, 24-33.

Platt, J. R. Strong inference. *Science*, 1964, *146*, 347-353.

Polanyi, M. *Personal knowledge*. University of Chicago Press, 1958.

Polya, G. *How to solve it: a new aspect of mathematical method*. Princeton, N. J.: Princeton University Press, 1945.

Popper, K. R. *Conjectures and refutations*. New York: Basic Books, 1962.

Posner, M. I. *Chronometric explorations of mind*. Hillsdale, N. J.: Erlbaum, 1978.

Posner, M. I., & Keele, S. W. On the genesis of abstract ideas. *Journal of Experimental Psychology*, 1968, *77*, 353-363.

Putnam, H. *Reason, truth, and history*. Cambridge University Press, 1981.

Raiffa, H. *Decision analysis*. Reading, Mass.: Addison-Wesley, 1968.

Ramsey, F. P. Truth and probability. In F. P. Ramsey, *The foundations of mathematics and other logical essays*. New York: Harcourt, Brace, 1931.

Rawls, J. *A theory of justice*. Cambridge, Mass.: Harvard University Press, 1971.

Reber, A. S. Implicit learning of synthetic languages: The role of instructional set. *Journal of Experimental Psychology: Human Learning and Memory*, 1976, *2*, 88-94.

Reisberg, D. Sources of selective failure. Manuscript, New School for Social Research, 1980.

Reisberg, D., Rappaport, I., & O'Shaughnessy, M. Limits of working memory: the digit digit-span. *Journal of Experimental Psychology: Human Learning and Memory*, 1984, *10*, 203-221.

Reitman, W. R. *Cognition and thought*. New York: Wiley, 1965.

Reitman, W., Malin, J. T., Bjork, R. A., & Higman, B. Strategy control and directed forgetting. *Journal of Verbal Learning and Verbal Behavior*, 1973, *12*, 140-149.

Rest, J. R. Morality. In P. H. Mussen (Ed.), *Handbook of child psychology* (Vol. 3). New York: Wiley, 1983.

Richards, D. A. J. *A theory of reasons for action*. Oxford University Press, 1971.

Rokeach, M. (Ed.) *The open and closed mind*. New York: Basic Books, 1960.

Rosen, B. C., & D'Andrade, R. The psychosocial origins of achievement motivation. *Sociometry*, 1959, *22*, 185-218.

Ross, M., & Sicoly, F. Egocentric biases in availability and attribution. *Journal of Personality and Social Psychology*, 1979, *37*, 322-326.

Rotter, J. B. Generalized expectancies for internal versus external control of reinforcement. *Psychological Monographs*, 1966, *80*, No. 1.

Rumelhart, D. Toward an interactive model of reading. In S. Dornic (Ed.), *Attention and performance VI*. London: Academic Press, 1977.

Russo, J. E., and Dosher, B. A. Strategies for multiattribute binary choice. *Journal of Experimental Psychology: Learning, Memory, and Cognition*, 1983, *9*, 676-696.

Savage, L. J. *The foundations of statistics*. New York: Wiley, 1954.

Scarr, S., & Carter-Saltzman, L. Genetics and intelligence. In R. J. Sternberg (Ed.), *Handbook of human intelligence*. Cambridge University Press, 1982.

Scheffler, I. *Conditions of knowledge: an introduction to epistemology and education*. Glenview, Ill.: Scott, Foresman, 1965.

Schneider, W., & Shiffrin, R. M. Controlled and automatic human information processing: I. Detection, search, and attention. *Psychological Review*, 1977, *84*, 1-66.

Schön, D. A. *The reflective practitioner: how professionals think in action*. New York: Basic Books, 1983.

Schroder, H. M., Driver, M. J., & Streufert, S. *Human information processing*. New York: Holt, Rinehart and Winston, 1967.

Schunk, D.H. Effects of effort attributional feedback on children's perceived self-efficacy and achievement. *Journal of Educational Psychology*, 1982, *74*, 548-556.

Schwartz, B. Does helplessness cause depression, or do only depressed people become helpless? Comment on Alloy and Abramson. *Journal of Experimental Psychology: General*, 1981, *110*, 429-435.

Schwartz, B. Reinforcement-induced behavioral stereotypy: how not to teach people to discover rules. *Journal of Experimental Psychology: General, 1982, 111*, 23-59.

Sears, R. S. Sources of life satisfaction in the Ternman gifted men. *American Psychologist, 1977, 32*, 119-128.

Segal, J. W., Chipman, S. F., & Glaser, R. *Thinking and learning skills* (2 vols.). Hillsdale, N. J.: Erlbaum, 1985.

Seligman, M. E. P. *Helplessness: on depression, development, and death.* San Francisco: Freeman, 1975.

Shafer, G. *A mathematical theory of evidence.* Princeton University Press, 1976.

Shafer, G. Constructive probability. *Synthese, 1981, 48*, 1-60.

Shafer, G., & Tversky, A. Weighing evidence: the design and comparison of probability thought experiments. Manuscript. Stanford University, 1984.

Shaffer, L. H. Multiple attention in continuous verbal tasks. In P. M. A. Rabbitt & S. Dornic (Eds.), *Attention and Performance V*. London: Academic Press, 1975.

Shaklee, H., & Fischhoff, B. Strategies in information search in causal analysis. *Memory and Cognition, 1982*, 520-530.

Shakow, D. Segmental set: a theory of the formal psychological deficit in schizophrenia. *Archives of General Psychiatry, 1962, 6*, 1-17.

Shapiro, D. *Neurotic styles.* New York: Basic Books, 1965.

Sharp, D., Cole, M., & Lave, C. Education and cognitive development: the evidence from experimental research. *Monographs of the Society for Research in Child Development, 1979, 44*, Serial No. 178.

Shepard, R. N. On selectively optimum selections among multi-attribute alternatives. In Shelly, M. W., & Bryan, G. L. (Eds.), *Human judgements and optimality*. New York: Wiley, 1964.

Shugan, S. M. The cost of thinking. *Journal of Consumer Research, 1980, 7*, 99-111.

Shweder, R. A. Likeness and likelihood in everyday thought: magical thinking and everyday judgments about personality. In P. N. Johnson-Laird & P. C. Wason (Eds.), *Thinking: readings in cognitive science.* Cambridge University Press, 1977.

Shweder, R. A., & D'Andrade, R. G. Accurate reflection or systematic distortion? A reply to Block, Weiss, & Thorne. *Journal of Personality and Social Psychology, 1979, 57*, 1079-1084.

Siegler, R. S., & Richards, D. D. The development of intelligence. In R. J. Sternberg (Ed.), *Handbook of human intelligence.* Cambridge University Press, 1982.

Simon, H. *Models of man: social and rational.* New York: Wiley, 1957.

Simon, H. A. Rationality as process and as product of thought. *American Economic Review, 1978a, 68* (2), 1-16.

Simon, H. A. Information-processing theory of human problem solving. In W. K. Estes (Ed.), *Handbook of learning and cognitive processes* (Vol. 5). Hillsdale, N. J.: Erlbaum, 1978b.

Slovic, P., & Fischhoff, B. On the psychology of experimental surprises. *Journal of Experimental Psychology: Human Perception and Performance, 1977, 3*, 544-551.

Slovic, P., & Tversky, A. Who accepts Savage's axioms? *Behavioral Science, 1974, 19*, 368-373.

Slovic, P., Fischhoff, B., & Lichtenstein, S. Facts versus fears: understanding perceived risk. In Kahneman, D., Slovic, P., & Tversky, A. (Eds.), *Judgment under uncertainty: heuristics and biases.* Cambridge University Press, 1982.

Smith, J. D., & Baron, J. Individual differences in the classification of stimuli by dimensions. *Journal of Experimental Psychology: Human Perception and Performance, 1981, 5*, 1132-1145.

Smith, L. B., & Kemler, D. G. Developmental trends in free classification: evidence for a

new conceptualization of perceptual development. *Journal of Experimental Child Psychology*, 1977, *24*, 279-298.

Smith, L. B., Kemler, D. G., & Aronfreed, J. Developmental trends in voluntary selective attention: differential effects of source distinctness. *Journal of Experimental Child Psychology*, 1975, *20*, 352-362.

Snapper, K. J., & Peterson, C. R. Information seeking and data diagnosticity. *Journal of Experimental Psychology*, 1971, *87*, 429-433.

Snow, C. E., & Hoefnagel-Höhle, M. The critical period for language acquisition: evidence from second language learning. *Child Development*, 1978, *49*, 1114-1128.

Snow, R. E., & Yalow, E. Education and intelligence. In R. J. Sternberg Ed.), *Handbook of human intelligence*. Cambridge University Press, 1982.

Spearman, C. "General intelligence" objectively determined and measured. *American Journal of Psychology*, 1904, *15*, 201-293.

Standing, L., Bond, B., Smith, P., & Isely, C. Is the immediate memory span determined by subvocalization rate. *British Journal of Psychology*, 1980, *71*, 525-539.

Steinlauf, B. Problem-solving skills, locus of control, and the contraceptive effectiveness of young women. *Child Development*, 1979, *50*, 268-271.

Stern, W. *Psychologische Methoden der Intelligenz-Prüfung*. Leipzig: Barth, 1912.

Sternberg, R. J. *Intelligence, information processing, and analogical reasoning*. Hillsdale, N. J.: Erlbaum, 1977.

Sternberg, R. J. Toward a triarchic theory of human intelligence. *Brain and Behavioral Sciences*, 1984, in press.

Sternberg, R. J., and Davidson, J. E. The mind of the puzzler. *Psychology Today*, June 1982, 37-44.

Sternberg, R. J., & Gardner, M. K. Unities in inductive reasoning. *Journal of Experimental Psychology: General*, 1983, *112*, 80-116.

Sternberg, R. J., & Salter, W. Conceptions of intelligence. In R. J. Sternberg (Ed.), *Handbook of human intelligence*. Cambridge University Press, 1982.

Stevens, A. L., & Collins, A. Multiple conceptual models of a complex system. In R. E. Snow, P. Federico, & W. Montague (Eds.), *Aptitude, learning, and instruction* (Vol. 2). Hillsdale, N. J.: Erlbaum, 1980.

Stevenson, H. W., Parker, T., Wilkinson, A., Bonnevaux, B., & Gonzalez, M. Schooling, environment, and cognitive development: a cross-cultural study. *Monographs of the Society for Research in Child Development*, 1978, *43*, Serial No. 175.

Stich, S., & Nisbett, R. Justification and the psychology of human reasoning. *Philosophy of Science*, 1980, *47*, 188-202.

Stroop, J. R. Studies of interference in serial verbal reactions. *Journal of Experimental Psychology*, 1935, *18*, 643-661.

Svenson, O. Are we all less risky and more skillful than our fellow drivers? *Acta Psychologica*, 1981, *47*, 143-148.

Terman, L. M. *The measurement of intelligence*. Boston: Houghton-Mifflin, 1916.

Terman, L. M., & Oden, M. H. *The gifted group at mid-life: Thirty-five years' follow-up of the superior child*. Stanford, CA: Stanford University Press, 1959.

Tetlock, P. E. Cognitive style and political ideology. *Journal of Personality and Social Psychology*, 1983, *45*, 118-126.

Tetlock, P. E. Cognitive style and political belief systems in the British House of Commons. *Journal of Personality and Social Psychology*, 1984, *46*,

Thaler, R. Toward a positive theory of consumer choice. *Journal of Economic Behavior and Organization*, 1980, *1*, 39-60.

Theil, H. *Economics and information theory*. Amsterdam: North Holland, 1967.

Thorndike, R. L., & Woodworth, R. S. The influence of improvement in one mental

function upon the efficiency of other functions. *Psychological Review*, 1901, *8*, 247-261, 384-395, 553-564.

Thurstone, L. L. Primary mental abilities. *Psychological Monographs*, 1938, *1*.

Treisman, A. M., & Davies, A. Divided attention to ear and eye. In S. Kornblum (Ed.), *Attention and Performance IV*. New York: Academic Press, 1973.

Tschirgi, J. E. Sensible reasoning: a hypothesis about hypotheses. *Child Development*, 1980, *51*, 1-10.

Tulving, E. Cue-dependent forgetting. *American Scientist*, 1974, *62*, 74-82.

Tversky, A. Additivity, utility and subjective probability. *Journal of Mathematical Psychology*, 1967, *4*, 175-202.

Tversky, A., & Kahneman, D. Availability: a heuristic for judging frequency and probability. *Cognitive Psychology*, 1973, *5*, 207-232.

Tversky, A., & Kahneman, D. The framing of decisions and the psychology of choice. *Science*, 1981, *211*, 453-458.

Tversky, A., & Kahneman, D. Extensional versus intuitive reasoning: the conjunction fallacy in probability judgment. *Psychological Review*, 1983, *90*, 293-315.

Tweney, R. D., Doherty, M. E., Worner, W. J., Pliske, D. B., Mynatt, C. R., Gross, K. A., & Arkkelin, D. L. Strategies of rule discovery in an inference task. *Quarterly Journal of Experimental Psychology*, 1980, *32*, 109-123.

Tweney, R. D., Doherty, M. E., & Mynatt, C. R. (Eds.) *On scientific thinking: a reader in the cognitive psychology of science*. New York: Columbia University Press, 1981.

Van Lehn, K., & Brown, J. S. Planning nets: a representation for formalizing analogies and semantic models of procedural skills. In R. E. Snow, P. Federico, & W. Montague (Eds.), *Aptitude, learning, and instruction* (Vol. 2). Hillsdale, N. J.: Erlbaum, 1980.

Vernon, P. E. *The structure of human abilities*. London: Methuen, 1950.

von Neuman, J., & Morgenstern, O. *Theory of games and economic behavior*. Princeton, N.J.: Princeton University Press, 1947.

Voss, J. F., Tyler, S. W., & Yengo, L. A. Individual differences in the solving of social science problems. In R. F. Dillon & R. R. Schmeck (Eds.), *Individual differences in cognition* (Vol. 1). New York: Academic Press, 1983.

Wagner, D. A. The development of short-term and incidental memory: a cross-cultural study. *Child Development*, 1974, *45*, 389-396.

Wagner, D. A. Memories of Morocco: the influence of age, schooling and environment on memory. *Cognitive Psychology*, 1978, *10*, 1-28.

Wald, A. *Sequential analysis*. New York: Wiley, 1947.

Wallach, M. A. Tests tell us little about talent. *American Scientist*, 1976, *64*, 57-63.

Ward, W. C., & Jenkins, H. M. The display of information and the judgment of contingency. *Canadian Journal of Psychology*, 1965, *19*, 231-241.

Wason, P. C. On the failure to eliminate hypotheses in a conceptual task. *Quarterly Journal of Experimental Psychology*, 1960, *12*, 129-140.

Wason, P. C. Reasoning about a rule. *Quarterly Journal of Experimental Psychology*, 1968a, *20*, 273-281.

Wason, P. C. 'On the failure to eliminate hypotheses . . . '—a second look. In P. C. Wason & P. N. Johnson-Laird (Eds.), *Thinking and reasoning*. Harmondsworth, Mddx.: Penguin Books, 1968b.

Wason, P. C., & Johnson-Laird. P. N. *Psychology of reasoning: structure and content*. Cambridge, Mass.: Harvard University Press, 1972.

Waugh, N. C. Associative symmetry and recall latencies: a distinction between learning and performance. *Acta Psychologica*, 1970, *33*, 326-337.

Weisberg, R. W., & Alba, J. W. An examination of the alleged role of "fixation" in the

solution of several "insight" problems. *Journal of Experimental Psychology: General*, 1981, *110*, 169-192.

Weiss, G., & Hechtman, L. The hyperactive child syndrome. *Science*, 1979, *205*, 1348-1354.

Weiss, S. M., Kulikowski, C. A., Amarel, S., & Safir, A. A model-based method for computer-aided medical decision-making. *Artificial Intelligence*, 1978, *11*, 145-172.

Wertheimer, M. *Productive thinking*. New York: Harper & Brothers, 1945. (Enlarged ed., 1959).

Whimbey, A., & Lochhead, J. *Problem solving and comprehension: a short course in analytical reasoning* (2nd ed.). Philadelphia: The Franklin Institute Press, 1980.

Whimbey, A., & Whimbey, L. S. *Intelligence can be taught*. New York: Dutton, 1975.

White, R. W. Motivation reconsidered: the concept of competence. *Psychological Review*, 1959, *66*, 297-333.

Wickelgren, W. A. *How to solve problems: elements of a theory of problems and problem solving*. San Francisco: Freeman, 1974.

Williams, B. *Moral luck*. Cambridge University Press, 1981.

Wissler, C. The correlation of mental and physical traits. *Psychological Monographs*, 1901, *3*, 1-62.

Wollman, W., Eylon, B., & Lawson, A. E. Acceptance of lack of closure: is it an index of advanced reasoning? *Child Development*, 1979. *50*, 656-665.

Woodworth, R. S., & Sells, S. B. An atmosphere effect in formal syllogistic reasoning. *Journal of Experimental Psychology*, 1935, *18*, 451-460.

Zajonc, R. B., & Markus, G. B. Birth order and intellectual development. *Psychological Review*, 1975, *82*, 74-88.

Index